"This edited volume is a comprehensive and thought-provoking exploration of the mechanisms and techniques of control used to keep the Palestinian people under settler colonial domination. The editors have brought together a team of brilliant scholars and experts to unravel the layers and intricacies that make this domination have such a devastating impact on Palestinian life. The result is an academically rigorous book that is an invaluable addition to the literature and for understanding the Palestinian experience."

Yara Hawari, Academic, Writer, and Co-Director of Al-Shabaka:
The Palestinian Policy Network

"Through an excellent choice of young and more senior researchers, this book provides a timely, innovative, and interdisciplinary analysis of the domination/resistance dynamics in the context of the Occupied Palestinian Territories since the post-Oslo Accords of 1993–4. During the past thirty years, the Zionist settler colonial framework characterized by its 'logic of elimination' has actually produced renewed modes of resistance among the Palestinian indigenous population. The volume definitely contributes to an emancipatory prose of knowledge production."

Riccardo Bocco, Emeritus Professor,
The Geneva Graduate Institute (IHEID)

"This superbly edited volume offers readers an illuminating series of scholarly studies of the extraordinary particulars of Palestinian resistance to decades of abusive Israeli domination, and in the course of doing so provides a vivid, unsurpassed account of the cruelties of settler colonialism."

Richard Falk, UN Special Rapporteur,
Occupied Palestine, 2008–14

"Although domestic politics has not evolved much since the 2007 division between Fatah and Hamas, the economic transformations around the power city of Ramallah are enormous. This excellent book tackles these new realities while continuing to document the new forms of encroachment by Israel in the West Bank. An essential and timely collection of essays that demonstrate how coloniality and settler colonialism are forms of control that shape and limit the Palestinian projects of autonomy and sovereignty but also lead Palestinians to use creative repertoires of mobilization."

Benoit Challand, Associate Professor of Sociology,
New School for Social Research

"*Resisting Domination in Palestine* has a simple but important premise: that Israeli domination and Palestinian resistance are intricately intertwined, and so they must be analyzed together. The strength of this edited collection lies in the multiplicity of sites and sectors selected to unpack this relationship. Interdisciplinary, insightful, and inspiring, the authors offer an abundance of rich empirical evidence to show how settler colonialism permeates all aspects of life. Such all-pervasive domination could dampen the spirits, but the book also provides hope by giving ample attention to how Palestinian *Sumud*, everyday resistance, and popular struggle exploit the weaknesses in Israel's mechanisms of control."

Mandy Turner, Professor of Conflict, Peace and Humanitarian Affairs, University of Manchester

"From medical permits to fiscal policy, from mechanisms of censorship to the intricacies of aid, this volume gathers scholars across disciplines to offer wide-ranging, empirically grounded, theoretically nuanced contributions that critique Israeli settler colonialism and uplift Palestinian resistance. Following the best radical traditions of producing knowledge as critique, the authors offer a powerful map of decoloniality, both epistemic and material."

Sherene Seikaly, Associate Professor, Department of History; Director, Center for Middle East Studies, University of California, Santa Barbara

"An illuminating and compelling study that examines Israeli settler colonialism in dimensions not typically seen but vital to understand. Full of critical and much-needed insights, this important book is essential reading for anyone seeking a deeper and more rigorous understanding of the reality that permeates Palestinian life and the ways in which Palestinian resist."

Sara Roy, Center for Middle Eastern Studies, Harvard University

Resisting Domination in Palestine

Unsettling Colonialism in Our Times

The Unsettling Colonialism in Our Times series publishes books at the intersection of settler colonialism studies, decolonization, and critiques of neoliberalism, illuminating the complex relationship between power and knowledge in the twenty-first century.

It encourages research which has previously been studied as "postcolonial" or as examples of successful "end of history" processes of modernization and Westernization to be viewed in light of the struggles for national liberation, democracy, and human rights. The series is a unique meeting point between new and established scholars who engage with activist intellectual work concerning the welfare and future of the most oppressed communities in the world.

Series Editors

William Gallois, Director of Research at the Institute of Arab and Islamic Studies
Ilan Pappe, Professor of History and Director of the European Centre for Palestine Studies
Both at University of Exeter, UK

Advisory Board

Lorenzo Veracini, Swinburne University of Technology in Melbourne, Australia
Robert J. C. Young, New York University
Eyal Weizmann, Goldsmiths Ruba Salih, SOAS
Katsuya Hirano, UCLA
Angela Woollacott, Australian National University

Resisting Domination in Palestine

Mechanisms and Techniques of Control, Coloniality and Settler Colonialism

Edited by
Alaa Tartir, Timothy Seidel and Tariq Dana

I.B. TAURIS
LONDON • NEW YORK • OXFORD • NEW DELHI • SYDNEY

I.B. TAURIS
Bloomsbury Publishing Plc, 50 Bedford Square, London, WC1B 3DP, UK
Bloomsbury Publishing Inc, 1359 Broadway, 12th Floor, New York, NY 10018, USA
Bloomsbury Publishing Ireland, 29 Earlsfort Terrace, Dublin 2, D02 AY28, Ireland

BLOOMSBURY, I.B. TAURIS and the I.B. Tauris logo are trademarks
of Bloomsbury Publishing Plc

First published in Great Britain 2024
This paperback edition published 2025

Copyright © Alaa Tartir, Timothy Seidel, Tariq Dana, and contributors, 2024

Alaa Tartir, Timothy Seidel and Tariq Dana have asserted their rights under the Copyright,
Designs and Patents Act, 1988, to be identified as Editors of this work.

For legal purposes the Acknowledgments on p. x constitute an
extension of this copyright page.

Series design by Toby Way
Cover image: *Nablus* © Irina Naji

All rights reserved. No part of this publication may be: i) reproduced or transmitted in any
form, electronic or mechanical, including photocopying, recording or by means of any information
storage or retrieval system without prior permission in writing from the publishers; or ii) used or
reproduced in any way for the training, development or operation of artificial intelligence (AI) technologies,
including generative AI technologies. The rights holders expressly reserve this publication from the
text and data mining exception as per Article 4(3) of the Digital Single Market Directive (EU) 2019/790.

Bloomsbury Publishing Inc does not have any control over, or responsibility for,
any third-party websites referred to or in this book. All internet addresses given
in this book were correct at the time of going to press. The author and publisher
regret any inconvenience caused if addresses have changed or sites have
ceased to exist, but can accept no responsibility for any such changes.

A catalogue record for this book is available from the British Library.

Library of Congress Cataloging-in-Publication Data
Names: Tartir, Alaa, editor. | Seidel, Timothy, editor. | Dana, Tariq, editor.
Title: Resisting domination in Palestine: mechanisms and techniques of control, coloniality and settler
colonialism / edited by Alaa Tartir, Timothy Seidel, and Tariq Dana.
Other titles: Mechanisms and techniques of control, coloniality and settler colonialism
Description: London; New York: I. B. Tauris, 2024. | Series: Unsettling colonialism in our times |
Includes bibliographical references and index. | Contents: Resisting Domination in Palestine / by Timothy Seidel,
Tariq Dana, and Alaa Tartir – Elimination by Other Means : Colonial Autonomy and Indirect Colonial Rule
in the Occupied Palestinian Territories / by Tariq Dana – The Bureaucracy of Mortality: the Structural Violence of
Medical Permits for Palestinians in the West Bank and Gaza Strip / by Yara M. Asi – Israeli Online Surveillance Regime:
Digital Colonization in Practice / by Nijmeh Ali – The Political Economy of Education and Technology:
a Focus on the Lived Experiences of Palestinian Digital Freelancers / by We'am Hamdan – Dislocating
Development: Palestinians in Israeli International Aid Imaginaries in the 1950s and 1960s / by Hebatalla
Taha – Banking in/on the Occupation / by Colin Powers – The Palestinian Authority: the Fiscal Contract
and Structural Constraints / by Anas Iqtait – Situating the Transnational in Agrarian Palestine / by
Gabi Kirk and Paul Kohlbry – Settler Colonial Violence and Indigenous Struggle: Land, Resistance, and
Refusal / by Timothy Seidel and Federica Stagni – International Holocaust Remembrance Alliance,
Academic Censorship and the Politics of Settler Colonial Erasure / by Somdeep Sen – Liberal Packaging
and Colonial Approaches: Problematizing Western Intervention in Palestine / by Jeremy Wildeman – Palestinian
Popular Education Post-Oslo / by Melanie Meinzer. Identifiers: LCCN 2023036818 (print) |
LCCN 2023036819 (ebook) | ISBN 9780755650835 (hb) | ISBN 9780755650873 (paperback) |
ISBN 9780755650842 (epdf) | ISBN 9780755650859 (ebook) | ISBN 9780755650866
Subjects: LCSH: Government, Resistance to–Palestine–History–21st century. |
Palestinian Arabs–Politics and government–21st century. | Settler colonialism–Palestine–History–
21st century. | Palestine–History–21st century. | Palestine–Economic conditions–21st century. |
Palestine–Social conditions–21st century. Classification: LCC DS119.76 .R464 2024 (print) |
LCC DS119.76 (ebook) | DDC 956.9405/5–dc23/eng/20231214956.9405/5
LC record available at https://lccn.loc.gov/2023036818
LC ebook record available at https://lccn.loc.gov/2023036819

ISBN: HB: 978-0-7556-5083-5
PB: 978-0-7556-5087-3
ePDF: 978-0-7556-5084-2
eBook: 978-0-7556-5085-9

Typeset by Deanta Global Publishing Services, Chennai, India

For product safety related questions contact productsafety@bloomsbury.com.

To find out more about our authors and books visit www.bloomsbury.com
and sign up for our newsletters.

Contents

List of Illustrations		ix
Acknowledgments		x
List of Abbreviations		xi

1 Resisting Domination in Palestine *Timothy Seidel, Tariq Dana, and Alaa Tartir* 1

Part I Political: Governmentality and Mechanisms of Control

2 Elimination by Other Means: Colonial Autonomy and Indirect Colonial Rule in the Occupied Palestinian Territories *Tariq Dana* 17

3 The Bureaucracy of Mortality: The Structural Violence of Medical Permits for Palestinians in the West Bank and Gaza Strip *Yara M. Asi* 36

4 Israeli Online Surveillance Regime: Digital Colonization in Practice *Nijmeh Ali* 51

5 The Political Economy of Education and Technology: A Focus on the Lived Experiences of Palestinian Digital Freelancers *We'am Hamdan* 68

Part II Economic: Exploitation, Dispossession, and De-Development

6 Dislocating Development: Palestinians in Israeli International Aid Imaginaries in the 1950s and 1960s *Hebatalla Taha* 91

7 Banking in/on the Occupation *Colin Powers* 108

8 The Palestinian Authority: The Fiscal Contract and Structural Constraints *Anas Iqtait* 126

Part III Environmental: Land, Indigeneity, and Settler Colonialism

9 Situating the Transnational in Agrarian Palestine *Gabi Kirk and Paul Kohlbry* 143

10 Settler Colonial Violence and Indigenous Struggle: Land, Resistance, and Refusal in Masafer Yatta *Timothy Seidel and Federica Stagni* 161

Part IV Epistemic: Local Knowledge and Global Norms

11 International Holocaust Remembrance Alliance, Academic Censorship, and the Politics of Settler Colonial Erasure *Somdeep Sen* 179

12 Liberal Packaging and Colonial Approaches: Problematizing Western
    Intervention in Palestine *Jeremy Wildeman*   194
13 Palestinian Popular Education Post-Oslo *Melanie Meinzer*   214

Note on Contributors   229
Index   233

Illustrations

Figures

3.1	Results of medical permit requests to cross Erez border from Gaza, 2011–19	43
3.2	Israeli fatalities/injuries, 2011–19	44
4.1	Suspected Pegasus infections	61
8.1	Palestinian Authority's revenue composition (including foreign aid allocated to the PA's budget) between 1996 and 2021	133
13.1	Excerpt from Ahmed Masri's "On This Earth We Deserve Life"	222
13.2	Excerpt from Sherien Habibah's "Curfew Challenge"	223

Tables

3.1	Global Terrorism/Peace Indices, Israel, 2014–19	44
13.1	Sources of Knowledge About Palestinian History and Identity	218

Acknowledgments

We would like to express our sincere gratitude and appreciation to those who have played integral roles in the production of this book. Firstly, our heartfelt thanks go to the contributing authors whose insights and perspectives have added depth and richness to the content of this work. The authors did not only write their own chapters and engage with us, the editors, but they also peer reviewed each other's chapters and offered thoughtful, valuable, and constructive feedback. As we have endeavored with our previous edited volumes, this is not merely a collection of chapters but a collaborative scholarly effort. Their outstanding scholarship, dedication and commitment, and courageous chapters are inspiring. We have learned so much from you and are grateful for the opportunity to be a part of this collective work.

We also want to express our sincere thanks to Irina Naji, whose beautiful art appears on the cover and whose creative talents have provided a visual dimension that enhances the book's overall impact. To our publishers at I.B. Taurus/Bloomsbury, and in particular the editorial team, we express our profound gratitude for their unwavering support and dedication. Special thanks to Sophie Rudland, Nayiri Kendir, Yasmin Garcha, and Faiza Zakaria, who have each contributed significantly to the success of this publication.

Our sincere appreciation extends to our colleagues and conversation partners who have offered invaluable feedback and guidance, including the reviewers of our proposal and draft manuscript. A big thank you to all the colleagues and scholars with whom we discussed individual chapters as well as the book as a whole, including those who participated in the conversations at panel sessions at the 2022 Middle East Studies Association and 2023 International Studies Association meetings. To the esteemed scholars and colleagues who endorsed our book, we are truly humbled, honored, and thankful for all your support.

On a more personal note, we express our deep gratitude to our families, whose encouragement and patience throughout this process have been instrumental. Finally, our most profound acknowledgment is dedicated to Palestine and its resilient people. This book is, in essence, a tribute to their enduring spirit, steadfastness, and resistance, and their unwavering pursuit of dignity and justice.

Abbreviations

ANERA	American Near East Refugee Aid
BDS	Boycott, Divestment, and Sanctions
BoI	Bank of Israel
COGAT	Coordinator of Government Activities in the Territories
DFID	Department for International Development, UK
DFLP	Democratic Front for the Liberation of Palestine
DoP	Declaration of Principles, Israel-PLO
EC	European Commission
EIB	European Investment Bank
ESCWA	United Nations Economic and Social Commission for Western Asia
EU	European Union
EUPOL	COPPS European Union Police Coordinating Office for Palestinian Police Support
GDP	Gross domestic product
GNI	Gross national income
GRM	Gaza Reconstruction Mechanism
HDI	Human Development Index
ICBS	Israeli Central Bureau of Statistics
ICC	International Criminal Court
ICJ	International Court of Justice
ICT	Information and communication technology
IDB	Islamic Development Bank
IDF	Israeli Defense Forces
IFI	International Financial Institution
IHL	International Humanitarian Law
IHRA	International Holocaust Remembrance Alliance
ILS	Israeli New Shekel
IMF	International Monetary Fund
INGO	International Nongovernmental Organization

JNF	Jewish National Fund
MNCs	Multinational corporations
MSW	Municipal solid waste
NGO	Nongovernmental organization
NSF	National Security Forces
OCHA	United Nations Office for the Coordination of Humanitarian Affairs
OECD	Organization for Economic Cooperation and Development
oPt	occupied Palestinian territory
PA	Palestinian Authority
PASF	Palestinian Authority Security Forces
PCBS	Palestinian Central Bureau of Statistics
PCP	Palestinian Civil Police
PER	Protocol on Economic Relations (Paris Protocol)
PIF	Palestine Investment Fund
PIPA	Palestinian Investment Promotion Agency
PFLP	Popular Front for the Liberation of Palestine
PLC	Palestinian Legislative Council
PLO	Palestinian Liberation Organization
PMA	Palestinian Monetary Authority
SDI	Sustainable Development Index
SSR	Security sector reform
UN	United Nations
UNCTAD	United Nations Conference on Trade and Development
UNDP	United Nations Development Programme
UNISPAL	United Nations Information System on the Question of Palestine
UNRWA	United Nations Relief and Works Agency for Palestine Refugees in the Near East
USAID	US Agency for International Development
USD	United States dollar
USSC	United States Security Coordinator
VAT	Value-added tax
WB	World Bank
WBGS	West Bank and Gaza Strip
WFP	World Food Programme

1

Resisting Domination in Palestine

Timothy Seidel, Tariq Dana, and Alaa Tartir

Introduction

In the midst of the "Sword of Jerusalem" battle in May 2021, a compelling real-life narrative emerged, encapsulating the paradoxes of domination and resistance in Palestine. This story centers around Muna El-Kurd, a young Palestinian activist from Sheikh Jarrah in Jerusalem, who became a formidable voice for her community as they confronted forced evictions by Israeli settlers.

Muna, alongside her twin brother Mohammed, harnessed the power of social media to share their experiences and chronicle the reality of life in occupied Jerusalem. Their candid videos and posts rapidly garnered global attention, illuminating the struggles of Palestinian families facing forced displacement and situating them within the broader context of Israel's settler colonial domination of Palestine.

In a pivotal moment in early June 2021, both Muna and Mohammed were arrested by Israeli authorities. Though they were released later, their detainment underscored the challenges and perils confronting Palestinians who dare to defy the forces of domination. Undaunted by these risks, Muna persisted in leveraging her voice and platform to champion the rights of her people and call for an end to the enduring occupation.

As Muna El-Kurd's story illustrates, multiple interlocking systems of control and domination continue to impact life and land in occupied Palestine. And, importantly, this story also gives one example of the ways Israel's control is challenged by Palestinian resistance in their struggle for freedom.

Power, Domination, and Resistance

The study of power relations often involves an investigation into the concepts of domination and resistance. Both concepts, domination and resistance, are defined by a dialectical interplay entailing a myriad of contradictions and tensions that have captivated scholars across a range of intellectual backgrounds and throughout different historical contexts, ranging from Gramsci's hegemony and Foucault's power relations to Fanon's politics of decolonization and postcolonial theories. On the one hand, domination is understood as a form of pervasive oppressive power that seeks to impose compliance and submission on individuals and groups by employing a spectrum of forceful and nonforceful methods. These methods encompass coercion and co-optation, whether through military strategies, legal, economic, institutional, and spatial pressures, overt or subtle, direct or indirect, or a tactically blended combination of these approaches. Resistance, on the other hand, entails actions of counterpower by individuals and groups that tend to deter, defy, and overcome the sources of domination. The approaches of resistance could be organized or disorganized, armed or peaceful, public or hidden, collective or grounded in everyday acts of resistance, or a combination of all.

Domination and resistance are sometimes depicted as diametrically opposed forces and are commonly assumed to be distinct and separate processes. However, the aim of this edited volume is to emphasize the ways in which these seemingly opposing forces are, in fact, intertwined and interdependent. Against this background, our book emphasizes James Scott's interpretation that "relations of domination are, at the same time, relations of resistance" (Scott 1990, 45). Such a perspective suggests that neither the power to dominate nor the counterpower to resist are all-encompassing but rather mutually inclusive and mutually enforcing practices and processes (Tartir and Seidel 2019).

Whereas questions of domination and resistance have been studied in almost every repressive context, they are arguably presented in their most striking form within the realms of colonialism and imperialism (Atkinson 2000, 93). The primary case study of this book accommodates this argument, whereby our understanding of Palestine has been constructed around the dialectical interplay of colonial domination and anti-colonial resistance. As Israeli settler colonial domination persists, so does Palestinian resistance. The context of Palestine-Israel exemplifies a vital site for scrutinizing the multifaceted and intertwined nature of domination and resistance, revealing the paradoxical aspects that lie at the core of colonial power dynamics.

The settler colonial paradigm serves as the foundational structure of the book, seamlessly integrating itself into the diverse themes and chapters. This is in line with the growing acknowledgment within critical academic circles that to truly comprehend the Israeli state and society, one must view them as a settler colonial formation in both their ideological, institutional, economic, and class dimensions. As Noam Chomsky has pointed out, settler colonialism reinterprets Israel as "the most extreme and sadistic form of imperialism" (cited in Shlaim 2020). In doing so, it offers both the moral and legal basis for Palestinian resistance against colonial domination. As a result, the settler colonial paradigm has evolved into an essential analytical and interpretive framework for the study and understanding of a century of Israeli domination over the Palestinians and the Palestinian myriad resistance to settler colonial domination.

Azmi Bishara contends that Palestine represents "the world's last remaining unresolved instance of settler colonialism" (2022, 6). The foundation for this argument lies in the essence of Zionism. As the late Edward Said observed, Zionism has never unreservedly identified itself as a Jewish liberation movement. Instead, it consistently presented itself as a Jewish colonial settlement in the Orient (Said 1997a, 24). The settler colonial framework helps to dissect the extremist ideological undertakings that form the foundation of Israel's domination as well as the resulting consequences for the colonized Palestinian population. By adopting this perspective to explore the interplay of domination and resistance, it becomes apparent that Palestinians have been subjected to a permanent state of exception, in which normal rules and rights are not only suspended but also outright denied (Lloyd 2012).

Building upon the previous discussion, Palestinian resistance emerges as a moral obligation, grounded in the principles of individual emancipation and collective liberation. The ongoing social, political, and conceptual (as well as narrative) struggles of Palestine against a settler colonial regime reveal a dynamic interplay between increasingly sophisticated forms of domination and the emergence of novel modes of resistance. As a late settler colonial formation that persisted through the global decolonization movements of the twentieth century and continued to endure into the first quarter of the twenty-first century with no apparent decline, Israel has systematically leveraged global trends to modernize its methods of colonization. By fusing multiple forms of colonialities, Israel has devised unique and innovative approaches to dominate and control the Palestinian population. To better understand Palestinian resistance to Israeli domination, clarity is needed as to Israel's settler colonial regime.

Coloniality, Settler Colonialism, and Resistance

Scholars like Anibal Quijano and Walter Mignolo write about modernity and coloniality as two sides of the same coin, supported by *both* a structure of knowledge *and* specific political economic institutions. As a logic, coloniality animates "racialized and gendered socio-economic and political hierarchies according to an invented Eurocentric standard" (Mignolo 2011, xxiv; see Quijano 2007). The structures and institutions of coloniality were produced and circulated globally as and through an epistemological system, which is why they do not disappear with the end of political institutional domination or the return of land after independence—and why decoloniality is both a political and epistemic project. Maldonado-Torres puts it his way:

> If coloniality refers to a logic, metaphysics, ontology, and a matrix of power that can continue existing after formal independence and desegregation, decoloniality refers to efforts at rehumanizing the world, to breaking hierarchies of difference that dehumanize subjects and communities and that destroy nature, and to the production of counter-discourses, counter-knowledges, counter-creative acts, and counter-practices that seek to dismantle coloniality and to open up multiple other forms of being in the world. (2016, 10)

Expressing coloniality in the present, settler colonialism is characterized by its "logic of elimination" (Wolfe 2006, 387–8). It is described as an ongoing structure, not an event confined to the past. This logic of elimination animates both the negative goal of the dissolution of Indigenous societies and the positive goal of constructing a new settler colonial society on expropriated land. Glen Coulthard describes the settler colonial relationship as a form of domination where power has been structured into "a set of hierarchical social relations that continue to facilitate the dispossession of Indigenous Peoples of their lands and self-determining authority" (2014, 6–7). It is fundamental to the work of both capitalism and colonialism requiring an emphasis on not only the *capital relation* but also the *colonial relation* (2014, 10).

Such structures and logics of elimination and replacement produce a particular kind of violence, settler violence, with a history in Palestine that can be traced back for over a century (Sayegh 1965; Salamanca et al. 2012; Hawari, Plonski and Weizman 2019; Khalidi 2020; Tartir, Dana and Seidel 2021; Dana and Jarbawi 2023). As this volume reveals, in occupied Palestine, this is seen in the confiscation of land and an intricate closure regime, forced displacement and ethnic cleansing of Palestinians, settlement building and expansion, water consumption and inequitable health access, mass surveillance and censorship, colonial population management, and institutional and economic subjugation. The social, political, and economic effects of this violence manifest in a system of domination that exploits, dispossesses, displaces, and constrains the livelihoods of Palestinians (Tartir and Seidel 2019).

This volume's exploration of settler colonialism and Indigenous resistance emphasizes that a decolonial analysis gives attention not only to enduring indigeneity but also to the role of land in the struggle for autonomy, sovereignty, and self-determination. This decolonial approach also acknowledges "everyday," alternative worlds where we observe "everyday" acts of resistance and popular struggle. As Seidel and Stagni discuss in their chapter, this framework and understanding of popular struggle and resistance illuminates a much larger and more powerful landscape of resistance to settler violence in occupied Palestine, for example, in Masafer Yatta in the South Hebron Hills.

This understanding of decoloniality has as its point of departure the enduring presence of Indigenous Peoples despite settler colonial projects of elimination (Kauanui 2016; Seidel 2021; Dana and Jarbawi 2023). The language or frame of indigeneity is important because it forces us to confront Palestinian dispossession and displacement within a specific framework of settler colonial history that "identifies a perceived sociohistorical familiarity with other dispossessed communities" (Salaita 2016, 2) rather than as a consequence of communal strife or an exceptional set of events brought forth by ahistorical circumstances.

Understanding Israel's mechanisms of domination through its settler colonial regime, and the enduring indigeneity of the Palestinian people whose lives and lands that regime violates, helps us see and understand the mutual and principled alliances of solidarity with Indigenous struggles around the world. This is another expression of resistance. This anti-colonial, internationalist framework illuminates the political economy of Israel's domination as well as the local, place-based struggles against it that are "embedded within, and empowered by, broader struggles" (Salamanca et al. 2012, 5; Seidel 2023). It also offers a way to "center indigenous, anticolonial frameworks that reconnect intellectual analyses of settler colonial relations, with political engagements in the praxis of liberation and decolonization" (Hawari, Plonski and Weizman 2019, 4).

Sites of Domination, Sites of Resistance

In this curated volume, we present an assemblage of insightful and contemporary perspectives on how Israeli domination has been reproduced in new forms and means. A number of scholars have already contributed valuable and thought-provoking analyses of Israeli practices of domination (for example, Pappe 2014; Zureik 2015; Dana and Jarbawi 2017; Turner 2019; Farsakh 2021; Tartir, Dana and Seidel 2021; Baconi 2022; Bishara 2022; Awad 2023). However, our aim in this edited volume is to offer a contemporary understanding by showcasing the work of a diverse array of scholars who delve into the complexities of the subject matter. The contributors to this book employ interdisciplinary approaches in their examination of the intricate functions, logics, and structures of domination that permeate Palestinian life while also shining a light on the resistance to those logics and structures that emerges in and about Palestine. Their collective expertise spans a wide range of disciplines, offering readers an opportunity to engage with various angles and nuances of the situation. Through their analyses, they illuminate the power dynamics at play and reveal the mechanisms that sustain Israel's settler colonial regime.

A closer look at these systems and mechanisms reveals the particular ways that Israel (as well as regional powers and global business) exerts control on Palestine and how this control infiltrates different spaces or what we are referring to here as "sites." This volume explores those systems by examining several "sites" of control and dominations and "sites" of resistance against settler colonial policies and institutions that the Oslo Accords perpetuated but whose histories can be traced back for over a century. This includes political (governmentality, institutions, and mechanisms of control), economic (exploitation, dispossession, and de-development), environmental (land, indigeneity, and settler colonialism), as well as epistemic (local knowledge and global norms) sites.

An important contribution this book makes is its emphasis on control, domination, and resistance in terms of *both* epistemic *and* material spaces. This signals our book's commitment to a decolonial politics and characterizes its critical approach in that it challenges prevailing neoliberal and settler colonial logics and structures. It offers critical perspectives as to how these various sites of control and domination—shaped by settler colonial processes of accumulation by exploitation and dispossession from both Israel and global business as well as from Palestinian elites—are also simultaneously sites of resistance and struggle for freedom.

This *thematic approach to understanding coloniality*, and more specifically *control, domination, and resistance*, provides a tangible way to approach each topic and presenting material. Our goal with this thematic approach, which covers knowledge production, land, governmentality, and political economy, is to provide useful categories through which to think about coloniality, settler colonialism, and neoliberalism. These categories also provide the reader with an additional layer of analysis to think through the various modes of domination and resistance reflected upon in the chapters. These categories reflect contemporary conceptual work on settler colonialism, and we find them useful for disentangling the various modes of domination and sites of resistance in occupied Palestine.

The *empirical material* covered in individual chapters is contemporary and timely. Contributors are working from new research, evidenced through the rich material exposed in this text. This empirical work is not only situated within Israel's colonialization of Palestine, but it also explains how this colonial relationship feeds into and shapes transnational and global circuits of power, knowledge, and exploitation. As such this volume attends to the importance of Palestine for understanding coloniality more broadly, and it brings Palestine into conversation with other sites through the analysis of exploitation, dispossession, development, and surveillance.

Contributions cover *a range of methods, qualitative and quantitative, foregrounding the interdisciplinary approach* of this volume. This approach is essential to understanding coloniality and settler colonialism in Palestine. The question of method and methodology is critical for our project's attention to knowledge production and signals the sort of politics of knowledge production we endeavor—one that points toward solidarity. It is a recognition that our intellectual work is always at the same time unavoidably political work, even struggle, *for someone*. This is based on field-work-driven scholarly exploration and research inquiries embedded in the realties on the ground. The purpose is not only to better explain these realities but also to contribute to an emancipatory process of knowledge production that aims to change those detrimental realities.

This approach to knowledge, politics, and struggle follows Stuart Hall, Robin D. G. Kelley, and Edward Said's recognition that "All knowledge is interpretation, and that interpretation must be self-conscious in its method and its aims if it is to be vigilant and humane" (1997b, 172). This methodological sensibility and reflexivity underlying every interpretation of politics and culture is attentive to what Said understood as "the choice facing the individual scholar or intellectual: whether to put intellect at the service of power or at the service of criticism, community, dialogue, and moral sense" (1997b, 172). This matters not least in terms of how the production of oppositional knowledges has the potential to articulate alternative imaginaries for political action and struggle. Hall understood this as engagement on two fronts simultaneously. It is intellectual theoretical work "to know deeply and profoundly" as well as a kind of activism that has the potential "to give politically useful tools of analysis to individuals who were on the disadvantaged end of the playing field" (Robbins 2016). In an *LA Times* interview, Robin D. G. Kelly put it this way:

> It's really important for me to be engaged in these movements, to make no pretense about some kind of dispassionate, detached objectivity. I think that we need to practice something that's even better than objectivity. And that is, as you know, critique. Critique, to me, is better than objectivity. Objectivity is a false stance. I'm not neutral. I've never been neutral. I write about struggles and social movements because I actually don't think the world is right and something needs to change. (Kelley and Cunningham 2021)

Finally, each chapter reflects on the *tension between domination and resistance* in a settler colonial context, considering their focus or "site" as one of both domination and resistance. This is an important analytic for our book. The chapters explore sites of control such as digital surveillance but then also the centrality of land in organizing. The chapters provide a compelling analysis of structures of domination in the post-Oslo period but situating this period in a longer history of struggle in Palestine. The book explores unique sites in the health sector, IT sector, development sector, education sector, and taken together, the chapters expose the tensions within these sites. They also expose weaknesses in the colonial system and what Palestinians have already been doing to exploit those weaknesses and remain steadfast in their efforts to do so.

Book Overview

This edited volume contains four parts, each exploring a particular site of domination and resistance. The first part focuses on *political* sites of control, domination, and refusal. Chapters elaborate the political aspects of settler colonialism through an analysis on governmentality and institutions and mechanisms of control. The health and technology sectors are analyzed for the ways they reveal Israel's control over access, life, and death. The structural violence manifest in occupied Palestine is also examined in terms of its governmentalizing effects and mechanisms of domination and control, including an intricate closure regime that renders movement a political act of refusal.

In his chapter, Tariq Dana explores Israel's capacity to dominate and control Palestinians through a "Palestinian autonomy" practiced by the Palestinian Authority (PA) since the signing of the Oslo Accords in 1993/4. Dana unpacks this form of autonomy as one designed to facilitate Israel's quest for indirect colonial rule—only feasible by subcontracting a segment of the Palestinian Liberation Organization (PLO) leadership to oversee the autonomy functions on behalf of Israel—while simultaneously separating Palestinians from their land, legally and physically. And yet, as Dana explains, Israel's relentless attempts to enforce this autonomy have often encountered effective resistance by the Palestinians.

Next, Yara M. Asi examines the structural violence of Israel's medical permit regime. Due to the inadequate Palestinian health system, many Palestinians must receive care in Israel, the West Bank, or East Jerusalem, leaving them at the mercy of a system of medical permits issued by Israel. In her chapter, Asi analyzes available medical permit data from the Gaza Strip and West Bank for the years 2011–19, assessing levels of conflict and security by evaluating the Israeli Global Peace Index (GPI) and Global Terrorism Index (GTI) scores and Israeli fatality and injury data from OCHA. She concludes that although Israel has arguably become more secure since 2011, the permit regime has grown more restrictive, disputing the claims that these permits and other movement restrictions imposed on Palestinians are necessary due to security concerns.

Nijmeh Ali explores digital expressions of domination and resistance. The digital era provides an open platform to practice freedoms in oppressive contexts. However, she argues, this view is incomplete, considering the counter-use of technologies as mass surveillance tools to spy, collect information, and restrict activities. Ali describes how Israel has become a leading exporter of this surveillance technology. And while this is particularly concerning for Palestinians, she points out that it is also dangerous for its potential to contribute more broadly to the shrinking global space for civil society organizations and the continued silencing of human rights defenders, activists, and organizations worldwide.

In the final chapter in Part I, We'am Hamdan explores the lived experiences of workers in the information and communications technology (ICT) sector. Despite the settler colonial context shaped by fragmentation, international interventions reflect a broader trend of experimenting with tech solutions to political economic problems in line with the neoliberal paradigm. In her chapter, Hamdan interviewed digital freelancers working in the ICT field and/or aspiring to join the global digital workforce. She finds that they experience a contradiction between aspirations that are believed to be universal and recurring structural barriers of de-development in occupied Palestine. Her study identifies three common themes in ICT workers' experiences: power relations resulting from the imposed Israeli occupation, capitalism's influence on education, and social constructs of the patriarchal family.

The second part of this book focuses on *economic* sites of exploitation, dispossession, and de-development. Chapters explore critical issues related to banking and taxation examining the relationships between finance capital, aid conditionalities, and military occupation as (neoliberal) technologies of exploitation and dispossession that are shaped by imperial histories and a settler colonial present.

In the first chapter in this part, Heba Taha explores the theoretical and empirical connections between Israel's economic and technical aid industry in African countries and colonial practices toward Palestinians in the decades immediately following Israel's establishment. This geographic entanglement, she argues, relied on global economic circuits, moral imaginaries, and cultural representations pertaining to the principles, practices, and promises of development. Such plans highlight the production of Palestinians as subjects of both Israeli capitalism and colonialism while at the same time revealing the ways in which Palestinian dispossession becomes part of global developmental imaginaries in the 1950s.

In his chapter, Colin Powers considers the interfacing between Israeli settler colonialism and endogenous Palestinian dynamics as it pertains to matters of monetary policy, money, and finance, tracing the effects of this dialectical exchange from 1967 through the present day. His analysis establishes that the Palestinian Authority's coerced adoption of the Israeli shekel curtails Palestinian development through a number of channels, and that the absence of independent payment and clearance systems keeps the Palestinian economy in a permanent state of vulnerability. He also finds that tendencies of credit intermediation in Palestine—which largely derive from the restraints imposed by the occupation—not only intensify macroeconomic distortions while heightening inequality but also render debt a sinew of social relations and foundation to the PA's fiscal viability.

Anas Iqtait closes out Part II with his chapter exploring the fiscal dynamics within the Palestinian Authority, shaped by the Paris Protocol and Israel's economic system of control. It delves into the politics of the PA's revenue mobilization, unpacks the influence of settler colonial structures on the PA's operations, and highlights the formidable challenges in formulating a fiscal contract amidst external influences and structural constraints. Findings reveal that despite three decades of public revenue administration and tax collection, the PA has not developed a foundational fiscal contract, with numerous structural constraints including the external nature of the PA's "institutions-building" process, its dependence on foreign aid and clearance revenue, Israeli extraction of taxes, and the proliferation of public service providers.

The third part of this edited volume explores *environmental* sites of domination and resistance and is situated within the settler colonial context. Chapters in this part focus on land, indigeneity, and space as critical elements to understanding settler colonialism, clarifying the context of racial capitalism in occupied Palestine.

In their chapter, Gabi Kirk and Paul Kohlbry make a case for approaching the study of rural Palestine through foregrounding the transnational forces that shape rural property, labor, and agriculture. After establishing some key concerns of this scholarship in Palestine, they sketch out the geography of how to study agrarian questions, distinguishing between studying Palestine and Palestinians, showing how what happens to and on rural land in the territory of historic Palestine must be comprehended by including Palestinian refugees, migrants, and exiles living abroad. Finally they show how framing local questions in Palestine through an international lens can productively approach long-standing concerns around class, gender, and space, as well as newer issues in the climate change era of commodity circulation and ecological resilience.

Timothy Seidel and Federica Stagni's chapter explores settler colonialism and Indigenous struggle in Palestine, emphasizing that a decolonial analysis gives attention not only to enduring indigeneity but also to the role of land in the struggle for autonomy, sovereignty, and self-determination. They examine "everyday" acts of resistance and popular struggle that take the form of *sumud*, or steadfastness, that may not be about a predetermined political economic telos per se but about existence, being, land, and a refusal of erasure and elimination. With this framework and understanding of popular struggle, they argue, we begin to hear and see a much larger and more powerful landscape of resistance to settler violence in occupied Palestine, for example, in this case of Masafer Yatta in the occupied South Hebron Hills.

Finally, Part IV of the book explores *epistemic* sites of domination and resistance, highlighting the ways norms, narratives, and knowledge production itself can demonstrate a commitment to liberation and freedom or perpetuate control and domination. Chapters in this part examine the definitions, methods, and frameworks used to study and teach as well as analyze policies and norms about Palestine that challenge the liberal peace.

In the first chapter of this final part, Somdeep Sen looks at the adoption of the IHRA definition of anti-Semitism at institutions of higher education, analyzing IHRA and academic censorship in view of the wider ideology and politics of settler colonialism. Sen notes that the IHRA definition seeks to circumscribe scholarship and pedagogical approaches that recognize the legitimacy, existence, and persistence of the Palestinian national cause as doing so undermines the myth of *terra nullis*—namely that Israel was built on a "land without a people for a people without a land." Sen concludes that IHRA is an extension of the settler colonial urge to erase the evidence of Indigenous existence. And its adoption across universities in the Global North is only evidence of the globalization of the politics of settler colonialism.

Next, Jeremy Wildeman traces how the intervention of Western liberal democracies has benefited Israeli settler colonial state-building, at the expense of Palestinian statehood and peace. His chapter explores how this process has unfolded, focusing on examples from three periods: the UN partition of Palestine (1940s), the Oslo Peace Process (1990s), and Western-led Palestine state-building after the Second Intifada (mid-2000s/2010s). This Western intervention has happened in an age of global decolonization and Western-driven global liberalism, where racist colonial ways of thinking remained inherent with how Western powers approached Palestine-Israel, demonstrably favoring the more "Europeanized" Israelis at the expense of the "Orientalized" Palestinians. The consistency with which Western states have prioritized Israeli perspectives and reinforced its illiberal settler colonial regime raises questions if Palestinians can trust Western intervention in the region.

In the book's final chapter, Melanie Meinzer takes a close look at Palestinian popular education post-Oslo. Palestinian NGOs' dependence on foreign aid during Oslo redirected civil society's energies toward donor priorities and weakened Palestinian resistance movements. Meinzer argues that despite these obstacles, the spirit and pedagogies of the Intifada-era popular education movement are alive today and serve as a bulwark against cultural erasure under donor-enabled Israeli settler colonialism. Drawing on interviews and surveys, she shows how NGOs, community-based organizations, and educators have reconstituted the popular education movement by using political theater, visual arts, debate, and storytelling to conscientize and mobilize young people. She concludes that while aid dependence restricts Palestinian self-determination, popular education continues to be a vehicle for personal and collective liberation.

Conclusion

Labeled by human rights organizations as the world's largest open-air prison, the occupied Gaza Strip is one of the most densely populated places on earth. Since 2007 Israel has imposed a blockade on Gaza that human rights organizations also call a form of collective punishment—an act in violation of international humanitarian and human rights law (UN OHCHR 2020; Middle East Eye 2020). During the Great March of Return in Gaza, a series of protests that began in March 2018 along the Gaza-Israel frontier to challenge the Israeli-imposed blockade, another poignant story emerged that embodies the contradictions between domination and resistance in Palestine. Razan Al-Najjar, a 21-year-old Palestinian volunteer medic, was a beacon of hope and compassion amid the chaos and violence that unfolded during the protests.

Razan dedicated herself to providing first aid to injured protesters, putting her own life at risk to save others. Her unwavering commitment to humanitarian aid and her bravery in the face of danger gained her recognition and admiration, both locally and internationally. In an interview with the *New York Times*, Razan said, "We have one goal: to save lives and evacuate people. And to send a message to the world: Without weapons, we can do anything" (Abuheweila and Kershner 2018). The Great March of Return was characterized by popular demonstrations and protests that were exploited by the Israeli military as a testing ground for its new high-tech weapons (Dana 2020). In the *Times* interview, Razan went on to describe her work and the work of the other volunteer medics as acts of humanitarianism and love. "We do this for our love for the country," she said. "We don't do it for money, we do it for God."

On June 1, 2018, while tending to the wounded during a protest, Razan was tragically killed by Israeli sniper fire. She was wearing a white paramedic's uniform, which clearly identified her as a medical worker. Her death shocked the world and served as a stark reminder of the perils faced by Palestinians who dare to defy the forces of domination and stand up for their rights.

The story of Razan Al-Najjar represents the courageous spirit of resistance against settler colonial oppression and serves as a testament to the selflessness and dedication of those who struggle tirelessly to alleviate the suffering of their people.

As we embark on the journey through this edited volume, we invite you to let the stories of both Muna El-Kurd and Razan Al-Najjar serve as an embodiment of the indomitable spirit of resistance in the face of domination and oppression and as a testament to the transformative power of grassroots activism, popular struggle, and resistance.

References

Abuheweila, Iyad and Isabel Kershner (2018), "A Woman Dedicated to Saving Lives Loses Hers in Gaza Violence." *New York Times*, June 2. https://www.nytimes.com/2018/06/02/world/middleeast/gaza-paramedic-killed.html.

Atkinson, David (2000), "Nomadic Strategies and Colonial Governance: Domination and the Resistance in Cyrenaice, 1923–1932." In J. Sharp, P. Routledge, C. Philo, and R. Paddison (eds), *Entanglements of Power: Geographies of Domination/Resistance*, 256–68. London: Routledge.

Awad, Hani (2023), "Israeli Colonial Governance vs. Palestinian Resistance: An Institutional Genealogy." *Middle East Critique*, 32 (3): 401–28.

Baconi, Tariq (2022), "Israel's Apartheid: A Structure of Colonial Domination since 1948." *Journal of Palestine Studies*, 51 (3): 44–9.

Bishara, Azmi (2022), *Palestine: Matters of Truth and Justice*. London: Hurst.

Coulthard, Glen Sean (2014), *Red Skin, White Masks: Rejecting the Colonial Politics of Recognition*. Minneapolis: University of Minnesota.

Dana, Tariq (2020), "A Cruel Innovation: Israeli Experiments on Gaza's Great March of Return." *Sociology of Islam*, 8 (2): 175–98.

Dana, Tariq and Ali Jarbawi (2017), "A Century of Settler Colonialism in Palestine." *The Brown Journal of World Affairs*, 24 (1): 197–220.

Dana, Tariq and Ali Jarbawi (2023), "Whose Autonomy? Conceptualizing "Colonial Extraterritorial Autonomy" in the Occupied Palestinian Territories." *Politics*, 43 (1): 106–21.

Farsakh, Leila (ed.). (2021), *Rethinking Statehood in Palestine: Self-Determination and Decolonization Beyond Partition*. Oakland: University of California Press.

Hawari, Yara, Sharri Plonski, and Elian Weizman (2019), "Settlers and Citizens: A Critical View of Israeli Society." *Settler Colonial Studies*, 9 (1): 1–5.

Kauanui, J. Kēhaulani (2016), "'A Structure, Not an Event': Settler Colonialism and Enduring Indigeneity." *Lateral*, 5 (1). http://csalateral.org/wp/issue/5-1/forum-alt-humanities-settler-colonialism-enduring-indigeneity-kauanui.

Kelley, Robin D. G. and Vinison Cunningham (2021), "The Future of L.A. Is Here. Robin D.G. Kelley's Radical Imagination Shows Us the Way." *Los Angeles Times*, March 17. https://www.latimes.com/lifestyle/image/story/2021-03-17/robin-dg-kelley-black-marxism-protests-la-politics.

Khalidi, Rashid (2020), *The Hundred Years' War on Palestine: A History of Settler Colonialism and Resistance, 1917–2017*. New York: Metropolitan Books.

Lloyd, David (2012), "Settler Colonialism and the State of Exception: The Example of Palestine/Israel." *Settler Colonial Studies*, 2 (1): 59–80.

Maldonado-Torres, Nelson (2016), *Outline of Ten Theses on Coloniality and Decoloniality*. Paris: Frantz Fanon Foundation.

Middle East Eye (2020), "Israel's 'Collective Punishment of Palestinians' Condemned by UN Expert." *Middle East Eye*, July 17. https://www.middleeasteye.net/news/israel-collective-punishment-gaza-palestinian-un.

Mignolo, Walter (2011), *The Darker Side of Western Modernity: Global Futures, Decolonial Options*. Durham: Duke University Press.

Pappe, Ilan (2014), *The Idea of Israel: A History of Power and Knowledge*. London: Verso.

Quijano, Anibal (2007), "Coloniality and Modernity/Rationality." *Cultural Studies*, 21 (2): 168–78.

Robbins, Bruce (2016), "A Starting Point for Politics: The Radical Life and Times of Stuart Hall." *The Nation*, October 27. https://www.thenation.com/article/the-radical-life-of-stuart-hall/.

Said, Edward W. (1997a), "Zionism from the Standpoint of its Victims." In Anne McClintock, Aamir Mufti, and Ella Shochat (eds), *Dangerous Liaisons: Gender, Nation, and Postcolonial Perspectives*, 15–38. Minneapolis and London: University of Minnesota.

Said, Edward W. (1997b), *Covering Islam: How the Media and the Experts Determine How We See the Rest of the World*. New York: Vintage.

Salaita, Steven (2016), *Inter/Nationalism: Decolonizing Native America and Palestine*. Minneapolis: University of Minnesota.

Salamanca, Omar Jabary, Mezna Qato, Kareem Rabie, and Sobhi Samour (2012), "Past is Present: Settler Colonialism in Palestine." *Settler Colonial Studies*, 2 (1): 1–8.

Sayegh, Fayez (1965), *Zionist Colonialism in Palestine*. Beirut: Research Center of the Palestine Liberation Organization.

Scott, James C. (1990), *Domination and the Arts of Resistance: Hidden Transcripts*. New Haven: Yale University.

Seidel, Timothy (2021), "Settler Colonialism and Land-Based Struggle in Palestine: Towards a Decolonial Political Economy." In A. Tartir, T. Dana, and T. Seidel (eds), *Political Economy of Palestine: Critical, Interdisciplinary, and Decolonial Perspectives*, 81–107. New York: Palgrave Macmillan.

Seidel, Timothy (2023), "'Emigrantes, Palestinos, Estamos Unidos': Anticolonial Connectivity and Resistance along the 'Palestine-Mexico' Border." *Postcolonial Studies*, 26 (1): 94–111.

Shlaim, Avi (2020), "Palestine and the West: A Century of Betrayal." *Middle East Eye*, February 17. https://www.middleeasteye.net/opinion/palestine-and-west-century-betrayal.

Tartir, Alaa, Tariq Dana, and Timothy Seidel (eds.). (2021), *Political Economy of Palestine: Critical, Interdisciplinary, and Decolonial Perspectives*. New York: Palgrave Macmillan.

Tartir, Alaa and Timothy Seidel (eds.). (2019), *Palestine and Rule of Power: Local Dissent vs. International Governance*. New York: Palgrave Macmillan.

Turner, Mandy (ed.). (2019), *From the River to the Sea: Palestine and Israel in the Shadow of "Peace"*. Lanham: Lexington Books.

UN OHCHR (2020), "Israel's Collective Punishment of Palestinians Illegal and an Affront to Justice: UN Expert." *UN Office of the High Commissioner for Human Rights*, July 17. https://www.ohchr.org/en/press-releases/2020/07/israels-collective-punishment-palestinians-illegal-and-affront-justice-un.

Wolfe, Patrick (2006), "Settler Colonialism and the Elimination of the Native." *Journal of Genocide Research*, 8 (4): 387–409.

Zureik, Elia (2015), *Israel's Colonial Project in Palestine: Brutal Pursuit*. London: Routledge.

Part I

Political Governmentality and Mechanisms of Control

In this first part, we consider *political* sites of control, domination, and refusal. Chapters elaborate the political aspects of settler colonialism, through an analysis of governmentality, structural violence, and institutions and technologies of control. The health and technology sectors are analyzed for the ways they reveal Israel's control over access, life, and death. The structural violence manifest in occupied Palestine is also examined in terms of its governmentalizing effects and technologies of domination and control, including an intricate closure regime that renders movement a political act of refusal.

In "Elimination by Other Means: Colonial Autonomy and Indirect Colonial Rule in the Occupied Palestinian Territories," Tariq Dana explores Israel's capacity to dominate and control Palestinians through a "Palestinian autonomy" practiced by the Palestinian Authority (PA) since the signing of the Oslo Accords in 1994. Dana unpacks this form of autonomy as one designed to facilitate Israel's quest for indirect colonial rule—made feasible by subcontracting a segment of the PLO leadership to oversee autonomy functions on behalf of Israel—while simultaneously separating Palestinians from their land, legally and physically. And yet, as Dana explains, Israel's relentless attempts to enforce this autonomy has often encountered effective resistance by the Palestinians.

Next, Yara M. Asi examines the structural violence of Israel's medical permit regime. One of the most pervasive barriers to Palestinian health is the restricted movement of Palestinians. An inadequate health system means many Palestinians must cross borders to receive care leaving them at the mercy of a complex system of medical permits controlled and issued by Israel. In her chapter "The Bureaucracy of Mortality: The Structural Violence of Medical Permits for Palestinians in the West Bank and Gaza Strip," Asi analyzes available medical permit data from the Gaza Strip and West Bank for the years 2011–19. She concludes that although Israel has arguably become more secure since 2011, the permit regime has grown more restrictive, disputing the claims that these permits and other movement restrictions imposed on Palestinians are necessary due to security concerns.

In "Israeli Online Surveillance Regime: Digital Colonization in Practice," Nijmeh Ali explores digital expressions of domination and resistance. The digital era provides an open platform to practice freedoms in oppressive contexts. However, she argues, this view is incomplete, considering the counter-use of technologies as mass surveillance tools to spy, collect information, and restrict activities. Ali describes how Israel has become a leading exporter of this surveillance technology. And while this is particularly concerning for Palestinians, she points out that it is also dangerous for its potential to contribute more broadly to the shrinking global space for civil society organizations and the continued silencing of human rights defenders, activists, and organizations worldwide.

In the final chapter in Part I, We'am Hamdan explores the lived experiences of workers in the information and communications technology (ICT) sector. Despite the settler colonial context characterized by fragmentation, international interventions reflect a broader trend of experimenting with tech solutions to political economic problems in line with the neoliberal paradigm. In "The Political Economy of Education and Technology: A Focus on the Lived Experiences of Palestinian Digital Freelancers," Hamdan interviewed digital freelancers working in ICT field and/or aspiring to join the global digital workforce. She finds that they experience a contradiction between aspirations that are believed to be universal and recurring structural barriers of de-development in occupied Palestine. Her study identifies three common themes in ICT workers' experiences: power relations resulting from the imposed Israeli occupation, capitalism's influence on education, and social constructs of the patriarchal family.

2

Elimination by Other Means

Colonial Autonomy and Indirect Colonial Rule in the Occupied Palestinian Territories

Tariq Dana

Introduction

In October 2018, the Israeli prime minister, Benjamin Netanyahu, speaking at the General Assembly of the Jewish Federations of North America, reiterated a long-held Zionist vision based on the notion of "Palestinian autonomy" to solve the Israeli-Palestinian conflict. This time, however, he expressed indifference toward the labeling of this entity by saying, "You can give it any name you want: state-minus, autonomy-plus, autonomy plus-plus." For Netanyahu and his right-wing bloc, one thing remains clear and firm: Israel would maintain sovereign control over the "area west of Jordan." Netanyahu's desire was taken up by Donald Trump's "Deal of the Century" plan, officially unveiled in January 2020 under the title "Peace to Prosperity: A Vision to Improve the Lives of the Palestinian and Israeli People." Trump's deal gives the Israeli settler colonial enterprise a leeway to legitimize its decades-long expansionism by authorizing it to annex major parts of the West Bank. In the remaining substantially diminished Palestinian areas, the plan envisions the establishment of a "demilitarized Palestinian state" that falls short of sovereignty. It lacks nominal power and limited jurisdiction within contiguous enclaves fully surrounded by Israel. It is also economically and spatially unviable for normal human activities, let alone for a meaningful polity. At best, such an entity would rather introduce a modified version of the Oslo-framed autonomy (Dana and Jarbawi 2023).[1]

The origin of these dramatic developments lies deep in the myth of "land without the people" that guided the Zionist movement in the pre-1948 era and its operational logic of "maximum land with minimum Arabs" that dominated the post-1967 Israeli strategies toward the occupied Palestinian territories (oPt). From a Zionist perspective, the Palestinian population living in the areas from the Jordan River to the Mediterranean Sea constitutes a demographic threat to the Jewish ethnonational character of the Israeli state. Thus, from the beginning of the Zionist colonization of Palestine, the interplay of demography and territory has been at the forefront of the

Israeli war against the Palestinians, seeking to neutralize the "demographic burden" to secure unchallenged Jewish hegemony and sovereignty over the territories.

In its first phase, the Zionist colonization instituted itself by inflicting a widespread violent depopulation of hundreds of Palestinian towns and villages in 1948, transforming the remaining Palestinians into an involuntary minority subjugated by Israel's discriminatory legal regime (Molavi 2013). The second phase is marked by the colonization of the West Bank, Gaza Strip, and East Jerusalem after the Arab-Israeli war in 1967. Israel's sudden takeover of these territories was not directed by a pre-orchestrated plan to replicate the 1948 eliminatory scenario. Moreover, the 1967 occupation coincided with the age of decolonization, the international recognition of the right to self-determination, and the rise of international law. All these complications forced Israel to deal with the Palestinian population density, which, for decades, rendered its settler colonial project incomplete and trouble ridden (Dana and Jarbawi 2017).

After 1967 occupation, Israeli strategists embarked on careful calculations that primarily aimed to redefine the territory/demography equation—to annex the land and exclude the Palestinians. Israel engineered complex governmentality methods to create legal and physical distinctions between the land and the Palestinians (Zureik 2016). Chief among these methods has revolved around the notion of "Palestinian autonomy." Indeed, far predating the Oslo autonomy arrangement in 1993, the autonomy vision has predominated the Israeli political thought since the aftermath of 1967 occupation, enjoying a quasi-consensus across the Israeli political spectrum—albeit with competing views regarding secondary details. Common to the different perspectives on the Palestinian autonomy is a number of conditions: it should be spatially limited, demographically dense, institutionally fragile, and able to administer the life conditions imposed by Israel. The overall objective for creating the Palestinian autonomy is to facilitate the annexation of vast territories and natural resources, enlarge the Jewish-only settlements, and counteract the Palestinian demographic challenge.

Strikingly, however, this autonomy vision does not resemble any other autonomy model implemented around the world. An examination of the Israeli envisaged autonomy, either as exemplified in the pre-Oslo plans or in its Oslo form, reveals numerous contradictions with the meanings, structures, functions, and relations common to the standard political autonomy. While scant studies casted doubt on the relevancy of autonomy in the Palestinian context, most studies have taken the notion of autonomy for granted. As such, the notion remains understudied and lacks a proper comparative explanation, despite the centrality of the autonomy to Israel's settler colonial design.

The Contemporary Usage of Political Autonomy

Academic debates point to the ambiguity of political autonomy, implying different meanings and manifestations across different temporal and geographical contexts. As noted by Pickerill and Chatterton (2006, 732), the conceptualization of political autonomy has been "moveable, historically specific, highly contextual and contested and used to pursue a variety of ends and ideologies." Despite the apparent lack of clarity, there persists a core aspect that enjoys broad agreement; that is, autonomy is the capacity of an entity/person to decide and act freely on their own affairs without interference and restraints by external forces. This core aspect made autonomy synonymous to, or associated with, independence, freedom, self-rule, self-government, self-determination, self-reliance, and self-direction. According to the *Encyclopedia of Global Justice*, political autonomy "means not under the control of another; the control is a matter of degree. Global justice, transcending both country boundaries and culturally based ethics, implies that not just minority groups but all persons individually have a human right to a significant degree of autonomy" (Foldvary 2011).

Today, political autonomy is almost exclusively associated with the "minority question" within the nation-state. This understanding has developed over centuries as a legal and political antidote to the inadequacies of the Westphalian conception of the nation-state, which resulted in troubled relationships between the state and its national minority. As evidenced in numerous historical and geographical instances, tensions between the state and the minority may escalate into a secessionist claim by the minority, repression by the state, and, at worst, lead to protracted violent conflicts. In this context, political autonomy is proposed as a conflict resolution instrument to compromise between the minority's secessionist claims and the state territorial integrity (Walsh 2018; Weller and Wolff 2005). It does so by offering a power-sharing mechanism and mutually agreed arrangements that stipulate the transfer of certain powers from the central government to the minority's self-governing institutions (Gagnon and Keating 2012). Thus, political autonomy transforms the conventional self-determination for independence to "internal self-determination" with guarantees of constitutional protection of the minority's political, religious, linguistic, and cultural rights through autonomous regulations and institutions (Moore 2003).

Political autonomy is often applied in two standard forms. The first is territorial, which is implementable in a territorially defined region where the minority is concentrated and constitutes the majority population. A key to this autonomy arrangement is the transfer of certain political and legislative powers from the central government to the self-governing institutions. In this case, the autonomous region is granted a special legal status under state sovereignty. The second is nonterritorial autonomy, sometimes called cultural or personal autonomy, and is granted to a minority group dispersed across the national territory. This form provides the minority the legal and institutional protection to express its distinctive cultural identity and establish autonomous institutions and regulations, including in the education, civil, legal, and religious spheres (see, e.g., Ghai 2001, 23).

In either case, political autonomy is regulated by three central conditions. First, it is an intrastate arrangement based on redefining the relationship between the state and a minority segment of its citizens (Brancati 2009). In this sense, political autonomy is *inclusionary* because it elevates the citizenship status of the minority through autonomous institutions and self-government mechanisms within the state. Political autonomy, therefore, is inconceivable between the state and non-nationals, noncitizens, or foreigners. Whereas, in some cases, autonomy is generated by international pressure or intervention, as in the post-Yugoslavia reconstruction of the

Balkans, the negotiation over its extent and provisions usually occurs within a national framework. This is because widespread public support is a key to successful and sustainable implementation of the autonomy (Ghai 2001). Second, political autonomy is implemented within the state's territorial domain, either within one region as in Kurdistan in Iraq or across the country as in the case of Spain *comunidad autónoma*. Therefore, autonomy is *unitary* in the sense that it promotes the uncontested territorial sovereignty of the state. In other words, political autonomy cannot be implemented in an alien region or enforced on an occupied territory outside the state's territorial jurisdiction. Third, the scope and degree of the autonomy arrangement are subject to internal statutes and national agreements (Heraclides 1990). By virtue of its consensual framework, political autonomy is implemented by a voluntary will and cannot be coercively enforced.

Nevertheless, political autonomy appeared in colonial history as a glass ceiling to emancipatory ambitions. Since the late eighteenth century through the decolonization of the Global South in mid-twentieth century, the British in particular and other colonial powers in general implanted a hybrid form of autonomy in distant colonies as part of the "indirect colonial rule" system. The indirect rule system was invented as a response to the crisis of the empire and its inability to continue preserving colonies through the conventional direct rule (Mamdani 2012, 8). Autonomy served as the institutional pillar of this arrangement because day-to-day governance was delegated from the colonial power to local power holders such as hereditary elite and domestic middlemen. The autonomy leaders relied on customary law and indigenous institutions to rule the population on behalf of the colonial power. Thus, autonomy was central to the reproduction of colonial governmentality in the form of indirect rule or in what Mamdani (2012) dubbed "decentralized despotism."

Three aspects characterize this colonial-sponsored autonomy. First, as a cost-benefit strategy, autonomy facilitated the colonial quest for further colonization beyond the metropoles' capacity and resources. Since the local autonomy took care of day-to-day governance, the colonial power was relieved from the costly deployment of vast militaries and bureaucracies in the colonies. Second, the local autonomy ensured better stability and security conditions for the colonial system. Given the decreased presence of the colonial troops on the ground, tensions that could arise from the direct encounter between the colonizer and the colonized were largely minimized. Well-trained and armed local security forces took internal policing responsibility, protecting the autonomy's ruling elite and suppressing resistance (Killingray 1986). Therefore, autonomy served as a deterrent mechanism to anti-colonial rebellion since people are expected to be less likely to rebel against their own leaders than against foreign rulers. Third, in terms of governance, the colonial power supported and sustained the traditional social system and encouraged patronage politics to stabilize the indirect rule system through the pacification of the population (Killingray 1986). Another aspect is the local ruling elite's acquiescence to the colonial decisions and interests in exchange for special privileges and protection. Failing to meet the colonial conditions would result in removing and replacing the noncompliant leaders with a "manufactured" loyal elite to the colonial system (Myers 2008, 4; Crowder 1964, 199).

Understanding Israeli Colonial Autonomy

What exists in the West Bank today is a peculiar form of autonomy that stands in sharp contrast to almost every aspect, structure, function, and objective of the contemporary autonomy models discussed in the previous section. It is colonial at its very core—a by-product of Israeli settler colonial expansion that requires innovative governance structures to reproduce colonial domination in more effective ways (Dana 2022).

Perhaps such uniqueness stems from the Palestinian context being the only active site for settler colonialism in the age, a matter that is often conducive to the emergence of unusual dynamics. This colonial autonomy has been developed and implemented to accommodate Israel's dual ambition for "maximum land with minimum Arabs." Moreover, although this form of autonomy shares striking similarities with the rationale that guided the past colonial-sponsored autonomy of indirect colonial rule, it is distinguished by major differences that make it largely unique.

First, the implantation of autonomy in a distant colony differs significantly from the contemporary settler colonial situation in the oPt. While the first relies on the autonomy of the native to facilitate the colonial exploitation of economic resources and labor, Israel uses autonomy as a transitional instrument for capturing more lands and resources while creating the conditions for the "transfer" of the Palestinians. The term "transfer" implies two meanings that collectively aim to empty the land of its Palestinian inhabitants. The first is immediate and is based on the legal exclusion of the Palestinians from the Israeli citizenship system to preserve the Jewishness of the state. The second denotes the long-term objective of forcing the Palestinians to leave their land, either by violent means or voluntarily by projecting a variety of political, social, economic, legal, and psychological pressure (Masalha 1997; Zureik 2003). Second, colonial autonomy reduces the costs on the colonial administration as in the past colonial autonomy. It seeks to redeploy the military forces and transfer the administrative costs to the autonomy's institutions. However, the different temporal context has offered Israel's colonial autonomy generous financial backing under the banner of "peacebuilding," exemplified by the flow of international aid and technical assistance by donor agencies and international organizations (Seidel 2019). Third, an acquiescent ruling elite is central to both forms of autonomy, mainly because it stands as intermediary between the colonial power and the local context. However, the main difference is that while the past colonial autonomy depended on the traditional elite to govern the autonomy, the colonial autonomy as embodied in the PA is legitimized by agreements with former leaders of the liberation movement. Fourth, the institutional aspect of both autonomy models is predicated on patron-client regime in an effort to stabilize the status quo. They, however, differ in the institutional setup. Whereas the past colonial autonomy was structured on traditional institutions combining tribal and religious authorities, the colonial autonomy is run by modern legal-bureaucratic apparatuses underpinned by neo-patrimonial networks.

Moreover, the Israeli colonial autonomy is specifically designed to obscure the struggle for self-determination and decolonization. It has affected the Palestinian population and their basic human and political rights at multiple levels.

1. *Perpetual statelessness*: The colonial autonomy is exclusionary by its very nature—mainly because it negates the existence of Palestinians as a discernable national community (Pace and Sen 2019, 3). The exclusionary dimension operates at dual levels: It excludes the Palestinians from the Israeli citizenship system and denies them the right to construct independent polity and nationality. In other words, it tends to inflect a status of perpetual statelessness by leaving the Palestinian population legally unrecognized, deprived of political rights, and unprotected by any sovereign polity. The stateless status and the lack of rights contribute to the Israeli long-standing policy of voluntary transfer. This is because the pressure caused by the statelessness status would push the Palestinians to search for personal recognition abroad, to immigrate to other countries where opportunities for citizenship and nationality are conceivable, and, by extension, the attainability of political and socioeconomic rights.
2. *Denial of residency and mobility*: Israeli colonial autonomy is shaped by myriad military and legal restrictions on the freedom of residency and mobility even inside and between the fragmented enclaves of the autonomous area. Denial of the residency right is expressed, for example, in Israel's control of the Population Registry to determine whether Palestinian individuals and families can qualify for identity documents and legal residency. The complex legal and bureaucratic procedures, often resulting in the rejection of family unification applications, have forced many Palestinian families, spouses, and children, to be torn apart. Another example is the military banning of the Palestinians from constructing houses, establishing businesses, and residing on their own private lands, as in Area C, which regularly results in the demolition of houses and properties by the Israeli forces. Similar restrictions are applied on the freedom of movement. This is particularly reflected in the so-called "closure regime," which restricts the movement of people, goods, and labor between the West Bank and Gaza, within the West Bank, and from these territories to Jerusalem and Israel (Peteet 2017).
3. *Deterritorialized jurisdiction*: This autonomy is deprived of the territorial base necessary to meet the basic requirements for a meaningful polity, economic development, and population growth. Its jurisdiction is confined merely to fragmented and discontinuous enclaves where the population is concentrated. This state of affairs corresponds to what Hanafi (2009, 107) terms "spacio-cide"—a process that "targets land for the purpose of rendering inevitable the 'voluntary' transfer of the Palestinian population, primarily by targeting the space upon which the Palestinian people live." The spacio-cidal regime is expressed in a wide range of policies and practices such as the confiscation of land and properties, the destruction of homes and infrastructure, and the physical and military besiegement of the Palestinian areas to cripple the urban growth.
4. *Fragile institutions*: The autonomy's institutions are regulated by various conditions and constraints. While they are expected to play a stabilizing role to prolong the status quo, the autonomy's institutions are purposefully kept weak and dependent on external financial and technical assistance. As demonstrated by extensive studies, the PA is devoid of key power resources for institution-building; its economy is structurally dependent on Israel; it cannot exert real

control over the narrow areas under its jurisdiction; and its security function is shaped by the Israeli security agenda. This led these institutions to become an informal extension to the colonial apparatus of control.

The Israeli Strategies for Colonial Autonomy in the oPt (1967–93)

Israel's victory in the 1967 Arab-Israeli war and the subsequent conquest of the oPt was marked by the rapid predominance of the maximalist claim for "Greater Israel" across the Israeli political spectrum (Masalha 2000). This ideological stance was expressed under different pretexts. Whereas the Labour Party and Zionist left subscribed to security considerations to justify tightening the grip on the oPt, the rising rightwing movements such as the Movement for Greater Israel and later the Likud Party embraced a religious-messianic and ethnonational narrative for annexing the oPt. Both the Zionist left and right implemented their visions simultaneously, combining the Judaization of the territories through the construction of Jewish settlements with a full-fledged military occupation and restrictive security conditions. Either way, both approaches are mutually inclusive and lead to dual separations. The first is the judicial and legal separation between the Palestinians and their lands, and the second is the racial and institutional separation between the Palestinians and the Jews (see, e.g., Lentin 2020; Lloyd 2012).

Central to the multilayered separation process is the idea of Palestinian autonomy, which developed over time and became a keyword in Israel's perception of "peace" to settle the Palestinian question. The early expression of Palestinian autonomy emerged immediately after the 1967 occupation and was central to two major plans that informed Israel's policy during the first decade (1967–77). The first is represented by the "Allon Plan," designed by the then Minister of Labor, Yigal Allon, and originally titled "The Future of the Territories and of the Refugees." The Allon Plan left a substantial imprint on the Israeli strategic planning in the spheres of security, borders, Jewish settlements, and the overall territorial divisions and the remapping of the oPt. Although the Allon Plan was not officially approved by the government at the time, its logic has influenced the subsequent Israeli policies including the Oslo-induced territorial division of the oPt (Achcar 2011).

While the Allon Plan was ostensibly driven by security considerations, it heavily draws on the long-held Zionist doctrine of "maximum territory for Israel with a minimum number of Arabs," as expressed in Allon's own words (quoted in Gordon 2008, 49). Elsewhere, Allon affirmed that his plan is designed "to ensure the fusion of the vision of Greater Israel from the strategic viewpoint with a Jewish state from a demographic viewpoint" (Quoted in Tzur 1982, 8).

Allon's strategic viewpoint has primarily projected extensive geographical reordering of the oPt, which encouraged annexing 40 percent of the West Bank areas considered of strategic significance, both in terms of security (e.g., defensible borders) and the economy (arable lands with abundant natural resources). These areas include the Jordan Valley along the borders with Jordan and the Dead Sea, large areas around Jerusalem, and within and around Hebron, leaving the town of Jericho as the only corridor for the Palestinians to interact with the outside world through Jordan (Shlaim 2015, 758–9; Raz 2012, 44). These areas would be Judaized through imposing "irreversible" facts on the ground such as Jewish settlements, military bases, and economic projects.

The geographical division in such a fashion complements Allon's demographic viewpoint. First, the areas to be annexed are thinly populated. In order to dispossess as many people as possible, Israel ethnically cleansed many villages along the eastern borders, the Jordan Valley, and several villages in Hebron after the 1967 war (Note by the UN Secretary-General, 1970). Second, densely populated towns would be left enclaved, disconnected, and encircled by Israeli settlements and military structures. This would equip Israel with the legal justification to exclude the Palestinians from the Israeli citizenship to prevent turning Israel into a binational polity.

The initial version of the plan favored granting the inhabitants a semiautonomous status under the direct Israeli control. This option, however, was short-lived. In 1969 Allon proposed amendments to the plan to promote the "Jordanian Option," which envisaged a limited Palestinian autonomy under the Jordanian sovereignty as the basis for a comprehensive peace agreement with Jordan (Khalifa 1981). Nevertheless, Allon promised to institute a deep-seated Israeli control over the autonomy arrangement through an implicit system of indirect rule. In 1976, he affirmed that the autonomy would be conditioned by "absolute Israeli control" and "effective demilitarization." By adopting the "Jordanian option," Allon intended to negate the Palestinian national identity, which he referred to as a "problem" that should "find its expression in a single Jordanian-Palestinian state" (Allon 1976).

The second plan, widely known as the "Open Bridges," was spearheaded by Moshe Dayan, then the Israeli minister of defense during the 1967 war. The Open Bridges acted as a counterinsurgency strategy that aimed to promote pacification and encourage self-management. Although Dayan did not explicitly use the term "Palestinian autonomy," his plan was primarily designed to institute the infrastructure of self-rule. Dayan's overall objective was "to leave the Arabs alone as much as possible while sustaining a Jewish presence and military control in the area" (Sicherman 2019, 102). Bishara notes that the implicit long-term objective of the Open Bridges was to impose a "functional compromise," where a limited autonomy administered by the traditional elite would satisfy Israeli needs for security and population management (Bishara 2020, 23).

The Open Bridges operated at two fundamental levels: the economy and local governance. The economic level was reflected in a set of policies of dual objectives. On the one hand, it aimed to pacify the population by supporting limited economic projects directly linked to the Israeli economy (Hever 2010). On the other hand, the policy implanted the seeds of Palestinian economic dependency on Israel through capturing the Palestinian natural resources, transforming the Palestinian peasants into unskilled labor in the Israeli marketplace, and turning the Palestinian businesses into subcontractors to Israeli companies (Abed 1988). In the governance realm, the Open Bridges promoted the local authority of the traditional elite and institutions that governed the Palestinian society during the Jordanian rule (1948–67) (Shafir 2017, 85).

First, this elite would facilitate the "Jordanian Option" through fostering the Jordanian influence on the Palestinian society. Second, the traditional elite was politically moderate and would accommodate much of the Israeli requirements for population management and retaining stability (Lukacs 1999, 141). Third, the traditional elite was positioned as a central force in Israel's effort to deter the raising power of the nationalist leadership affiliated with the PLO.

By the end of the first decade of Israel's occupation, the Open Bridges resulted in two contrasting outcomes. Whereas it created Palestinian dependency on the Israeli economy and consolidated Israeli control over the Palestinian life, the accompanying social and class changes have significantly weakened the traditional elite that Israel hoped to empower vis-à-vis the PLO leadership (Hilal 1977; Hiltermann 1993, 9). The erosion of the traditional elite power base is attributable to Israel's policy of land confiscation, which turned a large segment of the elite's constituents, mainly the peasants, into proletariats in the Israeli marketplace. As a result, the power over the population shifted in favor of the PLO nationalists.

The Open Bridges failure to secure pacification and to counterbalance the PLO was evidenced in the result of the municipal elections held in the oPt in 1976. Israel hoped that the elections would empower the traditional elite through whom Israel could legitimize the autonomy solution either within the framework of the "Jordanian option" or under the direct Israeli rule (Lukacs 1999, 141). However, the victory of pro-PLO representatives in most municipal councils constituted a source of disappointment to Israeli policymakers, and the elected mayors were faced by a series of repressive measures such as expulsion, imprisonment, and removal from office. By 1982, Israel replaced all elected mayors with military officers.

With Likud's victory in the 1977 public elections, the autonomy vision became a cornerstone policy to impose a political settlement. In a speech to the Knesset in December 1977, the Israeli prime minister, Menachem Begin, proposed the idea of "administrative autonomy," which would oversee civil matters in the Palestinian-populated areas. Begin's proposal signaled the maturity of the autonomy vision and was presented as part of the "Framework for Peace in the Middle East" during the Camp David talks between Israel and Egypt in 1978. Unlike the previous autonomy ideas, Begin's autonomy vision included concrete details about the organization and functions of the autonomy and its relations to Israel and the neighboring countries. Overall, Begin's autonomy plan was conditioned by three nonnegotiable principles: first, asserting the Jewish claim to sovereignty in the West Bank and Gaza; second, enforcing "a judicial separation of the people from the land"; and third, abolishing any possibility for a Palestinian sovereignty (Jensehaugen 2020, 53; Anziska 2018).

Practically, the implementation of the autonomy plan was based on establishing "self-governing administrative council," comprised of eleven elected members to administer social, cultural, and civil affairs, yet without executive and legislative powers. The "self-governing administrative council" should undergo a transitional period of five years during which "negotiations (are) conducted among Egypt, Israel, Jordan and the elected representatives of the inhabitants of the West Bank and Gaza . . . to determine the final status of the West Bank and Gaza and its relationship with its neighbors and to conclude a peace treaty between Israel and Jordan" (Framework for Peace in the Middle

East 1978). The plan stipulated that Israel would be responsible for security and public order but called for the establishment of "a strong local police force . . ., which may include Jordanian citizens." Israel would redeploy its military to the settlements and in other strategic positions around Palestinian towns. In essence, Israel would maintain control over the lands and the borders and rule the land, while the Palestinians could administer their own civil and cultural affairs (Jensehaugen 2020). Despite the seemingly gradual transfer of power to the autonomy in the context of the "Jordanian Option," the autonomy would in effect be regulated by the Israeli military governorate. As revealed by the *Washington Post* in 1979, the Palestinian administrative council would "derive its authority solely from the Israeli government [. . .] and could be dissolved by Israel if it failed to adhere to the principles laid down in its charter" (Claiborne 1979).

In response, the PLO leadership rejected the autonomy plan because "it is carefully designed to serve Israel's national interests and not satisfy the aspirations or realize the rights of the Palestinian people" (Sayegh 1979, 4). However, several analysts today contend that the Begin's autonomy framework has essentially inspired the Oslo Accords upon which the PA autonomy emerged (Anziska 2018).

Given the noncollaborationist stance of the Palestinians as proven in the municipal elections in 1976 and the opposition to the Camp David accords, Israel embarked on a policy change to handle the steadily growing power of the PLO and the increasingly radicalized population. The policy change implied a hybrid direct and indirect governance approaches to redefine the leadership and sociopolitical order. First, Israel sought to enforce compliance by appointing a new Palestinian leadership entrusted with certain civil and security matters. In 1979, Israel set up the federation of "Villages Leagues," comprised of a network of local collaborationists who operated under the direction of the Military Governorate and later the Civil Administration. According to the US Department of State, the Village Leagues aimed "to transfer patronage and authority from elected and established Palestinian nationalist leaders whom Israel objects to as being supporters of the Palestinian Liberation organization" (US Department of State, 1165–6). Moreover, by empowering the Villages Leagues, Israel sought to legitimize its colonial presence through a proxy governance that would set the foundation for a negotiated settlement based on the autonomy plan.

The Leagues networks originated in remote rural areas predominated by social conservatism, tribal and semi-feudal organization of social power, and the prevalence of illiteracy and patronage (Tamari 1983). The first League was founded in Dura's village near Hebron by the former Jordanian minister, Mustafa Dodin, who strove for negotiations and autonomy under the aegis of Israel. The initiative was then developed into a network of Leagues across multiple villages in the West Bank. The Villages Leagues presented itself as "the vanguard of the peace forces in the West Bank and Gaza—whose historic task is to mobilize the Palestinian people in a peace movement against bigotry and [Palestinian] terrorism" (Tamari 1983, 43). In order to enforce the local authority of the Villages Leagues, Israel exerted pressures on the head of villages to collaborate with the Leagues, and those who declined were forcefully removed and replaced by members of the Leagues (Litani 1981, 175).

The Leagues founded its armed militia to implement Israeli security policy. Israel equipped the Villages Leagues with extra-legal powers, provided them with arms, vehicles, and means of communication, and licensed the publication of a newspaper that often reflected the Israeli viewpoint (Tamari 1983). The Villages Leagues primarily resorted to coercive and violent means to enforce its authority on the population and waged frequent attacks against the civilians and their properties, as documented by human right groups (Al-Haq 1983). Alongside the violent approach, the Leagues attempted to expand its patron-client system to incorporate the largest possible segment of the population into the network of beneficiaries (Taraki 2006, 99). Israel supported this process by delegating basic social provision to the Leagues, such as permits concerning travels, family reunion, construction and trade, and driving licenses. The Leagues' distributive power of social services was used to punish and reward the population based on their resistance or compliance.

In conjunction with the Villages Leagues, Israel replaced the Military Governorate with the Israeli "Civil Administration" in 1981, which was tasked with "executing the autonomy plan" (Gordon 2008, 107). The idea of establishing the Civil Administration stemmed from what the Minister of Defense, Ariel Sharon, perceived as a convenient way to transfer the civil responsibilities to the Palestinian autonomy upon establishment. Although the characterization of this governing body as "civil" was meant to conceal the military nature of the Israeli occupation, the Civil Administration was in effect directed by the Israeli Ministry of Defense and the internal intelligence service, the Shen Bit. Indeed, the decision-making process within the Civil Administration strictly followed the military chain of command, where "the executive, legislative and judicial powers were concentrated in the person of the Military Governor and his deputies who reported directly to the Israeli Minister of Defense" (Shahwan 2003, 55).

The Civil Administration was an attempt to "alter some of the methods of control in order to make them more effective" (Gordon 2008, 107). The new methods are defined by a set of coercive and interventionist policies to regulate vital aspects of Palestinian daily life. In particular, the services provided by the Civil Administration were utilized as collective punishment measures against communities deemed noncompliant and involved in nationalist activism. These measures include, for example:

> marketing prohibitions, monetary restrictions, agricultural sanctions, fuel bans, closure of organizations and institutions, continued large scale arrests, the isolation of communities for long periods of time and the enforced payment of taxes. In order to increase Palestinian dependence upon the civil administration, Israeli authorities changed the license plates of all cars, made the granting of permits contingent upon the payment of tax, forced Gaza residents to obtain new identity cards, initiated tax raids against local communities, introduced new taxes and issued a host of new regulations. (Hunter 1991, 146)

The first Palestinian Intifada (1987–93) problematized Israeli approaches of the 1980s. The federation of the Villages Leagues was dissolved in 1987, and the Civil Administration was delegitimized by the popular resistance tactics of boycott and civil disobedience. This has accelerated the Israeli quest for a political compromise that would make the separation with the Palestinians realizable. By the early 1990s, new regional and global conditions drove Israel to reassess its approach to autonomy and indirect rule, especially by involving its long-standing foe, the PLO, as the main partner in the arrangement, or in what became known as the Oslo "peace" process.

Colonial Autonomy and Indirect Rule in Action

The Oslo Accords of 1993 and the subsequent agreements were signed in the framework of the "Declaration of Principles on Interim Self-Government Arrangements." The Oslo process, or the "peace process," was a direct by-product of major changes that engulfed the regional and the international system in the late 1980s and early 1990s, including the collapse of the socialist bloc, the second Gulf war, and the expansion of neoliberal globalization. This has forced a rapid shift in the strategic options, priorities, and policies of both Israel and the PLO. On the one hand, Israel's overriding priority was to end the First Intifada, enforce political stability, and ensure smoother integration into the neoliberal global economy. This orientation was particularly pronounced by the Labor government under the leadership of Ishak Rabin and Shimon Peres, who prioritized political settlement with the PLO through the US-brokered channels. On the other hand, the PLO rush for political comprise with Israel was primarily driven by a series of political, financial, and legitimacy crises that put the organization on the brink of irrelevancy (Dana 2019). Observers often attribute the signing of the Oslo Accords to the convergence of interests between Israel and the PLO leadership. As the Oslo Accords inaugurated a new chapter of the PLO-Israeli relations within asymmetric reality, the trajectory of the process was definitively determined in favor of the Israeli agenda. As observed by Bishara

> autonomy under a new Palestinian Authority was proposed as an interim solution. This was convenient for Israel. It absolved the occupying power of its civil responsibilities towards the local population (creating a luxurious situation for the occupiers, an occupation with costs, that numerous Israeli commentators have called "deluxe occupation") while requiring the PLO wield its authority on behalf of Israel's security interests in the name of counterterrorist security coordination. This was how the PLO was practically marginalized from the moment it was formally recognized. Not only did it become an authority without a state, but it became hostage to the Israeli occupation. (Bishara 2022, 171)

Echoing Israel's true intention for signing the Oslo Accords, the Israeli agenda was one of continuing the colonization by other means. This was enabled by a set of Israeli conditions that underpinned the Oslo process, which are barely new to Israel's post-1967 strategic planning in the oPt. Indeed, Israel used the Oslo framework as a fig leaf to consolidate its colonial project and to hinder the possibility for a Palestinian sovereign polity in the 1967 occupied territories. While the PLO embraced the Oslo Accords as a pragmatic route toward achieving the two-state solution, and as such provided substantial concessions, its decision was not anchored by any guarantee. In fact, the accords had many inherent flaws and ambiguities and did not assure ending Jewish settlements or establishing a Palestinian state. As the PLO's ultimate objective, the "Palestinian state" has neither appeared in the Oslo documents nor was it formally promised by the Israelis and the Americans.

Nonetheless, the Oslo Accords contained clear guidelines for implementing the "Self-Government Authority," or the Palestinian autonomy. In this sense, the very substance of the accords stipulated well-defined mechanisms to implement Israel's long-standing vision of autonomy in a way that was inconceivable in previous decades. The Israeli concept of autonomy was legitimized by the international community and the international organizations alike and most importantly by the contractual involvement of the PLO in the arrangement. In so doing, the occupying power could devise local autonomous structures in territories that are illegally conquered and do not fall under its recognized sovereignty while simultaneously legitimizing the legal exclusion of the population from its civil laws and citizenship system. Such legitimacy is further boosted by depicting the autonomy arrangement as a "peace process," thus nurturing the illusion of the PA autonomy as a vehicle for the Palestinian statehood. Instead, the "peace process" made the colonization proceed apace, resulting in an expanded territorial control and a contained Palestinian population in segregated, fragmented, and deterritorialized enclaves.

Intersecting perfectly with Israel's logic of colonial governmentality, Oslo repackaged and combined key aspects of the Israeli previous plans and transformed the direct military rule of the Palestinian lives into the indirect colonial rule system. This immediate and lasting outcome of Oslo was the establishment of the PA in 1994, which served as the institutional pillar of the autonomy. The Oslo framework entailed the gradual transfer of certain administrative powers from the occupation authorities to the newly established PA institutions in densely populated cities and towns in the oPt. In theory, the PA was supposed to undergo the five-year transitional period after which the PA-Israeli negotiations would lead to settling the final status agreement. The final status agreement was supposed to deal with major issues such as the status of Jerusalem, the Jewish settlements, the Palestinian refugees' right of return, and control over borders, water, and natural resources. With the failure of Camp David negotiations in 2000, the final status agreement was never reached, and the subsequent eruption of the Second Intifada (2000–5) drove many analysts to declare the end of the Oslo "peace" process. Despite this failure, the Oslo framework has never been readjusted, and instead it became the indefinite status quo defining the situation on the ground.

A closer look into the Oslo provisions suggests that it is a modified version of the Begin's autonomy plan. Such a conclusion has been affirmed by Palestinian and Israeli figures who participated in the negotiations. According to Joel Singer, a key Israeli member in both of Camp David and Oslo negotiating teams, the "arrangements contained in the Oslo Agreement are based on 'A Framework for Peace in the Middle East,' a part of the 1978 Camp David Accords" (Singer 2019). This includes, for example, the establishment of an administrative council in Camp David replaced by the PA after Oslo, the five-year transitional period, the formation of local police force, and the Israeli control over the borders. This comparison is also validated by the PA former foreign affairs minister, Nasser Alkidwa, who further admits that "the provisions of the accords fell short, even in comparison to the Framework for Peace in the Middle East which stipulated full autonomy, and not arrangements for self-government" (Alkidwa

2019). Interestingly, Anziska captures the extent to which the Oslo process reproduced the narrow conception of autonomy advanced by Begin's autonomy plan:

> By conditioning Palestinian political rights on a narrowly functionalist and nonterritorial definition of autonomy alongside continued Israeli settlement expansion in the occupied territories, the earlier talks undercut the possibility of Palestinian sovereignty long before the "peace process" of the 1990s had begun. Begin's autonomy plan, as both records from his time in office and later discussions make clear, became the basis for the US and Israeli negotiating positions—and the birth of the Palestinian Authority—in the years that followed. (Anziska 2018, 300–1)

If one aim of Begin's autonomy plan was to undermine the Palestinian sovereignty claim, Oslo has actualized this intention by not only creating a fragile autonomy as an endgame to the Palestinian question but also subordinating the Palestinian national movement to serve this purpose. This latter point makes the Oslo autonomy much more sophisticated and stable than Begin's envisaged autonomy. Whereas Begin proposed to form "administrative council" run by alternative leadership to exclude the PLO affiliates, a matter that would be challenged by the lack of popular backing, the engagement of the PLO leadership in Oslo has legitimized Israel's colonial autonomy as a Palestinian "national project."

By considering the central elements of the previous plans, it would be possible to comprehend the subtle roots of the Oslo autonomy. The spatial aspect of the Oslo autonomy is informed by the Alon Plan's territorial division of the West Bank. Oslo institutionalized the extensive reterritorialization of the oPt along the very logic of "maximum land and less Palestinians," causing the deterritorialization of the Palestinian space within which the autonomy is permitted, while conceding the lion share of the land to Israel. This was made possible by the division of the West Bank into Areas A, B, and C. Israel was granted full control over 60 percent of the land, known as Area C, where most settlements and natural resources are located. The PA autonomous zones comprise only 18 percent of the West Bank, mainly in densely populated areas, where it is allowed to exercise limited powers over civil and security affairs in coordination with the Israeli authorities. Israel militarily controls Area B, or 22 percent of the territories encompassing Palestinian rural areas, leaving the PA with some administrative powers to manage the population's civil affairs. Strikingly, the Oslo territorial divisions offered Israel control over a larger swath of the territories. Whereas the Alon Plan kept Israeli control over one-third of the West Bank areas considered strategically significant for security and economic purposes, the Oslo territorial division provided Israel with legal and military control of Areas C and B, estimated at 80 percent of the West Bank.

It can be observed that the Oslo context of territorial division accomplished two fundamental objectives of the Alon Plan. First, it facilitated large-scale colonization of the oPt. For instance, the number of settlers rose from 110,000, at the time of signing the Oslo Accords in 1993, to approximately 678,000 across 170 settlement blocs and 146 outposts in the West Bank by 2021, including East Jerusalem (European Union 2021). In the meantime, Israel institutionalized racial segregation where it applies its civil laws on Jewish settlers while governing the Palestinians directly through military orders and indirectly through the PA. This legal-racial segregation is bolstered by the physical separation between the Palestinians and Jewish settlers through myriad barriers such as bypass roads, checkpoints, the separation wall, and closed military zones. Moreover, this process is accompanied by swallowing up large swaths of the land, the incorporation of occupied East Jerusalem into the greater Jerusalem project, the division of Hebron, and the full colonization of the Jordan Valley with its abundant natural resources. Second, it enforced the "bantustanization" of the Palestinian autonomous cities and towns, rendering an independent polity impossible (Bishara 2020). As both Areas C and B completely encircle the PA autonomous zones, Israel ensured a fragmented and deterrorized Palestinian autonomy over isolated and scattered enclaves spatially detached from one another. Under these conditions, the Palestinians continue to live in a status of statelessness, either through the legal exclusion from the Israeli citizenship or the denial of independent Palestinian nationality.

No less important are the mechanisms of control that were incorporated into the very fabric of the Oslo autonomy. This was particularly inspired by the pacification approach and economic dependency utilized by the Open Bridges. Yet, unlike the Open Bridges' reliance on the Israeli state's financial resources to implement economic stimulus projects to stimulate pacification in the oPt, Oslo secured significant resources through donors' commitments to support the PA under the banner of peacebuilding and economic development. International aid has been instrumental to the pacification process in crucial ways: it mitigates the harmful consequences of Israel's colonization; it sustains the PA institutions; it provides salaries, social services, and humanitarian assistance to the population; and it supports the PA elite and its authoritarian and neo-patrimonial politics (Turner 2015). Therefore, donors' policies have been consistent with the Israeli position of keeping in place weak institutions and dependent economy through perpetuating the Oslo status quo. The complicity of donor-led peacebuilding in this arrangement is credited by Turner as being a form of counterinsurgency whose goal is to support compliant actors who have vested interests in ensuring stability and to help to embed their power in opposition to others who reject the autonomy arrangement (Turner 2015). Moreover, the oPt economic dependency on Israel meant the continuation of Israeli control over vital resources for the PA institutional sustainability. In this way, Israel managed to subjugate the PA to heavy pressure to accept its demands. A prominent example is Israel's control of the PA "tax clearance system," which is levied and transferred to the PA by Israel on a monthly basis. As the tax transfer accounts for more than 60 percent of all the PA revenues, Israel often uses this financial leverage to extract political concessions through withholding these amounts to force the PA to comply with its policies .

Even the logic that directed the Civil Administration and the Villages Leagues has been reproduced to underpin the Oslo model of indirect colonial rule. In this sense, the PA autonomy was designed to translate the Israeli conditions in the civil and security spheres into an institutionalized reality. Regarding the former, since the Civil Administration reflected Israel's willingness to delegate day-to-day administrative and civil affairs to a locally entrusted autonomous entity, the PA has absorbed much of these functions. The establishment of the PA in 1994 has been accompanied by a steadily growing public sector to administer all sectors that burdened the occupation's budget and bureaucracy in the oPt, such as health, education, social services, internal taxation, tourism, and employment. The costs of responsibility for all civilian matters have been transferred to international donors and the Israeli-controlled tax revenues, which subsequently structured the PA on rentierism and rent-seeking (Tartir, Dana, Seidel 2021). This has doubled the pressure on the PA, which in turn undercut its autonomous power to design and implement civil policies in accordance with national perceptions and local needs. In the field of education, for example, the Palestinian curriculum became subject to direct and indirect influence by Israel and donors. Whereas Israel vetoes topics that focus on Palestinian identity, rights, and accusing them of inciting hatred or violence against Israel, donors' conditionality has forced the PA to adopt liberal education curriculum as a prerequisite for further funding (Naser-Najjab 2020). Moreover, civil planning relating to the utilization of the territory, such as industrial zoning and urban planning, is denied, unless authorized by the Israeli authorities, a matter that is rarely approved (Zeid and Thawaba 2018). In the security sphere, the Oslo Accords stipulated the formation of a "strong police force" to enforce public order in the PA zones. As a key part of Begin's autonomy plan, which later inspired the failed Villages Leagues experiment, multiple PA security forces were formed, trained, and monopolized violence to police the status quo and ensure stability (Tartir 2019). The autonomy stability is secured at the internal and external levels. At the internal level, the PA security is the main guardian of the PA elite and institutions. Given the authoritarian character of the PA, security forces play a major role in the suppression of dissents and protests, preventing social unrest that would jeopardize the domestic security in area A where the PA autonomy operates. Externally, the PA security supplies Israel with an array of services that tend to accommodate Israeli security demands. This includes, for example, exchanging information, detecting potential threats, arresting Palestinian militants, and disbanding armed forces. The security dimension of the PA autonomy is a crucial pillar to the perpetuation of the status quo, without which the Israeli desired autonomy would inevitably collapse.

Note

1 This chapter is based on previously published article by the author. See Dana and Jarbawi (2023).

References

Abed, George T. (ed.) (1988), *The Palestinian Economy: Studies in Development under Prolonged Occupation*. New York: Routledge.
Achcar, Gilbert (2011), "The Allon Plan and the Impediments to Palestinian Statehood." In Helmot Krieger (ed.), *Perspectives Beyond War and Crisis III: What Kind of Palestinian State for what Kind of Peace?*, 73–91. Vienna: Vienna Institute for International Dialogue and Cooperation.

Al-Haq (1983), "Human Rights Violations in the West Bank: In Their Own Words." https://www.alhaq.org/publications/8173.html.

Alkidwa, Nasser (2019), "The Oslo Accords: A Closer Look." *The Cairo Review of Global Affairs*, February 24. https://www.thecairoreview.com/essays/the-oslo-accords-a-closer-look/.

Allon, Yigal (1976), "Israel: The Case for Defensible Borders." *Foreign Affairs*, January 28. https://www.foreignaffairs.com/articles/israel/1976-10-01/israel-case-defensible-borders.

Anziska, Seth (2018), *Preventing Palestine: A Political History from Camp David to Oslo*. Princeton: Princeton University Press.

Bishara, Azmi (2020), *The Trump-Netanyahu Deal: The Path that Led to the "Peace" Plan and What is to be Done*. Beirut: The Arab Center for Research and Policy Studies. (In Arabic).

Bishara, Azmi (2022), *Palestine: Matters of Truth and Justice*. London: Hurst Publishers.

Brancati, Dawn (2009), *Peace by Design: Managing Intrastate Conflict through Decentralization*. Oxford: Oxford University Press.

Claiborne, William (1979), "Begin Presents Palestinian Autonomy Plan to Cabinet Group." *Washington Post*, May 4. https://www.washingtonpost.com/archive/politics/1979/05/04/begin-presents-palestinian-autonomy-plan-to-cabinet-group/57bd15c6-07f2-4035-aee7-762706b2d09b/.

"Country Reports in Human Rights Practices." (1983), *United States Department of State*. Washington, DC: Committee on Foreign Affairs, February.

Crowder, Michael (1964), "Indirect Rule—French and British Style." *Africa*, 34 (3): 197–205.

Dana, Tariq (2019), "The Prolonged Decay of the Palestinian National Movement." *National Identities*, 21 (1): 39–55.

Dana, Tariq and Ali Jarbawi (2017), "A Century of Settler Colonialism in Palestine: Zionism's Entangled Project." *Brown Journal of World Affairs*, 24 (1): 197–219.

Dana, Tariq and Ali Jarbawi (2023), "Whose Autonomy? Conceptualising 'Colonial Extraterritorial Autonomy' in the Occupied Palestinian Territories." *Politics*, 02633957221128216.

European Union. (2021), "Six-month report on Israeli settlements in the occupied West Bank, Including East Jerusalem, (Reporting Period July-December 2020)." https://www.un.org/unispal/wp-content/ uploads/2021/11/EURPTSETTLE_221121.pdf (accessed September 27, 2022).

Foldvary, Fred. E. (2011), "Political Autonomy." In D. K. Chatterjee (ed.), *Encyclopedia of Global Justice*, 853–54. Dordrecht: Springer

"Framework for Peace in the Middle East (1978) 'Camp David' – Text/Non-UN Document." https:// www.un.org/unispal/document/auto-insert-210245/

Gagnon, Alain and Michael Keating (eds.). (2012), *Political Autonomy and Divided Societies: Imagining Democratic Alternatives in Complex Settings*. New York: Palgrave Macmillan.

Ghai, Yash (2001), *Public Participation and Minorities*. London: Minority Rights Group International.

Gordon, Neve (2008), *Israel's Occupation*. Berkeley: University of California Press.

Hanafi, Sari (2009), "Spacio-Cide: Colonial Politics, Invisibility and Rezoning in Palestinian Territory." *Contemporary Arab Affairs*, 2 (1): 106–21.

Heraclides, Alexis (1990), "Secessionist Minorities and External Involvement." *International Organization*, 44 (3): 341–78.

Hever, Shir (2010), *The Political Economy of Israel's Occupation: Repression beyond Exploitation*. London: Pluto.

Hilal, Jamil (1977), "Class Transformation in the West Bank and Gaza." *Journal of Palestine Studies*, 6 (2): 167–75.

Hiltermann, Joost R. (1993), *Behind the Intifada: Labor and Women's Movements in the Occupied Territories*. Princeton Studies on the Near East. Princeton: Princeton University Press.

Hunter, F. Robert (1991), *The Palestinian Uprising: A War by Other Means*. Berkeley: University of California Press.

Jensehaugen, Jørgen (2020), "*Terra Morata*: The West Bank in Menachem Begin's Worldview." *Contemporary Levant*, 5 (1): 54–63.

Khalifa, Ahmad (1981), "The 'Jordanian Option' Through Israeli Eyes." *Journal of Palestine Studies*, 10 (3): 153–9.

Killingray, David (1986), "The Maintenance of Law and Order in British Colonial Africa." *African Affairs*, 85 (340): 411–37.

Lentin, Ronit (2020), "Palestinian Lives Matter: Racialising Israeli Settler-Colonialism." *Journal of Holy Land and Palestine Studies*, 19 (2): 133–49.

Litani, Yehuda (1981), "Leaders by Proxy." *Ha'aretz*, November 30.

Lloyd, David (2012), "Settler Colonialism and the State of Exception: The Example of Palestine/Israel." *Settler Colonial Studies*, 2 (1): 59–80.

Lukacs, Yehuda (1999), *Israel, Jordan, and the Peace Process*. Syracuse: Syracuse University Press.

Mamdani, Mahmood (2012), *Define and Rule: Native as Political Identity*. 1st ed. Cambridge, MA: Harvard University Press.

Masalha, Nur (1997), *A Land without People: Israel, Transfer and the Palestinians 1949–96*. London: Faber and Faber.

Masalha, Nur (2000), *Imperial Israel and the Palestinians: The Politics of Expansion*. Sterling: Pluto Press.

Molavi, Shourideh C. (2013), *Stateless Citizenship: The Palestinian-Arab Citizens of Israel*. Leiden: Brill.

Moore, Margaret (2003), "An Historical Argument for Indigenous Self-Determination." *Nomos*, 45: 89–118.

Myers, Jason Conard (2008), *Indirect Rule in South Africa: Tradition, Modernity, and the Costuming of Political Power*. Rochester Studies in African History and the Diaspora. Rochester: University of Rochester Press.

Naser-Najjab, Nadia (2020), "Palestinian Education and the 'Logic of Elimination.'" *Settler Colonial Studies*, 10 (3): 311–30.

Note by the UN Secretary-General (1970), "Report of the Special Committee to Investigate Israeli Practices Affecting the Human Rights of the Palestinian People." December 15. https://web.archive.org/web/20140203074258/http:/unispal.un.org/UNISPAL.NSF/0/858C88EB973847F4802564B5003D1083.

Pace, Michelle and Somdeep Sen (2019), *The Palestinian Authority in the West Bank: The Theatrics of Woeful Statecraft*. Oxon: Routledge.

Peteet, Julie Marie (2017), *Space and Mobility in Palestine*. Public Cultures of the Middle East and North Africa. Bloomington: Indiana University Press.

Pickerill, Jenny and Paul Chatterton (2006), "Notes towards Autonomous Geographies: Creation, Resistance and Self-Management as Survival Tactics." *Progress in Human Geography*, 30 (6): 730–46.

Raz, Avi (2012), *The Bride and the Dowry: Israel, Jordan, and the Palestinians in the Aftermath of the June 1967 War*. New Haven: Yale University Press.

Sayegh, Fayez A. (1979), "The Camp David Agreement and the Palestine Problem." *Journal of Palestine Studies*, 8 (2): 3–40.

Seidel, Timothy (2019), "Neoliberal Developments, National Consciousness, and Political Economies of Resistance in Palestine." *Interventions*, 21 (5): 727–46.

Shafir, Gershon (2017), *A Half Century of Occupation: Israel, Palestine, and the World's Most Intractable Conflict*. Berkeley: University of California Press.

Shahwan, Usamah Salim (2003), *Public Administration in Palestine: Past and Present*. Lanham: University Press of America.

Shlaim, Avi (2015), *The Iron Wall: Israel and the Arab World*. London: Penguin.

Sicherman, Harvey (2019), *Palestinian Autonomy, Self-Government, and Peace*. New York: Routledge.

Singer, Joel (2019), "Developing the Concept of Palestinian Autonomy." *The Cairo Review of Global Affairs*, February 24. https://www.thecairoreview.com/essays/developing-the-concept-of-palestinian-autonomy/.

Tamari, Salim (1983), "In League with Zion: Israel's Search for a Native Pillar." *Journal of Palestine Studies*, 12 (4): 41–56.

Taraki, Liza (ed.). (2006), *Living Palestine: Family Survival, Resistance, and Mobility under Occupation*. 1st ed. Gender, Culture, and Politics in the Middle East. Syracuse: Syracuse University Press.

Tartir, Alaa (2019), *Outsourcing Repression: Israeli-Palestinian Security Coordination*. Johannesburg: Afro-Middle East Centre.

Tartir, Alaa, Tariq Dana, and Timothy Seidel (eds.). (2021), *Political Economy of Palestine: Critical, Interdisciplinary, and Decolonial Perspectives*. New York: Palgrave Macmillan.

Turner, Mandy (2015). "Peacebuilding as Counterinsurgency in the Occupied Palestinian Territory." *Review of International Studies*, 41(1): 73–98.

Tzur, Zeev (1982), *From the Partition Dispute to the Allon Plan*. Tel Aviv.

United States Department of State (1983), *Country Reports in Human Rights Practices*. Washington, DC: Committee on Foreign Affairs, February.

Walsh, Dawn (2018), *Territorial Self-Government as a Conflict Management Tool*. New York: Palgrave.

Weller, Marc and Stefan Wolff (2005), *Autonomy, Self-Governance, and Conflict Resolution: Innovative Approaches to Institutional Design in Divided Societies*. Oxon: Routledge.

Zeid, Maali and Salem Thawaba (2018), "Planning under a Colonial Regime in Palestine: Counter Planning/Decolonizing the West Bank." *Land Use Policy*, 71: 11–23.

Zureik, Elia (2003), "Demography and Transfer: Israel's Road to Nowhere." *Third World Quarterly*, 24 (4): 619–30.

Zureik, Elia (2016), *Israel's Colonial Project in Palestine: Brutal Pursuit*. Oxon: Routledge.

3

The Bureaucracy of Mortality

The Structural Violence of Medical Permits for Palestinians in the West Bank and Gaza Strip

Yara M. Asi

This is about freedom of movement at its most raw level- the right to access, literally, life-saving services for you, or an elderly parent or perhaps an infant child. The very idea that a fence, a wall, a security guard, a bureaucrat could stand between you and such life-saving services should fill us all with a sense of dread.
—Robert Piper, UN 2017

Introduction

The image of war to those fortunate enough to have never been exposed to its atrocities is largely based on what might academically be defined as direct violence: dramatic bombings and smoldering buildings, soldiers shooting guns, and tanks rolling through the streets. Representations of the idea of peace are similarly postured: quiet streets, children in classrooms, and bustling markets. But modern armed conflict, while still reliant on direct violence to devastating effect, effectively builds mechanisms of oppression that allow children to attend school and for citizens to shop. These mechanisms, long used in conflicts of all types, were first articulated by Johan Galtung in 1969 when he introduced the conceptualization of structural violence—man-made violence and oppression built into the edifices of everyday life, limiting some target population from achieving equity or their human rights. Structural violence is present throughout historical and contemporary settings of armed conflict but is also the prime mechanism with which other systems of domination, such as settler colonialism, become established and maintained.

While battle-related mortality is a significant threat to a country's health and well-being, decades of analysis have shown that health outcomes suffer long after wars are seemingly finished, and communities can be devastated for generations (Haar and

Rubenstein 2012; Ghobarah, Huth and Russett 2004; Sidel and Levy 2008). There are clearly factors outside of the direct violence associated with armed conflict, including entrenched parts of bureaucracy and administration, that lead to these poor social outcomes. Importantly, when there are broader political and territorial aims, as in settings of settler colonialism, structural violence is not just a tool of collective punishment but is also enacted as part of larger efforts to dispossess Indigenous populations, force dependence on external actors, and encourage migration so that territorial expansion is easier (Asi 2022).

In this chapter, I will describe the negative outcomes that can occur when structural violence manifests in the health care system of a population living under a highly securitized military occupation. This study will focus on the occupied Palestinian territory (oPt), considering decades of the manifestation and entrenchment of systems that almost completely encompass the lives of Palestinians, in service of Israeli settler colonialism. In this case, the structures are systems set in place by the Israeli state, as the primary actor in the military occupation and blockade of the oPt, and are either enforced or motivated by the two arms of Palestinian governance, the Palestinian Authority (PA) and Hamas, and to a lesser extent, surrounding Arab nations.

Although Israeli-imposed restrictions on movement are pervasive throughout Palestinian life—checkpoints, ditches, gates, a separation wall, and more— medical permits provide some of the only empirical long-term data of movement restrictions available, in terms of approvals and denials. These permits, along with all movement restrictions, are justified by Israel and its supporters as necessary for its security, despite their devastating effect on Palestinians. If these barriers are driven by security concerns, we would expect to see a relationship between threat levels and medical permit policies over time. If security does not play a significant role in guiding approval of medical permits, it would be an indication that there are structures driving these policies that are unrelated to security, as part of a broader mechanism of collective punishment and colonial structures of population control.

Structural Violence and Health

Because the mortality and injury caused by bureaucratic processes does not mimic the overt visibility of direct violence, it is not perceived as a shock to the status quo or even particularly harmful. Instead, as Galtung writes, "structural violence is silent, it does not show—it is essentially static, it *is* the tranquil water" (1969). As a result, these types of structures are less likely to be priorities of humanitarian agencies and peace efforts since the type of violence associated with battle-related traumas appears more urgent and compelling. This allows for unjust structures to persist under the guise of maintaining "normalcy," or, in some cases, even a false perception of security. The harm in this is that once structural violence has been allowed to develop in a period of minimal direct violence, it may then be perceived as a necessary component of that sense of "peace." Indeed, some would argue, disrupting this system, even though aspects may be unjust, will only serve to upset the so-called "peaceful" period.

Expounding on the concept of structural violence in health care, Paul Farmer described the importance of global health experts applying this idea to their understanding of the social forces outside of their patient's control. His analysis, however, maintained a level of optimism; because these structures were human-made, they were actionable. Interventions could be designed that countered or replaced the unjust structures, but first we must begin to see these structures for what they are, as Farmer et al. wrote, "because they seem so ordinary in our ways of understanding the world, they appear almost invisible" (2006). This echoes Galtung's "tranquil water" argument, and one of the most cogent contemporary examples is seen in the oPt, made of the geographically segregated Gaza Strip and West Bank. In such settings of settler colonialism, physical violence on behalf of the dominant entity is fundamental, but alone, "can be destabilizing to colonial dominance," leading to enactment of comprehensive and complex forms of control (Dana 2021) that are purposefully meant to obscure the violence underneath, while still fulfilling the "logic of elimination" (Wolfe 2006).

Palestinian scholars have long recognized the imposition of structural violence as a tool to further settler colonial aims under the guise of security needs, yet this framing remains underutilized as a way to critically assess Israeli policy toward Palestinians, especially in social sectors like health. Even when a Palestinian is in need of emergency medical care, and there is clearly no risk to security, they are still subject to the restrictions of structural violence: "even when on their deathbeds, Palestinians are situated as feared and monstrous others" (Shalhoub-Kevorkian, David and Ihmoud 2016). This "othering" is the underpinning of the structural violence that manifests across every aspect of Palestinian life, much of it in the form of severe restrictions on movement imposed by Israel. The structural violence enacted on Palestinians should then be more accurately situated under an umbrella of colonial violence with the goal of further colonizing Palestinian land and displacing the Palestinians on them, or, as said by former Israeli prime minister Yair Lapid, "Maximum Jews on maximum land with maximum security and with minimum Palestinians" (Hoffman 2016).

Movement Restrictions and Palestinian Health

Decades of armed conflict, occupation, and siege have led to a fragmented, underresourced, and inequitable health system that requires many to travel outside of the oPt for medical care, especially for chronic and critical ailments (Asi 2019). Distribution and diversity of health care facilities is poor throughout the territories; for example, hospitals are clustered in certain areas, such as Gaza City in Gaza and the center of the West Bank. There are almost no facilities for tertiary health care outside of East Jerusalem, which most Palestinians cannot travel to freely. It is easier for many Palestinians to travel to Egypt or Jordan to access care than to East Jerusalem, which is ostensibly Palestinian territory (Abu-Zaineh et al. 2011). Many also apply for permits to access such care in Israel, which features world-class health facilities with adequate personnel and resources—not to mention a universal health care system for its citizens but not the Palestinians living on the land Israel occupies.

As a result of the need to travel for health needs, movement restrictions for Palestinians are among the most insidious causes of poor quality of life, preventable physical and emotional suffering, and avoidable mortality (Kearney, Khdair and Muhareb 2020). The barriers have fluctuated over the years from more permissive to where they have landed today, which is among the most restricted they have been since the First Intifada in the early 1990s. The separation wall, which began construction in the early 2000s, the dozens of permanent and floating checkpoints throughout the West Bank, the blockade of the Gaza Strip, the increase in Israeli settlement construction and the subsequent geographic segregation in the West Bank, and the entrenchment of a bureaucratically opaque permit system have all led to significant decreases in Palestinians exiting their territories, especially to Israel, or even being able to travel freely within them.

There are essentially three layers of barriers to health that the movement restrictions impose: first, Palestinians report high unemployment due in large part to movement restrictions on people and goods (UNCTAD 2022). Thus, Palestinians are less able to afford care, causing many of them to avoid accessing health facilities unless necessary. Second, those who can afford care experience restrictions on their physical movement to hospitals and clinics due to physical barriers (like checkpoints and the separation wall) and political barriers (like medical permits and the blockade of Gaza). Lastly, if they can afford care and are able to access a health facility, movement restrictions on people and goods may prevent the facility from having the personnel (particularly specialists) or resources (like certain pharmaceuticals or advanced technologies) necessary to provide adequate and sustainable care.

As the negative economic effects of the movement restrictions have been documented (Brown 2004; World Bank 2007; United Nations 2016), less literature exists on its effects on health, but what has been published presents similarly discouraging evidence. A study shortly after the Second Intifada assessed hospital transportation delays in hospitals in the West Bank and found that patients who had been delayed presented more severe medical conditions (Rytter et al. 2006). The differences in how restricted movement affects Palestinian men and women were highlighted in a 2011 study that found that 10 percent of pregnant women were delayed at checkpoints on their way to give birth from 2000 to 2007 (Shoaibi 2011). Before the World Health Organization (WHO) data utilized in this chapter was available, a team used mixed methods to describe the experiences of Palestinians who had applied for medical permits, finding that the most common justification for a permit denial was an unexplained security basis (Vitullo et al. 2012), while a longitudinal study of movement restrictions on Palestinians focused on the years 1987–2011 found that 38 percent of participants reported being denied travel for medical care. Importantly, they also found that those who reported these denials had worse self-rated health and greater limits on functioning due to their health (McNeely et al. 2018). Investigations from the United Nations found that even for Palestinians granted permission to leave Gaza for medical treatment, some have been stopped and questioned about family members and political affiliations at the border crossing, with those who refused cooperation being prevented from traveling despite their acquisition of the permit (UN ESCWA 2018).

Studies assessing different aspects of Palestinian health have indirectly found the movement restrictions to be a major barrier to care, including for maternal and childcare (Leone et al. 2019), cancer diagnosis and treatment (Halahleh and Gale 2018), and cardiovascular health (Collier and Kienzler 2018). Similar reports have been issued by the WHO as well as Israeli and Palestinian human rights groups. However, to date, no study exists assessing movement restrictions using time-series WHO data on medical permits on both the Gaza Strip and the West Bank and examines them in relation to security measures. This chapter aims to fill that gap as well as provide tangible recommendations to minimize the negative health outcomes of these restrictions outside of the perpetually stalled peace process.

Why Do These Restrictions Persist?

The restrictions are held in place primarily by Israel with the blanket justification, seemingly accepted by its allies, that Palestinian movement in and out of the oPt is inherently dangerous. During the Second Intifada, the Israeli Ministry of Foreign Affairs claimed that several cases of ambulances and medical patients were used to assist or supply "terrorists" in some way, including transporting bombs and weapons (MFA 2004); however, a recent literature review found that between 1970 and 2018, only twenty instances of an ambulance being used for a terrorist attack were recorded globally (Jasani et al. 2021), calling into question the voracity of the Israeli claim. Suicide bombings out of the West Bank terrorized Israelis during the Second Intifada, killing nearly 1,000 civilians (B'Tselem 2010), and while such attacks have been virtually nonexistent since that period, occasional stabbings, shootings, and purported car attacks by Palestinian assailants toward Israelis, especially soldiers, have been branded "a new kind of terrorism" by former and current Israeli prime minister Benjamin Netanyahu (Booth and Eglash 2015). Many soldier accounts of these incidents, however, are discredited once video evidence is presented or independent investigations are conducted, calling into question how pervasive this type of violence is in reality.

To supposedly stifle these rare attacks, draconian policies equivalent to collective punishment have been imposed upon all Palestinians by Israel, despite no evidence that policies such as suppressing medical permit approvals have any effect on security. Further, Israel considers Hamas, the de facto governmental body in the Gaza Strip, a terrorist organization, which it then references in order to enact even more restrictive policies on the civilian population of the small territory. The permit system, like all the other restrictions on Palestinian life, is justified as a mechanism with which to protect Israelis from terrorism, prioritizing even the potential of threat to Israeli life over tangible and active threats to Palestinian life, like missing out on timely medical care. At the same time, Israel has not taken any step to mitigate its daily violent and oppressive treatment of Palestinians, which has led to multiple generations with no hope for justice or change, and has only continued to tighten its grip on Palestinian life while expanding its settler infrastructure and aims.

Medical Permits

When Palestinians seek the lifesaving care they are unable to find in the oPt, they face a "minefield of interviews, paperwork, opaque procedures, and logistical hurdles" before they are afforded permission to access the care they need elsewhere (PHR 2018). There are approximately 100 types of permits necessary for various types of Palestinian movement, from those needed to harvest agricultural land near the separation wall to those needed to travel for a wedding or funeral (Al-Qadi 2018). Permits for medical patients and their escorts to leave Gaza for any destination or enter Israel or East Jerusalem from the West Bank are all entirely different types of permits. In summary, patients must first receive a referral from a medical professional to receive advanced care. They must then apply for the travel permit itself through the Israeli Coordinator of Government Activities in the Territories (COGAT), and any companion (such as parents of young children, spouses, or adult children of elderly patients) must go through a similar permit process.

Israeli authorities introduced a directive in 2017 that applications should be processed within twenty-three days of their submission, but this time frame, already lengthy when considering very ill patients, is often not met, with 31 percent of applicants in 2018 not receiving an answer in time for an appointment or at all. Additionally, their escorts face additional wait times of up to seventy days. Humanitarian workers face similar restrictions—for example, in 2017 the WHO submitted 222 applications for health workers to exit or enter Gaza, only 61 percent of which Israeli authorities approved (WHO 2017).

Although permits may be denied with no explanation, typical reasons for permit denials rely on one of four premises. The first is age, with adults eighteen to forty-five the most likely to experience delays and denials. Next is gender, with men considered a greater security risk than women. Severity of the patient's medical condition is another consideration, with those not requiring immediate lifesaving care more likely to receive denials. Last is association, an imprecise indicator that means that patients who are related to or otherwise associated with a perceived security risk likely to be denied a permit (MAP 2017).

In 2016, in response to calls from human rights groups that patients with familial ties to Hamas members were being stopped and interrogated in their ambulances when attempting to leave Gaza, the Shin Bet responded that "time after time," Hamas would attempt to pass funds or instructions to other "terrorist cells" in the West Bank or Israel and accused senior medical officials in Gaza of falsifying medical referrals for money or other purposes. The Shin Bet recounted incidents of Palestinians crossing the Erez border with materials intended for explosives and abusing the humanitarian channels of travel (Cohen 2017). As a result, a change in Israeli Law in 2017 codified this practice, though several human rights organizations petitioned the Israeli High Court of Justice to revoke the decision, which eventually ruled that the practice was both ineffective and unlawful (Gisha 2019). In 2018, another directive was expanded to deny medical patients the ability to leave Gaza if a family member moved to the West

Bank without Israeli permission to do so, claiming suspicions that "the resident would exploit it for the purpose of illegal residency" (Hass 2018).

Methodology

I obtained medical permit data from the West Bank and Gaza monthly reports issued by the WHO (WHO 2020). This data set started in 2011, and the most recent data used was from December 2019 (data from 2020 to 2022 was not included in the statistical analysis due to the disruption in the permit process due to the Covid-19 pandemic). Data indicators used in this study included total applications from Gaza to cross the Erez border and the number of those applications that were approved, denied, or delayed. In 2018, the WHO also began including the same data about permits applied for, approved, denied, and delayed from the West Bank as well, which was also examined in this study but, due to the limited time frame, less scrutiny was possible. The number of medical patients able to cross the Rafah border to Egypt was available for parts of 2018 and 2019 but was too inconsistent for analysis.

To assess whether levels of conflict or security threats influenced the permit approval process, Israeli Global Peace Index (GPI)[1] and Global Terrorism Index (GTI)[2] scores were collected from the Institute for Economics and Peace Vision of Humanity reports (2020), and Israeli fatality and injury data was collected from OCHA (2020). Presence of an active military operation was entered as a binomial variable (0 = no, 1 = yes) for the Gaza data. Population data was captured from the Palestinian Central Bureau of Statistics (PCBS 2020). Statistics were compiled and analyzed using SPSS version 25.

Limitations

The time span for the permit data is limited, covering only seven years in the case of the Gaza data and one full year for the disaggregated West Bank data. Further, it is inconsistently collected and reported, with the WHO relying on local actors to report the data and not receiving information in some months. Although news stories and NGO reports on this topic have existed for years, there is little data-driven information accessible from before 2010 and especially from before the Second Intifada in the early 2000s. While many new movement restrictions were enacted during the Second Intifada, there is no data available to compare the current permit system with any other period as the situation has evolved. Similarly, health data and indicators were not available for consistent periods that would allow for more detailed analysis.

Factors outside of direct security threats likely influence permit policies, such as shifts in Israeli politics, which would not be captured by quantitative data. Lastly, there is no available database that outlines the types of terrorist incidents at the various border crossings. These had to be found by searching news organizations, NGO reports, and government press releases. Thus, it is possible that the level of terrorist threat was not captured in the injury/fatality or GPI/GTI data used in this analysis. Release of a more detailed record of incidences of suspected Palestinian medical permit abuse by Israeli authorities should be a bare minimum expectation to justify the enactment of these policies and would aid in a more detailed analysis.

Results

Descriptive analysis showed that from 2011 to 2019, medical permit applications from the Gaza Strip to cross Erez have slowly increased as Gaza's population has increased, with a peak of 2,851 permit applications in October 2018. However, the percentage of approved permits has decreased annually as the level of denied and delayed permits has increased (Figure 3.1). Approvals peaked in 2012 with a 92 percent approval rate but have been closer to 60 percent from 2015 to 2019. While denials generally stay below 10 percent, delays have increased by two to four times as much as 2011–2015 levels after 2016. In 2017, when the new decree of increased denials with any Hamas affiliation took effect, delays reached their highest point of the analysis, with 44 percent of all applications delayed, likely because all permit applications now had to undergo longer and more complex security screenings. Subsequently, 2017 was the year with the lowest approval rates in this analysis, at 57 percent. In years where such data was available, oncology, pediatrics, and cardiology were the primary reasons for medical permit applications out of Gaza.

I also conducted linear regression analysis of the relationship between the permit outcomes from Gaza (denied, delayed, and approved) and predictor variables such as Israeli Peace and Terrorism scores (Table 3.1), presence of active major conflict (Operation Pillar of Defense in 2012 and Operation Protective Edge in 2014), and Israeli casualty and injury numbers (Figure 3.2). None of the predictor variables—presence of active conflict, GPI, GTI, and number of Israeli injuries/fatalities—showed any statistically significant association with the level of permits approved, delayed, or denied in Gaza. In fact, approval rates from Gaza were among their highest in 2012 (92.41 percent) and 2014 (81 percent) when there were active ground wars. Analysis

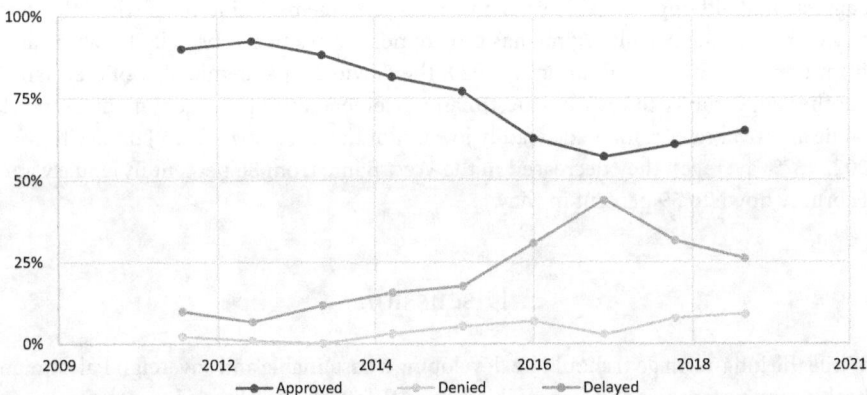

Figure 3.1 Results of medical permit requests to cross Erez border from Gaza, 2011–19.

Table 3.1 Global Terrorism/Peace Indices, Israel, 2014–19

	Global Terrorism Index*	Global Peace Index[1]
2019	4.522	2.779
2018	4.578	2.764
2017	5.062	2.707
2016	5.248	2.656
2015	6.034	2.781
2014	4.66	2.689

Data is from Vision of Humanity (2020), *Global Peace Index and Global Terrorism Index Reports*. http://visionofhumanity.org/reports/.
* Higher score indicates greater terrorism.
[1] Higher score indicates less peacefulness.

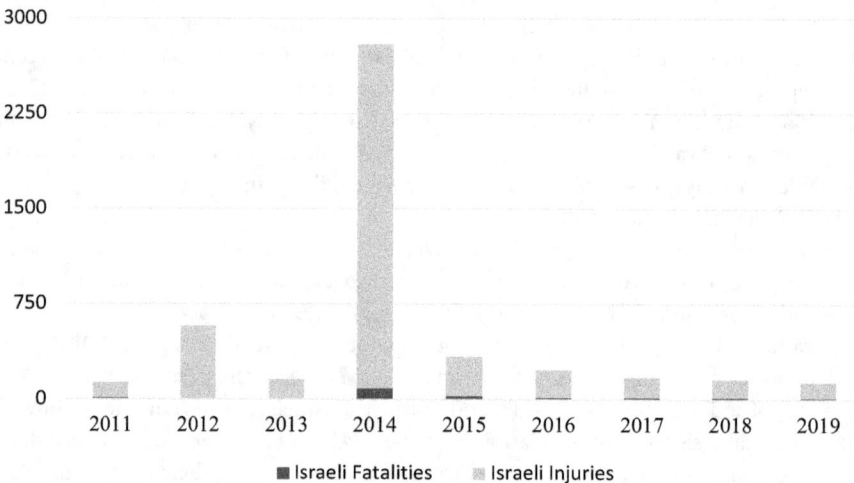

Figure 3.2 Israeli fatalities/injuries, 2011–19.

suggests that although Israel has become safer over the past nine years when the data was compiled, the permit regime has grown more restrictive, especially for applicants from the Gaza Strip.[3] Beginning in 2020, the Covid-19 pandemic also offered Israel another opportunity to restrict Palestinian movement, even for urgent medical travel; while approval rates remained steadily low out of the Gaza Strip from January to May 2022 (67% average), they decreased in the West Bank, from 86 percent in January and February down to 59 percent in May.

Discussion

While the long-term goal should be developing a sustainable and sovereign Palestinian health care system, for the foreseeable future Palestinians will need to access care in the more advanced medical facilities offered in Israel, East Jerusalem, and neighboring states. However, this analysis suggests that the system of medical permits has served to deny and delay needed access to health care. Approval rates have not exceeded 70 percent since 2015. In 2017, only 54 percent of patient applications from Gaza for medical permits were approved, the lowest rate of approvals since they began collecting this data. Fifty-four patients, primarily needing cancer treatments, died while awaiting their security permits. To explain the increases in denials, Physicians for Human Rights-Israel points to a decision made in 2017 by the Israeli Political-Security Cabinet to undergo "a number of operational steps to act as leverage on Hamas as regards the return of prisoners and missing persons" (PHR 2018).

The evidence seems to suggest that the rate of medical permit denials and delays, and the cumbersome nature of the process itself, is intentional and is largely meant to place pressure on Palestinian governance, especially Hamas. Permit denials from Gaza have reached their highest levels in recent years, with Hamas at their weakest point politically since their election in 2006. There are few if any publicly available reports of ambulances illegally used to transport weapons, let alone data that would justify denying more than 30 percent of permits, in over a decade. Moreover, the circumstances of the few reported incidents over two decades would likely not have been prevented by delayed or denied medical permits. A recent report by PHR Israel showed that in more than half of cases of permit rejections or delays in which they intervened, the rejection was eventually removed (2016). This indicates that these were not deemed legitimate security threats after cursory review, with PHR suggesting that "Israel makes completely arbitrary use of these claims" (Hass 2016).

Further, it is not only the level of denials that has decreased the numbers of approved application, but the applications where responses are delayed, often to the point of missed appointments. In 2017, the Shin Bet referenced increases in "terrorist" activity disguised as medical transport for the long delays: "Given the great danger this activity presents, strict security checks are performed on everyone applying to leave Gaza. Naturally, these checks take time" (Hass 2017). However, the nature of medical needs means that long-term planning is often not an option, and urgency in receiving care can mean the difference between life and death for very ill patients. Along with denials themselves, these long delays serve as significant threats to health that also cause stress to patients needing to travel yet are used as part of the overall security argument used to justify restrictions on Palestinians that clearly violate their human rights.

Recommendations

Michael Lynk, the former Special Rapporteur on the Palestinian Territories, issued a report in 2017 that called for, among other measures, Israel to "ensure freedom of movement and the establishment of an equitable permit system for the residents of the oPt" (Human Rights Council 2017). Ultimately, the short-term goal should be for Palestinians to attain the same levels of freedom of movement, under reasonable and standardized security procedures, as residents of other countries. This can occur under any combination of political outcomes. Yet, it has become increasingly clear that Israel has no interest in pursuing any outcome that leads to Palestinian sovereignty, as the direct and structural violence of Israeli settler colonialism continues. This is the root cause of many of the poor humanitarian outcomes reported by Palestinians, including those exacerbated by the broken medical permit system. However, to ease the medical burden on Palestinians today, there are reforms that are likely more palatable under the current political climate that are built upon decades of international humanitarian law, previously agreed-upon agreements, and countless statements and recommendations by multilateral and humanitarian organizations.

As the evidence suggests that the medical permit system is a tool of collective punishment with no legitimate security function, it should be dismantled. Like Al-Haq, a renowned Palestinian human rights organization, argues, "Israel's discriminatory restrictions on access to healthcare illustrate Israel's intention to punish the Palestinian civilian population of the Gaza Strip" (2021). Further, recognized as the occupying power of the oPt and thus conferred with certain responsibilities to Palestinian health and well-being, Israeli authorities should be expected to justify the existence of the onerous and destructive permit process to independent actors with empirical and abundant evidence that there is any security basis. As of yet, they have not done so. As long as the permit system is in place, which is likely for the foreseeable future, Israel must be compelled to maintain a transparent and efficient permit process, offer an immediate explanation in the event of a permit denial, and offer the opportunity for patients to quickly appeal a denied permit without need to acquire external advocacy. Actual empirical information about potential "terrorist" attacks that may have occurred without these restrictive systems should be made publicly available to justify their stringency. If such information is not available, global actors should openly question the legitimacy of such restrictive policies where Palestinians are neither able to build suitable health facilities nor easily travel to areas where they are available. Egypt, as the authority of the Rafah border, should maintain a consistent opening procedure for humanitarian cases, where closures have varied wildly in recent years and provide no ability to plan or act with urgency.

As this topic has increasingly grabbed the attention of human rights groups and NGOs, data collection and scholarship will persist, and more rigorous analysis will be possible. The next step would be to assess how the changes and trends in medical permit policies and outcomes have had a measurable impact on health and well-being in the Palestinian population outside of individual cases reported by NGOs. This would require a granular level of data that is not yet publicly available. Additionally, qualitative research on the perspectives of Palestinian patients and providers, as well as Israeli and Egyptian policymakers, would add a rich understanding on changes in these policies, their justifications, and their outcomes.

Conclusion

Most international entities proclaim broad support for Israel's "right to defend itself," especially when speaking of rocket attacks from the Gaza Strip. Yet this "security first" paradigm, bolstered over the fifty years of occupation, has justified tightened restrictions even in periods of relatively low active conflict or where the restrictions are collective and clearly out of proportion to the threat. Despite violating humanitarian law and multiple UN resolutions, and decades of condemnations by governments around the world, it has become clear that these restrictions have become a price the international community is willing to pay to guarantee the perception of Israel's security—or, at least, to avoid the issue altogether. However, these restrictions have real consequences for all Palestinians, to the point where the United Nations and other global entities regard many of these security measures as discriminatory, excessive, and a form of collective punishment, which is a violation of Article 33 of the Fourth Geneva Convention. Allowing these actions is implicitly accepting the dehumanizing narrative that every Palestinian is a potential terrorist if only given the opportunity. Further, only a just peace resolution, made less possible by the segregation and degradation of the movement restrictions, can bring durable security to either party.

In general, as much should be done within the oPt to minimize the need for patients to travel outside of the country to access care and shore up accessible health services to all Palestinians. In the absence of a resolution that would lead to such outcomes, examination of the merits of current policies is necessary and indeed should be considered welcome by all actors to ensure that the human security of one group is not sacrificed for the national security of another. This chapter suggests that the medical permit process serves as a political tool more than a policy built under evidence-based security concerns. External actors should use their political and diplomatic clout to further investigate and act accordingly to assure that Palestinians can access their human right to health.

Notes

1 A composite index measuring the peacefulness of countries made up of twenty-three quantitative and qualitative indicators. The lower the score, the more peaceful the country.
2 A composite measure made up of four indicators: incidents, fatalities, injuries, and property damage. To measure the impact of terrorism, a five-year weighted average is applied.
3 West Bank permit data was only available for 2018 and 2019, but initial findings make clear that approvals are much higher than from Gaza, with an average of 83 percent approved, 14 percent denied, and 3 percent delayed.

References

Abu-Zaineh, Mohammad, Awad Mataria, Jean-Paul Moatti, and Bruno Ventelou (2011), "Measuring and Decomposing Socioeconomic Inequality in Healthcare Delivery: A Microsimulation Approach with Application to the Palestinian Conflict-Affected Fragile Setting." *Social Science & Medicine*, 72 (2): 133–41.

Al Haq (2021), *On World Health Day, Al-Haq Recounts Israel's Systematic Denial of Palestinians' Right to Health*. https://www.alhaq.org/advocacy/18158.html.

Al-Qadi, Nasser (2018), "The Israeli Permit Regime: Realities and Challenges." *The Applied Research Institute-Jerusalem (ARIJ)*. https://www.arij.org/files/arijadmin/2018/permits1.pdf.

Asi, Yara (2019), "The Conditional Right to Health in Palestine." *Al-Shabaka*. https://al-shabaka.org/briefs/the-conditional-right-to-health-in-palestine/.

Asi, Yara (2022), "Palestinian Dependence on External Health Services: De-development as a Tool of Dispossession." *Middle East Law and Governance*, 14: 366–87. doi:10.1163/18763375-14030004.

Booth, William and Ruth Eglash (2015), "Israelis are Calling Attacks a 'New Kind of Palestinian Terrorism.'" *The Washington Post*. https://www.washingtonpost.com/world/middle_east/israelis-are-calling-attacks-a-new-kind-of-palestinian-terror/2015/12/24/e162e088-0953-4de5-992e-adb2126f1dcc_story.html.

Brown, Alison (2004), "The Immobile Mass: Movement Restrictions in the West Bank." *Social & Legal Studies*, 13 (4): 501–21.

B'Tselem (2010), *10 Years to the Second Intifada – Summary of Data*. https://www.btselem.org/press_releases/20100927.

Cohen, Gili (2017), "Cancer Patient Caught Smuggling Explosives for Hamas, Shin Bet Says." *Ha'aretz*, April 19. https://www.haaretz.com/israel-news/cancer-patient-caught-smuggling-explosives-for-hamas-shin-bet-says-1.5462792.

Collier, Jane and Hanna Kienzler (2018), "Barriers to Cardiovascular Disease Secondary Prevention Care in the West Bank, Palestine – A Health Professional Perspective." *Conflict and Health*, 12: 27. https://doi.org/10.1186/s13031-018-0165-x.

Dana, Tariq (2021), "Dominate and Pacify: Contextualizing the Political Economy of the Occupied Palestinian Territories Since 1967." In A. Tartir, T. Dana, and T. Seidel (eds.), *Political Economy of Palestine*, 25–47. Switzerland: Springer Nature.

Farmer, Paul, Bruce. Nizeye, Sara Stulac, and Salmaan Keshavjee (2006), "Structural Violence and Clinical Medicine." *PLoS Medicine*, 3 (10): e449. https://doi.org/10.1371/journal.pmed.0030449.

Galtung, Johan (1969), "Violence, Peace, and Peace Research." *Journal of Peace Research*, 6 (3): 167–91.

Ghobarah, Hazem, Paul Huth, and Bruce Russett (2004), "The Post-War Public Health Effects of Civil Conflict." *Social Science & Medicine*, 59: 869–84.

Gisha (2019), *In 2018, 31% of Applications Filed by Gaza Patients to Travel Via Erez Crossing for Medical Treatment were Answered Too Late, or Not at All*. February 11. http://gisha.org/updates/9766.

Haar, Rohini and Leonard Rubenstein (2012), "Health in Fragile and Post-Conflict States: A Review of Current Understanding and Challenges Ahead." *Medicine Conflict and Survival*, 28 (4): 289–316.

Halahleh, Khalid and Robert Gale (2018), "Cancer Care in the Palestinian Territories." *Lancet Oncol*, 19: e359–e364.

Hass, Amira (2016), "Ambulance Interrogations Delay Seriously Ill Patients Crossing into Israel from Gaza." *Ha'aretz*, July 20. https://www.haaretz.com/israel-news/.premium-seriously-ill-patients-crossing-from-gaza-interrogated-in-ambulances-1.5412315.

Hass, Amira (2017), "For Some Gazans in Need of Medical Treatment, the Wait for an Exit Permit Ends in Death." *Ha'aretz*, March 12. https://www.haaretz.com/middle-east

-news/palestinians/.premium-for-some-sick-gazans-the-wait-for-an-exit-permit-ends-in-death-1.5627529.
Hass, Amira (2018), "Israel Bars Gazans from Getting Medical Care in West Bank if They Have Relatives Staying There Without a Permit." *Ha'aretz*, October 20. https://www.haaretz.com/israel-news/.premium-gazan-patients-face-new-limitation-on-travel-for-medical-treatment-1.6573119.
Hoffman, Gil (2016), "Lapid: US Helped Iran Fund its Next War against Israel." *The Jerusalem Post*, January 26. https://www.jpost.com/israel-news/politics-and-diplomacy/lapid-us-helped-iran-fund-its-next-war-against-israel-442791#article=6017NzI0REQ2QkM2QkYyN0Y5NjU2NzRGQTVGRUZGQTBBQzA=.
Human Rights Council (2017), *Report of the Special Rapporteur on the Situation of Human Rights in the Palestinian Territories Occupied since 1967, Michael Lynk*. March 16. http://ap.ohchr.org/documents/dpage_e.aspx?si=A/HRC/37/75.
Jasani, Gregory, Reem Alfalasi, Garrett Cavaliere, Gregory Ciottone, and Benjamin Lawner (2021), "Terrorists Use of Ambulances for Terror Attacks: A Review." *Prehospital and Disaster Medicine*, 36 (1): 14–17. doi:10.1017/S1049023X20001260.
Kearney, Michael, Anna Khdair, and Rania Muhareb (2020), "COVID-19 and the Right to Health of Palestinians under Israeli Occupation, Colonisation, and Apartheid." *Al-Haq*. https://www.alhaq.org/cached_uploads/download/2020/12/08/covid-19-and-the-right-to-health-interactive-1-page-view-1-1607410547.pdf.
Leone, Tiziana, Diego Alburez-Gutierrez, Rula Ghandour, et al. (2019), "Maternal and Child Access to Care and Intensity of Conflict in the Occupied Palestinian Territory: A Pseudo-Longitudinal Analysis (2000–2014)." *Conflict and Health*, 13: 36. https://doi.org/10.1186/s13031-019-0220-2.
MAP (2017), *Access to Healthcare. Health Under Occupation: Volume 1*. https://www.map.org.uk/downloads/map-ch1--access-to-healthcare.pdf.
McNeely, Clea, Brian Barber, Rita Giacaman, Robert Belli, and Mahmoud Daher (2018), "Long-Term Health Consequences of Movement Restrictions for Palestinians 1987–2011." *American Journal of Public Health*, 108 (1): 77–83.
Ministry of Foreign Affairs (MFA)- Israel (2004), *Palestinian Misuse of Medical Services and Ambulances for Terrorist Activities*. October 13. https://mfa.gov.il/MFA/Government/Law/Legal+Issues+and+Rulings/Palestinian+Misuse+of+Medical+Services+and+Ambulances+for+Terrorist+Activities+13-Oct-2004.htm.
Palestinian Central Bureau of Statistics (PCBS) (2019), *Estimated Population in Palestine Mid-Year by Governorate, 1997–2021*. http://pcbs.gov.ps/Portals/_Rainbow/Documents/-2017%2097انجليزي%20المحافظات.html.
PHR (2018a), *Dramatic Increase in Refused Permits to Travel Out of Gaza*. August 20. https://www.phr.org.il/en/dramatic-increase-in-refused-permits-to-travel-out-of-gaza/.
PHR (2018b), *Israel: Record-Low in Gaza Medical Permits*. February 13. https://www.phr.org.il/en/israel-record-low-gaza-medical-permits/.
Physicians for Human Rights (PHR) (2016), *Denied 2: Harassment of Palestinian Patients Applying for Exit Permits*. August. https://www.phr.org.il/wp-content/uploads/2016/09/Denied-2.pdf.
Rytter, Maren, Anne-Lene Kjaeldgaard, Henrik Bronnum-Hansen, and Karin Helweg-Larsen (2006), "Effects of Armed Conflict on Access to Emergency Health Care in Palestinian West Bank: Systematic Collection of Data in Emergency Departments." *BMJ*, 13 (332): 1122–4.
Shalhoub-Kevorkian, Nadera, Yossi David, and Sarah Ihmoud (2016), "Theologizing State Crime." *State Crime Journal*, 5 (1): 139–62. https://doi.org/10.13169/statecrime.5.1.0139.

Shoaibi, Halla (2011), "Childbirth at Checkpoints in the Occupied Palestinian Territory." *The Lancet*. http://www.thelancet.com/pb/assets/raw/Lancet/abstracts/palestine/palestine2011-4.pdf.

Sidel, Victor and Barry Levy (2008), "The Health Impact of War." *International Journal of Injury Control and Safety Promotion*, 15 (4): 189–95.

United Nations (UN) (2016), *Freedom of Movement: Human Rights Situation in the Occupied Palestinian Territory, Including East Jerusalem*. https://www.ohchr.org/en/hrbodies/hrc/regularsessions/session34/documents/a_hrc_34_38_auv.docx.

United Nations Conference on Trade and Development [UNCTAD] (2022), *Report on UNCTAD Assistance to the Palestinian People: Developments in the Economy of the Occupied Palestinian Territory*. https://unctad.org/system/files/official-document/tdbex72d2_en.pdf.

UN United Nations Economic and Social Commission for Western Asia (ESCWA) (2018), *Support for the Palestinian People: Impact of the Israeli Occupation and Practices*. https://www.unescwa.org/sites/default/files/event/materials/1800228.pdf.

UN Office for the Coordination of Humanitarian Affairs (OCHA) (2020), *Data on Casualties*. https://www.ochaopt.org/data/casualties.

Vision of Humanity (2019), *Global Peace Index and Global Terrorism Index Reports*. http://visionofhumanity.org/reports/.

Vitullo, Anita, Abdelnasser Soboh, Jenny Oskarsson, Tasneem Atatrah, Mohamed Lafi, and Tony Laurance (2012), "Barriers to the Access to Health Services in the Occupied Palestinian Territory: A Cohort Study." *The Lancet*, 380 (1): S18–S19.

Wolfe, Patrick (2006), "Settler Colonialism and the Elimination of the Native." *Journal of Genocide Research*, 8 (4): 387–409, doi:10.1080/14623520601056240.

World Bank (2007), *Movement and Access Restrictions in the West Bank: Uncertainty and Inefficiency in the Palestinian Economy*. http://documents.worldbank.org/curated/en/964061468339036297/pdf/404450GZ0West0Bank0restrictions01PUBLIC1.pdf.

World Health Organization (WHO) (2017), *Health Access for Referral Patients from the Gaza Strip Summary: Annual Overview and December 2017*. http://www.emro.who.int/images/stories/palestine/documents/WHO_monthly_Gaza_access_report_Dec_2017-final.pdf?ua=1.

WHO (2020), *WHO Monthly Reports on Health Access in the Occupied Palestinian Territory*. http://www.emro.who.int/pse/publications-who/monthly-referral-reports.html.

4

Israeli Online Surveillance Regime

Digital Colonization in Practice

Nijmeh Ali

Introduction

In 2019, while I was traveling to Palestine and Israel, the Ben-Gurion/Tel Aviv airport security confiscated my laptop and forbade me from having it during the flight; since then, I have decided to travel with fewer electronic devices. However, in 2022, having only my backup, after a quick oral investigation, I was tagged as a "high-security threat."[1] My cell phone was taken on a scanning machine as part of the long security check process. A technical problem occurred, and the Israeli officer shouted in Hebrew that he could not copy it (my cellphone). These incidents inspired me to write this chapter, arguing that understanding and dismantling Israeli settler colonialism today, where technology emerges as a dominant tool in everyday human interactions, requires the mindset of an information technology (IT) scientist, not only a social scientist. The interaction between IT and social science in this chapter suggests a critical approach for examining the reinventing of colonial settler practices in a neoliberal context.

Undoubtedly, the new technology era is viewed positively and as part of a global liberation movement, providing various paths/spaces and tools to practice freedoms, particularly for those in oppressive contexts where freedom of speech and activism are restricted and under attack. Nevertheless, this view is incomplete. On the contrary, technology creates spaces where power and resistance are reflected. On the one hand, it made digital activism the new *Intifada*, where posts, videos, and photos become the "weapons of the weak," as James Scott wrote in 1985 in his description of the resistance of the oppressed. While on the other, digital colonization practices—defined as the use of digital technology for political, economic, and social control (Kwet 2019)—play into the hands of those who hold power; it flourishes and gains savage control and surveillance power. In this sense, this chapter exposes the Israeli settler colonial regime with attention to online surveillance, encapsulated with modernity and development, which secure the continuation of Palestinians' subjugation, oppression, and colonization. In a more comprehensive view, this chapter addresses the counter-use of technologies in spying and collecting massive data by applying and normalizing mass surveillance methods as a contemporary form of exercising oppression, subjugation, and authoritarianism.

Colonial Surveillance and Settler Colonialism

Settler colonialism is a project of racial domination. It is characterized by an ongoing effort to dispossess native peoples of their lands to replace their presence with a society dominated by settlers (Veracini 2011; Wolfe 1999; 2006). Therefore, settler colonialism normalizes the continuous settler occupation, exploiting lands and resources with which Indigenous Peoples have genealogical relationships; it includes oppression, racism, white supremacy, heteropatriarchy, and capitalism (Cox 2017). Wolfe (2006) articulates the "logic of elimination" that structures settler colonialism as a lasting system of native erasure rather than a historical event. In this sense, Bevilacqua (2022) understands settler colonialism as stratifications of an ethical and legal hierarchical system. It has constructed side by side the image of the "traditional" and "primitive" native/colonized and the image of the "human" and "progressive" newcomer/colonizer. The Zionist myth of "blooming the desert," thus, does not only refer to colonizing an empty land but also to bringing modernity to the noncivilized indigenous people. Therefore, and not surprisingly, colonial strategies of de-Arabization alongside policies of re-indigenizing Zionist settlers were applied to abolish the Palestinian landscape by using newly coined Hebrew nomenclature and biblical names for the villages, cities, and streets (Azaryahu and Golan 2001; Masalha 2015); this is how Street of the Mountain (Al-Jabal) in Haifa, which had been its name before the colonization of Palestine in 1948, turned to Hatzionut (Zionism) Avenue. Nevertheless, Palestinians resist these colonial elimination strategies by insisting on naming Al-Jabal street by its original name.

Ogasawara's statement that "nation building and colonialism are intervened in the development of surveillance systems" (2019, 727) also applies to Israel. To make this link clear, exposing the discourse on surveillance is essential. Helga Tawil-Souri says, "surveillance is double-sided" (2016, 57). It can be embracing and caring by providing benefits to citizens, as much as it can construct a system of inequality, oppression, and injustice (2016, 57).

David Lyon's definition identifies both its productive and repressive capabilities: surveillance, in his words, "the focused, systematic and routine attention to personal details for purposes of influence, management, protection or direction" (2007, 14). Therefore, governmental, military, educational, or corporate organizations use surveillance to achieve their goals. Elia Zuriek views surveillance "as a feature of power, surveillance in everyday life is involved in the constitution of subjectivities at the level of desire, fear, security, trust, and risk—all of which ultimately impact human dignity and individual autonomy" (2016, 12).

Surveillance, therefore, is considered a structure that supports the dominant relations of state power and control. However, as Tawil-Souri stresses, surveillance "cannot be divorced from the context of when, where, and by whom it is used" (2016, 57). In the context of Palestine-Israel, surveillance cannot be separated from Zionist strategies of categorization of people and places, which serves the continuing Zionist efforts of disposing and controlling the Palestinians.

Contextualizing the Israeli Colonial Surveillance Doctrine

Surveillance has consistently been an integral part of practicing oppression over Palestinians. This has been the case since the initial colonization of Palestine, even before the creation of the Israeli state. The prestate period, known in its Hebrew name as the *Yishuv* (settlement), designed and shaped the relational framework of the Zionist settler colonizers with the colonized Indigenous Palestinians, determining the domination of surveillance in the Israeli national security doctrine, and is sometimes described as Israel's "first line of defense" (Zaitun 2021). In 1953, David Ben-Gurion formulated the first and the only approved document on the Israeli national security doctrine, which was/still relies on three security elements: deterrence, intelligence, and a swift and decisive victory to end the war quickly (Amidror 2021).[2] Therefore, not surprisingly, the Directorate of Israeli Intelligence (DMI or AMAN—Hebrew acronym) determines Israel's policymaking process. AMAN's Research Division serves as the leading national intelligence estimator, not only in military matters but also in political, economic, and all matters considered relevant to state security (Bar-Joseph 2010).

Information, thus, is a cornerstone in the Zionist colonial project; since the late 1910s, they started gathering information about Palestinians for colonial purposes using various intelligence means, an activity that was intensified in the 1920s (Black and Morris 1991; Pappe 2006; Zureik 2015). Directing their first information gathering on land, in 1919, the World Zionist Organization (WZO) "Information Office," together with WZO Departments of Agriculture and Settlements, completed a detailed land survey of Palestine (Cohen 2010, 100). However, during the British Mandate, various British and Zionist organizations collected data about Palestinians.

A significant organization that collected maps for surveillance and population control of Palestine, constructing comprehensive lists of villagers and land holdings for military and settlement purposes, was *Shai*,[3] the intelligence arm of the *Hagana*, established in 1940; Zuriek (2016, 16) indicates that information included aerial photographs, maps, textual surveys, and socioeconomic data about the villages. Also, information on internal disputes, political affiliation, resistance involvement, water resources, and land ownership. Information on roads, the number of weapons available to Palestinians, and the presence of fighters during the 1936–9 Revolt. Later this information was used as an effective instrument in the ethnic cleansing of Palestine in 1948, also known as Plan *Dalet* (Pappe 2006). Zionists also established various bodies that later evolved into the state's "intelligence" institutions—Shin Bet and Mossad, among others (Tawil-Souri 2016, 58). This generated information constructed an accurate image to "know thy enemy," accumulated, after 1948, with the acquisition and theft of most British archives (Tawil-Souri 2016).

With the British withdrawal from Palestine in 1948, the Palestinian Nakba's new reality, and the establishment of Israel, Zionists had a state of their own, legislative powers, and complete control over law enforcement and intelligence apparatus, which allowed them to establish straightforward structures of colonial surveillance.

Israeli settler colonial practices were reflected through two parallel actions; the first was when Israel conducted its first census on November 8, 1948; the census included (1) a registry of the population and (2) a registry of Arab property. The former prepared the ground for Israel's war on "infiltration" or, as Robinson (2013) defines it, the "war on return," as it prevented the return of Palestinian refugees to their homes after the war; this includes the Palestinian Internal Refugees, those who became refugees in their homeland—which turned to Israel. The latter facilitated the mass confiscation of Palestinian land and property, which was later declared "absentees' property" under the 1950 Absentees' Property Law.[4] The census Israel conducted after it occupied the West Bank and Gaza in 1967 repeated the 1948 process, determining who was "in" and "out" by undercounting the resident population of the occupied territories. It then denied the right of return to Palestinian residents who were displaced during the fighting or absent from their place of residence for work, study, travel, or other reasons when the census was undertaken (Van Esveld 2012, 17–18).

The second action was the establishment of the Military Rule Administration, a comprehensive system of control and separation over the remaining Palestinians in Israel (48 Palestinians); that lasted for almost two decades (1948–66). However, despite becoming official Israeli citizens in 1952, the Military Rule continued to control the day-to-day aspects of Palestinians' lives who were deprived of fundamental freedoms, mainly freedom of movement, by imposing a permit system. As a classic settler colonial regime, the desire to place the 48 Palestinians under surveillance comes to fulfill the control of their lands, political life, and economic activity, restricting their capacity to organize and resist.

The Military Rule over the 48 Palestinians was officially dismissed in 1966. However, the Defense (Emergency) Regulations, which constituted the legal infrastructure for intrusively and systematically supervising and controlling the Palestinian, have never been revoked or canceled. Instead, the military government's functions were transferred to the police and Israeli intelligence service—*Shin Bet* (Zureik 2016, 12). Furthermore, with the occupation of the West Bank and Gaza Strip in 1967, the Military Rule Administration permit system was comprehensively refined and implemented in the newly occupied territories (Zureik 2016, 12). Following the same logic of surveillance, Israel expanded its means/institutions of surveillance—the police, the *Shin Bet*, the army, and the Civil Administration. In addition, it expanded its control over more Palestinian lands, resources and people.

Yael Berda (2013) singles out surveillance in the colonial state as signifying a shift from controlling the territory to managing the population. In comparison, Zuriek (2016) sees territory and population management as two parallel colonial activities. Two features are central to colonial surveillance for ruling: the production of objects of colonial surveillance and the quotidian context of people watching people and the formal aspect of colonial policies that are embodied in bureaucratic, enumerative, and legal measures aimed at controlling territory by classifying and categorizing the population (Zuriek 2016, 14).

Examining the Israeli surveillance structure of the Military Rule reveals four forms of surveillance (Grinberg 2009). *First, it was bureaucratic.* State institutions documented and stored detailed information about the lives of Palestinians. *Second, it was economical.* The state prevented the 48 Palestinians from establishing economic and development projects if its leaders refused to cooperate with the state. Furthermore, to a large extent, it dominated their life chances of work, education, land ownership, and travel. The military governor had absolute control over every aspect of the Palestinians, individually and collectively.[5] The massive land confiscations left the Palestinians with no economic resources and quickly turned them into "cheap labor" in the Israeli market—the joke about the Palestinians who constructed new buildings in Israel is not far from true. Later, after the West Bank and Gaza Strip occupation in 1967, Palestinians from the oPt became direct labor in Israel and the Settlements. Even those who were educated suffered from strict surveillance; until 2005, the employment of Palestinian teachers, for instance, was conditional on the approval of the security services. In local politics, the Israeli government relied on traditional Arab social structures by appointing subservient tribal/clan/familial chiefs, known as *Al Moukhtar* system, to provide votes for Zionist parties and administer the affairs of local councils but mainly to provide "local knowledge" to support the technical methods of surveillance. *The third form of surveillance was territorial control and geographical fragmentation*; surveillance alienated the Palestinian community by dismantling its spatial continuity. The state could continue its land confiscations by confining the Palestinians to geographically defined areas. *Fourth, it was social control and fragmentation.* Following the strategy of "divide and rule," Israeli authorities treated the Palestinians not as a single national unit but as divided into tribes and religious sectors—known as *al wasat*. Each of these *Wasat(s)* was treated according to its willingness to cooperate with the state. These colonial structures constructed the foundations that support the continuing of the Israeli settler colonial regime.

No doubt that surveillance takes place throughout the entirety of Palestine-Israel deploying different methods at different times onto different sets of populations. Israeli settler colonialism works by breaking apart and eliminating Palestinian communities, whether through the military violence of occupation and siege in the West Bank and Gaza Strip, the legal regimes of apartheid on the Palestinians in Israel, or the denial of refugees' right of return. However, this chapter sought to expand the observation of the Israeli settler colonial regime by examining the online surveillance reality where each individual becomes an independent entity targeted by surveillance authorities. By this, self-censorship behavior is boosted. Palestinians feel they are watched all the time and firmly believe the Israeli authorities know everything—this process leads to the construction of the "self-colonized." Particularly when the collection of intimate details and information, including the sexual orientation and political beliefs of Palestinians, has been used to recruit collaborators. Indeed, personal data has often been traded for information on security grounds, especially targeting groups such as women and LGBTQ people (al-Qaws 2014).

Constructing the Israeli Online Surveillance Regime: Digital Colonialism in Practice

Information researcher Michael Kwet (2019) describes digital colonialism as the use of digital technology for political, economic, and social control. In a time when enormous human communication is conducted via electronic media, controlling modern technology for comprehensive-scale collection, storage, and statistical data analysis can yield more productive and detailed intelligence information on surveillance targets than ever before. Couldry and Mejias (2018, 2) describe this as "data colonialism" similar to "digital colonization," a twenty-first-century expression of colonialism that normalizes "the exploitation of human beings through data, just as historic colonialism appropriated territory and resources and ruled subjects for profit." Israel, therefore, is the headquarters of more spyware companies than any other country (Shezaf and Jacobson 2018). Moreover, it became a "leading exporter of tools for spying on civilians. Dictators worldwide—even in countries with no formal ties to Israel—use them to eavesdrop on human rights activists, monitor emails, hack into apps and record conversations" (Shezaf and Jacobson 2018). These links generate an automatic suspect attitude toward technological changes even though encapsulated with modernity and development, mainly among Palestinians and human rights activists worldwide.

Neve Gordon (2009), who studied the Israeli security industry, draws our attention to the fact that Israel's surveillance industry stems from the close relations between Israel's military and the technology sector. For example, in 1960, the Israeli military was developing computer software—nine years before the Israeli software industry and university computer science programs even existed (Kane 2016). Moreover, Unit 8200, the Israeli intelligence unit responsible for Israeli cyber offence, is the largest unit of the Israeli military (WhoProfits 2021, 8). Of 2,300 Israelis who founded 700 Israeli cyber firms, 80 percent were graduates of Unit 8200. These founders use their military experience and connections as marketing tools for foreign investors (Shezaf and Jacobson 2018).

Gordon also emphasizes that the prolonged occupation of the West Bank, including East Jerusalem, the blockade of Gaza, and its periodic wars provide a laboratory for testing and modifying products that are created or different technologies.

Israeli surveillance has become an everyday reality for the Palestinians; in this regard it is crucial to emphasize that although according to the Oslo Accord (1993), Israel should have transferred the Information and Communication Technology (ICT) governance to the Palestinian Authority (PA), Israel has retained control over the internet backbone and service delivery infrastructure, hindering Palestinians' development of an independent network that would grant greater safety and freedom of expression (7amleh 2018). Israel's control over ICT is not only a matter of economic de-development—it has also been translated into the creation of new technologies for surveillance and repression (WhoProfit 2021; Bevilacqua 2022).

The impact of Israeli surveillance technology on human rights is undeniable. The UN special report on Surveillance and Human Rights (2019) warns that the surveillance of individuals—often journalists, activists, opposition figures, and critics—has led to arbitrary detention, torture, and extrajudicial killings. Journalists and media have also been subjected to military censorship, orders banning coverage of specific subjects, and private-sector lawsuits designed to gag them (Reports without Borders 2020). The Israeli online mass surveillance debate did not surprise the Palestinians, who have been struggling against mass surveillance technologies for years. Moreover, this technology for colonization purposes has been developed along with a set of laws and rules offering legitimacy for violating Palestinians' lives in the name of Israeli national security.

In particular, two significant laws related to internal surveillance of Israeli citizens caused a heated debate in the Israeli media and reached the court: "The Big Brother Law" and "The Biometric Database Law." The Big Brother Law, approved by the Knesset in 2007, allows the police to set up a database on citizens that contains telephone numbers, names of mobile telephone subscribers, serial numbers of mobile phones, and maps of antenna locations. The database has been described as the "biggest database in the West" (Shahar 2007). In addition, in 2009, Israel passed a law establishing a biometric database, collecting and storing biometric data, characteristic biological traits such as fingerprints, retina and iris patterns, DNA, and other unique identifiers (Lebovic and Pinchuk 2010). The motivation behind the biometric database is the argument that it ensures security and protection against the theft of personal information. However, human rights organizations opposed the biometric campaign in Israel for fear that it would compromise individual privacy and give governmental bodies full access to personal data without securing sufficient oversight (Klinger 2011).

In 2014, the Israeli government approved Resolution 1775 and established a strategy for increasing surveillance in East Jerusalem and Palestinians within the Green Line (Israel). Since then, the plan has been reinforced and expanded. For example, in 2015, the Jerusalem Police district plan included an investment of 48.9 million NIS to strengthen, purchase, and install CCTV cameras and surveillance technology in East Jerusalem (WhoProfits 2018). In addition, since 2015, Israel has been developing special units that report Palestinian content to social media companies—the Israeli Ministry of Justice developed a special "Cyber Unit" to support Israel's National Cyber Crime Unit (Lahav 433) and the Israeli Law, Information and Technology Authority at the Ministry of Justice.[6]

Moreover, the Israeli authorities have worked to legislate special laws to suppress Palestinians in the digital space, such as the Facebook bill, Prohibition Against Photographing and Documenting Israeli Soldiers law, and the Cyber Security and National Cyber Directorate Bill (7amleh 2018).

These laws and surveillance methods established a comprehensive monitoring system, violating Palestinians' right to privacy, limiting their freedom of expression, and "silencing" their voices, reflecting the continuing erasure of Palestinian narrative and content, which is the hardcore of the elimination logic of settler colonialism. Moreover, it expands the Zionist settler colonial regime practices to the online space as a continuity of strategies of colonial oppression in the offline, controlling actual and virtual territory.

With the outbreak of the discussion on using mass surveillance programs in Israel, Bergamn and Shabertoch revealed a vital piece in 2020, disclosing information regarding a secret database known as the "tool" or *Ha kle* in Hebrew. This revealed that the *Shin Bet* has been spying on all citizens using Israeli telecommunications since 2002, all the time, and most importantly, regardless of the coronavirus crisis. It is worth mentioning that the international debate at that time was shaped in the shadow of the September 11, 2001, attacks and the "war on terror," which gave the green light to the use of mass surveillance methods to face personal fears and national challenges.

Bergman and Shabertoch's (2020) investigation revealed that only five members of the Intelligence Subcommittee were aware of the "tool," and it was never brought to the public's attention in Israel. This means that an extensive system that collects information about all citizens in a country that considers itself a "democratic state" remains entirely in the dark, with no transparency and accountability (Ali 2020).

According to Bergman and Shabertoch (2020), apart from gathering information on everyone, the "tool" allows checking citizen life from when they became a subject of surveillance and back in time. The *Shin Bet* data collection makes it clear that the Israeli state surveillance is not limited to Palestinian citizens; it touches the lives of Jewish citizens as well, although it takes different forms and is not so bound up with nationalistic considerations (2020).

The panic of Israeli human rights organizations regarding their online safety while ignoring the impact of mass surveillance on the Palestinians for years indicates the dehumanization centrality in colonial practices. However, to understand the role of surveillance in maintaining and expanding the Israeli settler colonial regime, Handal and Dayan (2017, 472) suggest the "multilayered surveillance" model, presenting three types of surveillance (s): (1) "normalizing surveillance," performed on Israeli-Jews, whose loyalty is secured based on ethnic separation, emotional loyalty, and existential fears; (2) "exclusionary surveillance," enacted on different levels, mainly on the Palestinian inhabitants of the Gaza Strip and the West Bank but also on the Palestinian citizens of Israel; and (3) "globalizing surveillance," under which Jews and former Israelis serve as surveillance agents responsible for building a "domain of defense" for Israel in their own countries. This observation is interesting. However, it is missing the implications of the globalization (as a worldwide spread) of Israeli surveillance technologies and its economic and ethical role in maintaining the Israeli settler colonial regime.

Practices of Online Surveillance in Palestine and Israel

The coronavirus pandemic exposed comprehensive Israeli surveillance methods that were applied during the coronavirus outbreak openly and showed that—despite the pandemic—at least since 2002, there are records that include all conversations and messages (Ali 2020). In addition, text messages of all citizens of Israel are stored in a database that collects data under the control of the *Shin Bet*, and since 2013 there has been monitoring of citizens' movements. Those records are under the control of the Israeli police.

However, global crises (such as the current coronavirus pandemic and the Russian-Ukraine war) create a great fear among people that usually serves as an opportunity for states and governments to justify policies and practices that violate the fundamental rights of individuals behind the guise of providing protection. Also, in ethnic conflict realities, authorities can rule by capitalizing on citizens' fear, and surveillance in everyday life is promoted as necessary to reduce fear and risk (Zureik 2016, 12). Moreover, in the case of Israel, two justifications dominate the Israeli public discourse for applying surveillance toward Palestinians: (1) through creating a permanent "culture of fear," using the Jewish history of suffering and continuing reinventing the image of the "enemy" and (2) applying a securitization framework and portraying the Palestinians as a "security threat," "demographic bomb," and "fifth column." In this matter, Shalhoub-Kevorkian (2015, 7) argue that "fear and 'security claims' have become embedded in the Zionist anthology and epistemology, which, when partnered with power holders, enable surveillance technologies over feared Others that have assessed in disciplining, displacing and erasing communities maintaining spatial and racial dispositions."

In the name of security health, surveillance techniques applied to track Palestinians were used during the pandemic to track patients—using geolocation tracking, a mobile phone location tracking technology. Facial recognition is another powerful mass surveillance tool. It is a biometric software application that uniquely identifies or verifies a person by comparing and analyzing patterns based on facial contours (Omoyiwola 2018). Facial recognition is mainly used for security purposes. This surveillance method is profoundly used in the West Bank. The Old City of Jerusalem represents a microcosm of this method, where Israel seeks to create a coercive environment to drive Palestinians out of the city. To this end, Israel launched the "Mabat 2000" project in the Old City, consisting of 320–400 closed-circuit television (CCTV) cameras capable of maneuvering 360 degrees to follow and track movements (7amleh 2020). Also, face-scanning cameras were installed in the city of Hebron to help Israeli soldiers identify Palestinians at checkpoints even before they presented their ID cards. A more comprehensive network of CCTV cameras provides real-time monitoring and sometimes sees into private homes (Dwoskin 2021).

The "Hawk's Eye" cameras, in Hebrew "Ein H' Nets," are smart cameras that detect license plates and compare license numbers to predefined databases, such as the database of vehicles reported as stolen and the database of vehicles whose license has expired, and alert them in real time. However, these cameras have been deployed all over Israel, and information regarding civilian movement has been collected since 2013 (Dolev 2020). The police keep a database of the movements of civilians who have not committed any offence and are not even suspected of it, just in case their vehicle is involved in an offence in the future. In other words, the police hold a confidential database on civilian movement that may remain in the hands of the police for years. The Israeli police refuse to provide data regarding the deployment of the cameras, their number, the number of license plates captured on them, or the exact length of time the data was stored. "Ein H' Nets" database has not been reported as required to the

Registrar of Databases in the Ministry of Justice, and today there is not even a police procedure that regulates its use.

The Coordination of Government Activities in the Territories (COGAT)App related to Palestinians living in the occupied territories, which need to verify whether their permits to enter and remain in Israel are still valid, has been advised by Israel to download an app that enables the military access to their mobile phones. The app, known as *"Al Munasiq,"* in Arabic, or "The Coordinator," allows the army to track the user's phone location and access any notifications they receive, files they download or save, and the device's camera. During the coronavirus outbreak, the Coordination of Government Activities in the Territories (COGAT) offices were closed, and the COGAT app was the primary communication tool. In order to install the app, users need to approve the following terms: "We may make use of the information we collect for any purpose, including for security purposes" (Middle East Eye 2020). Another app involves a smartphone technology called Blue Wolf that captures photos of Palestinians' faces and matches them to a database of images described by a former Israeli soldier as "the army's secret Facebook for Palestinians" (Dwoskin 2021).

Online surveillance methods, therefore, include extensive monitoring networks, analysis and cross-referencing of large databases, monitoring citizens' geographical locations through their mobile phones, and using artificial intelligence, keeping the Palestinians "completely exposed" (WhoProfit 2021, 7) in an open prison.

Globalization of Israeli Online Colonialism

The Israeli online mass surveillance's impact is crossing borders, politics, regimes, and continents. In 2022, Israel's surveillance sector drew international condemnation after news of their abusive practices reached the headlines. At that time, a group of journalists and civil society organizations found that Israeli spyware was used to target some 50,000 journalists and human rights defenders worldwide (Citizen Lab and Amnesty 2021). This data shows the spread of Israeli surveillance technologies worldwide and challenges the acceptable observation that surveillance and control methods are frequently transferred from one colonial setting to another—it spreads worldwide and reaches everyone.

Not exclusive to Palestine, perhaps the most popular online mass surveillance technology is the Israel-based "Cyber Warfare" vendor NSO Group, which produces and sells a mobile phone spyware suite called Pegasus. The spies have been used to surveil journalists and political leaders from several nations worldwide (Levinson 2020).

In 2016, Citizen Lab revealed that Bahrain used the NSO Group's Pegasus to hack activists and members of *Waad*—a secular Bahraini political society. In Mexico, dozens of Mexican lawyers, journalists, anti-corruption activists, and human rights defenders were targeted by Pegasus in 2016. In Spain, Pegasus was used by the government of Spain against politicians active in the Catalan independent movement (Kirchgaessner and Jones 2020). Moreover, in 2020, it was reported that Saudi Arabia and the United

Arab Emirates deployed Pegasus software against two London-based reporters and thirty-six journalists at the Al-Jazeera Qatari television network (Marczak et al. 2020).

Citizen Lab organization (Marczak et al. 2018) conducted comprehensive research on Pegasus; the findings were shocking and raised ethical questions. For example, the Citizen Lab found suspected NSO Pegasus infections associated with thirty-three of the thirty-six Pegasus operators identified in forty-five countries: Algeria, Bahrain, Bangladesh, Brazil, Canada, Cote d'Ivoire, Egypt, France, Greece, India, Iraq, Israel, Jordan, Kazakhstan, Kenya, Kuwait, Kyrgyzstan, Latvia, Lebanon, Libya, Mexico, Morocco, the Netherlands, Oman, Pakistan, Palestine, Poland, Qatar, Rwanda, Saudi Arabia, Singapore, South Africa, Switzerland, Tajikistan, Thailand, Togo, Tunisia, Turkey, the UAE, Uganda, the United Kingdom, the United States, Uzbekistan, Yemen, and Zambia (Marczak et al. 2018). Figure 4.1 is to visualize the global spread of Pegasus.

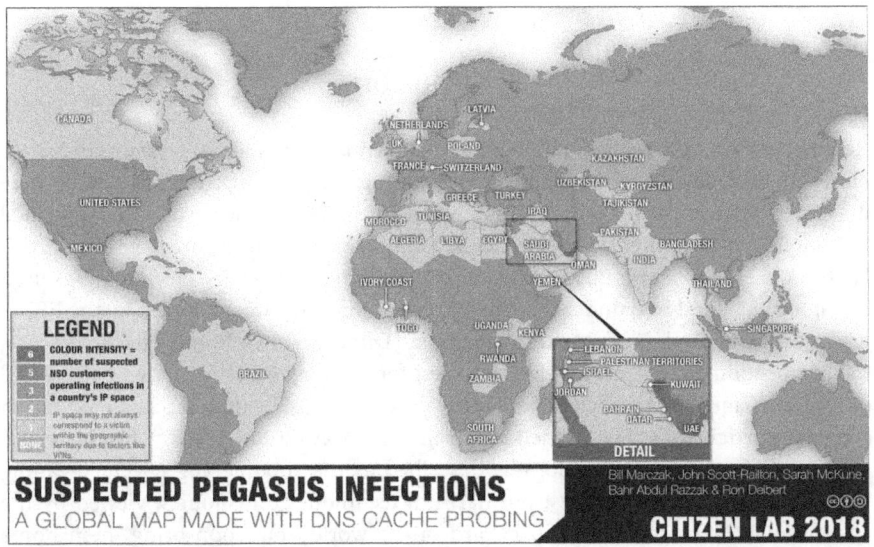

Figure 4.1 Suspected Pegasus infections. *Source*: https://citizenlab.ca/wp-content/webpc-passthru.php?src=https://citizenlab.ca/wp-content/uploads/2018/09/Hide-and-Seek-Figure-2.jpg&nocache=1.

Beyond the concerns over privacy and accountability, the implications of normalizing Israeli online mass surveillance methods are problematic and dangerous. While this is particularly concerning for Palestinians, it is also dangerous for its potential to contribute more broadly to the shrinking global space for civil society organizations and the continued silencing of human rights defenders, activists, opponents, and ordinary citizens worldwide.

The structures of Israeli settler colonialism, military occupation, and apartheid have enabled Israel to build one of the largest cyber industries in the world. Israel uses its surveillance power to market its surveillance technology as field-tested; as a result; the "colony becomes a laboratory for developing and testing surveillance technologies for home use and export" (Zureik 2016, 25). This tells about the profit-making of colonialism and the international collaboration that goes beyond nondemocratic regimes. In this regard, Israeli weapons exports significantly increased in 2021. The International Defense Cooperation Directorate showed that the Israeli military and security exports "surged by 30 per cent" (Asmar 2022), attributing this to the signing of normalization accords with four Arab countries and the war in Ukraine.

Thus, Israeli technologists sell the success of their surveillance technologies in putting down Palestinian opposition to its colonial practices (Zureik 2016, 25), and by doing this, Israel is widening its colonial practices, reaching out to the big world, and driving international legal experts to warn that Israeli surveillance technologies threaten human rights worldwide (DeSombre 2021). However, it seems that the Israeli management success of the coronavirus, the Abraham Accords, and the Ukrainian war contribute a lot to normalizing these technologies by considering and examining them through their efficiency.

Conclusion

Researchers on colonialism emphasize that primary surveillance methods, as we know them today, census taking, fingerprinting, mapmaking, and profiling, were developed and implemented in colonial settings. Surveillance was often invented for colonial management/control and later implemented in the metropolis (Zuriek 2016; Cole 2009; Parenti 2003). Thus, no surprise if drone (UAV) technologies used in Afghanistan and Iraq under the American war on terror were adopted by the FBI to use against the Black Lives Matter movement (Duncan 2015). In the Palestinian case, the geolocation surveillance technique used for tracking Palestinians was circulated during the pandemic to track patients and Israeli citizens. Later, it tracked Palestinian activists participating in Al-Sheikh Jarrah and May 2021 events. This historical trajectory of powerful technology is described as the "boomerang effect," meaning that Western countries first test out harmful techniques on colonies, viewed by the colonizers as "residence in the backyard of the world," but soon bring them home (Foucault 2003; McCoy 2009; Graham 2013). Colonies, therefore, have been the cradle and the laboratory of surveillance techniques for home use and export—the same story Palestine and Palestinians.

The chapter addresses the development of Israeli online surveillance as colonial practice. It sought to go beyond concerns about privacy, freedom of expression, and accountability, suggesting examining the impacts of normalization with online surveillance methods on the Palestinians and globally.

In its basic definition, surveillance is any collection and processing of personal data, whether identifiable or not, to influence or manage those whose data have been generated (Lyon 2001). However, with the development of technology, online surveillance also developed and became an active tool to support the Israeli settler colonialism and oppress the Palestinians harshly and precisely.

The colonial control of Palestinians' everyday life is individual and collective, and the geographic and temporal reach and breadth of the Israeli surveillance regime are formidable and all-encompassing. As a result, Israeli surveillance is a hybrid: an amalgam of low- and hi-tech means, a set of tools developed equally for defense and offense, security, and oppression, enacted on the entirety of the territory (Tawil-Souri 2016).

Just as power stands asymmetrically between colonizers and the colonized, surveillance systems reflect a sharp contrast between watchers and watched-in colonies (Ogasawara 2019, 727). Therefore, examining settler colonial practices via online surveillance is crucial for understanding contemporary Palestinian subjugation and resistance. The Israeli surveillance doctrine shows that Israel's colonial surveillance strength lies in the state's ability to change the rules, tactics, capacity, frequency of forces, strategies, techniques, and occupation techniques. Also lies on the capacity of Israel to establish a surveillance authority, creating a "big brother" atmosphere and managing the Palestinians' behavior by controlling and enhancing self-censorship.

In a global context, Israel is viewed with admiration and as a "model" state from which one must learn how to manage crises due to technological success. However, celebrating the Israeli settler colonial regime and portraying it as a pioneer, especially in the technological field, legitimize the oppression and colonization of Palestinians and others.

With the development of the internet and other electronic devices, people, governments, and countries have been attracted to technological novelties. Nevertheless, technology is not only technical and digital systems; it has social and political implications that shape our world, human relations, and power dynamics. Therefore, this chapter sought to expose the dark side of technology—by exploring its surveillance mechanisms on Palestinians and its power to maintain and expand the Israeli settler colonial regime. This chapter, in this sense, is a warning flag to remind us why Israeli colonial practices in all forms, particularly those encapsulated with development and modernity, should still be resisted. It is also a reminder of the heavy price Palestinians, journalists, human rights defenders, and other oppressed groups in the world pay for being a real-field laboratory.

Until this chapter's writing, I did not receive any information regarding my laptop that was confiscated from me in 2019, although I was promised by the Israeli airport authorities to receive it when arriving home. Undoubtedly, it was obvious to me that I would not use my laptop if I received it back. I am still waiting for it, however.

Notes

1 In the words of the checkup security officer on the personal security check stage stand after reading a serial number that was tagged to my passport after the quick oral investigation—conducted in the first stage of the security check.
2 A formal Israeli national security concept document has yet to be written since then, although there were several attempts to develop an overall defense doctrine.
3 Hebrew acronym for Sherut Yedi'ot—Information Service.
4 "Absentee means (1) a person who, at any time during the period between the 16th Kislev, 5708 (November 29, 1947) and the day on which a declaration is published, under section 9(d) of the Law and Administration Ordinance, 5708-1948(1), that the state of

emergency declared by the Provisional Council of State on the 10th Iyar, 5708 (May 19, 1948)"; for more information see: https://www.adalah.org/uploads/oldfiles/Public/files/Discriminatory-Laws-Database/English/04-Absentees-Property-Law-1950.pdf.

5 The military governor had the right to arrest people without a warrant and detain them without trial for long periods, the authority to ban them or expel them from their homes, and to put them under house arrest, in addition to the authority to close schools, businesses, newspapers, and banning demonstrations and protests. For further information, see Grinberg (2009).

6 The Office of the State Attorney. (n.y.): About the Cyber Unit. Retrieved from: https://www.gov.il/en/Departments/General/cyber-about.

References

7amleh- the Arab Center for the Advancement of Social Media (2018), *Connection Interrupted: Israel's Control of the Palestinian ICT Infrastructure and Its Impact on Digital Rights"*, December. https://www.apc.org/sites/default/files/Report_7amleh_English_final.pdf

7amleh- the Arab Center for the Advancement of Social Media (2020), *Facial Recognition Technology and Palestinian Digital Rights*, May. https://7amleh.org/2020/05/21/facial-recognition-technology-and-palestinian-digital-rights.

Absentees' Property Law, 5710–1950 https://www.adalah.org/uploads/oldfiles/Public/files/Discriminatory-Laws-Database/English/04-Absentees-Property-Law-1950.pdf.

Ali, Nijmeh (2020), "Israeli Impact on Palestinian Digital Rights During the Coronavirus Pandemic." *7amleh- the Arab Center for the Advancement of Social Media*. https://7amleh.org//storage/Research%20and%20Position%20Papers/Israeli%20Impact%20on%20Palestinian%20Digital%20Rights%20During%20the%20Coronavirus%20Pandemic%20.pdf.

Al-Qaws (2014), *Statement re: Media Response to Israel's Blackmailing of Gay Palestinians. alQaws for Sexual and Gender Diversity in Palestinian Society*. http://www.alqaws.org/articles/alQaws-Statement-re-media-response-to-Israels-blackmailing-of-gay-Palestinians.

Amidor, Yaakov (2021), *Israel's National Security Doctrine, The Jerusalem Institute for Strategy and Security (JISS)*. https://jiss.org.il/en/amidror-israels-national-security-doctrine/.

Amnesty (2021), "Amnesty International. Massive Data Leak Reveals Israeli NSO Spyware Used to Target Activists, Journalists, and Political Leaders." *Amnesty International*, July 9. https://www.amnesty.org/en/latest/press-release/2021/07/the-pegasus-project/.

Asmar, Ahmed (2022), "Israeli Arms Exports Mark Significant Increase in 2021." *AA News*, November. https://www.aa.com.tr/en/middle-east/israeli-arms-exports-mark-significantincrease2021/2745079#:~:text=Israel's%20weapons%20exports%20surge%20by%2030%20percent%20in%202021&text=Israeli%20defense%20industries%20reported%20new,in%202020%2C%20the%20report%20said.

Azaryahu, Maoz and Arnon Golan (2001), "(Re)naming the Landscape: The Formation of the Hebrew Map of Israel 1949–1960." *Journal of Historical Geography*, 27 (2): 178–95.

Bar-Joseph, Uri (2010), "Military Intelligence as the National Intelligence Estimator: The Case of Israel." *Armed Forces & Society*, 36 (3): 505–25.

Berda, Yael (2013), "Managing Dangerous Populations: Colonial Legacies of Security and Surveillance." *Sociological Forum*, 28 (3): 627–30.
Bergman, Ronen and Ido Shbertztuch (2020), "The 'tool' has Been Revealed: The Secret GSS Database That Collects Your SMS, Calla and Locations." *Ynet*, March 27. https://www.ynet.co.il/articles/0,7340,L-5701412,00.html.
Bevilacqua, Ivana (2022), "E-scaping Apartheid: Digital Ventures of Zionist Settler Colonialism." *Human Geography*, 15 (2): 220–8. https://doi.org/10.1177/19427786211055780.
Black, Ian and Benny Morris (1991), *Israel's Secret Wars: A History of Israel's Intelligence Services*. New York: Grove Press
Citizen Lab and Amnesty (2021), "Devices of Palestinian Human Rights Defenders Hacked With NSO Group's Pegasus Spyware." *University of Toronto's Citizen Lab and Amnesty International's Security Lab*. https://citizenlab.ca/2021/11/palestinian-human-rights-defenders-hacked-nso-groups-pegasus-spyware/.
Cohen, Hillel (2010), "The Matrix of Surveillance in Times of National Conflict: The Israeli–Palestinian Case." In E. Zureik, D. Lyon, and Y. Abu-Laban (eds.), *Surveillance and Control in Israel/Palestine*, 123–36. New York: Routledge.
Cole, Simon A. (2009), *Suspect Identities: A History of Fingerprinting and Criminal Identification*. Cambridge, MA: Harvard University Press.
Cox, Alicia (2017), "Settler Colonialism." In *Obo in Literary and Critical Theory*. https://www.oxfordbibliographies.com/view/document/obo-9780190221911/obo-9780190221911-0029.xml.
DeSombre, Winnona, Lars Gjesvik, and Johann Ole Willers (2021), "Surveillance Technology at the Fair: Proliferation of Cyber Capabilities in International Arms Markets." *Atlantic Council*. https://www.atlanticcouncil.org/in-depth-research-reports/issue-brief/surveillance-technology-at-the-fair/#conclusion.
Dolev, Daniel (2020), "Police Hold a Confidential Database on Civilian Movements." *Walla News*, May 6. https://news.walla.co.il/item/3355178.
Duncan, Ian (2015), "New Details Released About High-tech Gear FBI Used on Planes to Monitor Freddie Gray Unrest." *Baltimore Sun*.
Dwoskin, Elizabeth (2021), "Israel Escalates Surveillance of Palestinians With Facial Recognition Program in West Bank." *Washington Post*, November 8. https://www.washingtonpost.com/world/middle_east/israel-palestinians-surveillance-facial-recognition/2021/11/05/3787bf42-26b2-11ec-8739-5cb6aba30a30_story.html.
Foucault, Michel (2003), *Society Must be Defended: Lectures at the Collège de France 1975–1976*, trans. David Macey. New York: Picador, 2003, 242.
Gordon, Neve (2009), "The Political Economy of Israel's Homeland Security." *The New Transparency Project, Working Paper III*. https://www.sscqueens.org/sites/sscqueens.org/files/The%20Political%20Economy%20of%20Israel%E2%80%99s%20Homeland%20Security.pdf.
Graham, Stephen (2013), "The New Military Urbanism." In Kirstie Ball and Laureen Snider (eds.), *The Surveillance-Industrial Complex*, 11–26. Abingdon: Routledge.
Grinberg, Lev Luis (2009), *Politics and Violence in Israel/Palestine: Democracy Versus Military Rule*. New York: Routledge.
Handel, Ariel and Hilla Dayan (2017), "Multilayered Surveillance in Israel/Palestine: Dialectics of Inclusive Exclusion." *Surveillance & Society*, 15 (3/4): 471–6.
Kane, Alex (2016), "How Israel Became a Hub for Surveillance Technology." *The Intercept*, October 17. https://theintercept.com/2016/10/17/how-israel-became-a-hub-for-surveillance-technology/

Kirchgaessner, Stephanie and Sam Jones (2020), "Phone of Top Catalan Politician 'targeted by Government-grade Spyware.'" *The Guardian*, July 13. https://www.theguardian.com/world/2020/jul/13/phone-of-top-catalan-politician-targeted-by-government-grade-spyware.

Klinger, Jonathan (2011), "Israel to Start Collecting Fingerprints from All Citizens." *+972 Magazine*, June 4. https://www.972mag.com/israel-to-start-collecting-fingerprints-from-all-citizens/.

Kwet, Michael (2019), "Digital Colonialism: US Empire and the New Imperialism in the Global South." *Race & Class*, 60 (4): 3–26.

Lebovic, Nitzan and Avner Pinchuk (2010), *The State of Israel and the Biometric Database law: Political Centrism and the Post-democratic State*. The Israeli Democracy Institute. http://en. idi. org. il/analysis/articles/the-state-of-israel-and-the-biometric-database-law-politicalcentrism-and-the-post-democratic-state.

Levinson, Chaim (2020), "With Israel's Encouragement, NSO Sold Spyware to UAE and Other Gulf States." *Ha'Aretz*, August 25. https://www.haaretz.com/middle-east-news/2020-08-25/ty-article/.premium/with-israels-encouragement-nso-sold-spyware-to-uae-and-other-gulf-states/0000017f-dbf3-d856-a37f-fff3a4ba0000.

Lyon, David (2001), *Surveillance Society*. Buckingham: McGraw-Hill Education.

Lyon, David (2007), *Surveillance Studies: An Overview*. Cambridge: Polity Press.

Marczak, Bill, John Scott-Railton, Noura Al-Jizawi, Siena Anstis, and Ron Deibert (2020), *The Great iPwn: Journalists Hacked With Suspected NSO Group iMessage 'zero-Click' Exploit*. https://citizenlab.ca/2020/12/the-great-ipwn-journalists-hacked-with-suspected-nso-group-imessage-zero-click-exploit/.

Marczak, Bill, John Scott-Railton, Sarah McKune, Bahr Abdul Razzak, and Ron Deibert (2018), *Hide and Seek: Tracking NSO Group's Pegasus Spyware to Operations in 45 Countries*. Citizen Lab Research Report No. 113, the University of Toronto. https://citizenlab.ca/2018/09/hide-and-seek-tracking-nso-groups-pegasus-spyware-to-operations-in-45-countries.

Masalha, Nur (2015), "Settler-Colonialism, Memoricide and Indigenous Toponymic Memory: The Appropriation of Palestinian Place Names by the Israeli state." *Journal of Holy Land and Palestine Studies*, 14 (1): 3–57.

McCoy, Alfred (2009), *Policing America's Empire: The United States, the Philippines, and the Rise of the Surveillance State*. Madison: University of Wisconsin Press.

Mejias, Ulises A. and Nick Couldry (2018), "Consumption as Production: Data and the Reproduction of Capitalist Relations." In F. W. Frederick and W. Ian (Eds), *The Oxford Handbook of Consumption*, Oxford Handbooks (2019; online edn, Oxford Academic, October 9). https://doi.org/10.1093/oxfordhb/9780190695583.013.14.

Middle East Eye (2020), "'The Coordinator': Israel Instructs Palestinians to Download App That Tracks Their Phones." *Middle East Eye*, April 8. https://www.middleeasteye.net/news/coordinator-israel-instructs-palestinians-download-app-tracks-their-phones.

Ogasawara, Midori (2019), "Mainstreaming Colonial Experiences in Surveillance Studies." *Surveillance & Society*, 17 (5): 726–9.

OHCHR (2019), "Report of the Special Rapporteur on the Promotion and Protection of the Right to Freedom of Opinion and Expression." *United Nations: Human Rights Office of the High Commissioner*. https://www.ohchr.org/EN/Issues/FreedomOpinion/Pages/SR2019ReporttoHRC.aspx.

Omoyiwola, Damilola (2018), "Machine Learning on Facial Recognition." *Medium*, October 23. https://medium.datadriveninvestor.com/machine-learning-on-facial-recognition-b3dfba5625a7.

Oslo, I. (1993), *The Israeli-Palestinian Interim Agreement of the West Bank and Gaza Strip: Annex III, Protocol Concerning Civil Affairs*. https://www.mfa.gov.il/mfa/foreignpolicy/peace/guide/pages/the%20israeli-palestinian%20interim%20agreement%20-%20annex%20iii.aspx#app-36.

Pappe, Ilan (2006), *The Ethnic Cleansing of Palestine*. Oxford: Oneworld Publications.

Parenti, Christian (2003), *The Soft Cage*. New York: Basic Books.

Robinson, Shira (2013), *Citizen Strangers: Palestinians and the Birth of Israel's Liberal Settler State*. Stanford: Stanford University Press.

Scott, James (1985), *Weapons of the Weak: Everyday Forms of Peasant Resistance*. New Haven: Yale University Press.

Shahar, Ilan (2007), "Big Brother Law' Allows Biggest Database in West." *Ha'Aretz*, December 7. https://www.haaretz.com/1.4967126.

Shalhoub-Kevorkian, Nadera (2015), *Security Theology, Surveillance and the Politics of Fear*. Cambridge: Cambridge University Press.

Shezaf, Hagar and Jonathan Jacobson (2018), "Revealed: Israel's Cyber-spy Industry Helps World Dictators Hunt Dissidents and Gays." *Ha'Aretz*, October 20. https://www.haaretz.com/israel-news/.premium.MAGAZINE-israel-s-cyber-spy-industry-aids-dictators-hunt-dissidents-and-gays-1.6573027.

Tawil-Souri, Helga (2016), "Surveillance Sublime: The Security State in Jerusalem." *Jerusalem Quarterly*, 68: 56.

Van Esveld, Bill (2012), *"Forget About Him, He's Not Here": Israel's Control of Palestinian Residency in the West Bank and Gaza*. Human Rights Watch. https://www.hrw.org/report/2012/02/05/forget-about-him-hes-not-here/israels-control-palestinian-residency-west-bank-and.

Veracini, Lorenzo (2011), "Introducing Settler Colonial Studies." *Settler Colonial Studies*, 1 (1):1–12.

WhoProfits (2018), "Big Brother." In *Jerusalem's Old City: Israel's Militarized Visual Surveillance System in Occupied East Jerusalem*. WhoProfits, November. https://whoprofits.org/wp-content/uploads/2018/11/surveil-final.pdf

WhoProfits (2021c), "Repression Diplomacy: The Israeli Cyber Industry." *WhoProfits*, June. https://whoprofits.org/wp-content/uploads/2021/06/Repression-Diplomacy.-The-Israeli-Cyber-Industry.-June-2021.pdf.

Wolfe, Patrick (1999), *Settler Colonialism and the Transformation of Anthropology: The Politics and Poetics of an Ethnographic Event*. London: Cassell.

Wolfe, Patrick (2006), "Settler Colonialism and the Elimination of the Native." *Journal of Genocide Research*, 8 (4): 387–409.

Zaitun, Yoav (2021), "Chief of the IDI: We Practiced Intelligence Superiority." *Ynet*, (in Hebrew), July 20. https://bit.ly/3A00rTH.

Zureik, Elia (2015), *Israel's Colonial Project in Palestine: Brutal Pursuit*. New York: Routledge.

Zureik, Elia (2016), "Strategies of Surveillance: The Israeli Gaze." *Jerusalem Quarterly*, 66: 12.

The Political Economy of Education and Technology

A Focus on the Lived Experiences of Palestinian Digital Freelancers

We'am Hamdan

Introduction

Digitization—the mass adoption of information and communication technologies (ICTs)—has emerged in recent years and is considered, by governments and policy makers, a key economic driver that accelerates development and job creation (Sabbagh et al. 2012). The impact of digitization on economic growth, however, remains unequal across different regions, which highlights the importance of understanding the complex dynamics of the socioeconomic structures in the recipient contexts. Dominant strands of ICT research follow a technicist, instrumental, and deterministic approach to understanding technology, which often results in ahistorical work that is influenced by the latest trends but not previous structures of dominance and resistance (Oliver 2016). These approaches are market-driven in their essence as they are mainly focused on the concerns of governments with economic competitiveness. ICT development is thus presented as a process of knowledge diffusion—a transference from advanced economies and adapted to the conditions of the recipient economy, without considering the political economy of this technological encounter.

In the past decade, Palestinians have been inclining toward digital technologies as a source of employment, often referred to as the gig (or digital) economy. The nature of this labor is usually characterized in "freelancing" or "independent contracting" and also includes the effective use of ICTs as an important driver of economic optimization (Woodcock and Graham 2020, 20). Although only 24.7 percent of Palestinian tech graduates from the past decade have formal tech jobs, compared to 34.5 percent in Jordan, many Palestinian tech graduates, particularly those in Gaza, work as freelancers online, with a percentage of 31.8 percent of the talent pool, compared to 6 percent in Jordan (Portland Trust 2022). With the growing demand on the ICT sector as a driver of digitization, a question emerges about whether the Palestinian ICT market is well equipped to respond to the growing demands of digitization. The answer seems doubtful considering the barriers on the ground. Despite its proximity to the world-class Israeli hi-tech sector, and the combination of a highly educated young population with ample supplies of foreign aid, Palestine's tech industry lags far behind generating only $31.5 million in revenue in 2020, compared with $60 billion in Israel (Portland Trust 2022).

Current Landscape: An Instrumental Approach

The Palestinian context remains largely characterized by a crippling settler colonial regime, high unemployment rates, repeated budget shortfalls, a perpetual overdependency on international donor aid, and crony capitalism (Tartir, Dana and Seidel 2021). Although the World Bank and the International Monetary Fund (IMF) have been advising the Palestinian Authority (PA) since 1994, prescribing neoliberal policies as a framework for the development of Palestine, these policies failed to bring about sustainable growth. The strong potential of ICT on economic development has recently been advocated by the World Bank, mainly because it is less impacted by cross-border movement restrictions. This is exemplified in their $20-million grant allocated in 2021 to accelerate digital transformation under an ecosystem approach. World Bank Country Director for West Bank and Gaza, Kanthan Shankar, said:

> In a context of restrictions on movement and access of goods and people exacerbated even more by the COVID-19 crisis, the potential of the digital economy to thrive despite these constraints makes it a promising area for economic development and high-end jobs. While the potential is huge for the tech-savvy young population, it will also help bridge the digital gender divide in times of movement restrictions and social distancing. (World Bank 2021)

The crisis of the Palestinian economy and the outbreak of Covid-19 have suppressed economic activity, resulting in rates of growth reaching the lowest between 2015 and 2020 (Bezzina and El-Cassabgui 2021). The ICT sector's contribution to the Palestinian economy dropped significantly to just 2.3 percent of gross domestic product (GDP) in 2020 compared to an average of 5–7 percent of GPD in the past decade (Portland Trust 2022). The World Bank's optimistic lens, however, fails to consider how the chronic exposure to structural violence, constant humiliation, and the lack of basic human rights (such as freedom of movement) influence the lived experiences of Palestinian digital workers.

Funds from Western donors have comprised the majority of the more than 40 billion in development assistance spent on the Palestinian economy following the 1993 Oslo Accord (Wildeman and Tartir 2021). However, the lack of strong contextualized analysis among Western donors is observed in the way they frame or neglect key processes undermining the development of human capital, namely the occupation and settler colonialism. In enforcing its occupation of the West Bank, Israel employs movement restrictions as a key tool. These restrictions limit the movement of Palestinians within the West Bank, as well as travel between the West Bank and the Gaza Strip, into East Jerusalem, Israel, and other countries. Obtaining travel permits from Israel requires going through a lengthy, opaque, and arbitrary bureaucratic process. This creates a life of constant uncertainty for Palestinians, hindering their ability to perform everyday tasks and plan their lives and obstructing their professional development. West Bank and Gaza realities are thus masked by discourse of economic development that claims its potential to transcend restrictions on movement. Seidel (2019) notes that the language of sustainability is often present in the discourse surrounding political economies of resistance. These discourses frequently moralize neoliberal economics and fetishize resilience and adaptability, which are often used to govern vulnerable groups by promoting adaptation rather than resistance to these conditions. This can be observed to a certain degree in Kanshar's discourse, for example.

Instrumentalist and market-driven discourses, advocated by large international economic organizations such as the World Bank, are also adopted by Palestinian capitalist elites. One example of this is Rawabi Tech Hub, a technology and innovation center, which was founded along the new city of Rawabi by the Palestinian-American billionaire, Bashar Al-Masri, who called the hub a "Marshall plan to pick up the economy" (Jacobs 2018). The hub celebrates being the first to augment a national strategy to advance the Palestinian tech sector through state-of-the-art infrastructure, access to credit, investment capital, and training, as well as expanded access to local and international ICT markets, including outsourcing software services to the Israeli tech market. Dana (2020) examined how "crony capitalism" is a prevalent feature of the relationship between the PA and business elites. This system has emerged from the constraints of the Israeli colonial framework and was supported by international donors through the fostering of local political-business alliances. In the context of Rawabi, investment in the construction of the new city happened following the Palestinian Investment Conference (PIC), an event that was attended by American and EU officials as well as Palestinian, Arab, Israeli, and international investors and was facilitated by Israel's easing of control over checkpoints and borders to allow unhindered access to the business delegates (Dana 2020).

Tech hubs are part of venture education; education focused on collaborative investments from public- and private-sector actors. This type of education is argued to be linked to high-tech imaginaries and corporate actors' expanding investments in education technology sectors (Chan 2019). There is a danger, however, that it deploys strategies aimed at mobilizing its imagination in ways that may register for diversely situated global knowledge, dismissing as such the particularities of the Palestinian local community. Tech hubs also reflect a broader neoliberal trend to solve problems of economic integration. This optimistic discourse is also linked to corporate power, "Silicon Valley magic," which views technology as a lever of neoliberal reform in a digital, global, and knowledge-based world that is unresponsive to social pressures and choices (Hamilton and Feenberg 2005). For example, tech education has been highlighted as a solution to labor market and integration issues in connection with mass immigration. In 2016 alone, there were 106 tech projects for refugees in Germany. These attempted to promote "civic tech for social good" and were led by a "new breed of technologically savvy groups and organisations" (Rushworth and Hackl 2021). However, ethnographic fieldwork at coding schools in Berlin found that while migrants expected digital skills and training to lead to decent labor, dignity, and social mobility, their experiences revealed ongoing marginalization and precarity (Rushworth and Hackl 2021).

The success in deploying basic ICT infrastructure as well as the establishment of promising technology initiatives in Palestine, for example, the start-up accelerator *Gaza Sky Geeks*,[1] should, therefore, not overshadow the fact that Palestinians have been suffering the results of the draconian Israeli restrictions imposed on the sector. These barriers not only impair developing Palestinian start-ups into sustainable digital businesses but also hamper the reciprocation of good knowledge and practice between talented individuals and professionals from the West Bank, East Jerusalem, and Gaza Strip. Israel's recent announcement of the issuance of 500 work permits for Palestinian tech employees in the West Bank to work in Israel will pose another challenge as it is likely that the most qualified and experienced professionals will be drawn to the higher salaries offered in Israel.

Studies of the political economy of the occupied Palestinian territories (oPt) often examine the effects of Israel's economic policies and practices that maintain its colonial structure in the region. I challenge the neoliberal techno-optimistic lens by exploring the lived experiences of young ICT workers in the occupied West Bank, East Jerusalem, and Gaza Strip. In doing so, I argue for the need for nuanced and critical perspectives that emphasize power relations resulting from the complex interplay between individuals and their environment. Lived experience is a demonstration of how a setting may affect their choices and perception of knowledge (Boylorn 2012). In this chapter, lived experience reflects the personal and unique perspectives of Palestinian ICT workers, which are characterized by the tension between dominance and resistance in a settler colonial context and is shaped by factors relevant to their identity (including class, gender, and geopolitical status).

Methodology

I use two analytic frameworks for understanding the lived experiences of ICT workers. The first is drawn from the ethnographic tradition. It aims to provide a narrative snapshot of each interviewee's journey as they steer through their environment/setting. It thus focuses on power relations in their individualistic form. This process involves navigating barriers (i.e., geopolitical, education) but making choices based on personal motivation (i.e., aspirations, economic). The second framework is thematic focusing on power relations in their collective form. It draws outwardly from the individual to the collective meaning of lived experiences in a specific context (Dieumegard et al. 2021). I, therefore, identified two commonalities between the personal narratives to define ICT workers' experiences in the oPt. These pertain to structural barriers to ICT development and capitalism's influence on education. As such, I reconsider the effectiveness of the neoliberal framework of development advocated by large international funding bodies by giving a glimpse of how the life experiences of digital freelancers can resemble and respond to the wider political economy context.

By creating this unique space for storytelling, interpretation, and meaning-making, I show how life experiences can resemble and respond to the wider social and political context that is characterized by power relations (Boylorn 2012). I therefore conducted serial online interviews (total of twelve) with four ICT workers. Serial interviewing helps to counter biases (encountered by Palestinians in this case) resulting from a tendency to "flatten complexity" or "downplay socio political conflict" (Read 2018, 1). The interviews happened over three stages during the study. The first phase gave me the chance to navigate the personal journey of each participant. In the second phase, I asked follow-up questions and delved deeper into the information they had provided. In the third meeting, I cross-checked my understanding of their journey to ensure an authentic reflection of their experiences and mitigate any bias in the analysis. I paid particular attention to the geographic fragmentation of Palestinians, and hence my participants are from three parts of Palestine that are separated by various Israeli regimes: the West Bank, Gaza Strip, and East Jerusalem.

The History of ICT Development after the Oslo Accords

The Oslo agreement presented a breakthrough in the history of negotiations between Palestinians and Israelis. In this historical section, I show how the Israeli settler colonial regime that Palestinians are subjected to constitutes the cornerstone of the structural barriers to ICT development in occupied Palestine.

Following Oslo II (1995), the Israeli military withdrew partially from Palestinian cities in the West Bank and from Gaza City (Aly, Feldman, and Shikaki 2013). This period also marked the emergence of state-like institutions to prepare for the basic premise of the agreement, which would eventually allow for Palestinian self-government. With the creation of the Palestine Legislative Council (PLC), which served as an elected recognizable governmental body for the Palestinian people in the West Bank and Gaza Strip, the administration of the ICT sector in the West Bank and Gaza could be formally handed to the PA. Yet, East Jerusalem's ICT remained under the control of the Israeli government despite the international recognition as under PA jurisdiction. However, the reality fell far short of this expectation as the agreement would divide the West Bank into three areas: area "A," area "B," and area "C." Only area "A" comprising 18 percent of the West Bank would be under full PA control, while area "B" comprising 22 percent of the West Bank would be under both Palestinian civil control and Israeli military control. The remaining majority (60 percent of the West Bank) would be under full Israeli civil and military control. Article 36, Annex III of the Oslo II agreement (Israel Ministry of Foreign Affairs 1995) stated the following:

A. "In Area C, although powers and responsibilities are transferred to the Palestinian side, any digging or building regarding telecommunications and any installation of telecommunication equipment, will be subject to prior confirmation of the Israeli side."

B. "Notwithstanding paragraph a. above, the supply of telecommunications services in Area C to the settlements and military locations, and the activities regarding the supply of such services, shall be under the powers and responsibilities of the Israeli side."
C. "Israel recognises that the Palestinian side has the right to build and operate separate and independent communication systems and infrastructures including telecommunication networks, a television network and a radio network."

The Oslo agreement not only restricted Palestinians' autonomy over the sector but further legitimized the restrictions imposed and deepened dependency on the Israeli ICT sector. For example, Israel maintained a tight grip over the sector by ensuring that all communications in occupied Palestine go through an Israeli-controlled device that can break or open an electric circuit, as well as divert current from one conductor to another, often called a "switch," and, hence, granted Israel an estimate of up to 40 percent of the total revenue of the sector (Arafeh and Abdullah 2015). Israeli operators have also built switches in illegal settlements located in Area C while Palestinian operators were not given permission to build switches in Area C. Nor do they allow for switch building in area A, which is supposed to be under full PA control per Oslo agreement. Israeli cellular operators further profit from the Palestinian market as they directly benefit from the towers built in illegal Israeli settlements in Area C (Arafeh, Bahour, and Abdullah 2016). Whether in areas under Palestinian or Israeli Law, Palestinian ICT development is stunted by Israel's constant denial of permits to build switches. Therefore, Jawwal Cellular company was forced to locate its switches in London and Jordan while Wataniya's (or Ooredo) switches were located in East Jerusalem under Israel's control (Arafeh and Abdullah 2015). Israel ensures that any newly built Palestinian transmission lines function merely as extensions of Israeli backbone networks (Musleh 2022).

The launch of Palestine Telecommunication Group (Paltel), the leading company in the telecommunications sector in Palestine in 1995, is considered a major milestone in the development of the industry (The Portland Trust 2012). Until the late 1990s, Palestinians sought telephone service through the Israeli telecommunications company Bezeq and faced long wait times, sometimes up to seven years, as a means of controlling communication between Palestinians as well as collective punishment (Khoury-Machool 2007). It was widely understood that telephone lines also served as a source of intelligence for military authorities, and many Palestinians were aware of the connection between occupation and communication (Khoury-Machool 2007). Until the day, Bezeq still charges Hadara, an internet service provider owned by Paltel Group, connection and termination fees for using its backbone networks (Musleh 2022). As part of the Oslo agreement, negotiations between Bezeq and Paltel resulted in conditional access to exclusive monopoly rents (i.e., licenses) for the provision of fixed telephone lines as well as cellular services (Musleh 2022). Private monopolies refer to rights granted by the PA to certain private investors in accordance with the World Bank's recommendation to encourage private-sector-led development (Dana 2020). Paltel held a twenty-year monopoly (1996-2016), which was renewed for another twenty years in 2016, without consulting consumer protection groups or publicizing the details of the deal (Dana 2020).

When the first Palestinian mobile company Jawwal (subsidiary of Paltel) was established in 1999, it was licensed to access almost seven times less electromagnetic spectrum than that of Cellcom Israel for its approximately 2.5 million subscribers (Arafeh, Bahour and Abdullah 2015). Wataniya Cellular Company (currently operates under the name Ooredo) was established in 2007 and was granted fewer frequencies than that of Jawwal. The company further suffered a two-year delay in its operations as a result of Israel not agreeing to release frequencies for the company (Arafeh, Bahour and Abdullah 2015). Following eighteen months of negotiations led by the former British prime minister Tony Blair, in his quartet capacity, resulting in the "Frequency Allocation Agreement" in 2008, Israel agreed to allocate 4.8 MHz to Wataniya. However, the deal was further delayed following the political fallout of the 2008 Gaza war. Israel maintained the release of the Wataniya frequencies and made it conditional to the PA dropping its efforts to bring the Goldstone report to the ICC (Beckett, Hencke and Kochan 2015).

Since 2007, the PA claims to have taken serious measures to liberalize the ICT market. For example, the PA grants tax exemptions to ICT firms based on the number of employees rather than the size of the capital input (The Portland Trust 2012). The continued increase in the volume of the sector is evident (and has been encouraged by international funding for development assistance in support of the Oslo peace process). For example, the US State Department has sought to facilitate partnership between Palestinian ICT operators and American companies such as Cisco, which invested $15–20 million from 2008 to 2012 to boost the industry (PMDP 2014). However, the impact of such investments remains focused on recouping the lost revenue resulting from the asymmetrical power relations with Israel rather than achieving an authentic state of development.

In 2015, a deal mandating Israel to provide 20 MHz of 3G frequencies (the minimum to allow the operation of 3G services) was signed between Israel and the PA (Rasgon 2016). While Israel already offers 5G frequencies, the limited development of Palestine's ICT infrastructure is due to Israeli restrictions on optical fiber for Palestinian households and limitations on cellular usage of 2G frequencies in Gaza and 3G in the West Bank (Musleh 2022). According to the World Bank (2016), the losses inflicted on the Palestinian ICT sector as a result of the continuous delays and uncertainties, coupled with unauthorized competition by Israeli operators, are estimated between 436 million and 1.5 billion US$ in potential revenue from 2013 to 2015. Jawwal and Ooredoo still face intense competition from Israeli operators, who captured a significant portion of the market (at least 20 percent) in 2020 (Musleh 2022; World Bank 2020). Although the number of ICT firms has increased over the years, their overall contribution to the GDP has declined. The Palestinian ICT sector consisted of 677 registered companies with 8,815 employees in 2018 according to the Palestine Central Bureau of Statistics (PCBS), compared with around 250 ICT companies, over 5,000 employees, and up to approximately 10.5 percent of the GDP in 2012 (Tucker 2012). However, the sector still represents less than 1 percent of the Palestinian workforce with trade deficit of $200 million in 2017 alone (Musleh 2022).

Today, the Oslo Accord is still used to govern daily relations between the PA and Israel despite the set interim period having ended in 1999. The legal framework of Oslo remains fraught as it has undoubtedly intensified power gaps by making the PA more dependent on Israel and encouraging monopolistic control. This section, therefore, demonstrated how the asymmetrical power relations with Israel become highly relevant in the investigation of the political economy of edtech. As asserted by Roy (1999) in her definition of de-development, not only do these asymmetrical power relations deprive the economy of its capacity but further prevent the emergence of self-correcting measures, making change and reforms almost impossible. As the education system in Palestine is a product of the same environment, and only began to develop in 1994, it emerged against a backdrop of chronic crisis. With the absence of self-correcting measures, the PA is unable to directly solve infrastructural issues as they have no control over primary resources necessary to develop the ICT sector.

Fragmented Realities: Navigating Barriers

I used a purposeful sampling approach to recruit participants who can provide in-depth and detailed information about the topic in question. Three selection criteria were employed in order to increase variation and represent the broader population. First, my participants have worked in the Palestinian ICT sector, specifically as digital freelancers or entrepreneurs. The sample had diversity in terms of gender and finally reflected the fragmentation of the Palestinian identity resulting from the complex geopolitical status. A multi-sighted approach was therefore crucial to understanding how ICTs are taken up and received in different fragmented areas in the oPt. This allowed juxtaposing experiences and insights from fragmented entities, and to zoom in and out between localities.

In a context ruled by a settler colonial regime, the continuous military targeting of Gaza's infrastructure meant chronic power outages. Adjusting to eight hours of electricity a day and the low-speed 2G network remains a challenge to digital workers and citizens in the strip. On the other hand, young, educated professionals in the West Bank are driven to relocate to cities such as Ramallah, the de facto capital of the PA, where one can be misguided by the dominance of NGOs and the prosperous appearance of the city that masks a facade for the devastating effects of neoliberalism, internal corruption, and occupation. Although 3G was introduced in 2018, electricity cuts and slow internet connection (especially in remote areas far from Ramallah) are still major challenges. Conversely, East Jerusalem being under Israel's jurisdiction against international law is endowed with a 5G network and stable internet connection but remains fragmented with a two-tiered discriminatory system that aims to drive Palestinians out of the city.

While structural barriers to success were evident in the four cases, each individual navigated impediments differently. In all the interviews, the line between domination and resistance, and between structural barriers and opportunities that the tech sector provides, was blurred. Consequently, individuals experienced a contradiction between the lofty promises of global tech and structural barriers on the ground. While all individuals exhibited a remarkable degree of resilience and autonomy, a Palestinian ICT worker from Jerusalem does not experience the same barriers as a West Banker, neither a Gazan. For example, Jana survived four deadly wars by the age of twenty. For these reasons, my structure of the following four subsections follows a narrative form for each individual's navigational journey. These are:

1. From Gaza to Silicon Valley companies, Jana, the Gaza Strip
2. "I was both digitally-driven and design-oriented," Kadija, the West Bank
3. "I was enraged," Omar, the West Bank
4. "Separation is the rule here," Jad, East Jerusalem

From Gaza to Silicon Valley Companies

At that time I met her, Jana was a twenty-year-old female and a student of computer engineering in Gaza. She is passionate about full-stack software development and had recently been selected for a paid internship at Google in Germany. Her passion for programming was sparked in high school when she was selected to join a robotics competition. With her team members, she was able to build a robot using Arduino—an open-source prototyping platform that enables students to build digital devices without a background in electronics or programming. This was her first encounter with programming and that is where she decided to focus her aspirational and professional life. "I loved the logic behind programming, it is like poetry," Jana said. When I asked her about what she meant by that, she replied, "it is a harmonic process, every line makes way for the next to produce meaning."

Although her degree in computer engineering had been helpful in understanding the theoretical fundamentals, Jana thought it lacked the practical elements required for the market. "It is a rapidly evolving field and you need to always be aware of global advances to be successful," she elaborated. For these reasons, she enrolled in a number of online open courses to learn how to program. She also joined a competition through Gaza Sky Geeks—the first and only tech hub and start-up accelerator in Gaza. At the end of her first year at university, a friend shared an advertisement for a four-month immersive boot camp based in Jordan. "I did not expect to get accepted because I did not have a background in full-stack," said Jana.

Jana narrated the details of her journey to Jordan once she got accepted. "I doubted that I would be able to make it considering the complicated travel procedure imposed on Gazans," she said and summed up her experience with "it was a bumpy road, to say the least, but it was worth it." This was the first time Jana left Gaza—a journey that took her three months causing her to miss the first month of programming fundamentals. Jana was stressed but was delighted to have received support from other Palestinians joining the program from the West Bank. She observed the importance of exchanging knowledge in the field and explained how restrictions on movement are a huge barrier for Gazans. During the camp, Jana did not only learn hard skills but also soft skills that are deemed necessary in the tech industry. "I was the youngest in the cohort and at times, it felt like a marathon," said Jana. She further described how this boot camp changed her perception regarding learning for the tech world. "Teamwork and people skills are as essential as hard skills in this industry," she explained.

Upon returning to Gaza, Jana enrolled in a four-month job placement program. This included weekly lectures and assignments on topics related to hard skills, such as data structure, algorithm, and coding, as well as soft skills such as interviewing. "We practiced interviews virtually with Silicon Valley engineers and experts, which made all the difference," said Jana, who studied for a minimum of ten hours a day. The platform then provided referrals to Google, to which Jana then applied and was selected. Jana remarked that an increasing number of young people like herself are attracted to the ICT field because of the blockade imposed on Gaza. "It is a huge factor, but programming alone cannot solve Gaza's unemployment crisis," she explained. With a population of 2 million crippled by an ongoing siege and shattered infrastructure, Jana doubted that large-scale development of the ICT sector is possible in Gaza. "Two requirements are missing; Internet and electricity," she argued. "I am privileged because my family can afford to buy a generator, many of my friends do not have this basic requirement."

"I Was Both Digitally-Driven and Design-Oriented"

Kadija, a 27-year-old female, completed her bachelor's degree in international relations in Canada but chose not to work in this field. Instead, she joined an e-commerce start-up company in Ramallah in the West Bank—a city where the PA has its administrative headquarters with a small but burgeoning tech scene. The company where Kadija worked was one of the first local start-ups to secure an early-stage venture capital investment and to be widely recognized in the Middle East. When one individual in her team started giving her weekly lessons related to digital hard skills in user interface (UI) design and user experience (UX) design, as well as simple coding, Kadija was able to improve the product's usability. "Basically, it improves the experience of customers on the website and app using an attractive and friendly design," she elaborated. "I did not know much about UI and UX design[2] back then," remarked Kadija, "but I was both digitally-driven and design-oriented."

For four years, Kadija worked in product management; the product was a digital service for a tours and accommodation booking website. In her free time, Kadija found pleasure in creating content on her YouTube channel and Instagram social media platform, where she was able to gain hundreds of thousands of followers and views. "It certainly helped me in terms of gaining the skills necessary to communicate and present products for an online audience, but I would not classify myself as a geek," explained Kadija. She used the word "geek" in English—a slang term widely used in the tech scene to refer to someone who demonstrates knowledge and passion for computer technologies. Kadija worked with a team of software engineers, mostly males, which gave her initial exposure to the tech industry.

Although the start-up company provided a unique service and was able to expand the scope of its work within a short period of time, it did not survive during the outbreak of Covid-19. Kadija expressed her frustration regarding the operating environment.

She posits, "there is a pool of talent but manoeuvring around financing is a challenge," and she detailed the difficulties of negotiating with investors, many of whom were unwilling to invest during the outbreak of Covid-19 and the resurface of political tensions. Kadija then began her journey as a freelance digital designer. She described the advantages of being a freelancer, which in her opinion outweighed the hardships if compared with her previous start-up experience. "It is not easy to be visible for clients, not to mention the countless hours spent in researching and learning through open sources." In this sense, Kadija said that her undergraduate degree equipped her with the soft skills needed. "My undergraduate degree was not my dream major, but it certainly helped," she said. "I am competent in English and benefited from career services and critical thinking skills that my university provided us with," she added.

While Kadija considered electricity cuts and slow internet connection an impediment, she was delighted to have worked with Palestinian customers from across geographical locations. "Lately, I have had a customer from Haifa; I never thought I could reach our Palestinian community in Historical Palestine," she pointed out. Kadija expressed her lack of trust in the government (PA in this case) when reflecting on ICT development. "Occupation is one thing and corruption is another," she explained. "The PA is only concerned about maintaining their current status quo and their relationship with Israel." She recounted that education does not receive enough attention, and that the PA spends most of its budget on security, "but security of whom?" "Not Palestinians for sure," she exclaimed.

"I Was Enraged"

Omar, a 31-year-old male, held a degree in computer graphics and animation. When he graduated from high school, his father wanted him to pursue medicine. "All Palestinian parents want their children to become doctors," he said, laughing. Omar explained that he did not necessarily aspire to become a software engineer, but he "certainly did not want to be a doctor." At that time, computer sciences were newly introduced to local universities where they all offered a general course without providing specializations. However, the course Omar studied in Jordan was more specific. "I was attracted to it because it combined information technology and my passion for online gaming, so I thought why not create my own games?" Omar explained.

Omar worked as a game programmer for a year upon graduation. "I really enjoyed it and if given a choice, this is what I wanted to do for the rest of my life," he explained, "but the horizon is limited for us Palestinians." Omar is originally from Bethlehem but moved to Ramallah upon returning from Jordan. "The government does not see development beyond Ramallah, it is the Silicon Valley of NGOs," he sarcastically said. Omar then worked as a web developer before receiving another job offer. For the next six years, Omar worked in a start-up company where he strived in a "tough" environment due to the low salaries in comparison with the average salary of web developers worldwide. "We were featured in major global news agencies as a model for a successful tech scene," he said. Omar enrolled in a massive number of open online courses, as he believed in the significance of being autonomous in the field. "What I learned 10 years ago is from the past, programming languages are always evolving," he indicated.

Although Omar believed that working in the Palestinian context improved his nontechnical skills such as problem-solving, he observed that there was a significant gap in the local labor market. "The Palestinian market is limited and while numbers of ICT graduates may be increasing, it was difficult to recruit people who had the skills required for the industry," he asserted. Like many start-ups in Palestine, the company struggled during the Covid-19 outbreak until the business eventually closed down. "I was enraged because so many sleepless nights felt like a waste," Omar said about the termination. He noted that the start-up was remarkable in the service it provided and blamed the government for its inability to support digital businesses. He also thought that internet access, although slow at times, is no longer an issue. Rather, he cited the lack of policies to mitigate the risks of the market as a barrier.

Omar then decided to apply for a front-end engineer position at an international company using an online freelancing platform called Upwork where he now works. "You are your own boss as long as you complete the tasks required," he explained. Omar believed that the tech industry is an alluring field for young men given the higher average salaries. However, he remained critical of the local ICT market, which he thought exploited graduates by using them as cheap outsourcing capital for Israeli hi-tech firms. He explained that although salaries are lucrative for Palestinians working in outsourcing IT companies in the West Bank, it is still much lower than the average salary for the same positions in Israel and Europe. He also recounted the difficulties in retaining quality talent due to outdated curriculum, high international competition, and Israeli restrictions in Palestine. Omar doubted that the future of work would increasingly be freelancing in the digital economy in occupied Palestine: "It requires an open mindset and a demanding set of skills which our education system fails to deliver."

"Separation Is the Rule Here"

Jad, a 32-year-old male from East Jerusalem, completed his bachelor's degree in Ramallah and graduated with a degree in English literature. Jewish and Palestinian schools in Jerusalem have separate education systems, thus perpetuating divisions in society. While Jewish schools operate under the supervision of the Israeli Ministry of Education, the Palestinian Education Directorate of Jerusalem governs Arab schools in East Jerusalem, in accordance with the Oslo Accords. This means students are not taught Hebrew as they grow up. "It is one tactic to exclude us from studying in Israeli higher education institutions and further joining the Israeli labor market; separation is the rule here," says Jad. Palestinians in Jerusalem hold a permanent residency but not Israeli citizenship. While Jad mentioned that his residency does not restrict him from traveling to the West Bank and Israel, he still cited his identity as a barrier. "If I choose to live in the West Bank, it is a sufficient ground for the government to revoke my residency," he explained.

Jad believed that restrictions are manifested in other ways such as the municipality's "Arnona" occupancy tax, a property tax levied by the Jerusalem municipality in Israel. Jad viewed this as an impediment or a structural barrier because of the lower living standard of Arabs compared with Jews in the city. He also indicated the limitations of joining the Palestinian labor market of the West Bank due to the significant difference in the socioeconomic status compared with Israel. "While I can, in theory, join the market, they offer lower wages than what Jerusalem ID holders are accustomed to," he explained. In the past six years, Jad worked in a translation position for an NGO in Jerusalem. "I served as a translator for one tech project, and this is when I realised where the money is," Jad asserted. He then considered changing his career path to join the booming Israeli tech sector, but the road was not as easy as he anticipated.

He started taking Hebrew lessons and joined an intensive course at a coding academy. In addition to having a full-time job, Jad attended evening lessons and completed demanding assignments. He also felt the need to enroll in additional online courses, which he remarked as being "time and energy-consuming." Jad was nevertheless positive, citing his excellent English level as an advantage. "I do not need to be fluent in Hebrew because English dominates the sector," he said. However, he did not diminish the importance of Hebrew to communicate with other team members—most of whom are likely to be Israelis. Jad reflected on his dreams as a fresh graduate of becoming a playwright, but little did he know that "playwriting does not make a living for an Arab in Jerusalem."

An Instrumentalist Approach: Doomed to Failure?

The navigational journeys of my participants show a dichotomy between the instrumentalist and market-driven approaches, which have been advocated by large international organizations and funding bodies in Palestine, and the lived experiences of Palestinian ICT workers. Such approaches promote neoliberal assumptions and tend to decontextualize the environment. In doing so, they view ICT development as a process of diffusion, meaning a transference from advanced economies and adapting it to the conditions of the recipient country (Avgerou 2010). This is problematic, as it tends to gloss over two core issues pertaining to sustainability. These are geopolitical and economic fragmentation and structural barriers to success.

Geopolitical and Economic Fragmentation

Market-driven and instrumentalist approaches describe the potential of digital technologies in alleviating the high unemployment rate among graduates (White 2010; Tucker 2012; The World Bank 2016, 2018; Kashiwagi 2016). Technology is therefore seen as "enabling," "constraining," or "permitting" for development and economic revival (Oliver 2016, 44). The first drawback of these approaches stems from its treatment of Palestinians as a homogenous population without addressing the complex geopolitics and history of ICT development. The West Bank (including East Jerusalem) and Gaza are often treated as one entity in this literature. The navigational journey of ICT workers, however, shows that this solidified discourse is very simplistic and negates the reality on the ground. The experience of participants shows that the three contexts, although similar in many ways, are distinct from one another. Since the Palestinian people have never had sovereign control over the ICT sector, the engine of the digital economy remains largely stifled. This is evident in the daunting fragmentation of the Palestinians into three disintegrated regions: the West Bank, Gaza Strip, and East Jerusalem. The title of the first section of my findings "fragmented realities" alludes to this status quo as experienced by my informants.

For example, Jana, who has become a role model for aspiring "geeks" in Gaza, had experienced four wars by the age of twenty. Although she spoke highly about the potential of tech in providing opportunity for besieged Gazans, she paused at one point and said: "but they can cut that too just like when they destroyed Gaza's sole power plant." Omar and Kadija, on the other hand, witnessed the limitations of the ICT market of the West Bank, which is mainly centered in Ramallah. Not only is this tech scene highly dependent on cheap outsourcing contracts from Israeli hi-tech companies, which all of my participants refused to engage in and preferred to shift into freelancing activities, but is also reliant on early-stage venture capital investors, many of whom were unwilling to take a risk when political tensions began to resurface. Their frustration with the closure of their start-ups thus led to an independent activity characterized by digital freelancing. Conversely, Jad did not struggle with internet access; however, he experienced a sense of alienation as a result of the two-tiered system Israel maintains in Jerusalem. In his attempt to increase mobility and socioeconomic status, he sought in tech an opportunity to transcend exclusion. This aligns with Hackl's (2022) findings regarding the experiences of Palestinian workers in the neoliberal economy in settler colonial contexts. He posited that in an attempt to increase socioeconomic mobility, these individuals engaged in diverse tactics of "immersive invisibility" to transcend categorical differences and racial exclusion.

Structural Barriers to Success: De-development Revisited

The second problem arising from market-driven approaches (seen in the World Bank reporting, for example) manifests in how structural barriers are cited as a rationale for tech projects. This perspective, however, only greases the wheels of the ICT sector to recover lost revenue without addressing the urgency to remove structural barriers to growth. For example, a report by the World Bank (2018, 11) that analyses the internal dynamics of the start-up ecosystem in the West Bank and Gaza suggested the following: "Tech startups could provide access to employment opportunities (including self-employment) beyond the structural constraints of the West Bank and Gaza—by taking advantage of access to digitally connected markets."

The lived experience of ICT workers, however, shows that navigating structural barriers is not as straightforward as suggested in the report. Constraints facing Palestinian ICT workers are formidable, among them: a fragmented geography characterized by the isolation of Gaza; an internally cantonized West Bank that is divided into Areas A, B, and C; and an isolated East Jerusalem that remains inaccessible to most Palestinians. Restrictions on movement, therefore, should not be cited as a rationale—rather, a structural barrier. For example, Jana's "bumpy" journey to neighboring Jordan was her first time to leave Gaza to join a coding boot camp. She detailed the following:

> First, I had to apply for the Jordanian permit (only imposed on Gazans). It took a month to receive this document. I then applied for the Israeli permit, which in most cases is rejected. I was mentally prepared for that and started to eventually give up on the possibility of going, as I was almost a month late. Luckily, I received it; probably because the funding organisation of my Bootcamp scholarship was American. I then had to get a permit from the Government in Gaza. I packed my stuff and arrived at Erez border [. . . crossing, between Gaza and Israel] at 7:00 am. I was starting to get drained because there are so many security checks. [. . .] I finally arrived in Amman at 1:00 am the next day.

Another example of how structural barriers are oversimplified in NGO reporting is emphasized in the following report funded by the European Union and the UK government (White 2010, 48): "The Palestinian Authority needs to consider setting up political initiatives to aid structural development of the ICT sector, while also working with the banks to build a climate that is both sensible and encourages business growth."

The aforementioned extract is listed as one of the hindrances to ICT business development in the report. The lines suggest that resolving structural impediments is a matter of political negotiation that the occupied must initiate with their occupier. However, this rhetoric fails to acknowledge the Oslo agreement as sheer evidence of Israel's breach of political and economic initiatives to reach a resolution. Moreover, the severity of the structural barriers is normalized and Palestinians are simply expected to work around it. This is also exemplified in the World Bank report (2016) titled *A Missed Opportunity for Economic Development*. The word "missed" indicates a failure to notice the potential of ICT in economic growth. In so doing, the asymmetrical power and control over Palestinians is ignored in favor of recouping lost revenue. The words "occupation" and "infrastructure," for instance, remain absent in the sixty-page report (Tartir and Wildeman 2012; Wildeman 2019). In contrast, my interviewees gave explicit and vivid descriptions of these barriers. For example, Kadija stated:

> I struggle with slow Internet connection very often. I thought that registering in another more expensive company would solve the issue, but it did not. Whenever I call them, they ask me to turn the router off and turn it on again. And just before this call with you actually, the electricity was cut off the entire morning. It definitely slows my work down.

Another example is seen in how Jana described her experience with electricity outages in Gaza, she stated:

In the past my family had a generator that provided four hours of electricity only. No electricity meant planning my schedule around the clock and ensuring that all my devices are entirely charged before the next blackout. It also meant dealing with the constant humming of generators and having enough sockets to help out our neighbours who could not afford one.

Denying Palestinians of resources vital for their basic needs in the ICT sector lies at the heart of the dilemma. It prohibits creating a healthy environment for development and further burdens digital workers. This argument, however, negates the underlying neoliberal instrumentalist assumption that growth and development are solely driven by state, economic institutions, and policies. The dichotomy between the stories of my informants and the NGO reporting calls for the need to critically consider the political and economic forces at play in the development and use of technology for employment. Therefore, a nuanced debate about and including the political economy of edtech is important.

Silicon Valley Magic: Democratic Nature or Corporate Power?

There is increasing evidence of new forms of capitalism in the education field, namely "Californian capitalism" and "platform capitalism." These allude to the "Silicon Valley magic" and platform-based businesses such as Google, Microsoft, Facebook, Apple, and their influence on education. They describe a set of business methods that underpin the new high-tech economy and its increased interest in education (Selwyn, 2013, 2016; Srnicek 2017). The impact of capitalism's commercial involvement in education is worthy of analyses in the Palestinian context. This is because of the high dependency on internationally funded NGOs that work with tech hubs and university accelerators on edtech capacity-building programs to integrate graduates in the gig economy.

For example, twenty-first-century skills are advocated in most edtech capacity-building programs in Palestine and are depicted as a homogenous "one-size-fits-all" solution. Unlike technical (or hard) skills such as programming and coding, these encompass a set of "soft skills," such as interpersonal and "people" skills, as well as being "culturally fit" and adaptive of the cosmopolitan tech scene (Rushworth and Hackl 2021). While education for the digital era claims a nature characterized by democratic inclusiveness, which is consistent with the neoliberal assumption that human capital can be autonomously developed through open resources, my findings show that this inclusiveness and openness of resources is not enough for Palestinian ICT workers to develop professionally.

Biesta (2006, 169) posits, "under the conditions of the learning economy lifelong learning itself has become understood as an individual task rather than as a collective project and that this has transformed lifelong learning from a right to a duty." My participants indicated that they spend an average minimum of ten hours per week to fill the gaps between the labor market and their education and to stay well informed about the evolving requirements of the ICT field. Considering the market influences, they emphasized that the Palestinian education system lags far behind in comparison with global standards. This is due to its high dependency on rote-learning methods and theorization instead of communicative and practical skills teaching. Consequently, they classified the Palestinian education system as "incapable" for not being able to catch up with global trends. With the availability of open resources and private institutions (e.g., coding academies, mentor schemes, Massive Online Open Courses or MOOCs), learning becomes an individual responsibility rather than a collective concern (Biesta 2013, 2006). This is evident in how participants exhibited a high level of autonomy and resilience in searching and selecting from the multitude of resources. However, their awareness of their privilege signifies other hidden layers to the acclaimed democratic nature of education in the digital era.

Although the levels of "privilege" varied among the informants, for example, Jana having a generator and being able to leave Gaza; Kadija and Omar studying abroad and accumulating relevant work experience; Jad being able to join a blended learning program, one should question whether a large-scale sustainable development is viable within a context where basic human rights are missing (e.g., access to internet and electricity, freedom of movement). The vulnerability of the informants resulting from the limitations of the context (e.g., structural barriers, political tension, high unemployment rates) as well as the absence of real autonomy constitute serious impediments to a large-scale state of growth. Due to low living standards and lack of opportunity, these workers are more likely to be exploited. This is consistent with studies tackling digital labor for refugees in Germany (Rushworth and Hackl 2021; Embiricos 2020; Mason 2018).

The second reason behind the elusive nature of democratic inclusiveness of education for the digital era is the lack of a framework conceptualizing the so-called twenty-first-century skills. There is a tendency among stakeholders such as the Palestinian Ministry of Education, tech projects, as well as open sources to adopt the term "twenty-first-century skills" blindly. These actors promote an entrepreneurial attitude to economic challenges, framing digital skills as a speedy route to self-sufficiency and socioeconomic status (Rushworth and Hackl 2022; Liu-Farrer and Karen 2020). Therefore, reforms and capacity building are largely tied to the integration of these skills into the curriculum. However, determinants of twenty-first-century skills are limited to personality and digital skills, overlooking, for example, factors such as community-based learning, indigenous ways of learning in a colonial context, as well as "tacit knowledge." The latter encompasses a broad array of phenomena, including tangible skills gained through practicing, implicit understandings shared among group or profession members, and common patterns of acting acquired through society engagement (Collins 1974).

It is often argued that the gig/digital economy can transcend restrictions on travel and movement, for example, Kadija being able to reach the Palestinian community outside the borders of the West Bank and Omar utilizing online platforms to connect with other Palestinian programmers from Gaza. My participants, however, stressed the importance of learning from living through and within a community. The sense of defiance of geopolitical fragmentation (through online technologies) did not eliminate my informants' desire to build a community of professionals in reality (outside the digital realm). All of the participants emphasized that learning communities are important in the reciprocation of knowledge and good practice. Jad, for example, benefited from the blended approach used in the coding school as it enabled him to connect with like-minded people who are transitioning their careers. Jana and Kadija, on the other hand, reflected community-based future goals as they intend to establish a digital design school and a coding academy, respectively. Omar, despite his preference to remain a freelancer, indicated how communities can be key for growth. Therefore, there is a danger in capitalism's commercial involvement in education as it mobilizes the Silicon Valley magic and high-tech imaginaries, dismissing as such the particularities of local communities and their ways of resisting dominance and control.

Conclusion

Market-driven approaches, utilized by large economic institutions like the World Bank, promote digital labor as a potential source of income in Palestine because of its ability to transcend barriers of trade and movement imposed on Palestinians. My findings, however, reveal that this instrumentalist approach oversimplifies the reality of the ground. The navigational journey of my participants showed that the line between opportunity that high-tech promises and the barriers encountered by individuals is blurred. Nuancing the lens on edtech has to therefore factor in power relations resulting from the complex interplay between individuals and their context (e.g., political, economic, and educational forms of life). This angle allows for the treatment of ICT workers as individuals with agency, operating in a context of multilayered power dynamics. These include the imposed Israeli structural barriers that Palestinian ICT workers face, which not only leave them without any sovereignty over their own resources but also fragment them into three cantonized geographical areas. Another form of power results from capitalism's influence on education. I therefore questioned the democratic nature of education in the digital era, which marketizes a minimalist product for a mass market that "boxes in" or "dumbs down" education. These findings negate the neoliberal assumption that state and resources alone are drivers of growth and prosperity. Policy makers, educationalists, and international NGOs must therefore factor in the nuance of the debate around learning technology by reconsidering the lived experiences of Palestinian digital workers and promoting resistance rather than adaptability.

Notes

1 A joint venture between the international development organization Mercy Corps and Google for Entrepreneurs and is supported by other partners such as the US State Department and the World Bank. Gaza Sky Geeks provides resources and support to local entrepreneurs, including access to coworking spaces, business training, mentorship, and funding opportunities. For more information: https://gazaskygeeks.com/about/.

2   Both UI and UX designs are important for creating products that are functional, user-friendly, and enjoyable to use. While UI design focuses on the visual elements of a product, UX design considers the entire user experience, including how easy it is to use the product and how it makes the user feel.

References

Aly, Abdel Monem Said, Shai Feldman, and Khalil Shikaki (2013), *Arab and Israelis: Conflict and Peacemaking in the Middle East*. New York: Palgrave Macmillan.

Arafeh, Nur, Sam Bahour, and Wassim Abdallah (2015), *ICT: The Shackled Engine of Palestine's Development*, November 9. Retrieved July 7, 2021, from Alshabaka: https://al-shabaka.org/wp-content/uploads/2015/11/Arafeh_Abdullah_Bahour_PolicyBrief_Eng_Nov2015.pdf.

Arafeh, Nur, Sam Bahour, and Wassim Abdullah (2016), *Let Palestinians Control Their ICT Resources*. January 2. Retrieved July 7, 2021, from Aljazeera: http://america.aljazeera.com/opinions/2016/1/israel-must-let-palestinians-control-their-ict-resources.html.

Avgerou, Chrisanthi (2010), "Discourses on ICT and Development." *Information Technologies and International Development*, 6 (3): 1–18.

Beckett, Francis, David Hencke, and Nick Kochan (2015), *Blair Inc: The man Behind the Mask*. London: John Blake.

Bezzina, Jerome and Joseph El-Cassabgui (2021), *Unlocking the Potential of the Digital Economy in the Palestinian Territories*, March 30. Retrieved June 29, 2021, from The World Bank: https://blogs.worldbank.org/digital-development/unlocking-potential-digital-economy-palestinian-territories.

Biesta, Gert (2006), "What's the Point of Lifelong Learning if Lifelong Learning has no Point? On the Democratic Deficit of Policies for Lifelong Learning." *European Educational Research Journal*, 5 (3–4), 169–80.

Biesta, Gert (2013), "Responsive or Responsible? Democratic Education for the Global Networked Society." *Policy Futures in Education*, 11: 733–44.

Boylorn, Robin M. (2012), "Lived Experience." In L. M. Given (ed.), *The SAGE Encyclopedia of Qualitative Research Methods*, 490. Thousand Oaks: SAGE Publications.

Chan, Anita Say (2019), "Venture Ed: Recycling Hype, Fixing Futures, and theTemporal Order of Edtech." In J. Vertesi and D. Ribes (eds.), *DigitalSTS: A Field Guide for Science & Technology Studies*, 161–77. Princeton and Oxford: Princeton University Press.

Collins, H. M. (1974), "The TEA Set: Tacit Knowledge and Scientific Networks." *Science Studies*, 4: 165–86.

Dana, Tariq (2020), "Crony Capitalism in the Palestinian Authority: A Deal Among Friends." *Third World Quarterly*, 41 (2): 247–63, doi:10.1080/01436597.2019.1618705.

Dieumegard, Gilles, Magali Ollagnier-Beldame, Sandra Nogry, and Nicolas Perrin (2021), "Lived Experience as a Unit of Analysis for the Study of Learning." *Learning, Culture and Social Interaction*, 31(B): 100345. http://hdl.handle.net/20.500.12162/4461.

Embiricos, Alexandra (2020), "From Refugee to Entrepreneur? Challenges to Refugee Self-reliance in Berlin, Germany." *Journal of Refugee Studies*, 33 (1): 245–67.

Hackl, Andreas (2022), *The Invisible Palestinians: The Hidden Struggle for Inclusion in Jewish Tel Aviv*. Indiana University Press. https://doi.org/10.2307/j.ctv2cmr8s5.

Hamilton, Edward and Andrew Feenberg (2005), "The Technical Codes of Online Education." *E-learning and Digital Media*, 2 (2): 104–21.
Israel Ministry of Foreign Affairs (1995), *The Israeli-Palestine Interm Agreement-Annex III*, September 28. Retrieved July 17, 2021, from Israel Ministry of Foreign Affairs: https://mfa.gov.il/mfa/foreignpolicy/peace/guide/pages/the%20israeli-palestinian%20interim%20agreement%20-%20annex%20iii.aspx#app-36.
Israel Ministry of Foreign Affairs (1995), *The Israeli-Palestinian Interim Agreement Annex III*, September 28. Retrieved July 6, 2021, from mfa.gov.il: https://mfa.gov.il/mfa/foreignpolicy/peace/guide/pages/the%20israeli-palestinian%20interim%20agreement%20-%20annex%20iii.aspx#app-36.
Jacobs, Harrison (2018), *A Palestinian-American Billionaire Built a $1.4 Billion Luxury City From Scratch to be a 'Marshall Plan' for Palestine's Economy*, October 20. Retrieved December 10, 2022, from Insider: https://www.businessinsider.com/west-bank-palestine-rawabi-city-israel-news-2018-10?r=US&IR=T.
Kashiwagi, Kenichi (2016), "Productivity Growth and Technological Progress in the Palestinian Economy: Empirical Evidence From the West Bank." *Advances in Management & Applied Economics*, 6 (1): 69–88.
Khoury-Machool, Kenichi (2007), "Palestinian Youth and Political Activism: The Emerging Internet Culture and New Modes of Resistance." *Policy Futures in Education*, 5 (1): 17–36. https://doi.org/10.2304/pfie.2007.5.1.17.
Liu-Farrer, Gracia and Karen Shire (2020), "Who are the Fittest? The Question of Skills in National Employment Systems in an Age of Global Labour Mobility." *Journal of Ethnic and Migration Studies*, 47: 1–18. doi:10.1080/1369183X.2020.1731987.
Mason, Ben (2018), *Tech Jobs for Refugees: Assessing the Potential of Coding Schools for Refugee Integration in Germany*. Brussels: Migration Policy Institute Europe.
Musleh, David (2022), *ICT in Palestine: Challenging Power Dynamics and Limitations*, January 9. Retrieved December 10, 2022, from Al-Shabaka: https://al-shabaka.org/summaries/ict-in-palestine-challenging-power-dynamics-and-limitations/.
Oliver, Martin (2016), "What is Technology?" In N. Rushby and D. W. Surry (eds.), *The Wiley Handbook of Learning technology*, 63–57. Oxford: John Wiley & Sons, Inc.
Palestinian Market Development Programme (PMDP) (2014), *MNEs Outsourcing to Palestinians: Market System Analysis*. Ramallah: PITA.
Palestinian Market Development Programme (PMDP) (2015), *Rapid Market System Analysis Quality of Engineers for Multinational Enterprises (MNE's): Skills Gap Between Recent Graduate and MNE Outsourcing Job Market Needs*. Ramallah: PITA.
Rasgon, Adam (2016), *What Ever Happened to the Palestinian 3G Deal?* December 28. Retrieved July 10, 2021, from The Jerusalem Post: https://www.jpost.com/israel-news/what-ever-happened-to-the-palestinian-3g-deal-476732.
Read, Benjamin L. (2018), "Serial Interviews: When and why to Talk to Someone More Than Once." *International Journal of Qualitative Methods*, 17: 1–10.
Roy, Benjamin L. (1999), "De-development Revisited: Palestinian Economy and Society Since Oslo." *Journal of Palestine Studies*, 28(3): 64–82. JSTOR, https://doi.org/10.2307/2538308 (accessed October 16, 2023).
Rushworth, Philip and Andreas Hackl (2022), "Writing Code, Decoding Culture: Digital Skills and the Promise of a Fast Lane to Decent Work Among Refugees and Migrants in Berlin." *Journal of Ethnic and Migration Studies*, 48(11): 2642–58, doi:10.1080/1369183X.2021.1893159.
Sabbagh, Karim, Bahjat El-Darwiche, Roman Friedrich, and Milind Singh (2012), *Maximizing the Impact of Digitization*. Beirut: Booz & Company.

Seidel, Timothy (2019), "Neoliberal Developments, National Consciousness, and Political Economies of Resistance in Palestine." *Interventions*, 21 (5): 727–46, doi:10.1080/1369801X.2019.1585921.

Selwyn, Neil (2013), *Education in a Digital World: Global Perspectives on Technology and Education*. Abingdon: Routledge.

Selwyn, Neil (2016), *Is Technology Good for Education?* Cambridge: Polity Press.

Srnicek, Nick (2017), *Platform Capitalism*. Cambridge: Polity Press.

Tartir, Alaa, Tariq Dana, and Timothy Seidel (eds.) (2021), *Political Economy of Palestine: Critical, Interdisciplinary, and Decolonial Perspectives*. Cham, Switzerland: Palgrave Macmillan. Middle East Today.

Tartir, Alaa and Jeremy Wildeman (2012), *Persistent Failure: World Bank Policies for the Occupied Palestinian Territories*, October 9. Retrieved December 10, 2022, from Al-Shabaka: https://al-shabaka.org/briefs/persistent-failure-world-bank-policies-occupied-palestinian-territories/.

Tucker, Tremaine (2012), *The ICT Sector in Palestine: Current State and Potentials*. Ramallah: OPT, Palestine Economic Policy Research Institute.

The Portland Trust (2012), *The ICT Sector in the Palestinian Territory*, August. Retrieved July 9, 2021, from Portland Trust: https://portlandtrust.org/sites/default/files/pubs/ict_special_aug_2012.pdf.

The Portland Trust (2022), *The Palestinian Tech Echo System*, March. Retrieved December 10, 2022, from Portland Trust: https://portlandtrust.org/wp-content/uploads/2022/05/Palestinian-Tech-Ecosystem.pdf.

The World Bank (2016), *The Telecommunication Sector in the Palestinian Territories: A Missed Opportunity for Economic Development*. Washington: World Bank Group.

The World Bank (2018), *Tech Startup Ecosystem in West Bank and Gaza: Findings are Recommendations*. Washington: The World Bank.

The World Bank (2020), *Economic Monitoring Report to the Ad Hoc Liaison Committee* (English). Washington, DC: World Bank Group. http://documents.worldbank.org/curated/en/099407305062233565/IDU091fed1da019eb042d6090100a9320aa572de.

The World Bank (2021), https://www.worldbank.org/en/news/press-release/2021/03/26/us-20-million-to-boost-digital-development-in-the-palestinian-territories#:~:text=%E2%80%9CIn%20a%20context%20of%20restrictions,development%20and%20high%2Dend%20jobs.

White, Nicholas (2010), *ICT Business Development*. Ramallah: Mercy Corps.

Wildeman, Jeremy and Alaa Tartir (2021), "Political Economy of Foreign Aid in the Occupied Palestinian Territories: A Conceptual Framing. In A. Tartir, T. Dana, and T. Seidel (eds.), *Political Economy of Palestine*. Cham, Switzerland: Palgrave Macmillan. Middle East Today. https://doi.org/10.1007/978-3-030-68643-7_10.

Wildeman, Jeremy (2019), *Donor Perceptions of Palestine: Limits to Aid Effectiveness*, June 19. Retrieved December 10, 2022, from Al-Shabaka: https://al-shabaka.org/commentaries/donor-perceptions-of-palestine-limits-to-aid-effectiveness/.

Woodcock, Jamie and Mark Graham (2020), *The Gig Economy: A Critical Introduction*. Cambridge: Polity Press.

Part II

Economic Exploitation, Dispossession, and De-Development

In Part II of this volume, we focus on *economic* sites of exploitation, dispossession, and de-development. Chapters explore critical issues related to banking and taxation examining the relationships between finance capital, aid conditionalities, and military occupation as (neoliberal) technologies of exploitation and dispossession that are shaped by imperial histories and a settler colonial present.

In her chapter "Dislocating Development: Palestinians in Israeli International Aid Imaginaries in the 1950s and 1960s," Heba Taha explores the theoretical and empirical connections between Israel's economic and technical aid industry in African countries and colonial practices toward Palestinians in the decades immediately following Israel's establishment. This geographic entanglement, she argues, relied on global economic circuits, moral imaginaries, and cultural representations pertaining to the principles, practices, and promises of development. Such plans highlight the production of Palestinians as subjects of both Israeli capitalism and colonialism while at the same time revealing the ways in which Palestinian dispossession becomes part of global developmental imaginaries in the 1950s.

In "Banking in/on the Occupation," Colin Powers considers the interfacing between Israeli settler colonialism and endogenous Palestinian dynamics as it pertains to matters of monetary policy, money, and finance, tracing the effects of this dialectical exchange from 1967 through the present day. His analysis establishes that the Palestinian Authority's (PA) coerced adoption of the Israeli shekel curtails Palestinian development through a number of channels, and that the absence of independent payment and clearance systems keeps the Palestinian economy in a permanent state of vulnerability. He also finds that tendencies of credit intermediation in Palestine—which largely derive from the restraints imposed by the occupation—not only intensify macroeconomic distortions while heightening inequality but also render debt a sinew of social relations and foundation to the PA's fiscal viability.

Anas Iqtait closes out Part II with his chapter showing how Israel's colonization of the West Bank and Gaza Strip shapes Palestinian fiscal and economic policies at the local level. In "The Palestinian Authority: The Fiscal Contract and Structural Constraints," he delves into the politics of the PA's revenue mobilization, unpacks the influence of settler colonial structures on the PA's operations, and highlights the formidable challenges in formulating a fiscal contract amidst external influences and structural constraints. Findings reveal that despite three decades of public revenue administration and tax collection, the PA has not developed a foundational fiscal contract, with numerous structural constraints including the external nature of the PA's "institutions-building" process, its dependence on foreign aid and clearance revenue, Israeli extraction of taxes, and the proliferation of public service providers.

6

Dislocating Development

Palestinians in Israeli International Aid Imaginaries in the 1950s and 1960s

Hebatalla Taha

Introduction

In a commentary published in 1963 praising the economic "progress" of Palestinian citizens of Israel, Kamel Tibi, the director of the Tayibe branch of Bank Ha-Po'alim (then a national Israeli bank owned by the Histadrut, Israel's labor union), wrote:

> The development consciousness which has of late become so characteristic a component of African and Asian thinking has not bypassed the Middle East and has certainly influenced the Arabs in Israel, but the main inspiration has no doubt been provided by the development work performed in Israel during the last decades. (1963, 69)

Palestinians in Israel were still living under martial law at the time of his writing, requiring permits from the military government to move between different towns or to work. However, as his quote suggests, they had already become a main target of Israeli visions and discourses of economic development. Even more striking, Tibi's praise for Israeli development work in essence extricates third-world "development consciousness" from the larger phenomena of nationalism and decolonization that accompanied it at the time. In fact, he likens the situation of Palestinians of 1948—who after the Nakba had found themselves under Israeli colonial rule—to that of postcolonial or decolonizing states in Africa and Asia.[1] The quote simultaneously points to newly formed connections between these different regions, a geographic entanglement that shaped political imaginations. These connections were not a coincidence; they were a result of emerging material networks, linked to moral and political ideas pertaining to the practices and promises of economic development.

This liberal language of development was not at odds with Israeli policies of displacement. Israeli initiatives aiming to "develop" Palestinians of 1948 (Palestinians who have Israeli citizenship) have existed in some form since the establishment of the state, and they have consistently overlapped with processes of dispossession, proletarianization, and impoverishment (Shehadeh and Khalidi 2014; see also Taha 2021). This interplay between development and colonialism demonstrates that Israel has consistently relied on mutual practices of inclusion and exclusion (Robinson 2013; Getzoff 2020; Tatour 2019; Wesley 2006; Degani 2020; Kafkafi 1998).

Policies of development toward Indigenous people have been integral to the modus operandi of colonial states and colonial processes (Mitchell 1988; Getzoff 2020). The dialectical nature of development in Israel is illustrated in an anecdote of a Palestinian farmer who was given a tractor as part of an Israeli government project but whose land was expropriated. While Palestinian areas were placed under military rule until 1966, they were sometimes recipients of developmental and infrastructural projects during this period (e.g., Dallasheh 2015; Kamen 1998), though this was significantly lower compared to Jewish localities (Khalidi 1984, 69). The Israeli developmental state was designed to target the Jewish population, routinely and explicitly excluding Palestinians, but there were attempts to position Palestinians as recipients of Israeli development, adopting essentialist characteristics about the two groups of people. Narratives of development were a way to consolidate colonial control. Announcements of development projects were often made in the same declarations as changes to the elaborate bureaucracy of the military regime, indicating the extent of the intertwinement between developmental and security regimes, which have arguably always been mutually reinforcing (Duffield 2001).

This chapter focuses on development—as a political discourse and imagination[2]— in the early years of Israeli statehood, during the 1950s and 1960s. It aims to insert Palestinians of 1948 into analyses of Israeli developmental thought. It does so in two ways, highlighting the paradoxical status of development. First, I focus on the voices of Palestinians who, like Tibi, became involved in promulgating these policies and discourses of development. They sought to improve their political and material conditions by embracing developmental ideals, which were circulating globally and were depicted as a form of consciousness. Second, I look at how Palestinians were discursively used in Israeli marketing of development programs abroad and how this functioned as a form of dislocation as well as an affirmation of Israeli capitalism.

This research challenges the view of the Palestinians of 1948 as an internal Israeli issue, drawing on research on how they actively engaged in regional and global solidarity discourses, as they contested their position as colonized subjects in Israel (see Nassar 2014, 2017, 2019). I focus on development as part of transnational political imaginations and modes of negotiation, while aiming to understand how it was perceived in colonial and postcolonial contexts as potentially emancipatory, including from global capitalism. Developmental initiatives invoked science and technology, industriousness, and productivity; they sought to make agriculture more productive and to combat poverty. Palestinian modernizers in Israel took inspiration from nationalist elites in postcolonial states who pursued development projects. Development is seen not only as an economic endeavor but also as a political and even an ideological project (Escobar 1995; Ferguson 1990); and it is accordingly contested, enabling both dynamics of domination and resistance.

This chapter situates the developmental imaginary of Palestinians of 1948 in these transnational ideas and emerging discourses of development. It proceeds by first explaining the need to revisit the 1950s and 1960s, a period that offers insights regarding the consolidation and inner workings of the colonial process. I subsequently discuss attempts at replanning Palestinian villages and towns in Israel, advertised as a developmental project that will increase economic productivity but also framed through a moral discourse of self-rejuvenation. A third section places these projects into larger networks that had emerged during this period, particularly their intertwinement with Israeli foreign aid programs toward decolonizing states in Africa in the 1950s and 1960s. A final section offers concluding remarks on the intertwinement of liberal economic development, colonialism, and dislocation.

Revisiting the 1950s and 1960s

Numerous studies have analyzed relations between Palestinian workers and Zionist institutions as well as the politics of Palestinian capital and capitalism during the period of the British Mandate (Glazer 2001, 2007; Lockman 1996, 179–239; Seikaly 2015; Zu'bi 1984). However, there remains a gap in our understanding of how these dynamics played out following the consolidation of Israeli statehood. Similarly, in the literature on Palestinian political economy in Israel, the 1950s and 1960s are generally overlooked, with some key exceptions (e.g., see Ben Zeev 2019; Degani 2020; Lustick 1980a; Lustick 1980b; Shalev 1989), and Palestinians who embraced discourses of development have largely been forgotten (compared, for example, to systematic research on Palestinians in the communist party). This oversight can be attributed to several factors. One is the myth that the state's policies toward Palestinians were not yet systematic at this early stage, though this has been challenged by Ahmad Sa'di (2014, 1–11). A second factor is the dominance of the Israeli military government in nearly every aspect of Palestinian life; however, as this research contends, military rule was inseparable from developmental discourse and thought. As mentioned, development is understood not only, or even mainly, as an endeavor at economic improvement but also a mode of morality, political control, and governance.

The Palestinian "modernizers" this chapter focuses on worked within Zionist spaces, embracing subtle forms of resistance, and they saw discourses of economic development as a form of national rejuvenation. I consult written sources from the late 1950s until the mid-1960s, particularly journals and periodicals that identified both as liberal and Zionist, namely *Al-Ta'awun* and *New Outlook*. The former is a quarterly review published by the Arab Workers' Department of the Histadrut, which was a core institution of Labour Zionism. One of the associate editors was the same Kamel Tibi mentioned earlier. The articles were predominantly written in Arabic, with some editions including English translations or summaries. The latter publication, an English-language journal established after the Suez crisis, was led by Mapam, which had previously been the second largest party after Mapai, both proponents of Labour Zionism. Both parties depicted themselves as workers' parties, yet Palestinian labor was a subject of contention, with Mapam more in favor of equal pay while Mapai suggested the "national interests" of Arab and Jewish workers were too far apart to be bridged (Shalev 1989, 107–8). Articles in the journal criticized military rule but did not acknowledge the Nakba or the fundamentally exclusive nature of Zionism, focusing instead on "peace" and "cooperation." While the articles mainly discussed internal dynamics, they were written with a global audience in mind, suggesting that developmental narratives were both derived from and oriented toward the international sphere.

Both *Al-Ta'awun* and *New Outlook* were organs that sought to convince Palestinians that Labor Zionism could be beneficial to their interests, and these publications can effectively be characterized as propaganda. Nevertheless, an analysis of these sources can elucidate the dialectics of coloniality, such as its internal tensions and contradictions, while highlighting how it ironically drew upon the transnational grammars and networks of decolonization. A careful reading of Palestinian voices in these spaces, meanwhile, demonstrates the interplay between domination and resistance and reveals how Palestinians have navigated these "settler colonial assemblages" (Habbas 2021; Ghantous 2020).

The period in question was marked by political and economic shifts. The colonization of Palestinian labor underwent significant transformations after Israeli statehood: rather than displacing Palestinian workers, Israel sought a dependent labor force that could be strategically manipulated, resulting in widespread proletarianization. This process took place according to conditions of the labor market: when unemployment rose, the military government restricted the provision of transit permits (Rosenhek 2003, 236). Meanwhile, Palestinians were admitted to the Histadrut starting from 1959, a process that entailed selective distribution of benefits and sought to foster loyalty to Israel. The Histadrut, as a platform of integration, aligned with the primary objective of settler colonialism – both historically and in the present (Degani 2020; Englert 2023).

Even as Palestinians were admitted into the Histadrut, their labor was described as possessing polluting or parasitic characteristics. Essentialist descriptions of "Arab" and "Jewish" labor were widespread at the time and were even adopted as part of development policy, seeking to transform or "fix" Arab labor. Describing the success of Histadrut-led courses among Palestinian workers, Salah Safadi, a member of the Board of Directors of the Workers' and Farmers' Fund, which provided loans to Arab cooperative societies, local councils, and shareholders, wrote:

> A change of heart and outlook was experienced of such waterworks and housing units and the establishment of loan and savings funds. Had this momentum been maintained, we would today have witnessed also agricultural settlements modelled on Jewish experiments in this field. A development of this kind, however, will not come about until the Arabs adopt the initiative and resourcefulness that have characterized the Jewish endeavour. (1961, 1)

The quote reflects an embrace of modernization that emphasizes that people themselves must change—they must internalize certain logics of development. There is an emphasis on a development consciousness, which attributes the poverty of racialized groups to internal or inherent causes. Such an approach to development, mimicking colonial discourse, depicts Indigenous groups, their lives and livelihoods, as an obstacle to progress. Yet, it still saw modernization as possible, thereby legitimizing the role of Israeli developmental initiatives.

Development projects accordingly highlighted the supposedly positive role of the Israeli state and Zionism in supporting Palestinians in their quest to adopt a variety of moral traits—such as responsibility, self-initiative, and self-reliance—and providing them with opportunities, through programs of government assistance, to reach their potential as "modern" and productive citizens. The editor of *Al-Ta'awun* stressed, for instance, the "significant progress" and "economic revitalization" of the Arab village "as a result of the increase in its economic and professional production and integration in the life of the productive Israeli state" (Ben-Meir 1960, 15). Here, development becomes not only a state policy but also a political condition embraced by the people, a form of consciousness as Tibi described it—perhaps even a mode of recovery after the trauma of the Nakba. The rest of this chapter will explore developmental formulations in further depth, highlighting their embrace as potentially emancipatory but also their strategic use in support of dislocation. While the Palestinian "modernizers" who are described throughout this chapter saw themselves as resisting the intensity or negotiating the parameters of settler colonialism, the developmental projects they embraced arguably functioned as improved technologies and processes of domination.

Constructing the "Arab Village"

Israeli development discourse included proposals for reconstruction of Palestinian spaces, particularly the "Arab village," which was depicted as a problem upon which intervention was required. As several scholars suggest, the "Arab village" was itself a cultural construction within Israel, a site of expert mediation (Eyal 1996; Wesley 2006, 61) and "a source of colonial imagination" (Yacobi and Shadar 2014). This section will focus on development plans to restructure Palestinian villages. Detailed descriptions, models, and blueprints of "the" Arab village's development permeated the discourse of planners, academics, and experts (Flapan 1962; Rosenfeld 1961; Shamir 1962; Stan 1964; Weigert 1964). These invoked modernist ideals of progress and rationality, contrasted with Orientalist ideas of Palestinian landscapes as inefficient or in need of restructuring to a new, Zionist standard. This way, the function of Palestinian villages—as centers of Palestinian life—would be rendered anachronistic, a tourist site, or memory.

Often working in cooperation and consultation with Israeli developmental regimes, Palestinian experts formulated these plans, focusing on economic productivity, profit, and even peacemaking, alongside an emphasis on Palestinian rights to their lands. For instance, prominent architect Rustum Bastuni described Palestinian rural space in Israel as "a burden on the economy of the country" while still emphasizing Palestinian attachment to their land and their right of return (1957a, 21). Like other Palestinians in Israel, Bastuni described the right of return as a moral right (see Nassar 2011), based on "the deepest emotional bonds" (1957a, 21). "Land farmed by one's family for generations is more than just a means of making a living," Bastuni argued (1957a, 21). He proposed a pilot plan for resettlement projects to be undertaken by Israel for internally displaced Palestinian villagers (1957a, 1957b). The economic rationale underlying the reconstruction was explicit, as Bastuni proceeded to argue, "Settled on arable land, they would become productive citizens in a field where Israel seeks to close an import-export gap" (1957a, 21). Here, returning to one's land is narrated not only as a political or moral objective but also an economic opportunity.

Bastuni graduated from the Israel Institute of Technology, known as the Technion. He was the first Palestinian representing Mapam in the Knesset (1951–5), though it is important to note that he did not necessarily align with Zionist positions or thought (on Palestinians in Mapam, see Beinin 1991). For example, he rejected Israeli naturalization policies as "clear national discrimination" and attempted to develop a new "Israeli" identity that would be inclusive of Palestinians, facing significant backlash among the Jewish-Israeli political elite for this suggestion (quoted in Pappe 2011, 41; see also Lustick 1980a, 116–17). Bastuni emigrated to the United States in 1966, where he lived until his death in 1994 (*The New York Times*, 1994).

Before leaving, however, he was an adviser to Israel's housing ministry on dwellings for Palestinians, and it was in this capacity that he wrote extensively on the subject of how to reconstruct Palestinian spaces. While Bastuni's rhetoric of Palestinian modernization seemed to align with Zionist discourse, the idea of allocating land for a Palestinian village was subversive—and unsurprisingly, it was repeatedly rejected, while at the same time Israel built numerous Jewish settlements in the Galilee.[3] Bastuni's projects for new villages emphasized peace and coexistence:

> The refugee problem being one of the most painful and acute points of contention between the Arab states and Israel, a constructive solution within Israel would be the clearest evidence of Israel's goodwill and desire for peace. It would be a demonstration of Arab-Jewish cooperation within Israel in the settlement of a common problem. [. . .] The construction of modern Arab villages in Israel would make an outstanding contribution toward the solution of a problem vital to all the countries of the Middle East. (1957a, 21–2)

Bastuni continued:

> A mechanized, modernized Arab village can be the basis for real cooperation between Arabs and Jews and as a result can narrow the gap of enmity between the Arab states and Israel as well. A social and economic revolution in the Arab villages might find its effect not only within Israel's borders but ultimately in Arab countries beyond. (1957a, 22)

Bastuni laid out concrete examples of the model modern village, accommodating 600 families. These included detailed sketches along with a financial plan, including costs, investments, and projected economic-agricultural products. The plan was accompanied by a map of the village, including where the school and the mosque would be located, and a design of the structure of the individual home. Responding to a critique that his model village failed to accommodate current patterns of life, Bastuni declared, "I did not intend to copy the pattern of Arab life as it exists, without modifications according to the economic and social developments of the country," and insisted that the village's economy and inhabitants were suited for those who "need a new pattern of life" (*New Outlook* 1957, 57). Bastuni's efforts are part a rationalist-modernist project, seen at the time as a path to progress. These plans were ambitious, and Bastuni noted that smaller-scale models of cooperation between Arabs and Jews in Israel suggested that it is possible for Israel to be "integrated" within Afro-Asian spaces, including emerging networks of solidarity (1958, 34).

Bastuni was not alone in these efforts: others also challenged and criticized Israeli policy toward Palestinian land, particularly expropriation, while providing input on potential paths to development and insisting on the right of return (Makhoul 1957, 39–42; *New Outlook* 1963, 20–1). Israeli projects for land reform affecting Palestinians were often resisted by these intellectuals, who sought active involvement in the development of their own space, even as they adopted a patronizing tone toward working class Palestinians in the process (Bayadsi 1961). Tibi, who had been involved in the Arab department of the Histadrut prior to joining Bank Ha-Po'alim, argued, "We are in urgent need for more development and progress in all aspects of life, particularly the social and economic aspects" (1960, 22). To this end, he envisioned modern machinery for agriculture, alongside "the model home in its look and its residents" (1960, 22–3). These individuals believed they needed radical changes, ranging from ways of working the land and living on it to personal habits. While the number of individuals comprising this group of Palestinian modernizers and experts was not particularly significant, they had an impact on discussions surrounding Palestinian communities, through their access to centers of power, and they often successfully forced debates within Israeli society that Zionist elites did not approve of. Yet, their longer-term imprint is uncertain, as they were mostly unable to influence policy; Bastuni's detailed plans, for example, remained hypothetical.

The focus on changing Palestinians and Palestinian spaces aligned with Zionist objectives. Zvi Gluzman, in charge of Arab Housing at the Ministry of Labor, stressed that the aesthetics of rural Palestinian space were misaligned with Israel, declaring: "A synthesis must be achieved between these [agricultural] considerations and the fundamental aim of building a more solid, better-looking, healthier and cleaner house" (*Al-Ta'awun* 1961, 10). Such a link between lack of productivity and dirtiness, perhaps even disorder, has been noted in multiple contexts, in Israel and beyond, where cleanliness has been associated with progress and modernity (Levin 2019, 296; McKee 2015; Kallandar 2018, 297; Gupta 2013). Restructuring physical spaces was linked to ideas of economic revitalization—which, in Histadrut-related publications at the time, was emphasized through cooperative settlements (for a study of how this has evolved from the 1960s until the present, see Kaminer 2022). Describing new cooperatives in Palestinian towns, Yaakov Cohen, the head of the Arab Department of the Hisadrut, wrote: "We hope that this is a sign that the Arab *fellah* and worker are now ready to set out on new roads to cooperation which will lead to the development of the Arab village, raise its standard of living and create a productive working society" (Cohen 1963, 1). This language invokes the focus on internal characteristics of Palestinians as the obstacle to productivity, discussed earlier, which is racialized and which suggests that the state can help only if they are willing to modernize. It alludes to familiar ideas of self-reliance and self-responsibility, suggesting that thus far the main economic issue has been farmers' unwillingness to participate in "modern" ways of living.

Similar to Bastuni's project for reforming village architecture, Abd al-Majid al-Zu'bi, a member of the Executive of Arab Cooperatives affiliated with the Histadrut, proposed a plan to "fix" Arab agriculture through cooperatives—aligning with Israeli developmental objectives at the time, though the economy was still oriented within global capitalism. "As a result of the continuation of the communal tenure system," Zu'bi argued, "Arab agriculture suffers from the stagnation of techniques and methods of production" (1957, 10–16). He criticized the division of the land into small parcels, because it could not be operated upon using a machine:

> The tools used in the Arab village are added testimony to the backward nature of Arab agriculture. . . . These tools are the same as have been in use for hundreds and even thousands of years. . . . The costs of production with these primitive means is higher than with modern machines. Here, too, changes can only take place with the aid of long-term loans from the Ministry of Agriculture, the agricultural banks and the cooperatives. . . . The backwardness of his tools makes it impossible for the Arab agriculturist to adopt improved and more modern methods of cultivation or to raise his culture and social level of existence. (1957, 12)

This use of "agriculturalist" can be contrasted to the more familiar *fallah* or farmer, but there is also an embrace of "settler common sense" evident in the earlier passage, where Palestinian modes of existence are depicted as belonging firmly in the past (on the notion of "settler common sense" and its quotidian inscription into Zionist discourses of development, see Getzoff 2020). As mentioned, many Palestinian "modernists" openly criticized Israeli expropriation of Palestinian land and other acts of dispossession, yet they used these Israeli forums to articulate immediate policy changes. Zu'bi suggested extending technical training to Palestinian youth in kibbutzim and enabling them to enroll in agricultural schools.

Israel created institutions for this purpose, described as spaces to not only "transmit" Jewish ways of life but also create "fraternal coexistence," as described in one article (Stan 1964a, 42–5). Entitled "A step toward the future," the article is an indication of how developmental narratives are constructed temporally. Similarly, journalist 'Atallah Mansour, who himself spent time on an Israeli kibbutz and later wrote a novel in Hebrew about this experience, describes Palestinians who "fear contact with the 20th century" (1964b, 30). Elsewhere, he discussed "a cultural encounter between the conservative and feudal culture of Arab society and the free and industrial Jewish society" (1962b, 56; see also 1962a, 59–63). Mansour wrote extensively for Israeli newspapers like *Haaretz*. Despite his embrace of these essentialist dichotomies, Mansour did not merely adopt Israeli positions, and like the individuals discussed earlier, he sought to improve daily life for the Palestinian community. While he did not overlook Israeli violence or dispossession, Mansour nonetheless embraced developmental aspirations, a reflection of the prevailing atmosphere during this period but also a result of a unique class position that many of these individuals achieved (Mansour 1975). These Palestinian professionals placed themselves as "experts" vis-à-vis the rural Palestinian population, much like technocratic nationalist elites did elsewhere, but in this case, they also became intermediaries with the Israeli system.

There is no doubt that these developmental efforts corresponded with Zionist discourse: "Arab villages"—in the Israeli cultural conception of them—represented a problem. The intervention onto the space was depicted as a moral action. It combined both attempts to control Palestinian land with ways to create order and efficiency and consolidate control over space. Zionist officials embraced a distinction between the settlers, described as a "productive" labor force, and the Indigenous population, perceived as having failed to cultivate the land (Masalha 2007, 35; Levine 1995; Getzoff 2020). This discourse incorporated a view of Palestinian society—especially "the Arab village"—as timeless and unchanging, threatening Israel's future. And as scholars have highlighted, time has been used as a mode of governance, especially regarding development policies (Gutkowski 2018). This affected urban spaces too: in an article entitled "Nazareth looks for the future," Abd al-Aziz al-Zuʻbi, a Palestinian from Nazareth involved with Mapam, envisioned industrial plants and "modern hotels and restaurants" catering to tourists, alongside shops manufacturing souvenirs (1960, 32–4). These narratives have not dissipated in the contemporary period; they continue to frame discussions about Palestinian spaces in Israel (Kershner 2013), while the pace of settler colonialism has accelerated in the West Bank (Ghantous and Joronen 2022).

For many Palestinian intellectuals, development was an ambitious technological and ideological project of self-improvement; for others, it was a way to improve everyday life by increasing resources allocated to Palestinian areas. By highlighting the role of experts, my objective is to shed light on how development—as a technical and moral discourse—was not only a top-down state project but also a form of consciousness, which Palestinians also used and mobilized. In addition to allowing us to understand how development was mutually reinforcing vis-à-vis colonialism during this time, we can understand why and how different agents and subjects played a role in conceptualizing and negotiating development (for additional information, see Tartir, Dana and Seidel 2021).

Palestinians of 1948 and Israeli International Aid in Africa

Palestinians did not only play a role in envisioning development; they were also discursively integrated within Israeli aid in Africa and Asia. As Israeli developmental regimes became oriented toward international aid and assistance, the figures involved drew upon their experiences with the Palestinian community, economy, and land. As Ayala Levin argues (2022), Israel transformed its experience of settler colonialism into development expertise. For example, an Israeli architect who participated in numerous projects of town and master planning in Africa ultimately also designed Israeli settlements in the West Bank, and described the "Arab village" as "architecture without architects," alluding to its unplanned nature (Tamir-Tawil 2003, 160; on the use of this slogan more broadly, see Weizman 2017, 44). This can be contrasted with

Israeli architecture, which, as many scholars have argued, was not only aimed at nation-building but also a strategic weapon for displacement (Weizman 2017; Schwake 2010; Efrat 2004).

Around 2,000 Israeli experts working on foreign aid projects in African states between 1950 and 1970 participated in training and technical assistance programs (Oded 2010, 131). Israel established the Institute for Planning and Development to coordinate some of these activities, although many of the individuals involved in aid missions were affiliated with private companies or were individual consultants (Efrat 2004). Although technically run by the state, the Israeli aid industry seemed to operate as a laboratory and reflected an entrepreneurial ethos (Efrat 2004, 488). There were around 7,000 people from African states who were recipients of training in the Afro-Asian Institute for Labor Studies and Cooperation of the Histadrut (Nadelmann 1981). By the 1960s, MASHAV, Israel's Agency for International Development Cooperation, had grown significantly within the Israeli foreign ministry. The commercial aspects of the development industry, and the intertwinement of aid with exports, were discussed extensively during the time as a positive influence (Ben-Moshe 1961, 56–61). International aid to decolonizing states was mainly a strategic geopolitical tool, aiming to counteract Arab influence across the continent. Israeli international aid projects were combined with support for colonial powers in international forums like the United Nations. In other words, Israel supported developmental projects in African states using the language of national liberation and decolonization, yet it also sought to reassure colonial powers (Heller 2020b, 58).

Researchers have made reflexive arguments about the representations of "Africa" as a social and cultural category within Zionist ideology (Bar-Yosef 2013; Yacobi 2016). This has led to important insights about the constructions of race in this relationship, revolving around Israel's self-depiction as both "white" and "non-white." For instance, speaking to Kwame Nkrumah, Ben-Gurion described Jewish people as belonging "to the white race" but also victims of whiteness (Levey 2003, 157). Bar-Yosef accordingly outlines a sense of a sacred duty by a "civilized colonist" (2013, 94). Yacobi (2016) similarly invokes a "moral geography," which allowed Israel to "whiten" itself in the international arena. Networks of expertise and international aid reflected racial identities and hierarchies within Israel; for example, Mizrahi operatives were positioned between Ashkenazi and African identities (Yacobi, Misgav, and Sharon 2020, 948).

Israeli endeavors in African states also drew upon Israeli policies toward Palestinians who were still colonized subjects, even as they portrayed their involvement in aid as anti-colonial. As Daniel Kupfert Heller writes:

> To prove that their country was a "living laboratory" for women's advancement, Israeli officials took these students on tours of aid projects geared toward North African and Middle Eastern Jewish women living in Israeli development towns and Palestinian Arab women living in villages within the state of Israel's borders. These tours served as advertisements for the services of Israeli experts in Africa, who established on-the-ground women's programs tailored to specific countries. (2020b, 50)

The students who traveled to Israel as part of these schemes, Heller notes, went on guided tours to witness some of the development work carried out by Israel, particularly toward Mizrahim (Arab Jews) and Palestinians (2020b, 56). In international forums particularly, Israeli officials highlighted specifically its efforts with the "development" of women, especially Palestinian women (Heller 2020a, 682) who were depicted as strategic objects of modernization and described in patronizing terms. This aligned with ideas of the strategic role of women for national development in postcolonial states, and Israel highlighted in the international sphere that it was a laboratory for innovative solutions dealing with women's advancement in the Third World (Heller 2020b, 56).

This achieved several key objectives. First, it sought to situate Israel as an ally in the decolonizing world, sharing similar struggles. Furthermore, it allowed Israeli experts to highlight that they possessed a specialized knowledge and could deal with diverse groups. In doing so, Israel could establish its relationship with Palestinians as a model case of development, while emphasizing an image of state benevolence toward Palestinians in the international sphere. As Levin (2022) shows, the appeal of Israel, for several African states, was its ability to not only depict itself as distinct from the colonial powers but also draw upon its own history of development, since before the establishment of the state. Such claims of Israeli developmental success cannot be divorced from values associated with settler colonialism (Levin 2022) but also from the day-to-day experiences of Palestinians.

Furthermore, Israel could emphasize that its developmental projects were geared toward ethnic diversity and could therefore be appealing to decolonizing states with heterogenous groups. For example, while promoting a project in Mali, Israeli aid workers advertised in the local media their knowledge of various groups, including Palestinians in Israel, as part of their positioning of themselves as experts (Yacobi 2016, 66). Yacobi quotes Israel's first ambassador to the republics of Senegal and Mali, Yehuda Ben-David, who argued, "We made an effort to introduce diverse issues to Arabic programs, such as development-related problems, cultural practices of various ethnic groups, including Israeli Arabs, etc." (2016, 66). These narratives can be seen as aligning with the dislocation of Palestinians from their land, constituting a form of displacement. Through these emerging networks of expertise, Palestinian dispossession became discursively linked to global developmental imaginaries. Such dislocation is part and parcel with the development work of modernizing Palestinians, described earlier: both of these projects emphasized a discursive process of Palestinian development that is based on severing (or refusing to restore) existing connections with land. Instead, they seek to develop new forms of social and economic relations that can affirm, simultaneously, Israeli colonialism and capitalism.

Finally, the same colonial myths that Zionist settlers relied on in colonizing Palestine were used in descriptions of Israel's international development projects. An article on Israel's developmental role in Africa, for example, suggested that Israel was a preferred provider of aid because decolonizing states were "attracted by the vitality and dynamic character of Israel's society" (Shlomi 1957, 25). Yet, one observer could not help but highlight the ways in which some Israeli experts exhibited a degree of contempt toward the African people they were supposedly assisting, noting that this was not unlike the sense of superiority adopted by Zionist (Ashkenazi) elites toward Palestinians and Arab Jews (Wassermann 1959, 15). After the 1973 Arab-Israeli war, Israeli diplomats retreated rapidly from the African continent, as did its international aid to African states (Ojo 1988). Simultaneously, Israel's involvement in spaces of Afro-Asian solidarity, which was already tenuous, declined further, as support for the liberation of Palestine had become a core cause of the Third Worldist project (Chamberlin 2011). Today, Israeli experts are recognized globally for the country's security industry, which has become a strategic export, including in many states in the Global South (see Gordon 2010; Machold 2016).

Conclusion

This chapter has sought to situate Palestinians of 1948 within discussions of Israeli developmental policy and discourse in the early period when Israel was consolidating its control over the land. I have highlighted how Palestinian intellectuals and thinkers embraced aspects of development, in line with a global idea of development as a form of internal and spiritual consciousness and as potentially emancipatory. They did so while simultaneously seeking to negotiate and limit Israeli colonial policy and presence on their lands. This early optimism combined with their position of in-betweenness, produced these unique subjectivities that embraced a modernist orientation. At the same time, Palestinians became part of larger Israeli discourses of development abroad.

Although the rhetoric and policies of development have undergone significant shifts over the years, Israel has, since its establishment, framed Palestinians as objects of development. The framework of development has always played a role in the way the Israeli state engaged the Palestinian community, alongside securitization. Even during this early period, development did not only involve the state but also drew upon and fostered a professional Palestinian class, who embraced the terminology and technology of economic development, situating themselves within postcolonial language and frameworks, even as they were still colonized, and even as they were deliberately disenfranchised and proletarianized.

The approaches and infrastructures of development were part of a global industry: it operated as a site of technical expertise and a forum for economic networks, and at the same time, it was part of a larger moral project. Looking at development through these two frameworks—as a form of consciousness and desire for emancipation and as a depoliticizing mode of discursive displacement of Palestinians—allows us to understand its paradoxical role and make sense of how it aligned with and reaffirmed Israeli capitalism. Finally, many of the processes articulated in this chapter are continuously repackaged and renegotiated within contemporary discourses and policies of development. They can arguably be perceived as precursors to the modernization and professionalization of development in the contemporary era. The historical dimensions and narratives that have unfolded during Israel's attempt to manage relations with Palestinians within its borders have had implications for the subsequent adoption of economic policies toward Palestinians in the West Bank and

Gaza Strip (Gordon 2008, 29). Moreover, Israeli policies of economic development have become increasingly assertive toward Palestinians of 1948 in the past decade, producing new subjects, classes, and forms of projecting power but also creating new forms of resistance.

Notes

1   I would like to thank As'ad Zo'abi for help with collecting materials from Israeli libraries. An early draft of this research was presented at the Centre for Colonial and Postcolonial Studies at the University of Sussex in 2021, and I am grateful for the feedback I received from participants, particularly Heba Youssef and Ali Kassem. I thank the editors of this volume for their feedback on this chapter. Sai Englert, Pelle Valentin Olsen, Nikolas Kosmatopoulos, and Michael Shalev also provided helpful comments on an earlier draft. Derek Penslar offered crucial guidance as I started working on this project.
2   This refers to the ways in which development became an authoritative idea within both national and international frameworks, aligned with dreams of modernization and prosperity. As Escobar (1995) shows, international development depicted the Third World as a problem that required intervention, especially through the international economic system, yet it is also important to highlight that postcolonial programs have embraced ideas of developments and their associations with modernity and progress, including in Palestine (on development and colonialism in the West Bank, see Hanieh 2016; Salamanca 2016; for a critique of postcolonial elites' adoption of developmental projects, see Kapoor 2008).
3   In the past decade, there have been numerous plans to build a new "modern" Arab city in Israel, also depicted as a form of development, which have still not materialized (Khoury 2017).

References

Al-Ta'awun (1961), "Housing in the Arab Localities." January: 10.
Bar-Yosef, Eitan (2013), *A Villa in the Jungle: Africa in Israeli Culture*. Jerusalem: Van Leer Institute and HaKibbutz HaMeuchad.
Bastuni, Rustum (1957a), "Planning a Modern Arab Village." *New Outlook*, July: 21–4.
Bastuni, Rustum (1957b), "Planning a Modern Arab Village." *New Outlook*, August: 39–43.
Bastuni, Rustum (1958), "Towards New Jewish-Arab Relations." *New Outlook*, November/December: 39–43.
Bayadsi, Mahmud (1961), "Land Reform and the Israeli Arabs." *New Outlook*, February: 18–22.
Beinin, Joel (1991), "Knowing Your Enemy, Knowing Your Ally: The Arabists of Hashomer Hatza'ir (MAPAM)." *Social Text*, 28: 100–21.
Ben-Meir, Gad (1960), "Al-tatawur al-iqtisadi fi al-muhit al-'arabi [Economic Development in the Arab Sector]." *Al-Ta'awun*, March: 10–15.

Ben-Moshe, Eliezar (1961), "'Ilaqat isra'il al-iqtisadiyia bi-qarrat afriqiya [Israel's Economic Relations With the African Continent]." *Al-Ta'awun*, May: 56–61.

Ben Zeev, Nimrod (2019), "'We Built This Country' Palestinian Citizens in Israel's Construction Industry, 1948–73." *Jerusalem Quarterly*, 84 (11): 10–46.

Chamberlin, Paul Thomas (2011), "The Struggle Against Oppression Everywhere: The Global Politics of Palestinian Liberation." *Middle Eastern Studies*, 47 (1): 25–41.

Cohen, Yaakov (1963), "Al-jam'iyyat al-ta'awuniyya al-'arabiyya: tatawur mustamir [Arab Cooperatives: Continuous Progress]." *Al-Ta'awun*, Autumn: 1–9.

Dagani, Arnon (2020), "On the Frontier of Integration: The Histadrut and the Palestinian Arab Citizens of Israel." *Middle Eastern Studies*, 56 (3): 412–26.

Dallasheh, Leena (2015), "Troubled Waters: Citizenship and Colonial Zionism in Nazareth." *International Journal of Middle East Studies*, 47 (3): 467–87.

Duffield, Mark (2001), *Global Governance and the New Wars: The Merging of Development and Security*, London: Zed Books.

Efrat, Zvi (2004), *The Israeli Project: Building and Architecture 1948–1973*, trans. Dapha Raz. Tel Aviv: Tel Aviv Museum of Art.

Englert, Sai (2023), "Hebrew Labor without Hebrew Workers: The Histadrut, Palestinian Workers, and the Israeli Construction Industry." *Journal of Palestine Studies*, 52(3): 23–45.

Escobar, Arturo (1995), *Encountering Development: The Making and Unmaking of the Third World*. Princeton: Princeton University Press.

Eyal, Gil (1996), "The Discursive Origins of Israeli Separatism: The Case of the Arab Village." *Theory and Society*, 25 (3): 389–429.

Ferguson, James (1990), *The Anti-Politics Machine: "Development," Depoliticization and Bureaucratic Power in Lesotho*. Minneapolis: University of Minnesota Press.

Flapan, Simha (1962), "Integrating the Arab Village." *New Outlook*, March/April: 22–32.

Getzoff, Joseph F. (2020), "Zionist Frontiers: David Ben-Gurion, Labor Zionism, and Transnational Circulations of Settler development." *Settler Colonial Studies*, 10 (1): 74–93.

Ghantous, Wassim (2020), "Settler-Colonial Assemblages and the Making of the Israeli Frontier: Palestinian Experiences of (In)security, Surveillance and Carceral geographies." PhD diss., University of Gothenburg, Sweden.

Ghantous, Wassim, and Mikko Joronen (2022), "Dromoelimination: Accelerating Settler Colonialism in Palestine." *Environment and Planning D: Society and Space*, 40 (3): 393–412.

Glazer, Steven A. (2001), "Picketing for Hebrew Labor: A Window on Histadrut Tactics and Strategy." *Journal of Palestine Studies*, 30: (4): 39–54.

Glazer, Steven A (2007), "Language of Propaganda: The Histadrut, Hebrew Labor, and the Palestinian Worker." *Journal of Palestine Studies*, 36 (2): 25–38.

Gordon, Neve (2008), *Israel's Occupation*. Berkeley: University of California Press.

Gordon, Neve (2010), "Israel's Emergence as a Homeland Security Capital." In Elia Zureik, David Lyon, and Yasmeen Abu-Laban (eds.), *Surveillance and Control in Israel/Palestine: Population, Territory and Power*, 153–70. London: Routledge.

Gupta, Huma (2013), "Staging Baghdad as a Problem of Development." *International Journal of Islamic Architecture*, 8 (2): 337–61.

Gutkowski, Natalia (2018), "Governing Through Timescape: Israeli Sustainable Agriculture Policy and the Palestinian-Arab Citizens." *International Journal of Middle East Studies*, 50 (3): 471–92.

Habbas, Walid (2021), "The West Bank-Israel Economic Integration: Palestinian Interaction With the Israeli Border and Permit Regimes." In Alaa Tartir, Tariq Dana, and Timothy Seidel (eds.), *Political Economy of Palestine: Critical, Interdisciplinary, and Decolonial Perspectives*, 111–34. Cham: Palgrave Macmillan.

Hanieh, Adam (2016), "Development as Struggle: Confronting the Reality of Power in Palestine." *Journal of Palestine Studies*, 45 (4): 32–47.

Heller, Daniel Kupfert (2020a), "Gender, Development and the Arab-Israeli Conflict: The Politics of Study Tours for Women From the Global South in the State of Israel, 1958-1973." *History Australia*, 17 (4): 678–94.

Heller, Daniel Kupfert (2020b), "Israeli Aid and the 'African Woman': The Gendered Politics of International Development, 1958–73." *Jewish Social Studies*, 25 (2): 49–78.

Kafkafi, Eyal (1998), "Segregation or Integration of the Israeli Arabs: Two Concepts in Mapai." *International Journal of Middle East Studies*, 30 (3): 347–67.

Kallander, Amy Aisen (2018), "Miniskirts and 'Beatniks': Gender Roles, National Development, and Morals in 1960s Tunisia." *International Journal of Middle East Studies*, 50 (2): 291–313.

Kamen, Charles S. (1998), "After the Catastrophe II: The Arabs in Israel, 1948–51." *Middle Eastern Studies*, 24: (1): 68–109.

Kaminer, Matan (2022), "The Agricultural Settlement of the Arabah and the Political Ecology of Zionism." *International Journal of Middle East Studies*, 54(1): 40–56.

Kapoor, Ilan (2008), *The Postcolonial Politics of Development*. London: Routledge.

Kershner, Isabel (2013), "Mayoral Race Threatens to Shake Tradition Where Jesus Grew up." *The New York Times*, October 20. https://www.nytimes.com/2013/10/21/world/middleeast/mayoral-race-threatens-stability-in-jesus-childhood-home.html.

Khalidi, Raja (1984), "The Arab Economy in Israel: Dependency or Development." *Journal of Palestine Studies*, 13 (3): 63–86.

Khoury, Jack (2017), "Israel Promised to Build Its First Modern Arab City Since 1948. Here's What Came of It." *Haaretz*, October 17. https://www.haaretz.com/israel-news/2017-10-17/ty-article-magazine/.premium/israel-vowed-to-build-its-first-modern-arab-city-since-48-then-nothing/0000017f-e5d2-dc7e-adff-f5ff2d210000.

Levey, Zach (2003), "The Rise and Decline of a Special Relationship: Israel and Ghana, 1957–1966." *African Studies Review*, 46 (1): 155–77.

Levin, Ayala (2019), "South African 'Know-how' and Israeli 'Facts of Life': The Planning of Afridar, Ashkelon, 1949–1956." *Planning Perspectives*, 34 (2): 285–309.

Levin, Ayala (2022), *Architecture and Development: Israeli Construction in Sub-Saharan Africa and the Settler Colonial Imagination, 1958–1973*. Durham: Duke University Press.

Levine, Mark (1995), "The Discourses of Development in Mandate Palestine." *Arab Studies Quarterly*, 17 (1/2): 95–124.

Lockman, Zachary (1996), *Comrades and Enemies: Arab and Jewish Workers in Palestine, 1906–1948*. Berkeley: University of California Press.

Lustick, Ian (1980a), *Arabs in the Jewish State: Israel's Control of a National Minority*. Austin: University of Texas Press.

Lustick, Ian (1980b), "Zionism and the State of Israel: Regime Objectives and the Arab Minority in the First Years of Statehood." *Middle Eastern Studies*, 16 (1): 127–46.

Machold, Rhys (2016), "Learning From Israel? '26/11' and the Anti-politics of Urban Security Governance." *Security Dialogue*, 47 (4): 273–365.

Makhoul, Naʿim (1957), "The Arab Farmer." *New Outlook*, October: 39–42.

Mansour, Atallah (1962a), "Arab Intellectuals in Israel." *New Outlook*, November/December: 55–7.

Mansour, Atallah (1962b), "The Modern Encounter Between Jews and Arabs." *New Outlook*, March/April: 59–63.

Mansour, Atallah (1975), *Waiting for the Dawn*. London: Secker and Warburg.
Masalha, Nur (2007), *The Bible and Zionism: Invented Traditions, Archaeology, and Postcolonialism in Palestine-Israel*. London: Zed Books.
Mckee, Emily (2015), "Trash Talk: Interpreting Morality and Disorder in the Negev/Naqb Landscapes." *Current Anthropology*, 56 (4): 733–52.
Mitchell, Timothy (1988), *Colonising Egypt*. Cambridge: Cambridge University Press.
Nadelmann, Ethan A. (1981), "Israel and Black Africa: A Rapprochement?" *The Journal of Modern African Studies*, 19 (2): 183–219.
Nassar, Maha (2011), "Palestinian Citizens of Israel and the Discourse on the Right of Return, 1948–59." *Journal of Palestine Studies*, 40 (4): 45–60.
Nassar, Maha (2014), "'My Struggle Embraces Every Struggle': Palestinians in Israel and Solidarity with Afro-Asian Liberation Movements." *The Arab Studies Journal*, 22 (1): 74–101.
Nassar, Maha (2017), *Brothers Apart: Palestinian Citizens of Israel and the Arab World*. Stanford: Stanford University Press.
Nassar, Maha (2019), "Palestinian Engagement With the Black Freedom Movement Prior to 1967." *Journal of Palestine Studies*, 48 (4): 16–32.
New Outlook (1957), "Letters to the Editors." November/December: 56–7+60.
New Outlook (1963), "Only One Way to Peace." March/April: 20–1.
Oded, Arye (2010), "Africa in Israeli Foreign Policy—Expectations and Disenchantment: Historical and Diplomatic Aspects." *Israel Studies*, 15 (3): 121–42.
Ojo, Olusola (1988), *Africa and Israel: Relations in Perspective*. New York: Routledge.
Pappé, Ilan (2011), *The Forgotten Palestinians: A History of the Palestinians in Israel*. New Haven: Yale University Press.
Robinson, Shira (2013), *Citizen Strangers: Palestinians and the Birth of Israel's Liberal Settler State*. Stanford: Stanford University Press.
Rosenfeld, Henry (1961), "A Cultural Agenda for Arab Villages." *New Outlook*, January: 36–49.
Rosenhek, Zeev (2003), "The Political Dynamics of a Segmented Labor Market: Palestinian Citizens, Palestinians From the Occupied Territories and Migrant Workers in Israel." *Acta Sociologica*, 46 (3): 231–49.
Saʻdi, Ahmad (2014), *Thorough Surveillance: The Genesis of Israeli Policies of Population Management, Surveillance and Political Control Towards the Palestinian Minority*. Manchester: Manchester University Press.
Safadi, Salah (1961), "Madha yaʻbuq taqadum al-taʻawuniyat fi al-muhit al-arabi? [What Prevents the Development of Cooperatives in Arab Localities?]." *Al-Taʻawun*, January: 4–7.
Salamanca, Omar Jabary (2016), "Assembling the Fabric of Life: When Settler Colonialism Becomes Development." *Journal of Palestine Studies*, 45 (4): 64–80.
Schwake, Gabriel (2010), "Settle and Rule: The Evolution of the Israeli National Project." *Architecture and Culture*, 8 (2): 350–71.
Seikaly, Sherene (2015), *Men of Capital: Scarcity and Economy in Mandate Palestine*. Stanford: Stanford University Press.
Shalev, Michael (1989), "Jewish Organized Labor and the Palestinians: A Study of State/Society Relations in Israel." In Baruch Kimmerling (ed.), *Israeli State and Society: The Boundaries and Frontiers*, 93–133. Albany: State University Press of New York.
Shamir, Shimon (1962), "Changes in Village leadership." *New Outlook*, March/April: 93–112.
Shehadeh, Mtanes and Raja Khalidi (2014), "Impeded Development: The Political Economy of the Palestinian Arabs Inside Israel." In Mandy Turner and Omar Shweiki

(eds.), *Decolonizing Palestinian Political Economy: De-development and Beyond*, 115–37. Basingstoke: Palgrave Macmillan.
Shlomi, David (1957), "Israel Between Europe and Asia." *New Outlook*, September: 22–6.
Stan, Aviva (1964a), "'Landed Gentry' in an Arab Village." *New Outlook*, February: 54–8.
Stan, Aviva (1964b), "A Step Toward the Future." *New Outlook*, May: 42–5.
Taha, Hebatalla (2021), "Palestinians in Israel: Neoliberal Contestations and Class Formation." In Alaa Tartir, Tariq Dana, and Timothy Seidel (eds.), *Political Economy of Palestine: Critical, Interdisciplinary and Decolonial Perspectives*,155–76. Cham: Palgrave Macmillan.
Tamir-Tawil, Eran (2003), "To Start a City From Scratch: An Interview With Architect Thomas M. Leitersdorf." In Rafi Segal, Eyal Weizman, and David Tartakover (eds.), *A Civilian Occupation: The Politics of Israeli Architecture*, 151–62. London: Verso.
Tartir, Alaa, Tariq Dana, and Timothy Seidel (eds.) (2021), *Political Economy of Palestine: Critical, Interdisciplinary, and Decolonial Perspectives*. Cham: Palgrave Macmillan.
Tatour, Lana (2019), "Citizenship as Domination: Settler Colonialism and the Making of Palestinian Citizenship in Israel." *Arab Studies Journal*, 27 (2): 8–39.
The New York Times (1994), "Rustum Bastuni, 71, Builder and Teacher." May 14. https://www.nytimes.com/1994/05/14/obituaries/rustum-bastuni-71-builder-and-teacher.html.
Tibi, Kamel (1960), "Nahw islah al-qarya al-'arabiya [Towards Reform of the Arab Village]." *Al-Ta'awun*, March: 22–3+25.
Tibi, Kamel (1963), "Economic Progress for the Arab Community." *New Outlook*, March/April: 69–71.
Wassermann, Ursula (1959), "Israel in Africa." *New Outlook*, July/August: 11–16.
Weigert, Gideon (1964), "Women Want Freedom." *New Outlook*, June: 61–2.
Weizman, Eyal (2017), *Hollow Land: Israel's Architecture of Occupation*. London: Verso.
Wesley, David A. (2006), *State Practices and Zionist Images: Shaping Economic Development in Arab Towns in Israel*. New York and Oxford: Berghahn Books.
Yacobi, Haim (2016), *Israel and Africa: A Genealogy of Moral Geography*. New York: Routledge.
Yacobi, Haim, Chen Misgav, and Smadar Sharon (2020), "Technopolitics, Development and the Colonial- Postcolonial Nexus: Revisiting Settlements Development Aid From Israel to Africa." *Middle Eastern Studies*, 56 (6): 937–52.
Yacobi, Haim and Hadas Shadar (2014), "The Arab Village: A Genealogy of (Post)colonial imagination." *The Journal of Architecture*, 19 (6): 975–97.
Zu'bi, Abd al-Majid (1957), "A Plan for Arab Agriculture." *New Outlook*, September: 10–16.
Zu'bi, Abd al-Aziz (1960), "Nazareth Looks for the Future." *New Outlook*, October: 32–4.
Zu'bi, Nahla (1984), "The Development of Capitalism in Palestine: The Expropriation of the Palestinian Direct Producers." *Journal of Palestine Studies*, 13 (4): 88–109.

7

Banking in/on the Occupation

Colin Powers

Introduction

Israeli settler colonialism is the primary determinant of Palestinian economic performance. This is so not only because of how settler colonialism has and continues to act upon the Palestinian economy but also because of the ways through which its provocation of survival strategies among the Indigenous reformulates that economy's fundamental composition.

Works done within and outside the academy have unearthed causalities proximate, distal, and dialectical connecting Israeli settler colonialism to everything from contemporary business-state relations (Khalidi et al. 2019; Dana 2020) and class formation in Palestine (Hilal 1976; Samara 1989; Seikaly 2015; Smith 1986; Zureik 1976) to the consolidation of a growth model based on debt and aid-financed final consumption (Shikaki 2019). Though it would be an exaggeration to name them a lacuna, relatively neglected within this literature are analyses of money, monetary policy, and, to a lesser degree, finance (for exceptions, see Zaghah 1996; Cobhan and Kanafani 2004; Mitter 2014; Khalidi et al. 2021, Merrino 2021). This absence can be attributed to any number of things, including the somewhat technical nature of the matters at hand and the extent to which their discussion tends to be siloed—both within economics departments themselves and within the politically and sociologically blind frames of inquiry typically adopted therein. It may also follow from the perception that the issues in question are either of secondary importance to or epiphenomenal of the more tactile elements of Israel's system of oppression and control. A recent comment from Sara Roy captures the logic behind this second interpretation well: "the issue for the majority of Palestinians is not primarily a lack of control over their money, but their inability to generate money because their economy has been devastated" (Thier 2022).

Roy's claims are justified to no small degree. Stacked up against the direct, immediate, and devastating effects introduced via the likes of bombardment, blockade, outright theft, and the "logistics of occupation" (Alimahomed-Wilson and Potiker 2017), the consequence of money and finance does indeed pale. That money and finance constitute a relatively lesser weight upon the shoulders of Palestinian economic life, however, does not render them immaterial. Far from it. The Palestinian National Authority's (coerced) adoption of the Israeli settler currency markedly curtails the ability of Palestinians to "generate money" through a diversity of distinct and intersecting channels (Merrino 2021). By virtue of having been prevented from laying all its own plumbing when it comes to payment and clearance systems, the contemporary infrastructure of money can also be shown to keep the Palestinian economy in a state of acute vulnerability: The specter of enforced isolation haunts at all times, as Gaza painfully learned in the aftermath of Hamas's ascension to power in 2007.

Nor are processes operating in the realm of finance any less significant. Certainly, the dysfunction of credit intermediation in Palestine can, in the first instance, be attributed to Israel's successes in undermining the market viability of productive activities through the tactile forms of intervention that are referenced earlier. Nevertheless, the particular form of dysfunction evinced in Palestine engenders effects and externalities, which have gone on to retain an independent life of their own. Indeed, it is the self-propelling machinery of finance that today intensifies macroeconomic distortions, underwrites spiking inequality, reconstitutes the meaning and nature of both shelter and consumption, and consecrates debt as a sinew of both social relations and fiscal operationality. This being the case, to analytically marginalize the generative changes being catalyzed in the sphere of money and finance is to ignore critical mechanisms within Palestine's evolving sociology, politics, and economics.

Cognizant of extant gaps in the literature and the real-world gravity of these issues, this chapter is devoted to appraising money, monetary policy, and finance's varied effects on the Palestinian economy. In terms of organization, the chapter is structured as follows: to situate the reader in time, Section 1 furnishes a historical overview of monetary and financial developments in Palestine. Taking 1967 as its starting point, this review covers changes introduced in the aftermath of *al-Naksa* up until the signing of the Protocol on Economic Relations between the Government of the State of Israel and the PLO (henceforth the Paris Protocol) in 1994. Section 2 begins by probing how the Paris Protocol—through assigning the Israeli state vast powers over the monetary and financial infrastructure of the Palestinian economy—consolidates conditions unconducive to the growth of the Palestinian economy while simultaneously hardwiring conditions of "weaponized interdependence" (Farrell and Newman 2019). From there, it considers the developmental costs incurred as direct and indirect result. Finally, in the conclusion, the focus is turned inward to spotlight some financial effects induced through the Palestinian National Authority (PNA) and Palestine Monetary Authority's (PMA) attempts at navigating the post-Paris Protocol world.

Section 1: Currencies and Credit from al-Naksa to Oslo

Following Israel's swift victory in the war of June 1967, governance of the occupied Gaza Strip and West Bank was assigned to a freshly established Military Governorate, initially under the command of Belfast-born Chaim Hertzog. This division of the Israeli Army went on to unilaterally rule these parts of the occupied Palestinian territories (oPt) until 1981, at which point the Governorate was dissolved and replaced by a second entity called the Coordinator of Government Activities in the Territories

(COGAT). Still nested within the Ministry of Defense, COGAT was little different from its predecessor in substance. Its Civil Administration—directed in the final instance by officers from the military and Shin Bet—would serve as the public face of the Israeli state in the West Bank and Gaza through 1994.

Regardless of institutional form, the Israeli military's governance of economic matters was conducted in lockstep with elected governments and the Bank of Israel. Entrusted as Examiners of Banks within the oPt since the foundation of the Governorate, military personnel were empowered to administer prudential regulations; given jurisdiction over interest rate ceilings and the cross-border movement of foreign exchange; and granted discretion over the issuing of bank licenses, the liquidation of banks, and the freezing of accounts. Acting at one and the same time as a local surrogate for the central bank back in West Jerusalem and as an independent authority vested with wide powers within its designated geographic dominion, the army altered the order of economic life in the occupied territories *in toto*.

Over the course of its fourteen-year tenure, the Military Governorate issued 122 orders for the purpose of regulating monetary and banking activities.[1] Counted among the first—Orders 7, 18, 26, and 30—were those that shuttered (nearly all) the operations of the ten commercial banks hitherto managing thirty branches inside of the West Bank and Gaza, twenty-six of which were located in the West Bank.[2] Announced shortly thereafter and sending shock waves of a near equal size were orders installed to settle the currency question: A succession of military diktats established the Israeli pound as legal tender throughout the occupied territories, allowed the continued circulation and convertibility of the Jordanian dinar within the West Bank, and declared the Egyptian pound illegal.

The impact of these decisions was, expectantly, profound. Beyond the confusion and dislocation introduced through the abrupt monetary transition, the referenced changes to currency policy actuated a number of structural changes to economic life in the oPt. In the most immediate sense, they exposed Palestinians to the volatile monetary conditions which beset the Israeli economy up until the late 1980s. The availability of the Jordanian dinar in the West Bank and US dollar in both the West Bank and Gaza did, of course, furnish firms and households with alternative units of account and stores of wealth, even if the military's seizure of undeclared cross-border FX transfers always limited the supply of dinars to some degree (UNCTAD and ESCAWA 1989, 37). Regardless, Palestine and Palestinians had no surefire way of avoiding the uncertainty and wealth losses presented by the inflationary and hyperinflationary pulses running rampant inside the house of the occupier. This stemmed from the coalescence of three material facts, which together rendered the Israeli pound the primary means of exchange within the oPt: (1) a significant percentage of the Palestinian population secured its employment and wage either inside 1948 Israel or with the military government and was therefore paid in Israeli pounds; (2) dependency induced through the Open Bridges policy forced the oPt to import an enormous share of its goods and services from Israel; and (3) the stateless subjects of the oPt were obligated to pay their taxes in the currency of their foreign sovereign. Wealth and income losses incurred through the enforced use of the Israeli pound, moreover, were hardly the only corrosive consequence of monetary colonization. Colonization also meant that the vagaries credit and FX conditions in the oPt were decided by a central bank neither accountable to its people nor bearing any concern with their particular interests. Suffering the effects of second-hand inflation was, as a result, only the tip of the iceberg when it came to currency issues.

The damage caused to persons, firms, and the broader macroeconomy by dint of their being deprived of financial services was even more pronounced. This is not, of course, to say that credit intermediation prior to 1967 had been fully satisfactory.[3] Significant, however, as the shortcomings of the financial system in the oPt were before *al-Naksa*, it was the case that the West Bank in particular became host to a relatively well-functioning banking system as of the mid-1960s. By this juncture, aggregate deposits in local banks had crossed JD 14 million, the loan-deposit ratio in the banking sector was a healthy 71 percent, and aggregate assets of bank branches exceeded JD 15 million. To one degree or another, the extension of credit money was also helping facilitate the growth of tourism, trade, and small-scale manufacturing and agricultural industries (UNCTAD and ESCWA 1989, 34).

To disastrous effect, all this (uneven) progress was to be rapidly swept into the dustbin of history upon the commencement of the Israeli occupation. From the day the aforementioned military orders were announced until court victories in 1981 and 1986 secured a partial reversal of the orders' terms,[4] the domestic commercial banking industry was, for all effects and purposes, disappeared. The only institution retaining a degree of presence in the oPt was Arab Bank: Though disallowed like its peers from advancing loans or credit facilities to persons and companies in the West Bank, an Arab Bank branch in Nablus continued to accept deposits by way of opening new accounts for customers at sister branches in Amman and then transferring funds on their behalf. Derisked by way of Jordanian state guarantees and cofinancing arrangements organized by a specialized public institution then owned by the Jordanian government—namely, the Towns and Villages Development Bank—Arab Bank also managed to extend long-term loans to West Bank municipalities during the 1970s and early 1980s. Beyond that, however, no commercial banking was done by the local and foreign firms previously populating the sector. What is more, with the exception of the Towns and Villages Development Bank, these years also saw state-owned Jordanian financial institutions previously playing a critical if inadequate investment role in the West Bank—the Jordanian Agricultural Credit Corporation and the Industrial Development Bank most importantly—largely cease to operate.

Instances of impressive ingenuity notwithstanding, the vacuum of financial services created through the shuttering of the domestic banking sector could never be more than partially filled by *local* hands. Supplies dealers and agricultural cooperatives stepped up to provide seasonal loans to farmers in need—the cooperatives' facilities capitalized with funds sent by the US-based NGO American Near East Refugee Aid (ANERA) and the Jordanian-Palestinian Committee—though lacked the funds for extending lines of credit for long-term capital investment.[5] Along with the Housing Bank of Jordan, ANERA furnished some lending for housing construction and repair as well, though never at a level commensurate with need. Licensed and unlicensed money changers expanded their remits beyond currency exchange operations to provide services for remittance transfers, salary payments (for those employed by the

Jordanian state), deposit acceptance and storage, check cashing, and even short-term liquidity support. Lending at scale or at maturities in excess of a few months, however, was never in the cards (UNCTAD and ESCWA 1989, 56–64).

Interventions from the outside hardly helped plug the caps in the credit market, either. Israeli commercial banks ushered in on the back of the army's guns did, of course, step in to take deposits (including JD denominated ones) and provide some overdraft facilities and trade financing, albeit at exceedingly high interest rates and with sizable service fees tacked on. Beyond that, and despite having recourse to generous government guarantees on any loan issued in the oPt, these institutions largely refused to lend to the Palestinian economy: Using capital furnished by Palestinian subjects in the form of deposits to finance investment inside Israel and boost the country's foreign reserves, Israeli banks maintained deposit to loan ratios of just 10 percent in the oPt throughout their years of operation (UNCTAD and ESCWA 1989, 38–48).

It is difficult to overstate what a financial system rendered so patchy, informal, undercapitalized, and investment averse did to Palestine's real economy. The dissolution of commercial banking and the capital flight it precipitated brought about a near total collapse in fixed capital formation. In conjunction with effects introduced through a number of other Israeli policy initiatives—including the neglect of infrastructure, the flooding of the domestic market with final consumer goods and durables, and the extracting of the labor supply for employment in Israel—this collapse atrophied Palestine's productive base substantially (Roy 1987). In expediting the economy's premature dependence on final consumption, it also calcified structural distortions, which would constitute a semi-permanent impediment to economic growth henceforth. Hand in glove with Israel's attempts at obstructing the education of the occupied population, the hollowing of the financial sector would undergird to the Palestinian economy's increasing drift from the global technological frontier as well (Raz 2019; Shikaki 2021).

Section 2: Undermining Growth and Weaponizing Interdependence in the Present Day

In such a state was the Palestinian economy when the Rabin government, keen to extricate itself from the multilateral strictures imposed at the Madrid Conference of 1991, began bilateral negotiations with the lieutenants of Yasser Arafat in January 1993 with an eye on an interim political settlement. The economic aspects of the agreement reached at the end of these negotiations were decided through separate, highly mediated discussions held in Paris between late 1993 and early 1994. As was confessed by relevant principals, the Palestinian delegation dispatched to the French capital for these discussions was undermanned and admittedly underprepared (Merrino 2021). Per Haddad, the team also had the distinct disadvantage of sitting across the table from counterparts whose positions had the full backing of the US State Department and World Bank (Haddad 2016). Circumstance being as they were, that

Palestinian representatives ultimately proved unable to deliver a deal in the interest of the Palestinian people was something of a foregone conclusion.

On the monetary and financial front, arrangements established in the Paris Protocol structurally compromise the economies of the West Bank and Gaza in the post-Oslo period in two main ways. First, they deprive the Palestinian Monetary Authority, legally and materially, of conventional and unconventional monetary powers. Though central banking's developmental utility for Palestine would be limited regardless of the Paris Protocol—a reality of life for those with a subordinate position within regional and global economies (Alami 2019; Musthaq 2023)—denying Palestine's demi-state essential levers for managing the economy can nevertheless be shown to exert acutely negative effects. Second, the arrangements in question impose the condition of weaponized interdependence onto Palestine's payment infrastructure. Equipping the Israeli state to assert what Farrell and Newman describe as panopticon and chokepoint effects, weaponized interdependence puts Palestine's financial house in a state of constant existential peril while also allowing for more mundane forms of resource expropriation.

Conducting Monetary Policy without Monetary Policy Tools

Central banks possess distinct policy instruments, which may be deployed across a number of sites critical to an economy's functioning. One of the most important of these sites is the market for credit, where, depending on the structure of the national financial system, a central bank may take an assortment of "indirect" actions to affect short-term interest rates and, by extension, a country's money supply. The relation between the money supply and real economic activity, aggregate demand, inflation, and the distribution of income and wealth is, of course, ambiguous: It is a relation necessarily moderated by a host of other variables. Be that as it may, influencing the price of credit money represents a powerful mechanism for impacting dynamics of growth, employment, pricing, and inequality.

Due to a constellation of conditions—most of which derive from terms established in Article IV of the Paris Protocol—the PMA retains a limited capacity to act upon the credit market. Three provisions specified in Article IV are most salient to these limitations: The first designated that the New Israeli Shekel (NIS) would be one of the circulating currencies in the oPt, and that public and private institutions in the oPt must accept the NIS as a means of payment for any transaction; the second stipulated that Palestinian imports from both the outside world and from Israel be priced in NIS; and the third conditioned the possibility of an independent Palestinian currency on Israeli consent, the latter of which would need to be officially expressed via the Palestinian-Israeli Joint Economic Committee. Seen in the aggregate, the effect of these provisions was to create a monetary union, albeit one directed exclusively by the Bank of Israel.

Shekelization of the Palestinian economy functions to deny the PMA access to the credit market across many of the market's traditional entry points. Though empowered under the letter of Protocol law to operate a discount window,[6] the PMA's ability to do so is circumscribed by the size of its balance sheet—more specifically, by the volume of reserves it accumulates. This restraint follows from the fact that the PMA, lacking the power to issue legal tender currency, cannot simply create money out of thin air. The PMA's accumulation of reserves, meanwhile, is structurally bounded by Palestine's recurring current account deficits. These deficits are significant in magnitude and themselves overdetermined, both by alternative aspects of the Protocol itself and by Israel's unilateral violations of the Protocol (UNCTAD 2012). Materially, their effect is to refuse the PMA the resources required to safely operate a discount window. As is such, the PMA cannot use one of the primary means through which monetary authorities define a benchmark for credit markets.

In much the same way, the prospect of influencing interest rates through the interbank money market is at once legally possible and practically nonfeasible for the PMA. In this instance, policy transmission falters on the back of Palestine's low levels of bank-to-bank lending. These levels stem in large part from Jordanian chartered banks having recourse to home offices for their short-term liquidity needs (Hamed 2004). They also stem, however, from the tendency that locally operating banks demonstrate toward hoarding cash, which is itself partially a response to the high-risk business environment that the Israeli state purposefully cultivates (Nasir et al. 2012). Regardless of provenance, the effect from these low levels of lending is unchanged: the interbank lending is too marginal to the financial system's workings for PMA interventions to impact short-term interest rates.

Similarly off the table are open market operations, which represent the main instrument by which central banks in market-based financial systems indirectly affect interest rates. The reasons for this are perhaps obvious: The PNA has to date been unable to issue government securities, chiefly as a result of the economy's aforementioned external imbalances, the authority's weak and unpredictable revenue streams, *and* the legal risks that are presented by Hamas—designated as a terrorist organization in most Western capitals—potentially taking over the PNA. Nonissuance of treasuries is a problem in that the execution of open market operations—that is, a central banks' buying and selling of fixed-income assets with the intention of affecting liquidity conditions and the price of credit—presupposes the existence of highly liquid markets for either sovereign debt or an asset type equally able to function as collateral. Without the issuance of treasuries, no such markets have come into being, and without such markets, there can be no open market operations. This instrument too being unavailable, the PMA is left with but a singular tool for impacting credit conditions: reserve requirements. In adjusting the ratio of reserves to deposits that commercial banks must hold—and setting different ratios depending on asset classes and types of investment—the PMA can attempt to indirectly influence the supply side of the market for credit money. Doing so through this mechanism, however, infringes upon the PMA's ability to fulfill its mandate for prudential regulation, as will be discussed later.

Aside from closing down its options in the credit channel, the noncontrol of currency issuance naturally also disbars the PMA from conducting a second prerogative of a sovereign monetary authority: exchange rate policy. In this domain, the PMA does not just have limited power but no power at all, fully captive as it is to decisions rendered by the Bank of Israel. Freedom of maneuver in administering the third of its conventional prerogatives—prudential regulations—is also substantially compromised by the

Protocol, if indirectly so. First, by forcing the PMA to rely on reserve requirements to move credit markets, the Protocol paints Palestinian policymakers into a corner where overseeing the health of the wider financial system can only but become a lesser priority. This is because juicing the flow of credit via cutting reserve requirements by definition implies a rise in long-term systemic risk for the financial sector. The PMA's ability to honor responsibilities related to prudential regulations is also subverted by the Protocol vesting the Israeli state with control over critical chokepoints within the PNA revenue system: While granting the PNA power over the specification and collection of taxes within Areas A and B of the West Bank—be those taxes levied on business transactions, income, capital gains, asset sales, or anything else—the Protocol delegates Israel control over all other elements of Palestinian tax collection.[7] Consequentially, the proportion of PNA revenues that first run through the hands of the Israeli state is in the area of 70–75 percent (Iqtait 2021). By withholding the timely transfer of the amounts in question, the Israeli state can swiftly precipitate a liquidity crisis for the PNA. Such a crisis redounds onto the PMA and its prudential mandate by leaving the institution with little choice but to acquiesce to violations of exposure limits put in place to regulate the banking sector's accumulation of public sector debts.

Lastly as relates to conventional prerogatives, note that the PMA is again deeply hamstrung when it comes to the supporting of public finances. Deprived by law and other means from issuing government securities, the PMA can make no contribution to the diversification of the state's revenue streams. The absence of a secondary market for government securities also means the PMA cannot indirectly monetize the state debts through open market operations. Lacking currency issuance power, the institution's facility for directly financing the PNA's deficits is exceedingly limited, too.[8]

Turning to unconventional prerogatives and policies, by dint of many of the causes already foregrounded, the PMA's capacity to execute mandates once thought the preserve of emergency times though now increasingly central to monetary authorities' everyday remits is narrowly delimited. Devoid of money-creating powers or an asset portfolio of a sufficient magnitude, the PMA cannot act as a lender of last resort beyond a defined threshold. By extension, it cannot act as a buyer, dealer, or market maker of last resort either. One can debate, of course, whether unconventional interventions of these types ultimately serve to generate beneficent effects for anyone beyond those in the financial sector or with exposure to asset markets (Musthaq 2021). That they have demonstrated a decisive effect on countries' differential abilities to absorb financial shocks—and thereby a significant effect on the wealth of nations in the final instance—is, however, beyond dispute.

Weaponizing Interdependence

The Paris Protocol does not only deprive the PMA of powers and instruments needed to conduct monetary policy: it also structures the plumbing of the payments system in a manner institutionalizing weaponized interdependence.

As concerns payments, the PMA was empowered under the Protocol to oversee and administer clearing and settlement systems at a domestic level. And to the PMA's credit, a number of steps would be taken with an eye on better positioning the institution for fulfilling these tasks.[9] All these efforts have certainly streamlined local payment processes and addressed some of the blockage points creating cash flow and liquidity-related issues. They have not, however, provided an infrastructural workaround of, or alternative to, the system handling cross-border transactions with Israel. And it is from this system that the conditions of weaponized interdependence derive.

Though the Paris Protocol stipulates cross-border transactions be processed through the coordination of Israeli and Palestinian clearance houses, failure to actually integrate clearing houses on both sides of Green Line has meant such transactions run via Palestinian banks establishing correspondent banking relationships (CBRs) with Israeli counterparts. Functionally, this arrangement means that Israeli banks act as the Palestinian banks' conduit to the Israeli economy, and, to a large degree, to the outside world. As such, public and private Palestinian actors' ability to execute an import transaction, receive a capital inflow, or transfer excess liquidity ultimately hinges upon Israeli financial institutions choosing not to jam up the cross-border channel. Certainly, the inverse is also true: A Palestinian financial institution could itself theoretically block the payments' channel. The relative marginality of Palestine to the Israeli economy, however, renders the consequence of such a prospective action less meaningful to their Israeli peers: Averaging at approximately NIS 44 billion per year, payment activity between Israel, the West Bank, and Gaza equates to roughly 80 percent Palestine's GDP but just 3.6 percent the GDP of Israel (Toffano and Yuan 2019). Given the imbalance, interdependence can be seen to belie a relation of power, and Israeli dominance.

Developmental Costs Incurred

The development costs incurred to Palestine on the monetary front are diverse and sizable. To begin, restraints on the PMA's ability to indirectly affect the supply of credit to the economy imbricate Palestine's low levels of investment. Recall that the benchmark for interest rates in the oPt since the dawning of the two-state solution era has been (predominantly) set by the Bank of Israel. For its part, through the mid-2000s, the Bank of Israel showed itself to be committed to aggressively fighting inflation and seeking credibility in international capital markets. By consequence, the benchmark in question ran between the low and high teens up until 2003 before tracking steadily downward thereafter, with credit conditions inside Israel increasingly converging upon those witnessed within much of the Global North during the post-financial crisis age of cheap money.

Interest rates in Palestine are generally coming in at twice the rates on offer in Israel due to the cost of credit money inside the oPt being mediated by the vast legal and material apparatus through which the Israel Army manipulates the country's business climate. Beyond being subject to a risk premium, interest rates in the oPt are of course further elevated by the noncompetitive nature of the commercial banking sector. This all being the case, the effects of the expansionary turn in Israeli monetary policy have always been somewhat muted for Palestinians. During the years when the Bank of Israel (BoI) established its monetarist bona fides—the 1990s–early 2000s—the price of debt in Palestine exceeded 20 percent, with marginally cheaper rates available for

USD- and JD-denominated loans. When the BoI turned to a sustained loosening of monetary conditions post-2012—a time during which the NIS's appreciation against the USD and JD did not cease, leading Palestinians to increasingly seek out NIS-denominated debts as a way of hedging against foreign exchange losses—rates still settled between roughly 7 and 9 percent. Given market conditions and the occupation's dexterity in disrupting any business's revenue stream, such borrowing costs have proven prohibitively high for a great many enterprises.

The pass-through effects of these firms staying away from debt markets are significant. Unable or unwilling to finance investments, levels of fixed capital formation have remained consistently and dangerously depressed. Compounded by capital depreciation, the relative withering of industrial capacity has kept potential output low, which has in turn restricted the economy's capacity to create jobs. At the macro level, meanwhile, private-sector disinvestment has left aggregate demand structurally dependent upon final consumption, final consumption that is today increasingly sustained by debt and the expenditures of the PNA.

Certainly, it would be naive to presume that a truly sovereign PMA might unilaterally resolve Palestine's investment issues and, through them, unleash a productivity boom. Issue its own currency or not, the need to attract and retain foreign investment will always put upward pressure on interest rates in Palestine, as it does everywhere else in the Global South. Lest the occupation be brought to an end, the investment effects of any actions the PMA might take on the supply side of the credit market would also be attenuated by enduring demand-side issues: So long as firms are unable to bring in desired inputs, develop land, access resources and infrastructure, or export freely, they will have little reason to go searching for debt—and banks will have little reason to extend it (Barnett et al. 1998). Be that as it all may, the consequence of the PMA's being made bereft within the credit market ought not be diminished. It is the case, after all, that Palestinians businesses show an extreme sensitivity to changes in the cost of credit: estimates suggest that a single percentage point increase in interest rates causes nearly 20 percent declines in private investment in the West Bank and Gaza (Awad, al-Jerashi and Alabaddi 2021). Leaving aside whether a free PMA might ever be allowed play a heroic developmental role, then, in merely rendering the institution powerless before prospective interest rate hikes, the Protocol arrangement can clearly be seen to exert unique and acutely corrosive effects.

The consequences of the PMA being unable to implement exchange rate policy have proven corrosive as well. Reflecting the movement of the Israeli economy toward the global technological frontier, as mentioned, the NIS has steadily and significantly appreciated against major international currencies over the last twenty years. This secular shift has transmitted myriad negative effects to Palestine through the mechanism of the country's real effective exchange rate (REER). Certainly, one should not discount the degree to which Palestine's REER has also been inflated throughout by the persistent receipt of high levels of capital inflows, be they in the form of international aid, remittances from abroad and Israel, and diaspora transfers. Nevertheless, the advance of the Israeli economy (and its currency) is at the heart of these dynamics and of the developmental malady that has resulted: Dutch disease.[10] For the oPt as anywhere else, Dutch disease has resulted in increased import consumption and in the country's export industries growing less sophisticated and less competitive. Both elements serve to undermine productive sectors of the economy and to worsen external imbalances. By lowering the attractiveness of investments into tradables, the overvaluation of the NIS also led to capital flows being steered into speculative nontradables, financial assets, and property most especially (Khalidi et al. 2021, 46). Expediting processes of financialization and supercharging the West Bank's property boom, such investment-related effects only intensify the macroeconomic distortions already riddling the Palestinian economy.

Strictures imposed on the PMA's recourse to unconventional policy instruments have not been without consequence either. This is most easily observed within the comparative light cast by differential monetary responses to SARS-CoV-2. At this time, global behemoths like the Federal Reserve and European Central Bank were seen to expand their respective balance sheets without apparent limit—including through directly purchasing corporate debt for the first time. Monetary authorities of peripheral countries like Tunisia, though far more restrained in action, were also able to mobilize emergency supports, typically through some form of deficit monetization. In contrast, the record shows that the PMA was largely handcuffed in terms of direct action in these crucial days, only able to institute regulatory changes like moratoriums on debt repayments and fee collections. Given the scale of growth losses that the pandemic precipitated, one can only wonder what having a lender, buyer, or market maker of last resort might have done for the Palestinian people.[11]

The PMA's being prevented from properly fulfilling prudential regulatory obligations due to Protocol-enabled circumstances has had negative developmental effects, too, despite credit-market-minded reductions in reserve requirements having yet to threaten financial instability much. By virtue of Israel regularly withholding and now systematically reducing monthly clearance revenue transfers,[12] the PNA has been pushed into frequent liquidity crises over the past decade. As the stacking of arrears owed to employees, private contractors, and the pension system has been insufficient to resolve such crises, the PMA has needed to respond to these crises by allowing limits on banks' exposure to public sector debt to be breached: As of December 2021, Palestinian banks directly held $2.5 billion worth of PA debt on their balance sheets. Factoring in the debts of PA employees, that figure jumps to $4.3 billion (World Bank 2022). Such sums are well in excess of the regulatory ceiling the PMA has defined and imperil Palestine's developmental outlook through two channels. First, they create the possibility of cascading fiscal and financial crises, whereby a PNA liquidity squeeze sets off a banking sector liquidity squeeze, which in turns sets off a run of defaults in the wider economy. Second, they crowd out private-sector lending: Able to collect relatively high returns (6 percent interest on loans to the PNA, per Merrino) through extending short- and medium-term credit lines to a demi-state driven to desperation by Israeli machinations, Palestinian commercial banks have less reason and ability to offer debt to the real economy. The second of these perils is not a prospective one haunting some unknown future but a present-day reality: the state broadly defined presently accounts for 40 percent of total banking sector credits (World Bank 2022). Crowding out is very much upon Palestine.

Effects introduced through the consolidation of weaponized interdependence within the underlying plumbing of the monetary system have proven deleterious to

Palestinian development as well. In the first instance, weaponized interdependence allowed exploitation and rent-seeking: In exchange for access to Israeli clearinghouses in the 1990s and early 2000s, Israeli banks charged their Palestinian counterparts high service fees and placed limits on transfer volumes, the second of these actions allowing for commissions on fund conveyance to be grossly inflated. In demanding excessive cash collateral for their trouble, the practices of Israeli banks also served to tie up an enormous of Palestinian capital in a kind of economic purgatory (Coalition of Women for Peace 2010). These types of practices have not ceased in more recent times. Israeli-imposed drags on Palestine's capital efficiency continue through today, most prominently through the arbitrary restrictions that are imposed on cash deposit transfers between Palestinian banks and the Bank of Israel. This policy leaves Palestinian banks with excess NIS holdings equivalent to 7.9 percent of their total assets, pulling down sector profitability substantially (World Bank 2022).

More dangerously from a developmental perspective, weaponized interdependence in the monetary system has also been leveraged for punitive purposes. In conjunction with restrictions imposed on cash movements between the West Bank and Gaza, Israeli banks' severing of correspondential relations with Gazan counterparts in 2009 allowed the Israeli state to create liquidity crises in Gaza at its discretion. It has used this power regularly since, rendering any import transaction into a minefield while subjecting firms and households to an economic climate defined by grave uncertainty and the impossibility of planning. Lest swift progress be made between the PMA and Bank of Israel as relates to the establishment of publicly owned correspondent companies, there is reason to think that the people of the West Bank may suffer the same fate soon. Under the pretext of concerns about money laundering and terrorism financing, Israeli banks began breaking off correspondential relations with their West Bank peers in 2016. This continued even after the Israeli government approved a temporary indemnity and immunity package for Israeli banks working with Palestinian counterparts in 2017—a measure since renewed on an annual basis. Should the last two Israeli banks offering services to West Bank institutions stop doing so—and correspondent services with external banks fail to be established—things could get very ugly very quickly: In the eventuality where money can only move as cash, trade will collapse, financial services will dissolve, and the PNA will approach obsolescence in short order. Weaponized interdependence in the payments system, then, is hardly a triviality.

Conclusion

Today as a century before, the character and performance of the Palestinian economy remain determined not by endogenous developments but exogenous ones. Inducing the macro and micro properties of the economy alike and vesting each with the fixity of a path dependency, the external is decisive.

That is not to say, however, that local actors are devoid of agency. The material and institutional edifice structuring the contemporary Palestinian economy did require a cosigner, after all, and found one in the coterie surrounding Yasser Arafat. If not setting the course itself, it has subsequently also been Palestinian policymakers who, in negotiating the restraints and incentives thereby imposed, accelerated the economy's drift into exceedingly hazardous waters.

Powering this drift as much as anything else has been national leadership's many attempts at harnessing finance for development, efforts in which the Palestine Monetary Authority has featured prominently. Unable to act indirectly via interest rates, the PMA imposed shifting minimum credit-deposit ratios on commercial banks in its early days of operations in hopes of juicing lending (it did away with such provisions in 2007). With an eye on keeping capital at home, the institution leveraged regulations on the percentage of deposits that could be allocated for foreign investment—set at 55 percent since 2009—and supported the establishment of a credit information system to help banks evaluate the risk of local borrowers. Seeking to facilitate innovation, the PMA also steadily rolled back regulations on the provision of credit facilities from 2008 onward (Khalidi et al. 2021, 55). Measures were taken to expedite the growth of the financial sector itself, too, including initiatives aimed at opening specific areas of the economy for credit money expansion.

Housing is of course central to this last prong of the PNA's finance promotion push. Toward facilitating its growth as a financial asset, the Palestine Mortgage and Housing Corporation was established in 1997 with World Bank support, henceforth acting as a secondary mortgage facility meant to derisk the wider lending market. Upon the ascension of Salam Fayyad, the Palestine Investment Fund (PIF)—a quasi-sovereign wealth fund of the country established in 2003 and capitalized with funds transferred from the Ministry of Finance—was enlisted into service as well: Through its subsidiary Amaar Real Estate, the PIF spearheaded mega property developments. By way of a collaborative effort backed by private partners and what was then the US Overseas Private Investment Corporation, the PIF also launched Palestine's largest mortgage lending facility (the Affordable Mortgage and Loan Program, or AMAL). Inside the PMA, meanwhile, housing financialization was advanced via the definition of a dynamic loan-to-value ratio in 2014, which, in conjunction with the onlining of the credit scoring system, rationalized and streamlined borrower evaluation and mortgage extension processes. In other domains, regulatory changes to contract and property law and land titling combined with land registration efforts led by the Land and Water Settlement Commission to subsume long-standing practices of land defense within market logics (Kohlbry 2018; Radi 2022). Where necessary, the PNA also evoked eminent domain to clear land for luxury developments, most famously in the case of Rawabi, boosting banks' housing portfolios further.

Beyond property, finance's growth would also be promoted through the diversification of lending markets. Consumer debt has been cultivated as an asset class, in part due to the vast majority's struggles with income stagnation and rising costs of living but also through the active messaging and public education campaigns, which the PNA has both greenlit and directly participated in (Harker 2020).[13] A poverty finance sector has similarly received public supports: this is evinced in the launch of an assortment of aid community-backed financial inclusion schemes as much as it is in the many ways through which the PNA has promoted microfinance-styled programs, whether by lowering reserve requirements for loans to small and microenterprises, directing public lending facilities, or granting private entities a lax regulatory environment.

If misguided in any context, the bet on finance in Palestine was especially reckless. Encountering an environment carefully curated to ensure industry and agriculture cannot scale, the guidance of the profit rate, after all, could only ever but direct credit money to what Shikaki and Springer have called "occupation circumventing activities"—and that is without investment into those same activities being expressly encouraged through policy, as it has been (Shikaki and Springer 2015). The consequence of the modality of credit intermediation thereby fostered has proven predictably disastrous: Worse than merely going bust, the PNA's wager on finance created all kinds of novel pathologies. Developmentally, they include: (1) the hypertrophy of the nontradables sector, expressed most obviously through the extreme housing valuations observed in parts of Area A in the West Bank (Khalidi et al. 2021); (2) macroeconomic dysmorphia, actuated through the financial sector's disproportionate growth and evinced in the decoupling of finance's profit rate from wider economic conditions; (3) structural divestment from domestic agriculture and manufacturing, as attested by 74 percent gross fixed capital formation concentrating in the built environment between 2008 and 2021; (4) accelerating the economy's premature transition into service sector-biased growth; (5) consolidating a *dukan* nation via microenterprise support, wherever more low-productivity firms fight to service a domestic market with relatively fixed demand; and (6) deepening aggregate demand's dependence on final consumption. On the social front, meanwhile, consequences count rising income and wealth inequality, mass joblessness, a stark expansion of formal and informal debt relations, and a housing crisis for the nonwealthy, to name but a few.

These tragic returns on investment in many ways encapsulate what have been the defining properties of economic life in Palestine during the post-Oslo period. On the one hand, conditions imposed through Israeli settler colonialism hem in the possible and elicit structural changes nonconducive to development. On the other hand, remedies selected to treat the problems thereby arising often only serve to make ailments worse—and to trigger unpredictable processes of metastasis.

This chapter has attempted to cast light on how such dynamics have and continue to play out in the domains of money and finance. Due to the relative size and reach of the Palestinian financial sector today, it should be clear that what goes on in these domains has now become elemental to all the major questions of social, economic, and political life in Palestine. If not too big to fail, these matters are certainly too big to ignore.

Notes

1. Within annexed East Jerusalem, the activities in question were immediately made subject to the financial legislation prevailing within Israel's post-1948 borders.
2. At this time, all extant accounts with the banks in question were frozen and all cash deposits transferred to the Bank of Israel, where they were held in accounts designated in the respective banks' names. See Shikaki (2019, 35).
3. Excepting the Bank of Alexandria, Arab Bank, and the Shawwa family's Bank of Palestine—the latter of which restricted operations to the financing of trade—the Palestinian banking sector forewent any effort at extended services within Gaza

throughout the years in question. Major foreign banks operating in 1948 Israel and the West Bank, meanwhile, had always "refrained from financing any local investment," repatriating abroad whatever capital remained in excess of their short-term cash and payment needs. And indiscriminate of place of domicile, all locally operating financial institutions evinced a tendency toward avoiding lending for productive activities, especially when it came to the agrarian economy.

4   The legal cases in question cleared the way for Bank of Palestine and Cairo-Amman Bank, respectively, to relaunch some lending operations in Gaza and the West Bank. Even after greenlit to reopen its doors, the desperate nature of the business climate and the need to clear any potential investment with the military authorities saw both institutions avoid extending loans of a maturity greater than ten months throughout the remainder of the 1980s, though.

5   After the Likud's rise to power in 1977, Palestinian farmers also evinced a disinclination toward investment, fearful that their land might soon be expropriated.

6   Through a discount window facility, central banks furnish domestic commercial banks with a theoretically unlimited source of short-term credit designated at escalating interest rates.

7   Charged with administering the Israeli-Palestinian customs' union, it is saliently Israeli tax authorities who collect import taxes on the behalf of the PNA. It also the Israeli tax authorities who collect value-added taxes on goods and services sold by Palestinian firms inside of Israel and who collect income taxes levied on Palestinian laborers working side both 1948 Israel and West Bank settlements. The Israeli state retains 25 percent the sum raised by taxes on Palestinian wages inside 1948 Israel.

8   The PNA's ability to stimulate the economy via deficit spending is itself limited by Law no. 24 of 2005, which defined a public debt ceiling of 40 percent GDP.

9   The BURAQ system, which is comprised of a Real-Time Gross Settlement System and an Automatic Clearing House Module, was inaugurated in 2010, considerably abbreviating the time required to clear checks and transfer funds and credit between accounts with local banks. The National Switch was launched in 2015, expediting transfer time for card-based transactions and facilitating the use of electronic retail payments. Decree Law no. 17 of 2012 was passed, lending clarity as concerns the PMA's precise powers and responsibilities. The following year, a Payment Systems Oversight Unit (PSOU) was established as well, charged not only with reducing risk attaining to large value and retail transactions and the clearance of securities and remittances but also with implementing other key PMA objectives like ones related to money laundering and terrorism financing. More recently and in accordance with the National Payment Development Strategy 2018–23, a number of steps have also been taken to further build up the back and front ends of the digital payments system, inclusive of (worrisome) efforts for promoting and a nascent fintech sector. See: Toffano and Yuan 2019.

10 The real exchange rate in the West Bank and Gaza jumped by 10 percent in 2021 alone, suggesting these exchange rate-related dynamics are set to get even worse in the era of the coronavirus.

11 The Palestinian economy contracted by 11.3 percent GDP in 2020. Recovery in 2021 and 2022 has been relatively weak, set back considerably of course by Israel's bombing of Gaza in the spring of 2021.

12 Since 1997, Israel has suspended clearance transfers on eight occasions for periods lasting between one month and two years. The most recent suspension of transfers was in April 2015. Beginning in 2012, Israel also began unilaterally deducting

from clearance revenue transfers. Initially, it did so to pay off Israeli electricity and water firms for debts owed by Palestinian municipalities. In 2019, Israel also began implementing terms of a law passed in July 2018, which stipulated that tax authorities reduce from the clearance transfers sums equivalent to what the PA pays into the Martyrs' Fund, the latter of which predominantly supports Palestinians in Israeli prisons. As of August 2021, Israel was reducing NIS 100 million per month from clearance revenue transfers.

13 The volume of personal consumer loans, which exclude loans for housing and automobiles, grew 2000 percent between 2008 and 2021. See Khalidi et al. (2021, 56).

References

Alami, Ilias (2019), *Money Power and Financial Capital in Emerging Markets: Facing the Tsunami*. Oxon: Routledge.

Alimahomed-Wilson, Jake and Spencer Louis Potiker (2017), "The Logistics of Occupation: Israel's Colonial Suppression of Palestine's Goods Movement Infrastructure." *Journal of Labor and Society*, 20 (4): 427–47.

Awad, Ibrahim, Ghada al-Jerashi, and Zaid Alabaddi (2021), "Determinants of Private Domestic Investment in Palestine: Time Series Analysis." *Journal of Business and Socioeconomic Development*, 1 (1): 71–86.

Barnett, Steven, Dale Chua, Nur Calika, Oussama Kanaan, and Milan Zavadjil (1998), "Monetary Policy in the West Bank and Gaza Strip in the Absence of a Domestic Currency." In *The Economy of the West Bank and Gaza*. Washington, DC: International Monetary Fund.

Coalition of Women for Peace (2010), "Financing the Israeli Occupation: The Direct Involvement of Israeli Banks in Illegal Settlement Activity and Control Over the Palestinian Banking Market." *Report: Who Profits From the Occupation*.

Cobham, David and Nu'man Kanafani (eds.) (2004), *The Economics of Palestine: Economic Policy and Institutional Reform for a Viable Palestinian State*. London: Routledge.

Dana, Tariq (2020), "Crony Capitalism in the Palestinian Authority: A Deal Among Friends." *Third World Quarterly*, 41 (2): 247–63.

Farrell, Henry and Abraham L. Newman (2019), "Weaponized Interdependence: How Global Economic Networks Shape State Coercion." *International Security*, 44 (1): 42–79.

Haddad, Toufic (2016), *Palestine Ltd.: Neoliberalism and Nationalism in the Occupied Territory*. London and New York: IB Tauris.

Hamed, Osama (2004), "The Role of the Financial Sector." In David Cobham and Nu'man Kanafani (eds.), *The Economics of Palestine: Economic Policy and Institutional Reform for a Viable Palestinian State*, 93–106. London: Routledge.

Harker, Christopher (2020), *Spacing Debt: Obligations, Violence, and Endurance in Ramallah*. Palestine: Durham: Duke University Press.

Hilal, Jamal (1976), "Class Transformation in the West Bank and Gaza." *Middle East Research and Information Project (MERIP) Reports*, 53: 9–15.

Iqtait, Anas (2021), "The Palestinian Authority Political Economy: The Architecture of Fiscal Control." In Alaa Tartir, Tariq dana, and Timothy Seidel (eds.), *Political Economy of Palestine*. London: Palgrave Macmillan.

Khalidi, Raja et al. (2019), "Political Economy Analysis of the Palestinian Private Sector." *Report, Palestine Economic Policy Research Institute (MAS)*.

Khalidi, Raja et al. (2021), "Prospects for Development in Palestine: Weathering the Storm, Mobilizing Together." *Report, Palestine Economic Policy Research Institute (MAS)*.

Kohlbry, Paul (2018), "Owning the Homeland: Property, Markets and Land Defense in the West Bank." *Journal of Palestine Studies*, 47 (4): 30–45.

Merrino, Serena (2021), "Currency and Settler Colonialism: The Palestinian Case." *Review of International Political Economy*, 28 (6): 1729–50.

Mitter, Sreemati (2014), *A History of Money in Palestine: Form the 1990s to the Present*. PhD Dissertation, Harvard University.

Musthaq, Fathimath (2021), "Dependency in a Financialised Global Economy." *Review of African Political Economy*, 48 (167): 15–31.

Musthaq, Fathimath (2023), "Unconventional Central Banking and the Politics of Liquidity." *Review of International Political Economy*, 30(1): 281–306.

Nasir, John et al. (2012), "West Bank and Gaza: Towards Economic Sustainability of a Future Palestinian State: Promoting Private Sector-led Growth." *Report*. World Bank.

Radi, Tareq (2022), "Cultivating Credit: Financialized Urbanization is Alienation!" *Journal for Palestine Studies*, 51 (1): 4–26.

Raz, Adam (2019), "'The Formation of an Educated Class Must be Averted': How Israel Marginalized Arabs From the Start." *Haaretz*, March 28.

Roy, Sara (1987), "The Gaza Strip: A Case of Economic de-development." *Journal of Palestine Studies*, 17 (1): 56–88.

Samara, Adel (1987), "The Political Economy of the West Bank Peasants Under the Israeli Occupation: From Peripheralization to Development 1967–1987." PhD Diss., Exeter University.

Seikaly, Sherene (2015), *Men of Capital: Scarcity and Economy in Mandate Palestine*. Stanford: Stanford University Press.

Shikaki, Ibrahim (2019), *The Political Economy of Growth and Distribution in Palestine: History, Measurement and Application*. PhD Dissertation, The New School University.

Shikaki, Ibrahim (2021), "The Political Economy of Dependency and Class Formation in the Occupied Palestinian Territories Since 1967." In Alaa Tartir, Tariq Dana, and Timothy Seidel (eds.), *Political Economy of Palestine*. London: Palgrave Macmillan.

Shikaki, Ibrahim and Joanna Springer (2015), "Building a Failed State: Palestine's Governance and Economy Delinked." *Policy Brief 21*. Al Shabaka.

Smith, Pamela Ann (1986), "The Palestinian Diaspora, 1948–1985." *Journal of Palestine Studies*, 15 (3): 90–108.

Thier, Hadas (2022), "Bitcoin Cannot Free Palestine." *Middle East Research and Information Project (MERIP)*, 303.

Toffano, Priscilla and Kathy Yuan (2019), "E-Shekels Across Borders: A Distributed Ledger System to Settle Payments Between Israel and the West Bank." *Paper: LSE Middle East Centre Paper Series*, 28: 1–36.

UNCTAD (2012), "The Palestinian Economy: Macroeconomic and Trade Policy Under Occupation." *Report*.

UNCTAD and ESCWA (1989), "The Palestinian Financial Sector Under Israeli Occupation." *Report*. United Nations.

World Bank (2022), "Economic Monitoring Report to the Ad Hoc Liaison Committee." *Report*.

Zaghah, Adel (1996), "A Monetary Alternative for the Palestinian Currency: A Palestinian Currency." *Middle East Forum*, 1: 254–63.

Zureik, Elia (1976), "Transformation of Class Structure Among the Arabs in Israel: From Peasantry to Proletariat." *Journal of Palestine Studies*, 6 (1): 39–66.

8

The Palestinian Authority

The Fiscal Contract and Structural Constraints

Anas Iqtait

Introduction: Fiscal Dimensions of Paris Protocol

Since the Palestinian Authority's (PA) inception in 1993/4, it has set up institutions that were intended to form the core of a future Palestinian state. It has established state institutions such as ministries and embassies and built a public revenue mechanism that has enabled domestic taxation and distribution of external public revenues. These taxation and public revenue policies were shaped by the parameters of the 1993 Oslo Accords, which instituted a legal framework dictating Palestinian economic activity with Israel and the rest of the world. The "Protocol on Economic Relations" (also known as the Paris Protocol), signed in 1994, regulated matters related to trade, monetary and financial issues, taxation, labor, agriculture, industry, tourism, and insurance issues. The fiscal section of the Protocol defined public revenues available to the PA. It allocated the roles and responsibilities associated with the collection of public revenues including income taxes, customs duties, value-added taxes (VAT), and petroleum excises, among others. The PA was accorded the right to extract direct and indirect taxes from the majority of Palestinians residing in the West Bank and Gaza. It further stipulated that Israel would remit taxes collected from Palestinians residing in the West Bank and Gaza levied from imports; purchases from Israeli markets; and Palestinian laborers working in Israel and settlements. These sums were to be remitted to the PA on a monthly basis after the deduction of 3 percent "handling" fee (Gaza-Jericho Agreement 1994).

The Paris Protocol envisioned fostering favorable fiscal and economic conditions for the PA to establish state institutions. It projected a sustainable tax system would be developed with foreign aid assisting in the establishment of needed infrastructure and in facilitating the provision of public services (Kanafani 2001). It further anticipated favorable developmental and growth conditions by binding the Palestinian economy to Israel's well-developed economy. These anticipated outcomes have largely not manifested. After nearly thirty years of economic engagement and integration under the Paris Protocol umbrella, the Palestinian economy and the PA's fiscal health are today dependent on Israel's political economic system of control (Tartir, Dana and Seidel 2021). Indeed, the PA's finances and Palestinian economic enterprises have never been more integrated with Israel's economy (Iqtait 2022a). While scholarship has delineated the characteristics of this integration and its consequential impact on the Palestinian economy, society, and politics, this chapter explores the fiscal dimensions concerned with this dependence and integration (Dana 2021; Hanieh 2016; Iqtait 2022b; Shikaki 2021; Taghdisi-Rad 2015; Wildeman 2019; Wildeman and Tartir 2014). In particular, this chapter investigates the politics of the PA's revenue mobilization and how it is dictated and relates to the wider political economic circumstances of the oPt.

Issues of taxation are central to the political and economic development of any state and have been particularly vital to the study of state formation among Westernized nations. It remains a central feature of the current-day study of political economics including state-society relations given the centrality of taxation in enabling public services provision, influencing state-society relations, and shaping the effectiveness of foreign aid. However, notwithstanding the depth of the existing literature and its widespread applicability, our understanding of the politics of revenue mobilization of the PA remains rudimentary (Fjeldstad and Al-Zagha 2004; Levi 1988; Moore 1998). A crucial distinction of studying the politics of revenue mobilization in the Palestinian context is the overarching settler colonial structure dictating the PA's formation and operations. This context has been a key factor in shaping the PA's ability to mobilize revenues and devise fiscal policy. Previous work by the author has explored the effects of the PA's fiscal structure on its relationship with Palestinian society, including the composition of the PA's public revenues and the Israeli fiscal structure of control over these revenues (Iqtait 2020a, 2021, 2022b). These studies highlight the need to deconstruct the political and economic context of revenue mobilization in the oPt.

While previous works have taken the fiscal composition of the PA as a starting point of analysis, this chapter shifts the focus to the dimensions shaping and hindering the formation of a fiscal contract between the PA and Palestinians. Building and contributing to the literature of fiscal sociology and fiscal theories of governance, it argues that the PA's inability to formulate a fiscal contract with its society can be shaped by structural constraints. These include the external nature of the PA's "state-building" process, the proliferation of public service providers, the PA's sources of external income, and Israeli extraction of taxes in the oPt.

The main objective of this chapter is to provide a better understanding of the structural constraints that may be impacting the formation of a fiscal contract in the oPt. This is a crucial topic because understanding the politics of fiscal mobilization in the oPt can shed light on the inner workings of the PA and its relationship to colonial and neoliberal control structures. This is especially relevant in light of the declining aid flows and the increasing pressure on the PA to rely on domestic taxation. The chapter presents four arguments in an effort to understand this topic, but it also recognizes that this is just the starting point for further research on the subject. By examining the fiscal-historical and fiscal-political connections, this chapter aims to provide a deeper understanding of the PA's fiscal affairs under enduring settler colonialism.

State Revenues and the Fiscal Contract

Sources of state revenue are fundamental in understanding patterns of policymaking and state-society relations. Scholars have long argued that state revenues are one of the best starting points for an investigation of society and its political life (Schumpeter 1991). Margaret Levi contended that "the history of state revenue production is the history of the evolution of the state" (Levi 1988). Levi defined revenue as the "income of the government" and argued that "the greater the revenue of the state, the more possible it is to extend rule" (Levi 1988, 2). State revenues improve the ability of governments to shape the institutions of the state, to expand the domain of those institutions, and to expand the provision of public goods through the state (Levi 1988; Schumpeter 1991).

The relationship between the government and the governed can further be used to help explain public policy outcomes and the emergence of a fiscal contract. Fiscal theories of governance, which are largely derived from Western historical experiences, investigate this relationship and argue two main points. The first is that the shape political institutions assume reflects a government's need for revenue (Bates and Lien 1985; Levi 1988; Moore 1995; Hoffman and Gibson 2005). Only when a government is dependent on its citizens for revenue does it have the incentive to defer to its citizens' policy preferences (Moore 1998). The second is that taxpayers benefit from government policies roughly in proportion with the share of government revenue they finance (Hoffman and Gibson 2005; Sacks 2012). In accordance with this point, comparative historical scholarship shows that governments have incentives to accord citizens representation and provide them with public goods. In return, it is argued that citizens are more likely to comply with tax demands when representation and public goods are provided. Both are further likely to reduce the costs to governments associated with ensuring compliance (Levi 1988; Sacks 2012). There is also strong evidence to suggest that governments which rely on a wide range of taxes are more likely to establish a fiscal contract with citizens (Bergman 2003; Fjeldstad and Semboja 2001; Guyer 1992; Levi and Sacks 2009; Lieberman 2001; Sacks 2012).

Fiscal theories of governance were largely constructed from observations of Western experiences of taxation and state formation. However, fiscal dimensions of governance vary in non-tax-dependent and non-Western states. For example, rentier states derive the majority of their revenue from external funds, such as the sale of oil and natural gas. In these states, external funds impede the development of a representative form of governance as they reduce the dependence of the government on the governed (Ross 2001; Tornell and Lane 1998). Rentier governments are autonomous from citizens because the "state apparatus, and the people who control it, have a 'guaranteed' source of income that makes them independent of their citizens" (Moore 2004, 306).

Ross argued that there are three causal mechanisms that engender authoritarian rule from dependence on oil and mineral wealth (Ross 2001). The first is the rentier effect, whereby the absence of wide taxation in society, large-scale spending on patronage, and forceful inhibition of the formation of societal groups keep society disengaged and buy political acquiescence for the state. The second is the "repression effect," whereby rentier income leads to the creation of a repressive apparatus either for containing local dissent or for protecting resource wealth from regional or ethnic conflict. The third is borrowed from modernization theory, according to which, in order for economic development to lead to democratization, a combination of societal and cultural changes must occur, mainly in educational level and occupational specialization, whereas in rentier states sociopolitical stagnation persists, inhibiting democratization (Ross 2001).

An expanding body of literature has extended the logic of rentier economics to suggest that foreign aid and other forms of political rents generate similar political incentives impeding government's incentives and efforts to generate domestic revenues through taxation (Bizhan 2018; Iqtait 2022b; Knack 2009; Moore 2001; and Svensson 2000). Smith (2008) and Morrison (2009) argued that aid and oil are both fungible and a free resource for the state. Feyzioglu, Swaroop and Zhu (1998, 54) analyzed the impact of international aid on recipient country's budgetary allocation in different components and across different sectors and found that aid was used to free up resources for the state and that "part of the funds are used for tax reduction." This evidence reaffirms earlier findings by Griffin and Enos (1970) about the likelihood that political rents lead governments to increase domestic consumption and abstain from raising domestic taxes. Moore (2001) found that political rents increase the financial autonomous nature of the state from its society by eliminating the need for taxation and consequently diverting funds as it deems necessary. Djankov, Montalvo and Reynal-Querol (2008, 171) noted that "natural resources and foreign aid share a common characteristic: they can be appropriated by corrupt politicians without having to resort to unpopular, and normally less profitable, measures like taxation."

These works help us to understand that the origin of public revenues has a pronounced effect on the structure and policies of government as well as on the establishment of a fiscal contract. Public revenues derived from taxation, as opposed to external sources of income in the form of natural resources or foreign aid, are likely to result in governments upholding their end of the fiscal contract through the provision of public services and representation. In turn, citizens are more likely to comply with tax extractions when it is linked to existing or new public services provisions. Both lead to better government and greater compliance.

Tax, Compliance, and Absence of Statehood

Theories on fiscal contracts between governments and the governed are broadly underpinned by an assumed functionality inherent within sovereign states. Less frequently investigated are fiscal contracts where statehood is limited or in instances whereby nonstate actors assume the role(s) of government. As a result the literature has a tendency to conceptualize the state as the only relevant actor engaging in the provision of public goods and taxation. Crucially this assumption underplays the contributions of donors and nonstate actors, especially in instances of limited statehood. More broadly, however, in states lacking the capacity to perform basic government functions, other actors step in to fill this gap. Such actors can include donors, nongovernment organizations (NGOs), international organizations, rebel groups, and religious institutions. These donors and nonstate actors provide essential public services including education, health care, water, electricity, infrastructure, and municipal services (Sacks 2012). Furthermore, in cases where a government operates under occupation, the occupying power and its colonial system of control plays a role in shaping the fiscal contract (Iqtait 2021).

Scholarship in the fields of governance, taxation, and compliance in developing countries can provide important insights to begin to understand how fiscal contracts operate in such cases. Willingness to comply with government extraction seems to increase when citizens observe a direct relationship between their taxes and services received (Fjeldstad and Semboja 2000). Additionally, citizens are more likely to comply with taxation when there is a positive perception of governance, even when public goods are provided by donors or nonstate actors (Krasner and Risse 2014). Compliance is further dependent on simplification and clarity; complex tax systems not only make compliance difficult but can also obscure the link between taxes and service provision (Levi and Sacks 2009).

The manner in which governments implement their authority coupled with the extent of such authority shapes the citizenry's perceptions of their government's legitimacy and, in turn, their own deference (Levi, Sacks and Tyler 2009). Two factors impact whether governments are perceived as fair and therefore deserving of compliance. The first is the perception of impartiality. Governments viewed as biased in their implementation and enforcement of taxation are likely to face increased disobedience (Fjeldstad and Semboja 2000). The second factor is the perception of influence on making policy. Political representation and meaningful community-wide consultation are likely to lead to higher compliance. An unequal distribution of income can also increase perceptions of bias by fostering objections among nonelites to being taxed to provide privileged services to elites or when nonelites believe that high-income individuals can purchase tax exemptions (Bird, Martinez-Vazquez and Torgler 2004; Levi 1988).

The earlier literature paints a broad picture of factors influencing the evolution and relationship of fiscal contracts in developing countries. It is likely that these factors play a similar role in the Palestinian context. However, a consideration of Israel's colonial system of economic control, the unique historical circumstances that accompanied the PA's establishment, and the proliferation of public service providers in Palestine are likely to also enhance our understanding of the fiscal contract in the oPt. The later segments provide a conceptual and empirical exploration of these factors.

PA Revenues and International-led State-Building

State formation in the oPt was hardly a native process. The emergence of the PA and its governing bodies was largely the outcome of an internationally led state-building agenda. Donors and international organizations, such as the World Bank, played an instrumental role in establishing and building the PA, including its public revenue systems (Wildeman and Tartir 2021). Khalidi described the involvement of donors and international organizations in the PA's economic and public sector management as "international financial trusteeship" (Khalidi 2005, 79). Donors drove an agenda influenced by institutional neoliberalism, whereby neocolonial relations of production and exchange strengthened liberal economic models that fostered state minimalism; subsequently, the PA continuously concerned itself with maximizing revenues, minimizing spending, and controlling fiscal deficits (Haddad 2016; Iqtait 2022b).

In addition to neoliberal economic policies, donor's efforts in state-building were largely securitized (Tartir 2015b). Internationally led state-building efforts of the PA were arguably implemented in two distinct waves. The first established the institutions of the PA during the Oslo process, and the second was led by the state-building and reform agenda of PA prime minister Salam Fayyad between 2007 and 2013 (Iqtait 2019). Andres Persson contends that the internationally led state-building agenda of the PA was driven by three objectives. The first was centered on security with the aim of reforming the sector and monopolizing violence by the PA. The second objective focused on expanding the PA's legitimacy through public spending and investments in public institutions. The third and final objective focused on economic development through good governance, economic liberalization, and fiscal conservatism (Persson 2018, 435). International donors disproportionally favored the security objective; as Persson explained: "The belief in the U.S. and Europe has traditionally been that only when the Palestinians were able to guarantee their own security and the security of Israel would Israel be ready for a major withdrawal from the West Bank" (Persson 2018, 426). Consistent with this approach, 27 percent of total PA expenditure between 2008 and 2017 was devoted to the security sector (Iqtait 2020a; Tartir 2017a).

Scholarship on the outcomes of the securitization of the internationally led state-building process described it as detrimental to political representativeness and an accelerant of political polarization (Bouris 2012; Lia 2007; Monaghan 2016; Sayigh 2011; Tartir 2017b). Palestinians were stripped of any level of ownership over this process, which was designed, financed, and implemented by international actors (Tartir 2015a). In turn, internationally led state-building empowered authoritarianism and insulated the PA and its political elites from those they were supposed to serve and govern—Palestinian society (El-Kurd 2019). It further instituted a governance structure dependent on the PA's collaboration with Israel in security and economic fields, which was devoid from both the larger political context and the PA's own constituents (Iqtait 2019). Therefore, the PA's domestic legitimation or the formation of a fiscal contract in the form of provision of public services and representation in exchange for taxation compliance was overlooked as an underlying policy of internationally led state-building.

PA Lacking a Monopoly over Public Goods Provision

The West Bank and Gaza are home to a multitude of donors and nonstate actors involved in the provision of public goods. These include, but are not limited to, the United Nations Relief and Works Agency; international donors such as USAID and DFID; international organizations, such as the World Bank and UNDP; international and domestic NGOs such as Care International, Save the Children, and Palestinian Red Crescent Society; Hamas de facto institutions in the Gaza Strip; and Israeli state agencies. The vast proliferation of public service providers in the oPt is driven by two factors.

The first is the historical legacy of the Israeli occupation of the West Bank and Gaza between 1967 and 1994. Underinvestment in governance and economic infrastructure during this period prompted many donors, international organizations, and Palestinian civil society to engage in public services provision (Nakhleh 1989; Mansour 1988; Roy 1998). Palestinian civil society played a leading role in this period. Civil society in sovereign states mediates and bridges relations between society and the state and, at times, provides services to marginalized or underrepresented segments of society. By definition, civil society operates under the umbrella of a national central authority (Challand 2008). In the oPt, however, civil society emerged as an alternative to the state, to compensate for the absence of a government capable of providing basic services (Al-Barghouthi 2009). When the PA was established in 1993, there were approximately 1,500 NGOs operating in the West Bank and Gaza, employing up to 30,000 people and receiving more than US$ 220 million per year in external funding (Brynen 2000).

The second factor is based on the rationale of many donors and international organizations, such as the World Bank, which generally stresses the inability of state institutions to meet basic public goods needs in addition to the greater perceived ability of civil society to identify and tailor projects to local-level needs (Edwards and Hulme 1996; Marcussen 1996; Mansuri and Rao 2004). Smith and Lipsky (1993) further argue that donors award contracts of public goods provision to private or nonstate actors to create competition where government is viewed as corrupt or inefficient. In the West Bank and Gaza, donors dedicated large sums of foreign aid to civil society often funding NGO projects, which duplicated or overlapped with PA-provided services (Iqtait 2022b; DeVoir and Tartir 2009). Since 1994, the PA competed for foreign aid disbursements against at least 3,000 Palestinian NGOs operating in the West Bank and Gaza (Atia and Herrold 2018). A 2018 study examining the evolution of NGO's technologies of governing via professionalization, bureaucratization, and upward accountability concluded that Palestinian NGOs have developed into an effective "apparatus of governing" (Atia and Herrold 2018).

Palestinians living away from urban city centers have little interaction with the PA. This limited interaction makes these regions a fertile ground for the operation of NGOs that can provide replacement governmental services through donor-funded projects. The PA's inability to provide adequate services in many areas is in part due to the arrangements stipulated in the Oslo Accords. The Accords divided the West Bank into three distinct administrative areas with Areas B and C falling under partial or complete administrative and security control of Israel. The PA's limited interaction with—and therefore governmental services provision and delivery to—Palestinians residing in Areas B and C was embedded within the political arrangements it created with Israel during the Oslo Accords.

PA Revenues: A Tale of External Income

With the creation of the PA in 1993/4, international donors envisaged the establishment of local state institutions capable of financing activities through domestic revenue. Donors had not initially envisioned the need to support the PA directly via external budgetary transfers (Beck 2000). Instead, donors sought to support long-term developmental plans for the wider Palestinian economy, which was necessary after decades of underinvestment and the confiscation of Palestinian public revenue by Israeli military authorities (Roy 1995, 192). However, by 1997 it was clear this plan had failed when donor funding had to be diverted from humanitarian and development projects to ensure the survival of the PA as it faced its first fiscal crisis. This fiscal crisis stemmed from Israel's refusal to transfer clearance revenue, which resulted in the PA's near insolvency (Mosse 2015). Subsequently, budgetary support from donors became an essential part of the PA's revenue and accounted for nearly 30 percent of all PA public revenue between 1996 and 2021 (Iqtait 2020b).

The extent to which donor funding became embedded within the PA's budgetary requirements is perhaps best reflected through an assessment of the PA's development plans. Since 1994, nine development plans have been formulated (Iqtait 2020a). The first four plans were based on donors' interests in funding humanitarian relief and infrastructural projects and were prepared by international organizations and donors in accordance with their priorities and policies. The other five development plans were thematic and focused more on structural reform and wider economic objectives. Although the plans did not include a clear funding component, they were laden with appeals to donors for foreign aid. This appeal was often juxtaposed with PA's alignment with the World Bank and other donors' priorities, such as economic and security commitments toward Israel. In the construction and research of all these plans, the Palestinian public was rarely consulted in the plan formation and drafting process (Iqtait 2020a).

In addition to donor funding, clearance revenue represents a significant component of the PA's overall available revenue. As Figure 8.1 showcases, the PA's reliance on clearance revenue has more than doubled since 1996 increasing from 25 percent of public revenue to 64 percent in 2021. Initially, clearance revenue could be mistaken for

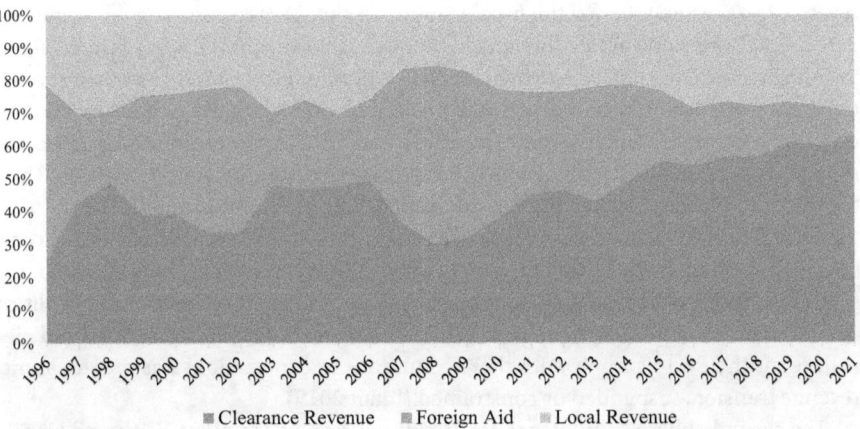

Figure 8.1 Palestinian Authority's revenue composition (including foreign aid allocated to the PA's budget) between 1996 and 2021. *Source*: Author's calculations based on data publicly available from the World Bank and IMF's reports to the Ad Hoc Liaison Committee (AHLC).

typical indirect taxes levied by states, but the conceptualization of clearance revenue as an external income to the PA stems from two notable factors.

The first notable factor is that external income is unearned, requiring little effort on behalf of the receiving government. Clearance revenue is comprised of two major components. The larger component consists of customs duties, VAT, and petroleum excises imposed on the Palestinian private economy by the Israeli government. The other component consists of income taxes imposed on Palestinian laborers working in Israel or in Israeli settlements. Both components of the clearance revenue had historically existed before the creation of the PA; the PA does not have the institutional capacity or the sovereign status to collect these taxes independently; and although Palestinian laborers working inside of Israel consume social services in the oPt, their productive output is harnessed in Israel benefiting the productivity level of the Israeli economy not the Palestinian. The second reason for conceptualizing clearance revenues as external income is the conditionalities associated with their consistent disbursement by Israel to the PA (Iqtait 2017). Israel has routinely exploited its control of the clearance revenue by withholding their transfer in exchange for political acquiescence by the PA.

Israel as a Tax Extractor

In addition to Israel playing a role in the provision of public services, primarily in the West Bank, it is extensively engaged in the extraction of direct and indirect taxes from Palestinians who reside in the West Bank and Gaza. This extraction can be divided into three spheres. The first, and most influential, is Israel's control over the clearance revenue mechanism. The clearance revenue mechanism came into effect as part of the Oslo Accords, as agreed in the Protocol of Economic Relations (UNCTAD 1994). The revenue is comprised of customs duties, VAT, petroleum excises, and income taxes of Palestinian workers in Israel and settlements. Although clearance revenue is a cornerstone for the fiscal viability of the PA (representing on average 68 percent of PA revenue before foreign aid between 1996 and 2021), it has limited ability to influence or control this mechanism. The PA's role in receiving clearance revenue transfers from Israel is mired with technical and policy-related conditionalities. In order to receive clearance revenue transfers, the PA has to continually balance two separate conditionality mechanisms. The first is a set of technical conditionalities. These technical conditions involve the PA submitting VAT and clearance bills (invoices) to the Israeli authorities to collect the tax rebate on these bills. Nondelivery of clearance bills by importers from or though Israel cost the PA treasury hundreds of millions of dollars per year (World Bank 2016). The second mechanism comprises a set of political conditionalities imposed by comprehensive economic, political, and security policies. Failure for the PA to comply with these conditions or expectations has seen clearance revenue transfers suspended or constrained (Iqtait 2019).

The second sphere of influence for Israeli taxation in the West Bank and Gaza is embodied in its taxation over Palestinian traders and trade activity. The Palestinian economy is home to more than 80,000 economic establishments operating in trade, representing more than 50 percent of all economic establishments and housing nearly 40 percent of all private sector employment (Shikaki 2021). Trade services are heavily dependent on two-way trade with Israel, with 54 percent of total imports and 89 percent of total exports in 2021 originating from Israeli market (PCBS 2022). Trade services importing from Israeli or international markets pay taxes to the Israeli government. These taxes can be in the form of import taxes and/or VAT. For example, importers from the Israeli market pay VAT to the Israeli authorities. In addition, importers from international markets pay import taxes and VAT to Israel at points of entry. In fact, the importation process is composed of eleven procedural steps, including VAT and customs payments, and only three of these producers fully or partially include the PA, with the Israeli public and private sectors processing and monitoring the entire transaction (Iqtait 2022b).

The third sphere included taxes and fees unrelated to trade activity or employment in Israel. Such fees include exit fees collected at the King Hussein/Allenby Bridge crossing—a border crossing between the West Bank and Jordan. The crossing facilitates the movement of nearly two million passengers and 57,000 truckloads of goods each year (Office of the Quartet 2021). The Paris Protocol stipulated that exit fees should be shared between the PA and Israel on 46/54 basis for the first 750,000 passengers and on a 62/38 basis for each passenger thereafter. However, Israel has on several occasions suspended the full or partial transmissions of these funds (World Bank 2020).

Conclusion: Understanding the Fiscal Contract in Palestine

This chapter has explored the contextual setting of revenue mobilization of the PA. It has demonstrated how after nearly thirty years of public revenue administration and domestic tax collection, the PA lacks the foundational context to develop a fiscal contract. While previous work on taxation and the PA assessed its administrative effectiveness and institutional capacity to develop a taxation system (Fjeldstad and Al-Zagha 2004), this chapter investigated the effects of the PA's contextual setting on the formation of a fiscal contract. Relying on an extensive review of literature on theories of fiscal governance and tax compliance, the chapter advanced four themes constraining the fiscal contract in the oPt. The internationally led state-building agenda's fixation on instilling a neoliberal economic development model as well as securitized approach to development hindered the PA's domestic legitimation or its formation of a fiscal contract. While the PA employs more than 200,000 people and provides about 25 percent of its budget in the form of social transfers, it remains one of many public service providers in the West Bank and Gaza (Iqtait 2022b). Scholarship assessing the impact of public services provision by donors and nonstate actors argues that they could reinforce the fiscal contract if providers were perceived to be associated with the state (Sacks 2012). However, in the case of the PA, a lack of presence and/or control over the majority of the oPt as well as a perceived independence of other public service providers have undermined the PA's legitimacy and ability to forge a fiscal contract.

The PA's excessive dependence on external income through both foreign aid and clearance revenue has undermined its ability to extract domestic legitimacy through taxation. The PA's dependence on foreign aid has resulted in donors exerting influence on the drafting and implementation processes of the PA's developmental policies and plans. The plans were top-down in their design and were drafted as a technical process with little public consultation. The clearance revenue mechanism, shown to form another source of external income, prevented the PA from exerting a monopoly over Palestinian taxes. Indeed, clearance revenue represents an important mechanism of Israeli control over tax extraction in the oPt. The mechanism also granted Israel de facto control over the essential trade process with Israeli and international markets. This fostered a divide between the PA and Palestinian traders and fortified pre-PA economic links between Palestinian and Israeli traders, as well as between Palestinian traders and the Israeli government. Israeli extraction of other forms of fees, such as the exit fee, further demonstrates its expansive taxation reach in the oPt.

More work is needed to determine the empirical effects of the contextual setting of the PA. However, the earlier analysis draws parallels to a wide body of literature on taxation and legitimation, which could provide avenues for further explanations. For example, individuals are likely to pay taxes when they can observe a direct relationship between their taxes and services received. It is further essential for the government to be seen as competent providers of public services. The existence of multiple services providers in the oPt and the PA's dependence on external income can have direct effects on shaping these relations. Israel's taxation is likely to increase complexity in the tax system and break down perceived links between taxes and public services provision, which is known to hinder the process of compliance.

This chapter contributes to the nascent field of fiscal sociology and fiscal governance in the oPt. Shifting the focus to the machinations dictating public revenues, taxation, and public service provision in the oPt has the potential to advance our understanding of Israel's colonial economic and fiscal system and the inner workings of the PA. It can also further contribute to the study of the politics of tax mobilization where statehood is limited or in instances where nonstate actors and occupying powers assume the role(s) of government. It is even more salient given the PA's recent push toward increased domestic taxation in an environment of diminishing foreign aid and increased Israeli deductions from clearance revenue.

References

Al-Barghouthi, Samar (2009), *The Characteristics of the Palestinian Political Elite Before and After the Establishment of the Palestinian National Authority*. Beirut: Al-Zaytouna Centre.

Atia, Mona and Catherine E. Herrold (2018), "Governing Through Patronage: The Rise of NGOs and the Fall of Civil Society in Palestine and Morocco." *VOLUNTAS: International Journal of Voluntary and Nonprofit Organizations*, 29 (5): 1044–54.

Bates, Robert H. and Da-Hsiang Donald Lien (1985), "A Note on Taxation, Development, and Representative Government." *Politics & Society*, 14 (1): 53–70.

Beck, Martin (2000), "The External Dimensions of Authoritarian Rule in Palestine." *Journal of International Relations and Development*, 3 (1): 47–66.

Bergman, Marcelo (2003), "Tax Reforms and Tax Compliance: The Divergent Paths of Chile and Argentina." *Journal of Latin American Studies*, 35 (3): 593–624.

Bird, Richard M., Jorge Martinez-Vazquez, and Benno Torgler (2004), "Societal Institutions and Tax Effort in Developing Countries." CREMA Working Paper, No. 2004-21, Center for Research in Economics, Management and the Arts (CREMA), Basel.

Bizhan, Nematullah (2017), *Aid Paradoxes in Afghanistan: Building and Undermining the State*. London: Routledge.

Bouris, Dimitris (2012), "The European Union's Role in the Palestinian Territories: State-building Through Security Sector Reform?" *European Security*, 21 (2): 257–71.

Brynen, Rex (2000), *A Very Political Economy: Peacebuilding and Foreign Aid in the West Bank and Gaza*. Washington, DC: United States Institute of Peace Press.

Challand, Benoit (2008), *Palestinian Civil Society: Foreign Donors and the Power to Promote and Exclude*. London: Routledge.

Dana, Tariq (2021), "Dominate and Pacify: Contextualizing the Political Economy of the Occupied Palestinian Territories Since 1967." In Alaa Tarir et al. (eds.), *Political Economy of Palestine*, 25–47. Cham: Palgrave Macmillan.

DeVoir, Joseph and Alaa Tartir (2009), "Tracking External Donor Funding to Palestinian Non-Governmental Organizations in the West Bank and Gaza 1999-2008." *Palestine Economic Policy Research Institute (MAS)*.

Djankov, Simeon, Jose G. Montalvo, and Marta Reynal-Querol (2008), "The Curse of aid." *Journal of Economic Growth*, 13 (3): 169–94.

Edwards, Michael and David Hulme (1996), "Too Close for Comfort? The Impact of Official Aid on Nongovernmental Organizations." *World Development*, 24 (6): 961–73.

El Kurd, Dana (2019), *Polarized and Demobilized: Legacies of Authoritarianism in Palestine*. Oxford: Oxford University Press.

Feyzioglu, Tarhan, Vinaya Swaroop, and Min Zhu (1998), "A Panel Data Analysis of the Fungibility of Foreign aid." *The World Bank Economic Review*, 12 (1): 29–58.

Fjeldstad, Odd-Helge and Adel Al-Zagha (2004), "Taxation During State Formation: Lessons From Palestine, 1994–2000." *Forum for Development Studies*, 31 (1): 89–113.

Fjeldstad, Odd-Helge and Joseph Semboja (2000), "Dilemmas of Fiscal Decentralisation: A Study of Local Government Taxation in Tanzania." *Forum for Development Studies*, 27 (1): 7–41.

Fjeldstad, Odd-Helge and Joseph Semboja (2001), "Why People Pay Taxes: The Case of the Development Levy in Tanzania." *World Development*, 29 (12): 2059–74.

Griffin, Keith B. and John L. Enos (1970), "Foreign Assistance: Objectives and Consequences." *Economic Development and Cultural change*, 18 (3): 313–27.

Guyer, Jane (1992), "Representation Without Taxation: An Essay on Democracy in Rural Nigeria, 1952–1990." *African Studies Review*, 35 (1): 41–79.

Haddad, Toufic (2016), *Palestine Ltd.: Neoliberalism and Nationalism in the Occupied Territory*. London: Bloomsbury Publishing.

Hanieh, Adam (2016), "Development as Struggle: Confronting the Reality of Power in Palestine." *Journal of Palestine Studies*, 45 (4): 32–47.

Hoffman, Barak D. and Clark C. Gibson (2005), *Fiscal Governance and Public Services: Evidence From Tanzania and Zambia*. San Diego: Department of Political Science, University of California, San Diego.

Iqtait, Anas (2017), "The Palestinian Authority and the Rentier State." *Siyasat Arabiya*, 26: 55–66.

Iqtait, Anas (2019), "The Political Economy of Taming the Palestinian Authority." In Tristan Dunning (ed.), *Palestine: Past and Present*, 145–75. New York: Nova Science Publishing.

Iqtait, Anas (2020a), "The Political Economy of Rentierism of the Palestinian Authority." PhD diss., The Australian National University.

Iqtait, Anas (2020b), "Economic Desperation and Dependence are Driving the Palestinian Authority's Political Decisions." *Middle East Institute*, December 2. https://www.mei.edu/publications/economic-desperation-and-dependence-are-driving-palestinian-authoritys-political.

Iqtait, Anas (2021), "The Palestinian Authority Political Economy: The Architecture of Fiscal Control." In Alaa Tartir et al. (eds.), *Political Economy of Palestine*, 249–70. Cham: Palgrave Macmillan.

Iqtait, Anas (2022a), "The Palestinian Authority's Economic 'disengagement' Looks a Lot Like the Status quo." *Middle East Institute*, May 24. https://www.mei.edu/publications/palestinian-authoritys-economic-disengagement-looks-lot-status-quo.

Iqtait, Anas (2022b), *Funding and the Quest for Sovereignty in Palestine*. Cham: Palgrave Macmillan.

Kanafani, Numan (2001), "Trade – A Catalyst for Peace?" *The Economic Journal*, 11 (1): 276–90.

Khalidi, Raja (2005), "Reshaping Palestinian Economic Policy Discourse: Putting the Development Horse Before the Governance Cart." *Journal of Palestine Studies*, 34 (3): 77–87.

Knack, Stephen (2009), "Sovereign Rents and Quality of Tax Policy and Administration." *Journal of Comparative Economics*, 37 (3): 359–71.

Krasner, Stephen D. and Thomas Risse (2014), "External Actors, State-building, and Service Provision in Areas of Limited Statehood." *Domestic Politics and Norm Diffusion in International Relations*, 197–217.

Levi, Margaret (1988), *Of Rule and Revenue*. Berkeley: University of California Press.

Levi, Margaret and Audrey Sacks (2009), "Legitimating Beliefs: Concepts and Indicators." *Regulation and Governance*, 3 (4): 311–33.

Levi, Margaret, Audrey Sacks, and Tom Tyler (2009), "Conceptualizing Legitimacy, Measuring Legitimating Beliefs." *American Behavioral scientist*, 53 (3): 354–75.

Lia, Brynjar (2007), *Building Arafat's Police: The Politics of International Police Assistance in the Palestinian Territories After the Oslo Agreement*. London: Ithaca Press.

Lieberman, Evan (2001), "National Political Community and the Politics of Income Taxation in Brazil and South Africa in the Twentieth Century." *Politics & Society*, 29 (4): 515–55.

Mansour, Antoine (1988), "The West Bank Economy: 1948–1984." In George Abed (ed.), *The Palestinian Economy: Studies in Development Under Prolonged Occupation*, 71–99. Oxon: Routledge.

Mansuri, Ghazala and Vijayendra Rao (2004), "Community - Based and - Driven Development: A Critical Review." *The World Bank Research Observer*, 19 (1): 1–39.

Marcussen, Henrik Secher (1996), "NGOs, the State and Civil Society." *Review of African Political Economy*, 23 (69): 405–23.

Monaghan, J. (2016), "Security Development and the Palestinian Authority: An Examination of the 'Canadian Factor.'" *Conflict, Security & Development*, 16 (2): 131.

Moore, Mick (1995), "Promoting Good Government by Supporting Institutional Development?" In *Institute for Development Studies*. Brighton: University of Sussex, IDS Bulletin 26 (2).

Moore, Mick (1998), "Death Without Taxes: Democracy, State Capacity, and Aid Dependence in the Fourth World." In Robinson and White (eds.), *The Democratic*

Developmental State: Politics and Institutional Design, 84–124. Oxford: Oxford University Press.

Moore, Mick (2001), "Political Underdevelopment: What Causes 'bad Governance'." *Public Management review*, 3 (3): 385–418.

Moore, Mick (2004), "Revenues, State Formation, and the Quality of Governance in Developing Countries." *International Political Science Review*, 25 (3): 297–319.

Morrison, Kevin M. (2009), "Oil, Nontax Revenue, and the Redistributional Foundations of Regime Stability." *International organization*, 63 (1): 107–38.

Mosse, William (2015), *Israel's Retaliatory Seizure of Tax: A War Crime to Punish Palestinian ICC Membership*. Ramallah: Al-Haq.

Nakhleh, Khalil (1989), "Non-Governmental Organizations and Palestine: The Politics of Money." *Journal of Refugee Studies*, 2 (1): 113–24.

Office of the Quartet (2021), *Annual Report: January–December 2021*. Jerusalem. http://www.quartetoffice.org/page.php?id=5eba80y6208128Y5eba80.

PCBS (2022), "Registered Palestinian Exports, Imports of Goods for 2021 and 2022." https://www.pcbs.gov.ps/statisticsIndicatorsTables.aspx?lang=en&table_id=1346.

Persson, A. (2018), "Palestine at the End of the State-Building Process: Technical Achievements, Political Failures." *Mediterranean Politics*, 23(4): 433–52.

Ross, Michael L. (2001), "Does Oil Hinder Democracy?" *World politics*, 53 (3): 325–61.

Roy, Sara (1995), *The Gaza Strip: The Political Economy of De-development*. Washington, DC: Institute of Palestine Studies.

Roy, Sara (1998), "The Palestinian Economy After Oslo." *Current History*, 97 (615): 19–25.

Sacks, Audrey (2012), "Can Donors and Non-state Actors Undermine Citizens' Legitimating Beliefs?" World Bank Policy Research Working Paper 6158.

Sayigh, Y. (2011), *Policing the People, Building the State: Authoritarian Transformation in the West Bank and Gaza*. Beirut: Carnegie Middle East Center.

Schumpeter, Joseph A. (1991), "The Crisis of the Tax State." In Richard Swedberg (ed.), *The Economics and Sociology of Capitalism*, 99–140. Princeton: Princeton University Press.

Shikaki, Ibrahim (2021), "The Demise of Palestinian Productive Sectors: Internal Trade as a Microcosm of the Impact of Occupation." *Al-Shabaka*, February 7. https://al-shabaka.org/briefs/demise-of-palestinian-productive-sectors/.

Smith, Alastair (2008), "The Perils of Unearned Income." *The Journal of Politics*, 70 (3): 780–93.

Smith, Steven Rathgeb and Michael Lipsky (1993), *Nonprofits for Hire: The Welfare State in the Age of Contracting*. Cambridge, MA: Harvard University Press.

Svensson, Jakob (2000), "Foreign Aid and Rent-seeking." *Journal of International economics*, 51 (2): 437–61.

Taghdisi-Rad, Sahar (2015), "Political Economy of Aid in Conflict: An Analysis of Pre- and Post-Intifada Donor Behaviour in the Occupied Palestinian Territories." *International Journal of Security and Development*, 4 (1): Art. 22.

Tartir, Alaa (2015a), "Securitised Development and Palestinian Authoritarianism Under Fayyadism." *Conflict, Security & development*, 15 (5): 479–502.

Tartir, Alaa (2015b), "The Evolution and Reform of Palestinian Security Forces 1993–2013." *International Journal of Security and Development*, 4 (1): 1–20.

Tartir, Alaa (2017a), "Criminalizing Resistance: The Cases of Balata and Jenin Refugee Camps." *Journal of Palestine Studies*, 46 (2): 7–22.

Tartir, Alaa (2017b), "The Palestinian Authority Security Forces: Whose Security?" *Al Shabaka: The Palestinian Policy Network*. https://al-shabaka.org/briefs/palestinian-authority-security-forces-whose-security/.

Tartir, Alaa, Tariq Dana, and Timothy Seidel (eds.) (2021), *Political Economy of Palestine: Critical, Interdisciplinary, and Decolonial Perspectives*. Cham: Palgrave Macmillan.

Tornell, Aaron and Philip R. Lane (1998), "Are Windfalls a Curse?: A Non-representative Agent Model of the Current Account." *Journal of International Economics*, 44(1): 83–112.

UNCTAD (1994), "Gaza-Jericho Agreement Annex IV-Economic Protocol."

Wildeman, Jeremy (2019), "Neoliberalism as Aid for the Settler Colonization of the Occupied Palestinian Territories After Oslo." In Alaa Tartir and Timothy Seidel (eds.), *Palestine and Rule of Power: Local Dissent vs. International Governance*, 153–70. London: Palgrave.

Wildeman, Jeremy and Alaa Tartir (2014), "Unwilling to Change, Determined to Fail: Donor Aid in Occupied Palestine in the Aftermath of the Arab Uprisings." *Mediterranean Politics*, 19 (3): 431–49.

Wildeman, Jeremy and Alaa Tartir (2021), "Political Economy of Foreign Aid in the Occupied Palestinian Territories: A Conceptual Framing." In A. Tartir, T. Dana, and T. Seidel (eds.), *Political Economy of Palestine*, 223–47. Cham: Palgrave Macmillan.

World Bank (2016), *Palestinian Authority Incurs US$285 Million in Annual Fiscal Losses*. Washington, DC: World Bank.

World Bank (2020), *Economic Developments in the Palestinian Territories*. Washington, DC: World Bank.

Part III

Environmental

Land, Indigeneity, and Settler Colonialism

The third part of this volume explores *environmental* sites of domination and resistance and is situated within the settler colonial context. Chapters in this part focus on land, indigeneity, and space as critical elements to understanding settler colonialism clarifying the context of racial capitalism in occupied Palestine.

In "Situating the Transnational in Agrarian Palestine," Gabi Kirk and Paul Kohlbry make a case for approaching the study of rural Palestine through foregrounding the transnational forces that shape rural property, labor, and agriculture. After establishing some key concerns of this scholarship in Palestine, they sketch out the geography of how to study agrarian questions, distinguishing between studying Palestine and Palestinians, showing how what happens to and on rural land in the territory of historic Palestine must be comprehended by including Palestinian refugees, migrants, and exiles living abroad. Finally they show how framing local questions in Palestine through an international lens can productively approach long-standing concerns around class, gender, and space, as well as newer issues in the climate change era of commodity circulation and ecological resilience.

Timothy Seidel and Federica Stagni's chapter "Settler Colonial Violence and Indigenous Struggle: Land, Resistance, and Refusal in Masafer Yatta" emphasizes that a decolonial analysis not only gives attention to enduring indigeneity but also to the role of land in the struggle for autonomy, sovereignty, and self-determination in Palestine. They examine "everyday" acts of resistance and popular struggle that take the form of *sumud* or steadfastness, that may not be about a predetermined political economic telos per se but about existence, being, land, and a refusal of erasure and elimination. With this framework and understanding of popular struggle, they argue, we begin to hear and see a much larger and more powerful landscape of resistance to settler violence in occupied Palestine, for example, in this case of Masafer Yatta in the occupied South Hebron Hills.

Situating the Transnational in Agrarian Palestine

Gabi Kirk and Paul Kohlbry

Introduction

Agriculture makes Palestine visible internationally. The mainstreaming of organic certification and fair trade has made products like Palestinian olive oil and dates available to ethically minded consumers around the world. Interest in international foods and debates over culinary origins have brought Palestine to popular cooking shows and best-selling recipe books (Gaul and Pitts 2021). And just as the guerilla fighter and the stone-throwing youth captured the imagination of older generations of solidarity activists, today the Palestinian peasant as an Indigenous steward of the land inspires activists for whom climate catastrophe, not international revolution, is the concern of the day. Of course, many are still likely to understand Palestine through long-standing geopolitical concerns or religious traditions. But they are increasingly likely to encounter Palestinians as producers of organic olive oil and practitioners of environmentally sound farming techniques.

Transnational forces are key to understanding agrarian Palestine today. By this, we mean that transnational capital, markets, regulations, and technologies shape the production, circulation, and consumption of Palestinian agriculture: from soils and seeds; to the labor of planting, care, and harvesting; to marketing and circulation; to consumption both in Palestine and in places like Oakland and Chicago where we were writing from. A transnational framing, we think, has much to offer the critical scholarship of agrarian life in Palestine that is emerging in the field of Palestinian studies.

The first body of such work is agroecological. It engages with traditional forms of Palestinian agriculture as living techniques and puts agricultural technoscience in the context of the settler colonial project (Tesdell 2017; Tesdell, Othman and Alkhoury 2019; Tesdell et al. 2020). The Makaneyyat research group has, among other projects, developed a database of wild plants; the Palestinian Heirloom Seed Library project preserves threatened seeds and promotes their use among farmers; and the Applied Research Institute-Jerusalem worked during Covid-19 to develop organic urban gardens (Arraf 2020). Such agroactivism, according to Anne Meneley, offers a means of salvaging hope from the ruins of occupation (2021). Scholarly attention to agrarian political economy, especially regarding rural labor, land ownership, and commodity circulation, has much to offer agroecological framings. Such questions are especially critical at a time when concerns about climate change and ethical consumption are creating openings for corporations to capture sustainable practices and hollow out their radical potential.

The second body of work explores the relationship between agriculture and resistance. Writing during the First Intifada, Adel Samara (1988) emphasized popular protection and delinking from the Israeli economy, seeing in peasant agriculture not only the basis for autonomy and subsistence but also envisioning how cooperation and collectivization might be scaled up. George Kurzom (2001) developed a similar line at the beginning of the Second Intifada. Against dependency and trade integration with Israel, he advocated for Palestinian "national resistance" through "investment in popular agricultural production, whether through communal, collective or individual projects" (11) that eschewed chemical inputs and export in favor of traditional knowledge and local consumption. Most recently, scholars calling for a resistance economy have argued that smallholder farming and sustainable agricultural practices can contribute to rebuilding a devastated agricultural sector and build the basis for collective action (Sansour and Tartir 2014; Dana 2014; Seidel 2021). Critical agrarian studies can help this body of scholarship explore relationships between subsistence and commercial farming and between smallholders and large commercial operations and illuminate the ways that international competition and local pressures on land are transforming agriculture. This is especially important for smallholders, many of whom face the double squeeze of colonial dispossession and the conversion of agricultural land into real estate.

The third body of work is rural critique. Ted Swedenburg argued that the peasantry worked as a "national signifier," stripped of its "distinctive class features, rough edges, subversive capacities, and past treacheries" (1990, 19). Salim Tamari was harsher, arguing that urban Palestinian intellectuals turned the "fallah into a faceless collective identity" that, in the 1970s and 1980s, elevated the peasantry to "a condition of uncontaminated purity" (1992, 82). Rayya El Zein is critical of a middle-class back to the land discourse "that romanticizes the relationship of the Palestinian farmer to her land" (2017, 16), while Kareem Rabie shows how "proponents and opponents of development" share common assumptions about rural life that "rely on a version of Palestinian history that has obscured class and economic change" (2021, 159). We agree with these critiques. They point to the ways that nationalist and class ideologies have made it difficult to understand the ways that rural Palestine has changed; how peasant agriculture has disappeared and smallholder production has been reconfigured; and how private development has integrated villages into global circuits of capital. They clear the ground to ask what agrarian Palestine *is* rather than what it *isn't* and what it potentially *could be*.

In what follows, we will focus on olives, dates, sheep, and goats to illuminate a few of the transnational processes that shape agrarian life in Palestine today. We draw on our own fieldwork and archival research in the West Bank, as well as published scholarship, to situate the transnational in the formation of rural people, places, and struggles. We offer the following account as a set of notes that, we hope, will raise questions about agrarian Palestine and invite further conversation and research.

Palestine and Agrarian Studies

Writings on and from Palestine have long been concerned with questions of the peasantry, agrarian space, and land transformation—not simply due to the 1967 occupation but also in the *longue durée* of capitalist development and successive imperial and colonial structures in the Levant. Today, research based on fieldwork in rural Palestine—at least in geography and anthropology, the disciplines with which we are most familiar—focuses on issues of traditional knowledge, identity, and state violence. Issues of class formation, land ownership, the division of labor, and social reproduction get far less attention, especially when we look back at the debates post-1948 and post-1967.

Agrarian studies in Palestine coalesced during two crises in rural life. The first body of scholarship critically analyzed the impacts of the *Nakba* on rural communities and livelihoods, specifically examining how Palestinians were proletarianized within the boundaries of the new Israeli state (e.g., Asad 1975; Rosenfeld 1978; Makhoul 1982). Such scholars traced the dispossession of Palestinian land within the 1948 borders through both legal and economic means, arguing decades before the rise of "settler colonial studies" that "the definition of state land under Israel's rule . . . is built on racist and national criteria" (Zureik 1976, 44). Such analysis of Israel's legal structures of confiscating Palestinian land (including from those that remained within the boundaries of the new Jewish state and/or successfully returned after a short time away) brought together the materialist description of dispossession with Israel's racialized legal structures, which defined citizenship as an exclusively Jewish province. Zureik argued that Palestinian proletarianization, rather than a "natural shift" of a rural to urban society in the mid-century, was directly "in the context of colonization with strict patterns of domination and dependency" (48).

The second major wave of agrarian studies came about in the 1980s. It primarily focused on sociological and political studies of farmers and pastoralists in the Occupied West Bank. Primary rural sociological research included in-depth village surveys alongside historical analysis to show the persistence of the peasantry despite political, economic, and technoscientific pressure from Israel's occupation and the Green Revolution to proletarianize them (Tamari 1983; Tamari and Giacaman 1997). Work like Hisham Awartani's (1982) took the needs of Palestinian farmers as central to the national struggle against occupation, through an exploration of the impediments to improving traditional Palestinian rainfed agriculture and the formation of Palestinian agricultural development organizations preceding and then during the First Intifada. Such themes continued to show up in Palestinian political economy on labor writ large (e.g., Farsakh 2005) but with less of a specifically agrarian focus.

By the Oslo Accords, agrarian studies in Palestine as a cohesive project had nearly fallen off the map. Politically, the entrenchment of neoliberalism and the state-building project initiated post-Oslo brought a political-social shift marked by increased government attention to urban spaces—investment in real estate and the development of a service economy. Meanwhile, Israel prevented agricultural development. It blocked access to farms, confiscated land, and forced smallholders, who were unable to make a living from agriculture, into interminable struggles for access and ownership. Furthermore, the transformation of rural lands—into industrial sites or, more commonly, housing developments—by the PA and private investors, for instance, has been analyzed less for its spatial-social impact on Palestinian farmers and more for issues of international development, labor migration, or international diplomatic impacts on a potential Palestinian state.

Second, a larger cultural turn in critical studies writ large meant that agrarian studies even outside of Palestine diminished, as non-Marxist approaches gained credence. This is not to say no research was conducted in the post-Oslo period. Palestinian research organizations carried out extensive research on agricultural development and undertook development projects themselves. Studies from the Land Research Center (LRC), Applied Research Institute-Jerusalem (ARIJ), and applied research and development projects from Palestinian Agricultural Relief Committees (PARC), the Union of Agricultural Work Committees (UAWC), and more broadly Ma'an Development Center aimed at developing and protecting a largely destroyed sector. However, this was in service of a nascent national economy that never materialized. Therefore, such work tended to focus more on issues of political economy in the agricultural sector and less on agrarian livelihoods.[1]

Third, as the twentieth century came to a close, peasant movements around the world came to the forefront as major sites of struggle against neoliberal globalization. However, representation from Palestinian agricultural organizations or leaders—and in fact, from the Arab world writ large—was nearly absent from such formations (Ajl 2021). La Via Campesina was founded officially in 1993 and is often considered the heart of the modern global peasants' movement (Martínez-Torres and Rosset 2010). It still does not have a region covering the Middle East and North Africa. The Union of Agricultural Work Committees (UAWC) did not join as a Palestinian affiliate of the movement until 2017 and today is listed as an "emerging region." This is not to say that no work on agrarian life happened in the past thirty years; important work, especially on issues of gender and development, continued (Hammami 2000, 2005). However, it must be contextualized that the emergence of the peasant studies tradition in the rest of the world was specifically a political and economic movement against Green Revolution technoscience and structural adjustment (and its precedents). Occupation shaped both neoliberal development and its technoscientific tools in unique ways (Haddad 2016). The reconnection to a settler colonial studies framework to describe all of historic Palestine has led to significant and important work that contextualizes Israel's structural and direct violence against Palestinian agriculturalists as a form of racial colonial dispossession (Sansour and Tartir 2014; Tartir 2018). Any criticism of global agribusiness, international aid, or "land reform" in Palestine always keeps Israel's settler colonial dispossession project squarely in the center of its sights. This criticism can still contend with how Palestinian farmers enlist and embrace Green Revolution technology if it kept farmers on their lands, especially from Palestinian-led development organizations. Such ambivalent engagement can put them in conflict with global peasant movements' demands.

We join in the renewed interest in critical agrarian studies, which "share[s] a concern with the ways in which agrarian life and livelihoods shape and are shaped by the politics, economics and social worlds of modernity" (Edelman and Wolford 2017, 960). There is a strong need for this body of literature to engage more deeply with the Arab world more broadly and Palestine specifically (Ajl 2021); here, we focus on what critical agrarian studies might bring to Palestine studies. It offers a corrective to the ways that critiques of international development and Israeli colonization can miss how Palestine opens up opportunities to understand agrarian change both because of occupation and because of the global capitalist system that continues to impact, and in many cases eliminate, a global peasantry. Olives, dates, and sheep and goats allow us to explore agrarian labor, commodity circulation, and capital accumulation, offering different views on transnational processes that are long-standing, interrupted, and emerging.

The Transnational Commodity: Olive Oil

One would be hard-pressed to find a field of Palestinian agriculture that has received as much attention as olive farming, and for good reason. Olives make up a major part of Palestinian agrarian life, spatially, economically, culturally, and politically. It is estimated that olives make up 57 percent of cultivated land in the West Bank (predominantly rain-fed) and 15 percent of income from agricultural products, yet concerns have grown on the declining amount of land and yield from olive production due to Israel's occupation (UNCTAD 2015). Historically and in the present, olives serve as a major cultural symbol and a synecdoche for *fellahin*'s persistence on their lands and in their lifestyles (Abufarha 2008).

Olive oil and its attendant products, notably olive oil soap, topped Palestine's exports out of Jaffa and Haifa in the late nineteenth century under Ottoman control (Owen 1982). Annual production tends to fluctuate on a two- to three-year cycle, as olive trees are alternative bearing trees, oscillating between "mast" years of major production with off years of lower yield. The first major expansion of olive-growing areas began in the late nineteenth century due to increased demand from European markets, focused especially in the Nablus areas where olive oil and soap production became vertically integrated (Doumani 1995). However, the First World War devastated the olive market. Despite destruction of some olive groves by Ottoman soldiers, by and large the expanded planted area led to a glut after military demand evaporated, coupled particularly by British Mandate tariff policies that led to a massive import of cheap oil and soap despite surplus domestic production. This combined with the general economic depression in Palestine in the interwar period led directly to smallholder debt—and limited land sales to Zionists (Anderson 2018). Thus, a historical look at the relationship between politics and economy in olive farming shows how issues of legal and extralegal settler colonial dispossession have always been tied to global capitalism's booms and busts.

In the past fifteen years, scholarship on olive farming has emphasized the cultural significance of olives and the legal dimensions of land dispossession, which we might call the *sumud* turn in scholarship on agrarian Palestine writ large. This turn focuses on the Palestinian ethos of *sumud*, or steadfastness, as political and cultural resistance against Israeli occupation usually through rural practices and in rural spaces—but often leaves out the transnational materialist structures that impact and undergird agrarian life. Recent anthropological and geographic scholarship on olive trees and Palestinians who care for them has fallen into one or multiple of a few categories. The first aims to chronicle the violent impacts of Israeli occupation on olive trees themselves: how Israel targets olive trees for destruction because of their specific legal status that affords Palestinians persistence on their lands (Cohen 1993; Braverman 2009; Fields 2017). Such violence has been termed "eco-occupation" (Sharif 2015)—Israel's continued actions condemned as a specific form of racial violence with a genocidal logic as enacted against the land itself, sometimes positioning olive trees as more-than-human agents against the occupation (Fields 2012; Hanafi 2013; Jaber 2019; Pugliese 2020). Relatedly, work on olive harvest describes the affective labor of and relations between Palestinian farmers and international volunteers in solidarity with the Palestinian struggle (Meneley 2014a, 2014b; Simaan 2017; Kelly 2020). Both intellectual and political work on olive farming as a form of decolonial resistance often draws a transnational connection between Palestinian farmers remaining on their land through olive farming and global Indigenous struggles against settler colonialism (Collins 2010; Ayyash 2018; Tannous and Zahzah 2018). Some of this work, which looks closely at how the legal structures of the occupation impact land use, access, and rights, refers to impacts on Palestinian economy and livelihoods. However it often does not define them or delve deeply into structures and processes; political economy is mentioned only in passing, if at all.

It is important to bring to the work on contemporary olive farming the attention that olives are not simply culturally important to the Palestinian cause but also their place in larger Palestinian agroecosystems and political economy. Olive oil forms a unique role in being a great cash crop for export, and olive trees are comparatively low maintenance (as opposed to, for instance, almonds, which have higher susceptibility to disease and often need to be irrigated to reach economically desirable yields). Yet Palestinians' political planting of olive trees creates problems as well as solutions, including what to do with the massive increase in olive oil production before a strong export market was in place. This limitation of exports has both political (notably, Israeli restrictions on export from the Occupied Territories) and economic causes (e.g., Italian, Greek, and Spanish olive oil is cheaper; increased production competition from other Arab states and China). While olive growing has long followed expansion and contraction cycles, the current major expansion of planted orchards began after the *Nakba*, when Palestinians who remained or returned to their villages in the Galilee expanded olive production against Israel's attempts to restrict their cultivation (Reger 2017). The 1967 occupation brought similar dynamics to the West Bank highlands, but by the 1980s the expansion of olive production had unintended deleterious effects. Palestinian olive oil faced a major marketing problem, as the amount of olive oil produced exceeded the domestic market's demands. Jordan increased its domestic production and no longer purchased as much Palestinian olive oil, which was in both quality and price uncompetitive with other Mediterranean producers from both southern Europe and northern Africa (Reger 2018, 460). Yet olive oil marketing internationally was not the only cause of expanded production, as Jeffrey Reger notes: "family production for one's own consumption remained a key motivating factor for the extensive scale of olive production, especially considering the increasingly thin profit margins" (470). However, "even with the switch to uncompensated household members for most of the harvesting labor, the consequence was that Palestinian olive oil had become more and more internationally uncompetitive" (477). The 1990s and 2000s saw the First Gulf War and then the Second Intifada cut off major international markets for Palestinian olive oil. The direct establishment of fair trade (Palestine is the first place to develop a fair trade olive oil certification) and the "solidarity market" to sell Palestinian olive oil to non-Palestinians in the West has not been without its problems (Meneley 2008).

One author of this piece conducted ethnographic interviews from 2018 to 2022 with Palestinian fair trade olive farmers in the Jenin governorate, which today produces more olive oil than any other in the West Bank (Palestinian Central Bureau of Statistics 2019). These farmers described how olives have replaced almond production and even row and field crops in the *sahel* (plains). Farmers find this promising, both due to olive oil's consistent higher price per dunam because of low input needs and fair trade's raising of prices both in the domestic and foreign markets. But they are also concerned. They describe a cultural and agroecological loss of diversity from the diminishing cultivation of almonds, grazing land, and wheat in favor of olive trees. It is worth asking what political work international actors focusing on olives does and how separating olives out from their agroecological context may jeopardize the overall environmental and economic health of rural landscapes. Additionally, the Covid-19 pandemic caused major challenges for Palestinian olive oil production and exports (OCHA 2021). Covid-19 movement restrictions made it difficult for farmers to access their lands, and Israel denied more permits to farmers to access their lands in the "seam zone," citing public health concerns. Export out of the West Bank was already challenging due to Israeli restrictions, but the so-called public health justification of the pandemic meant that Israel closed West Bank export crossings for months and continues to close them on and off. Israel put harsh restrictions on the movement of West Bank Palestinians and their products under a pandemic public health justification (as has long been done for "security reasons"), but similar restrictions were not put on Israeli settlers or settlement goods, casting a spurious meaning over such public health justifications. One staff member at a fair trade organization in the West Bank said that Covid-19 made them think that "maybe this was it, it was over forever" for the international export of olive oil, and that attention needed to be renewed toward domestic consumption of olive oil—or diversifying agroecosystems away from olive monoculture. More research could be done as to the economic diversity of household farms and the balance of their reliance on local versus international markets and what structures should be put in place to better support adaptation to global market shocks and disruptions.

Finally, a transnational attention to olive production shows how Palestinian farmers have become cultural symbols, not just as an embodiment of Palestinian nationalism, but also for a global audience who sees Palestinian agricultural resistance and heritage as a vanguard against the impacts of climate change. Palestinian agriculturalists are increasingly positioned as a global symbol of land protection because olives are a drought-tolerant, rainfed tree. Climate change's impacts on olive yield are lamented while Palestinian farmers are also seen as those who can provide lessons to the rest of the world as to how to farm with fewer resources through traditional farming practices which are climate adaptable. Yet the expansion of olive orchards into areas that cannot be rainfed (as well as the expansion of other non-drought-tolerant crops for export, notably irrigated almonds) challenges a monolithic image of Palestinian agriculturalists as fixed in their practices and livelihoods. Activists and NGOs position Palestinian agriculturalists as global environmental stewards by focusing in on their practices as unchanged—reproducing the same figure of the Palestinian peasant lauded by nationalists and demonized by Zionists. If the national signifier of the pure peasant was about the crisis of the nation, and the ideal countryside and back to the land is about the crisis of capitalist development, then the peasant as an unchanging environmental steward is about the next global crisis: climate change.

Interrupted Transnationalism: Goats and Sheep

Pastoralism in Palestine is a story of an interrupted transnationalism. While common imagery of pastoralism is associated with semi-nomadic and nomadic practices of the Bedouin, rural communities across historic Palestine have long kept large flocks of goat, sheep, and camels, and migratory practices occurred across historic Palestine as documented even by the British Mandate government (Fakher Eldin 2014). The creation of colonial borders cut across traditional territory and grazing areas. Inside Israel after 1948, and in the occupied territories after 1967, state-orchestrated land dispossession, population transfer, and movement restrictions all further constrained Palestinian pastoral practices. As a source of livelihood and mode of life, pastoralism has drastically diminished over the twentieth and into the twenty-first century; that people are still able to keep flocks of goats and sheep today attests both to their expansive knowledge of animal husbandry and remarkable social tenacity.

In southern Palestine, Bedouin communities cultivated land and grazed flocks of animals across large territories. In the Naqab (Negev) desert, there were eight main tribal confederations. Their territories allowed land use and access, forming part of a larger, singular "spatial unit" that encompassed "the Negev, today's southern Jordan, the Sinai in Egypt, and northern Saudi Arabia" (Amara 2013, 29). As Ahmad Amara has shown, Bedouin mixed pastoralism with farming; drawing from British census data, he argues that by 1931, "89.3 percent of the Negev Bedouins mentioned that they relied on agriculture as their main source of livelihood" (30).

Under Israeli rule, Bedouin Palestinian communities have faced extreme forms of land dispossession and movement restriction. Under Ottoman and British administrations, the Bedouin were rather autonomous (Amara 2013, 34). After 1948, as part of turning the Naqab into Israeli territory, Israeli forces expelled thousands of Bedouin from their homelands into the West Bank and Gaza (Hunaiti 2008). Those who remained have been subjected to various legal and administrative powers that have sought to dispossess them of land, restrict movement, contain them in reservations, and settle them in segregated towns (Amara 2013; Plonski 2018; Gutkowski 2021). Israel's attempts at expulsion and forced sedentarization in the Naqab connects the Israeli state's settler colonial project to other attempts by colonial powers to restrict the movement of semi-nomadic pastoralists in arid lands around the world (Davis 2016).

The Bedouin expelled from their homes in the Naqab sought to rebuild their lives in the West Bank in the 1950s and 1960s, settling around Jerusalem, Hebron, Bethlehem, Ramallah, and Jericho, grazing their flocks across the West Bank (and sometimes crossing into Jordan) and selling meat, dairy products, and wool to residents of the villages, camps, and cities (Hunaiti 2008, 18). The Jahalin, for instance, fled to an area outside of Hebron and Bethlehem before moving to the hills southeast of Jerusalem in 1953. They planted limited crops, mostly for animal feed, on the dry hills; moved as far north as Jenin and east as Jordan for pasture; sold dairy products and sheep in the Jerusalem market; took jobs in construction; and entered into sharecropping agreements with local landowners (Hunaiti 2008, 34–8).

This process was not without friction. In the 1960s, villagers filed dozens of complaints against owners of sheep, goats, and camels to the Jordanian government. Many of these, filed by villagers in the hinterlands of Ramallah, Bethlehem, and Jerusalem, alleged that Bedouin who were grazing their flocks had allegedly damaged crops.[2] In 1963, for instance, a complaint read that Bedouin were "wrecking trees (*kharabu al-ashjar*)" in Silwan. Inspectors assessed damages, and police imposed fines, mostly around 3–5 Jordanian dinar (JD) (although one case went as high as 43 JD). At other times, filing a complaint was not to obtain compensation but to get the Bedouin to move on. Regarding a complaint raised in al-Jib in 1962, the police informed the governor of Jerusalem that "the point of the complaint is to expel (*tarhil*) the Bedouin that come down with their animals to the village land and its crops. Now that the Bedouin have left (*rahalu*) on their own, please consider the matter closed."

Israel's occupation of the West Bank devastated pastoralists. State land declarations, settlements, closed military zones, and nature reserves have all closed off huge areas of the West Bank and restricted access to Jordan. The military kept shepherds out of pasture lands, prevented access to water, confiscated animals, and, if owners were unable to pay the fines, sold them on public auction (Hunaiti 2008; Gutkowski 2021). According to statistics compiled by Hisham Awartani in the early 1980s, the number of sheep dropped by 33 percent in the "early years of the occupation [and then] 57% during the period of 1977–79)" (1982, 291).

The experiences of the isolated communities in the Jordan Valley clarify how colonial power has restricted pastoralism. In the northern Jordan Valley, between military zones and settlements, lies al-Hadidya, where one of the authors conducted interviews for the Land Defense Coalition; we draw on this material here. In 2016, al-Hadidya was home to ninety people who lived in sturdy tents surrounded by animal barracks—and the wreckage of structures bulldozed by the Israeli Civil Administration. Residents kept sheep and chicken and planted the surrounding lands with grain, alfalfa, olive trees (in an attempt to stake a legal claim), and vegetables. Prior to 1967, these shepherds moved with their animals north to Ein al-Beida, south to Jiftlik, and east beyond the Jordan River. In 1970, the creation of military zones and nature reserves closed off hundreds of thousands of dunams of former pasture. Military patrols enforced these new borders, confiscating sheep and imposing holding fees on their owners. Today, the Israeli agricultural settlement of Ro'i, as well as the nearby military training base, ensures that military patrols are a constant presence in the area. There is no public transportation, and roads turn to impassable mud after heavy rains. Like other communities located in Area C, the Israeli Civil Administration prevents residents of al-Hadidya from building permanent structures, paving roads, or irrigating crops. Instead, since 1997, the community has faced multiple waves of home demolitions and expulsion orders (Stop the Wall 2017).

These conditions have transformed pastoralism in several ways. First, restrictions have forced residents into risky forms of agriculture. The surrounding areas are owned by families from the nearby town of Tubas, who cultivated the land until 2001. Since then, people in al-Hadidya have rented this land on a yearly basis, paying 5 JD for each dunam they plant and hoping that the level of rainfall is sufficient to make the investment worth it. Second, the lack of paved roads and reliable transportation creates serious difficulties for those who still are able to maintain flocks of sheep. The lack of refrigeration limits production of meat and dairy products, and residents find themselves at the mercy of merchants who visit the area to buy and transport products to Palestinian cities. Finally, isolation has created a private water market. Water sellers purchase water from wells in Tammun and Tubas, transport it to al-Hadidya, and sell it for a significant markup (Stop the Wall 2017). Colonial control does not only dispossess or limit access to land but also shapes the political economy of pastoralism that people are able to maintain.

Thinking about the political economy of pastoralism can provide a powerful compliment to studies of law and resistance. There is a large literature, primarily focusing on the struggle of Bedouin in the Naqab/Negev region, that shows how colonial laws and regulations displace and erase Bedouin communities and the ways that these communities resist and rebuild (Amara 2013; Weizman and Sheikh 2015; Plonski 2018; Tatour 2019). There is ample room to build on this literature and see how those forms of governance and territory can become questions of production, commodities, labor, and livelihood. Combining a critical agrarian perspective with a critical legal one can clarify not only how people resist but also the forms of production, consumption, distribution, and accumulation that this resistance helps create and the individual and collective aspirations it gives rise to.

Finally, pastoralism could provide a lens for understanding the relationship between colonialism and concerns about food sovereignty and environmental degradation. While there has been rising interest in pastoralists as potential stewards of land in arid regions of the Middle East (Nori et al. 2009), in the West Bank and Gaza Strip there has been little concerted focus on pastoralists or rangeland preservation (Baumgarten-Sharon 2017). As Ian Scoones argues (2021), since pastoralists are experts in dealing with uncertainty and variability, attention to pastoralism may be of heightened importance at a time of planetary climate change and local ecological transformation. At the same time, colonial powers across the Middle East and North Africa have long blamed pastoralists for ecological degradation, falsely claiming that grazing causes desertification (Davis 2007). There is, we think, an opportunity to bring research about

Palestinian pastoralism into these discussions. One way to do so might be to focus on the animals themselves. In the 1980s, Hisham Awartani noted that the dominant Palestinian sheep, the Awasi, produced less milk than the Assaf variety, which was locally bred on Israeli farms. However, it was the Awasi that displayed a "marked tolerance to the local environment, dominated by frequent droughts, scanty pastures, and poor nutrition" (1982, 300–1).³ Attention not only to land and market but also to the changing breeds of animals and the knowledge that pastoralists have about them could be vital research questions as climate change and colonial rule transform the environment of the West Bank.

Emerging Transnationalism: Dates

The Jordan Valley is of central importance for Palestinian commercial agriculture. The Valley's soil, water, and climate are uniquely conducive to the production of vegetable and fruit crops, among them the topic of this section: dates. While date farming has been practiced in the Valley for centuries, it was, according to Julie Troitter (2020), Israeli settlers who introduced the medjool variety. She calculates that Israeli settler farms covered 524 hectares in 1999 and 2,560 hectares in 2016, while Palestinian farms grew from 25 hectares to 1,584 hectares over the same period. Dates are a lucrative Israeli export crop, and a majority of Israeli date production occurs in farms located in and around settlements in the Jordan Valley (Who Profits 2014). Dates are also part of an emerging Palestinian transnationalism, one in which Palestinian capitalist agriculture is reworking notions of sustainability, land defense, and solidarity through market relations.

We should understand Palestinian date farming as a result of liberalization in the 1990s. While the peace process did not lead to peace, it did create institutional frameworks that could support free markets, concentrating power into a small number of companies controlled by an international Palestinian capitalist class (Hanieh 2011; Khalidi, and Samour 2011). In a 2016 radio interview, Samir Hulileh (one of the West Bank's most powerful businessmen) argued that Palestinian date farms not only effectively hold land but also they employ Palestinians who would otherwise be doing similar jobs in the nearby settlements. Hulileh likely had Nakheel Palestine in mind, which was founded in 2010 by Palestine Development and Investment Company (PADICO) (of which Hulileh was its CEO). Oslo also created opportunities for diaspora investors who are not as involved in PA state-building. Ziyad Brothers, for example, was founded by two Palestinian brothers in the 1960s in Chicago; the company became one of the dominant importers and distributors of Arab and Middle Eastern food in North America. The company obtained land for date cultivation outside of Jericho and opened Palestine Dates in 2007. In 2019, the operation expanded with the completion of a large packing facility.

These larger corporate concerns organize date production through large commercial farms. To allow for efficient harvesting they are planted only with rows of palm trees, with on-site processing facilities for sorting, packaging, and refrigeration. These operations do not require much full-time labor, relying instead on seasonal workers during the two-month harvest (Trottier, Leblond and Garb 2020, 128). Such farms also enter into outgrowing arrangements with smaller farmers, buying their dates and selling them under company labels (133).

Date farming is transforming agricultural labor, in particular sharecropping (Trottier, Leblond and Garb 2020). Unlike the highlands of the West Bank, where agriculture is primarily done by smallholders, sharecropping has been important for agriculture in Jordan Valley. After the Nakba, the Jordan Valley was the only place in the West Bank that could absorb huge numbers of Palestinian refugees. According to Salim Tamari, refugees became sharecroppers and agricultural workers, their labor fueling the introduction of capitalist agriculture to the Valley, encouraging land purchases, and rapidly bringing nearly all land under cultivation (1983, 274–8). In his study of the northern Jordan Valley, Alex Pollock argued that sharecropping allowed impressive returns without the risks of capital investment (and its potential loss by Israeli policies). In combination with Green Revolution technologies that increased yields, the cultivation of tomatoes, aubergines, and other vegetables brought more women into wage labor and allowed powerful Palestinian merchants to seize control of agricultural surplus (Pollock 1990, 112–17). Today, Trottier, Leblond, and Garb (2020) warn that the spread of date cultivation is replacing banana crops, leading to the loss of stable work, subsistence farming, and the mass displacement of sharecroppers.

The use of water in date farming links environmental sustainability to international markets. The idea of sustainable agriculture in the Jordan Valley has long been shaped by concerns of farmer livelihood, on the one hand, and ecological constraints of water and salinity, on the other. Both are inseparable from settler colonial rule. In the early 1980s, Alex Pollock (1990) described Green Revolution innovations through the tomato. Tomatoes were a key cash crop because of their resistance to salinity, combined with drip irrigation, which allowed more extensive cultivation. Today, the date is part of a similar set of claims, one that has shifted with the addition of climate change. According to date advocates, the trees require less water than other cash crops, and their ability to thrive in highly saline soil makes them a bulwark against desertification. Trottier, Leblond, and Garb (2020, 120–2) call this the "mainstream" argument and argue that it misrepresents both water use and impact on local livelihoods. These issues are part of a larger, international debate about sustainability. It is not only a problem of making sure there is enough water or that Palestinians can move product. It also is about how huge, mono-cropped commercial farms and short-term profits come to be understood as sustainable, and how this project is (or is not) contested politically.

In the Jordan Valley, date plantations blend commercial agriculture with the protection of Palestinian territory. This is not the first time commercial agriculture has been seen as a means to protect land. In the 1930s, Palestinian investors established banana plantations in Beisan in an attempt to hold land against Zionist purchases. Hindered by Jewish National Fund (JNF) land purchases and poor planning, the effort collapsed after several years (Fakher Eldin 2008, 133). In the Jordan Valley today, date farms are part of a land defense discourse. Take the motivations of Ismael Daiq, one of the founders of the Palestinian Agricultural Relief Committees (PARC) and active in various sorts of land defense activities in the 1980s (see, e.g., Daiq 1986). In the 1990s, Daiq and his brother opened Alwadi farms, which they claim was the first Palestinian date palm plantation; part of the company's current mission is to hold land in Area C. Land defense is not only the concern of those with a background in agrarian politics. One of the authors of this chapter was once contacted by a lawyer representing Palestinian-American investors interested in investing in dates in the Jordan Valley. They hoped for returns on investment but also to prevent the expansion of settler colonial control.

Finally, dates are a commodity sold on the international market. Palestinian producers compete globally, including with Israeli producers who enjoy far more state support. One marketing angle has involved building a Palestinian brand that addresses environmental and political concerns, similar to what Anne Meneley (2011) describes for olive oil. Take Zaytoun, a fair trade Community Interest Company based in the UK. The founders of Zaytoun come from the international Palestine solidarity movement, active originally in visiting and working in Palestine in the mid-2000s. Today, they help distribute the dates of Palestine Gardens and Nakheel to buyers interested in ethical consumption.

Dates raise important questions. They bring Palestine into debates about sustainable agriculture and climate change in arid zones, and they bring the problem of territorial defense into new regulatory regimes and the vicissitudes of demand for a luxury commodity. In short, dates help show how we might think of long-standing concerns about land and labor in terms of new political discourses about the environment, conflicts over what sustainability means, and different expressions of solidarity whose political commitments emerge in attempts to make markets more just.

Conclusion

Critical agrarian studies can bring to Palestine studies a transnational approach to studying local political economy. It reminds us to decenter and nonexclusively examine urban spaces and industrial concerns when looking at questions of political economy and to reorient studies of rural spaces and agrarian livelihoods, lifestyles, and people out of exclusively being seen as either objects of development intervention or of cultural signifiers against legal dispossession. We have shown here how attention to different agricultural crops, methods, and spaces—olives and the smallholder peasant; grazing livestock and the pastoralist; and dates and the sharecropper and corporation—opens up possibilities and directions for critical agrarian studies in Palestine to be revitalized.

We also wish to highlight what Palestine brings to critical agrarian studies, not simply as an interesting case study example but also as a site of theorizing rural life and local and transnational struggle. For instance, scholars in peasant studies have recently called to better think about issues of global capitalism and climate change together (Borras et al. 2022), following wider Marxian concerns with the ecological dimensions of capitalist extraction and dispossession (Moore 2015). Agrarian Palestine brings to that conversation a continuous attention to the historical and persistent colonial dimensions of both capitalist expropriation and climate change's causes and effects. We have laid out here some of those potential threads that bring together critical political economy with cultural and legal studies of rural life in Palestine. Transnational circuits of both capital and knowledge shape how rural people resist, engage, and adapt to changing political, economic, and environmental regimes. Analyses of Palestinian agrarian formations and development bring much to conversations on peasant politics happening across the Global South, and they allow us a deep look at the forces that shape how people live, what they plant, and how they imagine their future.

New critical frameworks have done a lot to de-exceptionalize Palestine and to bring in comparative framings. But thus far, they have done little to make agrarian life and rural worlds visible. Palestine is part of an agrarian and rural world, one that is transnational, both in its geographic and scholarly connections. Scholars of Palestine can bring a lot to these transnational conversations, and we can learn a lot as well.

Notes

1 More also should be written about the history of these organizations and their role in agrarian class formation and struggle. Work on this, which does exist but could be expanded, includes Abu Sada (2007); and Robinson (1993).
2 Israel State Archives 39/15 and 39/20. These files contain dozens of complaints from 1961 to 1964. Under the provision of Preservation of Crops and Saplings No. 20, 1937 (*Siyanat al-Mazru'at wa al-Gharasat*), West Bank residents would file official complaints to the Jordanian government, which would send a team to the area to survey the damages, assess the validity of the complaint, and determine which party was responsible for damages. The files contain correspondence between the Jordanian authorities, witness statements, and descriptive reports of the land in question. All of the complaints are about goat and sheep (and in one case, chickens) damaging trees, vines, and vegetables. They are filed against individuals or groups of people. One man, unable to determine who exactly was responsible for the loss of his saplings, filed a complaint against every single shepherd in Beituna in 1964.
3 In the same section, Awartani draws a similar distinction between the distinctively black Sa'aneen goat and the Shami variety. The latter produces more milk and due to the availability of "certified goats from near-by Israeli sources" increased in number in the West Bank. However, Awartani notes, the Shami goat does not do well in open pastures and as such cannot replace the Sa'aneen.

References

Abufarha, Nasser (2008), "Land of Symbols: Cactus, Poppies, Orange and Olive Trees in Palestine." *Identities*, 15 (3): 343–68.

Abu Sada, Caroline (2007), *ONG palestiniennes et construction étatique. L'expérience de Palestinian Agricultural Relief Committees (PARC) dans les Territoires occupés palestiniens, 1983–2005*. Beyrouth: Institut Français du Proche-Orient.

Ajl, Max (2021), "Does the Arab Region Have an Agrarian Question?" *The Journal of Peasant Studies*, 48 (5): 955–83.

Amara, Ahmad (2013), "The Negev Land Question." *Journal of Palestine Studies*, 42 (4): 27–47.

Anderson, Charles (2018), "The British Mandate and the Crisis of Palestinian Landlessness, 1929–1936." *Middle Eastern Studies*, 54 (2): 171–215.
Arraf, Suha (2020), "Home Gardening Plants Seeds for Palestinian Self-sufficiency." *+972 Magazine*, June 12. https://www.972mag.com/palestinian-home-gardens-coronavirus/.
Asad, Talal (1975), "Anthropological Texts and Ideological Problems: An Analysis of Cohen on Arab Villages in Israel." *Economy and Society*, 4 (3): 251–82.
Awartani, Hisham Masoud (1982), "Agricultural Development in the West Bank: An Economic and Political Study of the Development of Rain-Fed Farming in the West Bank." PhD dissertation, University of Bradford.
Ayyash, Mark Muhannad (2018), "An Assemblage of Decoloniality? Palestinian Fellahin Resistance and the Space-Place Relation." *Studies in Social Justice*, 12 (1): 21–37.
Baumgarten-Sharon, Naama (2017), *Towards Sustainable Food Security in the Occupied Palestinian Territory: Strengthening Rangeland Governance*. Oxfam. https://policy-practice.oxfam.org/resources/towards-sustainable-food-security-in-the-occupied-palestinian-territory-strengt-620254/.
Borras Jr., Saturnino M., Ian Scoones, Amita Baviskar, Marc Edelman, Nancy Lee Peluso, and Wendy Wolford (2022), "Climate Change and Agrarian Struggles: An Invitation to Contribute to a JPS Forum." *The Journal of Peasant Studies*, 49 (1): 1–28.
Braverman, Irus (2009), *Planted Flags: Trees, Land, and Law in Israel/Palestine*. Cambridge: Cambridge University Press.
Cohen, Shaul Ephraim (1993), *The Politics of Planting: Israeli-Palestinian Competition for Control of Land in the Jerusalem Periphery*. Chicago: The University of Chicago Press.
Collins, John (2010), "Between Acceleration and Occupation: Palestine and the Struggle for Global Justice." *Studies in Social Justice*, 4 (2): 199–215.
Daiq, Ismail (1986), "Dur Al-Munthamat al-Jumhariyya Fi al-Tanmiyya al-Rifiyya Li-l-Ard al-Muhtalla [The Role of Mass Organizations in Rural Development for Occupied Land]." *Samed Al-Iqtisadi*, 61: 41–53.
Dana, Tariq (2014), "A Resistance Economy: What Is It and Can It Provide an Alternative?" Rosa Luxemburg Stiftung PAL Papers Series.
Davis, Diana K. (2007), *Resurrecting the Granary of Rome: Environmental History and French Colonial Expansion in North Africa*. Athens: Ohio University Press.
Davis, Diana K. (2016), *The Arid Lands: History, Power, Knowledge*. Cambridge, MA: The MIT Press.
Doumani, Beshara (1995), *Rediscovering Palestine: Merchants and Peasants in Jabal Nablus, 1700–1900*. Berkeley: University of California Press.
Edelman, Marc and Wendy Wolford (2017), "Introduction: Critical Agrarian Studies in Theory and Practice." *Antipode*, 49(4): 959–76.
El Zein, Rayya (2017), "Developing a Palestinian Resistance Economy Through Agricultural Labor." *Journal of Palestine Studies*, XLVI (3): 7–26.
Fakher Eldin, Munir (2008), "Communities of Owners: Land Law, Governance, and Politics in Palestine, 1858–1948." PhD diss., New York University.
Fakher Eldin, Munir (2014), "British Framing of the Frontier in Palestine, 1918–1923: Revisiting Colonial Sources on Tribal Insurrection, Land Tenure, and the Arab Intelligentsia." *Jerusalem Quarterly*, 60: 42–58.
Farsakh, Leila (2005), *Palestinian Labour Migration to Israel: Labour, Land and Occupation*. London and New York: Routledge.
Fields, Gary (2012), "'This Is Our Land': Collective Violence, Property Law, and Imagining the Geography of Palestine." *Journal of Cultural Geography*, 29 (3): 267–91.

Fields, Gary (2017), *Enclosure: Palestinian Landscapes in a Historical Mirror*. Berkeley: The University of California Press.
Gaul, Anny and Graham Auman Pitts (2021), "Introduction: Making Levantine Cuisine." In Anny Gaul, Graham Auman Pitts, and Vicki Valosik (eds.), *Making Levantine Cuisine*, 1–20. Austin: University of Texas Press.
Gutkowski, Natalia (2021), "Bodies That Count: Administering Multispecies in Palestine/Israel's Borderlands." *Environment and Planning E: Nature and Space*, 4 (1): 135–57.
Haddad, Toufic (2016), *Palestine Ltd: Neoliberalism and Nationalism in the Occupied Territory*. London: I.B. Tauris.
Hammami, Rema (2000), "Palestinian NGOs Since Oslo: From NGO Politics to Social Movements?" *Middle East Report*, 214: 16–19.
Hamamami, Rema (2005), "Women in Agricultural Production in the Palestinian Authority." In Pnina Motzafi-Haller (ed.), *Women in Agriculture in the Middle East*, 47–92. London: Routledge.
Hanafi, Sari (2013), "Explaining Spacio-Cide in the Palestinian Territory: Colonization, Separation, and State of Exception." *Current Sociology*, 61 (2): 190–205.
Hanieh, Adam (2011), "The Internationalisation of Gulf Capital and Palestinian Class Formation." *Capital & Class*, 35 (1): 81–106.
Hunaiti, Hadeel (2008), *'Arab Jahalin: From the Nakba to the Wall*. Ramallah: Palestinian Grassroots Anti-Apartheid Wall Campaign.
Jaber, D.A. (2019), "Settler Colonialism and Ecocide: Case Study of Al-Khader, Palestine." *Settler Colonial Studies*, 9 (1): 135–54.
Kelly, Jennifer Lynn (2020), "Subjection and Performance: Tourism, Witnessing, and Acts of Refusal in Palestine." *Feminist Formations*, 32 (2): 79–110.
Khalidi, Raja and Sobhi Samour (2011), "Neoliberalism as Liberation: The Statehood Program and the Remaking of the Palestinian National Movement." *Journal of Palestine Studies*, 40 (2): 6–25.
Kurzom, George (2001), *Towards Alternative Self-Reliant Agricultural Development*. Birzeit: Development Studies Program / Birzeit University.
Makhoul, Najwa (1982), "Changes in the Employment Structure of Arabs in Israel." *Journal of Palestine Studies*, 11 (3): 77–102.
Martínez-Torres, María Elena and Peter M. Rosset (2010), "La vía Campesina: The Birth and Evolution of a Transnational Social Movement." *Journal of Peasant Studies*, 37 (1): 149–75.
Meneley, Anne (2008), "Time in a Bottle: The Uneasy Circulation of Palestinian Olive Oil." *Middle East Report*, 248: 18–23.
Meneley, Anne (2011), "Blood, Sweat and Tears in a Bottle of Palestinian Extra-Virgin Olive Oil." *Food, Culture and Society*, 14 (2): 275–92.
Meneley, Anne (2014a), "Resistance Is Fertile!" *Gastronomica: The Journal of Critical Food Studies*, 14 (4): 69–78.
Meneley, Anne (2014b), "The Accidental Pilgrims: Olive Pickers in Palestine." *Religion and Society: Advances in Research*, 5: 186–99.
Meneley, Anne (2021), "Hope in the Ruins: Seeds, Plants, and Possibilities of Regeneration." *Environment and Planning E: Nature and Space*, 4 (1): 158–72.
Moore, Jason W. (2015), *Capitalism in the Web of Life: Ecology and the Accumulation of Capital*. London: Verso.
Nori, Michele, Mohamed El Mourid, Pamela Giorgi, and Ali Nefzaoui (2009), "Herding in a Shifting Mediterranean Changing Agro-pastoral Livelihoods in the Mashreq & Maghreb Region." EUI Working Paper RSCAS 2009/52.

OCHA (United Nations Office for the Coordination of Humanitarian Affairs) (2021), "2020 Olive Harvest Season: Low Yield Amidst Access Restrictions and Settler Violence." https://www.ochaopt.org/content/2020-olive-harvest-season-low-yield-amidst-access-restrictions-and-settler-violence.

Owen, Roger (ed.) (1982), *Studies in the Economic and Social History of Palestine in the Nineteenth and Twentieth Centuries*. London: MacMillan Press.

Palestinian Central Bureau of Statistics (2019), "Quantity of Olive Pressed and Oil Extracted for Olive Presses Activity in Palestine by Governorate/ Automation Level, 2019." https://www.pcbs.gov.ps/statisticsIndicatorsTables.aspx?lang=en&table_id=902

Plonski, Sharri (2018), "Material Footprints: The Struggle for Borders by Bedouin-Palestinians in Israel." *Antipode*, 50 (5): 1349–75.

Pollock, Alex (1990), "Sharecropping in the North Jordan Valley: Social Relations of Production and Reproduction." In Kathy Glavanis and Pandeli Glavanis (eds.), *The Rural Middle East: Peasant Lives and Modes of Production*, 95–121. London: Birzeit University and Zed Books.

Pugliese, Joseph (2020), *Biopolitics of the More-Than-Human: Forensic Ecologies of Violence*. Durham: Duke University Press.

Rabie, Kareem (2021), *Palestine Is Throwing a Party and the Whole World Is Invited: Capital and State Building in the West Bank*. Durham: Duke University Press.

Reger, Jeffrey D. (2017), "Olive Cultivation in the Galilee, 1948–1955: Hegemony and Resistance." *Journal of Palestine Studies*, 46 (4): 28–45.

Reger, Jeffrey D. (2018), "Planting Palestine: The Political Economy of Olive Culture in the 20th-Century Galilee and West Bank." PhD dissertation, Georgetown University.

Robinson, Glenn E. (1993), "The Role of the Professional Middle Class in the Mobilization of Palestinian Society: The Medical and Agricultural Committees." *International Journal of Middle East Studies*, 25 (2): 301–26.

Rosenfeld, Henry (1978), "The Class Situation of the Arab National Minority in Israel." *Comparative Studies in Society and History*, 20 (3): 374–407.

Samara, Adel and Shehada Awda (1988), *Al-Himayya al-Sha'biyya [Popular Protection]*. Damascus: Dar Kan'an li-l-Darasat wa-l-Nashr.

Sansour, Vivien and Alaa Tartir (2014), "Palestinian Farmers: A Last Stronghold of Resistance." *Al-Shabaka, the Palestinian Policy Network*. https://al-shabaka.org/briefs/palestinian-farmers-a-last-stronghold-of-resistance/.

Seidel, Timothy (2021), "Settler Colonialism and Land-Based Struggle in Palestine: Toward a Decolonial Political Economy." In Alaa Tartir, Tariq Dana, and Timothy Seidel (eds.), *Political Economy of Palestine: Critical, Interdisciplinary, and Decolonial Perspectives*, 81–107. Switzerland: Palgrave Macmillan.

Scoones, Ian (2021), "Pastoralists and Peasants: Perspectives on Agrarian Change." *The Journal of Peasant Studies*, 48 (1): 1–47.

Sharif, Lila (2015), "Savory Colonialism: Land, Memory, and the Eco-Occupation of Palestine." *Journal of Middle East Women's Studies*, 11 (2): 256–57.

Simaan, Juman (2017), "Olive Growing in Palestine: A Decolonial Ethnographic Study of Collective Daily-Forms-of- Resistance." *Journal of Occupational Science*, 24 (4): 510–23.

Stop the Wall (2017), *The Palestinian Periphery: Home Demolitions and Settler Colonialism in the Jordan Valley and South Hebron Hills*. Ramallah: Palestinian Grassroots Anti-Apartheid Wall Campaign.

Swedenburg, Ted (1990), "The Palestinian Peasant as National Signifier." *Anthropological Quarterly*, 63 (1): 18–30.

Tamari, Salim (1983), "The Dislocation and Re-Constitution of a Peasantry: The Social Economy of Agrarian Palestine in the Central Highlands and the Jordan Valley, 1960–1980." PhD dissertation, University of Manchester.

Tamari, Salim (1992), "Soul of the Nation: The Fallah in the Eyes of the Urban Intelligentsia." *Review of Middle East Studies*, 5 (5): 74–83.

Tamari, Salim and Rita Giacaman (1997), *The Social Impact of Agricultural Technology on the Life of a Peasant Community in the Jordan Valley*. Birzeit: Birzeit University.

Tannous, Nadya Raja and Omar Zahzah (2018), "The Scarred Land: Settler Imprints and Indigenous Futures." *The Funambulist*, 20. https://thefunambulist.net/magazine/turtle-island/scarred-land-settler-imprints-indigenous-futures-nadya-raja-tannous-omar-zahzah-palestine-youth-movement.

Tartir, Alaa (2018), "Farming for Freedom: The Shackled Palestinian Agricultural Sector." In Rami Zurayk, Eckart Woertz, and Rachel Bahn (eds.), *Crisis and Conflict in Agriculture*, 144–56. Wallingford: CAB International.

Tatour, Lana (2019), "The Culturalisation of Indigeneity: The Palestinian-Bedouin of the Naqab and Indigenous Rights." *The International Journal of Human Rights*, 23 (10): 1569–93.

Tesdell, Omar Imseeh (2017), "Wild Wheat to Productive Drylands: Global Scientific Practice and the Agroecological Remaking of Palestine." *Geoforum*, 78: 43–51.

Tesdell, Omar Imseeh, Yusra Othman, and Saher Alkhoury (2019), "Rainfed Agroecosystem Resilience in the Palestinian West Bank, 1918–2017." *Agroecology and Sustainable Food Systems*, 43 (1): 21–39.

Tesdell, Omar, Yusra Othman, Yara Dowani, Samir Khraishi, Mary Deeik, Fouad Muaddi, Brandon Schlautman, Aubrey Streit Krug, and David Van Tassel (2020), "Envisioning Perennial Agroecosystems in Palestine." *Journal of Arid Environments*, 175: 104085.

Trottier, Julie (2020), "Debate: In the West Bank, the Palm Trees of Discord." *The Conversation*, February 25. https://theconversation.com/debate-in-the-west-bank-the-palm-trees-of-discord-132041.

Trottier, Julie, Nelly Leblond, and Yaakov Garb (2020), "The Political Role of Date Palm Trees in the Jordan Valley: The Transformation of Palestinian Land and Water Tenure in Agriculture Made Invisible by Epistemic Violence." *Environment and Planning E: Nature and Space*, 3 (1): 114–40.

UNCTAD (2015), "The Besieged Palestinian Agricultural Sector." *United Nations Conference on Trade and Development*.

Weizman, Eyal and Fazal Sheikh (2015), *The Conflict Shoreline: Colonization as Climate Change in the Negev Desert*. New York: Steidl Verlag/Cabinet Books.

Who Profits (2014), "Made in Israel: Agricultural Export From Occupied Territories." April. https://www.whoprofits.org/report/made-in-israel-agricultural-export-from-occupied-territories/.

Zureik, Elia T. (1976), "Transformation of Class Structure Among the Arabs in Israel: From Peasantry to Proletariat." *Journal of Palestine Studies*, 6 (1): 39–66.

10

Settler Colonial Violence and Indigenous Struggle

Land, Resistance, and Refusal in Masafer Yatta

Timothy Seidel and Federica Stagni

Introduction: Settler Colonialism in Palestine

Settler colonialism in Palestine has received increased attention in recent years (Salamanca et al. 2012; Barakat 2017; Hawari, Plonski and Weizman 2019; Amoruso, Pappé and Richter-Devroe 2019; Tartir, Dana and Seidel 2021). As a particular kind of colonialism, settler colonialism is characterized by its "logic of elimination" (Wolfe 2006, 387–8). It is described as an ongoing structure, not an event relegated to the past but a structure marked by settler colonizers who "come to stay" on the land and "destroy to replace" (Wolfe 2006, 387–8). This logic of elimination animates both the negative goal of the dissolution of Indigenous societies and the positive goal of constructing a new colonial society on expropriated land.

Such structures and logics of elimination and replacement produce a particular kind of violence, settler violence, with a history in Palestine that can be traced back for over a century (Sayegh 1965; Barakat 2017; Khalidi 2020). This includes violence against Indigenous people and against the land. In occupied Palestine, this is seen, for example, in the confiscation of land, forced displacement and ethnic cleansing of Palestinians, settlement building and expansion, water consumption, and inequitable access. The social, political, and economic effects of this violence manifest in a system of domination that exploits, dispossesses, displaces, and constrains the livelihoods of Palestinians (Seidel 2019). This chapter explores Israel's settler colonial violence as well as Palestinian resistance and struggle that expresses a kind of refusal or *sumud* (steadfastness) emerging out of Palestinians' experiences with the land.

This exploration of settler colonialism and Indigenous resistance emphasizes that a decolonial analysis gives attention not only to enduring indigeneity but also to the role of land in the struggle for autonomy, sovereignty, and self-determination (Seidel 2021). This chapter makes the case for investing agency in both the Palestinian communities and their relation with the land of historic Palestine as an inseparable part of those communities—defining enduring indigeneity in political and economic terms that defy the logics of settler colonialism and capital. This chapter then explores this subjectivity through land-based struggles. In occupied Palestine, in particular, this resistance and refusal takes the form of *sumud* or steadfastness considering alternative subjectivities that may not be about a predetermined political economic telos per se (e.g., in terms of the modern/colonial telos of the nation-state and the market economy) but about existence, being, land, and a refusal of erasure and elimination.

This approach challenges the dismissal of political economic activity that is not formal or legible to the state or the market by articulating a decolonial political vision of pluriversality that visibilizes land-based livelihoods and struggles and their multiple networks of relationships. In contrast to formal activity, informal activities include those that are not legible and governable by the state and the market, that is, that can be tracked, taxed, and managed by the state or by global business. Importantly this often includes the labor and economic activity of women who do not have access to formal institutions or whose labor goes undervalued by the market despite its essential contribution to everyday livelihoods. By challenging the erasure of informality, a decolonial approach acknowledges (the simultaneity and heterogeneity of) everyday, alternative worlds—where alternative imaginaries animate; alternative sovereignties define. This chapter considers the experience of Palestinian communities in the South Hebron Hills, in the southern occupied West Bank. These communities have all experienced settler violence in an attempt to eliminate or erase through different colonial strategies, but they have all resisted in similar ways. By embracing popular resistance they engage in an act of refusal, of not-leaving their land vis-à-vis eviction orders and frequent demolitions. We might call these practices "everyday" acts of resistance and popular struggle (Scott 1985; Zaru 2008; Qumsiyeh 2011; Johansson and Vinthagen 2016) that take the form of *sumud* or steadfastness, accessible to and embodied by Palestinian communities, especially in places like Area C in the occupied West Bank (Seidel 2017). With this framework and understanding of popular struggle, we begin to hear and see a much larger and more powerful landscape of resistance to settler violence in occupied Palestine, for example, in the case of Masafer Yatta in the South Hebron Hills.

This area in the southern Hebron district of the occupied West Bank constantly experiences settler violence as it is surrounded by a belt of illegal Israeli settlements. The focus of the chapter will be on this particular area for three reasons. First of all, because the area of Masafer Yatta is right now at risk of ethnic cleansing and, despite the campaign launched by local activists such as the Youth of Sumud collective,[1] demolitions are proceeding relentlessly (Al Tahhan 2023). Second, the Palestinian communities of this area still live a place-based lifestyle grounded in a relationship of resistance, steadfastness, and presence on the land of their ancestors. Third, despite the Israeli Civil Administration giving these communities the option to move to Yatta or other urban areas, the inhabitants of this region have always refused and continued to live in their villages facing both the institutionalized colonial violence of the Israeli Civil Administration and daily violent attacks on the ground from Israeli settlers. The Israeli Civil Administration[2] overtly prevents construction in almost all Palestinian villages in the South Hebron Hills. One way to do this is to not authorize master plans that would allow for the legalization of existing construction as well as future developments. The Civil Administration relies on the system of master plans that was formalized by the British mandatory authorities in 1942. According to that master plan, the area was devoted to agricultural use and not construction (Amnesty International 2022, 157).

Settler Violence in Occupied Palestine and Enduring Indigeneity

The settler colonial relationship, writes Glen Coulthard, is characterized by a form of domination found in a relationship where "power ... has been structured into a relatively secure or sedimented set of hierarchical social relations that continue to facilitate the dispossession of Indigenous Peoples of their lands and self-determining authority" (2014, 6–7). Coulthard identifies territoriality—access to territory—as settler colonialism's "specific, irreducible element" (2014, 7). It is fundamental, in his analysis, to the work of both capitalism and colonialism and requires a contextual shift in our investigation "from an emphasis on the *capital relation* to the *colonial relation*" (2014, 10).

> The theory and practice of Indigenous anticolonialism, including Indigenous anticapitalism, is best understood as a struggle primarily inspired by and oriented around *the question of land*—a struggle not only *for* land in the material sense, but also deeply informed by what the land as a system of reciprocal relations and obligations can teach us about living our lives in relation to one another and the natural world in nondominating and nonexploitative terms. (2014, 13)

This signals a commitment toward decoloniality and decolonization as both a political and epistemic project (Mignolo 2011). J. Kēhaulani Kauanui talks specifically about decoloniality as an approach that gives attention to the erasure of history and to the history of erasure, which has as its point of departure the enduring presence of Indigenous peoples despite settler colonial projects of elimination (2016). This is a commitment, then, to historical interpretations, and studies of race and indigeneity, that challenges the logic of elimination and gives attention to histories of erasure as well as land and the livelihoods and struggles around land.[3]

Indeed, politically and economically, erasure is necessary to invalidate Indigenous land claims. This is an important function of statements like "there is no such thing as a Palestinian" as well as "land without a people." The erasure of a whole people necessarily includes their claims to, and existence on, land.

The language or frame of indigeneity is also important for the way it historicizes the situation in Palestine. It forces us to confront Palestinian dispossession and displacement within a specific framework of settler colonial history rather than as a consequence of communal strife or historical misfortune or as an exceptional set of events brought forth by ahistorical circumstances. Steven Salaita points out that the language "identifies a perceived sociohistorical familiarity with other dispossessed communities" (2016, 2).

It is also important to locate a settler colonial analytic within an Indigenous framework. In other words, settler colonialism must be read from within a Palestinian narrative in order to understand Palestinian indigeneity. This offers "a way to read Palestinians as the makers of Palestinian history as opposed to Palestinians as a part of a Zionist narrative" (Barakat 2017, 350). It also sees Indigenous as a political category, within a political project, in which Palestinians narratives of resistance to imperial and settler colonial powers include elements such as Indigenous sovereignty and Palestinian resistance and endurance (Barakat 2017, 361).

Despite the logic of elimination, Indigenous peoples as individual and collective polities "exist, resist, and persist" (Kauanui 2016). Where the hegemony of settler governmentality forecloses the possibility of imagining otherwise, a decolonial approach challenges the unmarkedness of settler colonialism, working to visibilize "settler common sense" as well as Indigenous subjectivity (Kauanui 2016).

As we will discuss later, expressions of Indigenous resistance and steadfastness take multiple shapes, including living in sustainable, right relationship with the land, challenging settler violence and the destructive forces of colonization by "struggling to reclaim and regenerate one's relational, place-based existence" (Corntassel 2012, 88).

Indigenous resistance also manifests through transnational solidarities—an internationalism that draws from intergenerational tradition of resistance to colonialism and global capitalism (Simpson 2008; Estes 2019; Seidel 2023).

Finally, we observe a kind of Indigenous resistance that expresses alternative politics and sociality through struggles for sovereignty. An example of this in North America was the community of resistance that emerged at Standing Rock struggling against the Dakota Access Pipeline (Estes 2019).

In what follows, we explore examples of this Palestinian subjectivity, resistance, and refusal as enduring indigeneity in the face of settler violence in the South Hebron Hills. The testimonies shared were taken from interviews and ethnographic fieldwork conducted in October 2021 and April 2022.

Contention, Resistance, and Refusal: *Sumud* in the South Hebron Hills

The South Hebron Hills region is located in Area C of the West Bank, under full Israeli control. Israeli authorities constantly threaten the very existence of the Palestinian villages in this area.[4] The region, part of which is also known as Masafer Yatta (referring to the villages in the southern occupied West Bank near the town of Yatta), is home to around 4,000 people, most of whom are farmers and herders who mainly live off what they produce (OCHA 2020, 2022; Al Tahhan 2022, 2023). This chapter focuses on this site of contentiousness because it exemplifies the tension between resistance, expressed in the terms of *sumud*, and the violent efforts by the settler colonial power to expel and erase these communities.

In the 1980s Israel declared areas of Masafer Yatta a "firing zone" and a closed military zone. This set the stage for a series of demolitions and forced evictions of the Palestinians in this region. More recently in May 2022, the Israeli high court ruled that Israel could expel more than 1,000 Palestinians from their homes in Masafer Yatta to make way for a training zone for Israel's occupying army.

While Israel routinely destroys Palestinian homes, this is the largest forced displacement carried out by Israel since it began its military occupation of the West Bank in 1967. The United Nations condemned the ruling as a serious breach of international humanitarian and human rights laws, and human rights group Amnesty International described it as "a pillar of Israel's system of apartheid" (Al Tahhan 2023).

The Palestinian Authority also condemned it saying "the demolitions would be a flagrant violation of international law" (Al Tahhan 2023). However, the PA remains an absentee from this area of the Occupied Territories. The PA plays a limited role in Area C, where Masafer Yatta is located. It underscores the ongoing effects of the Oslo process that literally fragmented not only the land of Palestine but also the Palestinian national movement. In fact, the PA has very limited authority in Area C: the educational and administrative aspects of social health services, but as mentioned, it is excluded from urban planning, which Israel deals with. If on the one hand, this has meant that the urbanization and transition to a neoliberal market economy did not fully develop, on the other it begs the question of what role the PA plays in parts of occupied Palestine experiencing settler violence. This is keenly felt by Palestinians who experience little support or acknowledgment let alone policies from the PA that support them and respond to their needs.

The South Hebron Hills and Masafer Yatta, specifically, are just examples; settler violence can be observed in many other places from Jericho to Gaza and from Jenin to Jerusalem. It takes different forms and manifests in different ways even though the final goal is always the erasure of the Palestinian Indigenous population. Likewise, farmers' and shepherds' struggles are present in many other parts of the occupied Palestinian territories (oPt) both in the West Bank (e.g., in the Jordan Valley) and in the Gaza Strip.

Without approved construction plans, Palestinians cannot obtain building permits, both for housing and for public buildings such as schools and medical clinics. Nor can they get approval for paving streets. Furthermore, Palestinians are prevented from connecting to either the electricity grid or the water pipes that Israel has laid in the area for settlements and so-called outposts that are usually built without any proper permits. Although the Civil Administration drafted several master plans for Palestinian villages in Area C, these plans were usually aimed at limiting the real development options for these villages. For example, in the early 1990s, the Civil Administration prepared a plan for the village of At-Tuwani in Masafer Yatta. In 2009 the plan was updated and the coverage area was expanded. However, the plan was prepared without a previous planning survey that accounted for the demographic needs of the village. The Civil Administration plan allocated only 52 dunams (5.2 hectares) to the village and did not allocate any land for future development. At the same time, the Civil Administration allocated 385 dunams (38.5 hectares) to the nearby Israeli settlement of Ma'on, regardless of the similarly sized populations of the two communities (B'Tselem 2013).

The Palestinian village of Susiya, also in the South Hebron Hills, has experienced a similar story albeit under different pretexts. It houses around 250 people, who make a living from pastoralism, agriculture, and olive trees. In 1983, the Israeli settlement of Susya, which currently has a population of 1,170 settlers, was established near the village on Palestinian private land that Israeli authorities have declared state-owned land. In 1986, when about twenty-five families lived on their private land in ancient Khirbet Susiya, the Israeli Civil Administration declared the village land an "archaeological site" and the land was confiscated "for public purposes." As a result, the Israeli Army expelled Palestinian residents from their homes without further notice and compensation. The families then moved to what was left of their agricultural lands outside the archaeological site, about 500 meters from their village.[5] Israeli authorities have issued demolition orders against 170 structures in the village. As in At-Tuwani, Palestinian residents have repeatedly tried to obtain building permits, but the Israeli authorities refused to release them, and instead, in 1999, 2001, and 2011, they demolished several of these new Palestinian shelters. Again, in 2012, the Israeli Civil Administration issued demolition orders for more than fifty structures in Khirbet Susiya (B'Tselem 2018). The loss of land, here as in other villages, forced the inhabitants of Susiya to reduce the size of their herds. One resident of Susiya Azam Nawaj'a said that before he had 150 sheep, but now he can only keep 25. He also told Amnesty International that often the settlers come to destroy the olive trees of the village. He said three years earlier they had cut down 300 of his olive trees. According to OCHA, Israeli settlers vandalized and damaged 800 olive trees and saplings in Khirbet Susiya in 2014 alone (Amnesty International 2022).

Concrete Manifestation of the Settler Colonial Effort to Replace the Indigenous People in the South Hebron Hills Region

The settler colonial logic to replace Indigenous people manifests in different ways. One of these efforts is to replace Indigenous people by "becoming" Indigenous, which requires, among other things, eliminating the actual Indigenous people. Trying to prove their ancestral belonging to Samaria and Galilee[6] is not a new strategy for Israeli settlers. Zionist elites have always mobilized academics, theologians, religious leaders, cartographers, and geographers to legitimize the Israeli Jewish presence on the territory of what they consider Eretz Israel (Kedar 2003; Barakat 2017; Benvenisti 2000). All these efforts served to justify the existence and the legitimacy of the state of Israel from an institutional point of view (Pappé 2017). The appropriation from certain groups of settlers of a Palestinian Indigenous lifestyle is something different and aims at providing a legitimation that is not political or formal but sociocultural. Nevertheless, some settler communities in the area are starting to appropriate Palestinian lifestyles. Israeli settlements in the region such as Ma'on[7] or Susya settlement are famous for their agricultural production of milk, olive, grains, and wine that they export all over Israel and the world.[8] Palestinians living in these areas have a similar type of agricultural production but most of the time it is aimed at the self-sufficiency of the communities. This is a first major difference with the settler society. The settler society uses dispossession from an export-oriented economy perspective in order to keep pace with both colonial and capitalist expectations. By contrast, the Indigenous population lives in relationship with the land for sustainability and well-being. There is evidence not only from the agricultural sector but also from the pastoralist one. Israeli settlers are increasingly approaching Palestinian shepherds grazing with their flocks of sheep on their agricultural properties not with sticks and clubs but with their own flocks.

The purpose of these clashes is twofold. In the first place, Israeli settlers can present themselves as agricultural communities with a strong relationship with the land claiming to be more deeply rooted than Palestinian communities among whom there are also groups of nonpermanent but mobile Bedouins. On the other hand, by mixing the flocks, they have the opportunity to appropriate a greater number of sheep. This example of theft is a direct consequence of the land theft carried out by the Zionist movement for almost a century. One example from our fieldwork while accompanying a shepherd in the hills of Masafer Yatta illustrates this strategy. What follows are fieldnotes from that encounter:

> The settlers approach with their sheep the Palestinian shepherd with his flock that I and other activists are escorting. I did not immediately understand well the situation. It is very different from usual clashes which are certainly more confrontational and violent. My fellow Israeli activist tells me that flocks absolutely must not mix. I still don't understand exactly what is happening here but I begin to push the settler's sheep in the opposite direction to that of the Palestinian herd. A confrontation with settlers and the arrival of the military follow but we manage not to mix the herds. When the situation calms down, I ask our Palestinian partner the reasons for this strategy. He explains to me that a few days earlier the settlers did the same thing. The herds mixed up and once the matter was reported to the Civil Administration, it was decided that the Palestinian shepherd was trying to steal the settler's sheep. He was then fined and forced to give to the settler that invaded his land part of his flock. The settler de facto stole his sheep.

In Palestine, the legacy of settler colonialism is that it destroys in order to replace and renames in order to erase (Tartir and Wildeman 2020). And yet, as this example illustrates, not simply to replace but a process of replacement that "maintains the refractory imprint of the native counter-claim" (Wolfe 2006, 389), asserting false narratives and structures of settler belonging. Settler colonialism endeavors to recast indigeneity onto the settler, requiring the violence of elimination and erasure of the native population. This is another key feature: settler colonialism seeks its own end in that it trends toward the ending of colonial difference in the form of a supreme and unchallenged settler state and people.

In Susiya the settler colony used a different pretext to demonstrate the same forged ancestral connection to the land. The first time the inhabitants of Susiya were expelled was due to the discovery of the archaeological remains of an ancient synagogue (Patel 2018). Archaeological sites have always been a common pretext for Israel to expel Palestinians living in those lands without any possibility of appeal or compensation. Think for example of the "King David City" in Silwan, a predominantly Palestinian neighborhood of occupied Jerusalem, where a theme park has been built to recount the exploits of the biblical figure.[9] Similarly, to access the synagogue in the caves where Palestinian families lived, you have to pay a ticket. It is now a "National Heritage Site."[10] The use of archeological ruins as an excuse aims to create an alleged connection with an historical past in which Israeli Jews were the natives of that land (Abu El-Haj 2001). During an action together with other international and Israeli activists, Susiya inhabitants started to tell the old stories of the village. They proposed, as a political act, to go all together to visit the archeological site:

> We said, we want to go home. We want the whole village to walk across the highway and to go to our original village of Susiya where we were, where many of us were born in the caves, many of us lived and died in these caves and on the agricultural land that's now been turned into a settlement/archaeological site. Before that action, I think maybe three or four people from the community had ever gone back since they were forced off that land when the Israeli government expelled them and turned it into an archaeological site. I was born here. I want to see where I was born, even though it's literally across the road, literally across the road. This would be the most meaningful thing for the grandparents and the children to go back and visit. We won't stay. We can't stay at that time. We can't stay. Maybe in the future will do something where they can reclaim it. I want the kids of Susiya to get to see where their parents were born, where their Grandparents grew up. (Susiya community organizer)

The community of Susiya now lives on part of its agricultural land. Therefore, the subsequent pretext used by Israel to expropriate those lands and force the community to disintegrate by moving to the town of Yatta was to blame its poor sanitary conditions. In 2013, the Israeli Civil Administration rejected a zoning plan that would have given villagers legal permission to build and extend their homes. Its rejection was based in part on the Israeli government's contention that the distance of the village from the nearest urban center would keep villagers, and particularly women, trapped in a "cycle of poverty," despite the fact that the center in question is less than three kilometers away. They stated: "We see the current plan [prepared by the village] as yet another attempt to keep a poor, downtrodden population from advancing; from choosing between partial income and other resources; it is an attempt to prevent the Palestinian woman from breaking the cycle of poverty and depriving her of educational and professional opportunities" (Beaumont 2015).

The decision to demolish Susiya and the other villages of the area fits into the larger Israeli plans for colonization of the West Bank. The simple goal is to force Palestinians off their land and into major urban areas like Hebron or the city of Yatta, where they can be easily contained by Israel. The colonial power does it in several ways. As exposed in this section there were at least three different methods applied in the same zone. First, what we can call "indigenous mimic"; second, archeological heritage; and third, false humanitarianism. Susiya, At-Tuwani, and the area of Masafer Yatta are among the few villages still fighting this plan in the southern occupied West Bank becoming a symbol of struggle through different initiatives, such as the Sumud Freedom Camp that we discuss in the next section.

Concrete Manifestations of Indigenous Resistance

There are two things to consider when it comes to this type of resistance in the South Hebron Hills. First, it is *land-based*, and second, it is *community-based*. These two elements make Indigenous resistance strong and durable through time in this area. The first point is explained by a young At-Tuwani activist interviewed in October 2021. While many of the youth move to urban centers to obtain better working conditions, a new generation of Palestinian activists has tried to remain on their ancestral land. One of them explained why this effort is so important and how much the colonial power tries to prevent any type of struggle to remain:

> This is our land and we won't give up and leave. This is why existing is resisting in the South Hebron Hills. Despite all these aggressive rules, Palestinians remain here. The goal of the settler state is to empty the land from Palestinians and steal the land piece by piece. This is the general policy of the occupation. This is why in 2017 we created the "Sumud Freedom Camp" in Sarura village that was supposed to be demolished to make room for the nearby settlement to expand. Our activity targeted going inside the village and telling the story of the original inhabitants of the caves. Therefore, during that summer, we lived inside the caves, planted trees, and fixed stonewalls, really to repeat that traditional type of life generally inside the village. This idea went on for months because what was going on was a good process, but the occupation on the third day of our presence in the village raided the village. They started to beat us and beat everyone destroying property and stealing and confiscating most of the properties that we have. (Youth of Sumud organizer)

The camp represented a direct action of civil disobedience in the South Hebron Hills. Since May 2017, the project has reclaimed homes for two families who were displaced by military and settler violence, rehabilitated the area, and established a community center for nonviolent resistance events and peace education. At-Tuwani residents and the village's Popular Resistance Committee are currently sustaining the project. The camp stands for an end to the systematic displacement of Palestinians and the rights for all to live free from violence and to actualize their human rights of home, livelihood, and safety. Expected to last only a few weeks, subjected to consistent military and settler violence, the camp has sustained itself until today.[11]

The Sumud Freedom Camp is an emblematic example of the various forms that Indigenous resistance can take. For example, it bears resemblances to the Oceti Sakowin Camp at Standing Rock in that it is not simply a site of protest but a community of mutual support and aid and collective resistance against settler violence (Estes 2019, 58–9).[12] In areas subject to settler violence, the act of refusal by staying where one is—which is what the term *sumud* expresses—is understood as an act of resistance. Similarly, maintaining a place-based lifestyle such as that which many shepherds and farmers continue to preserve in the area not only tangibly resists settler colonialism but also the uncontested exploitation of the land and its resources, as it offers a way of subsistence that challenges capitalist forces.

> Here we are talking about simple farmer people. We used to live in tents and in caves, and our primary source of income is the sheep, the sheep grazing. Everyone has his own flock, and every family has its own sheep and sometimes agricultural fields. We live a very simple life, but at the same time, occupation is deploying really complex Apartheid policies against us. They are strangling us. This is why we need to resist. (Youth of Sumud organizer)

The other strongly anti-capitalist character is that of the relationship with the community that one inhabits. The community element and the responsibility to keep one's community united play a very important role in the decision to engage in campaigns to challenge house demolitions and displacement of people. It is evident that if people were to move to Yatta or other large urban centers their lives would change enormously. As pointed out earlier, one of the arguments used by the Civil Administration was that such displacement would have improved the lives of women who have no possibility of advancing their conditions in rural communities. This humanitarian frame of settler militaries "protecting" Indigenous peoples is fundamentally racist. It claims that the colonial power is more advanced and knows what is "best" for an Indigenous population. And yet once displaced to a city it is not automatic or guaranteed that women find jobs either. The risk is the opposite: once in the urban context some of them may find themselves confined to the home where they would live an even more isolated life without the support of other women in the community.

> [in Susiya] we are living as farmers, shepherds. We gain our income from milk products and farming the land, which is, from my point of view, one of the reasons behind the success of the movement: [not evicting the people from their village]. If we were employees we wouldn't stay there, we would move to area A or B. But being a shepherd means being resistant by nature. Being a farmer means being in the field. I think without the power of the people, nothing can happen even if all of Europe, all of Israel, and all of the world, stand beside us. [. . .] When it comes to the people who feel the threat for the land, the olive trees, the crops, the sheep, the livestock, everything becomes clear: this is not an abstract occupation. Some of us had the choice to be in Yatta, a bigger town, where some have houses but we prefer to live in caves instead of living in houses. We are doing our daily lives so the everyday actions that people are doing are very important because the nature of this is everyday embedded resistance. We are the community. We want to do this. We care about the protection of our land, which is similar to many farmers all over the world. (Susiya community organizer)

This last testimony also demonstrates how the relationship between the land and the community that inhabits it goes hand in hand. The decision to resist and to remain where one's community can develop according to Indigenous traditions that include an anti-capitalist logic is another manifestation of the will to confront a colonial regime that aims at the total elimination of both the Indigenous people and their traditions by either erasing or appropriating.

Conclusion

All this settler violence, and we never leave.
(At-Tuwani community organizer)

That Palestinians in Area C in the occupied West Bank rarely get permits to build, while nearby Israeli illegal settlements are growing disproportionately is one of the many examples that shows how Israel's settler colonialism defines it as a settler state. The resources of the state are used to build settlements—the buildings, the surrounding infrastructure—while the state uproots Palestinians, expropriates land, demolishes homes, and disrupts livelihoods.

The Israeli settler state also supports settlers and settler violence in all of occupied Palestine. Israeli soldiers in the South Hebron Hills routinely protect Israeli settlers, then stand by while those settlers attack Palestinians. This is another characteristic of a settler state: the security apparatus of the state is used to protect and defend its settler population while it makes a disproportionate use of violence against Palestinians, terrorizing schoolchildren or shepherds and farmers by cutting down olive trees, poisoning sheep and water wells. Additionally, the Israeli military constantly discriminates against Palestinians when it comes to political and civil rights: Palestinian land is often declared closed military zones as a pretext to detain Palestinians protesting nonviolently. Similarly, Masafer Yatta was defined as a firing zone with the precise aim of the Israeli military to train near Palestinian villages, invoking fear and a pretext for evicting Palestinians from their homes (in addition to the permit regime). Masafer Yatta has become one of the largest eviction efforts in decades, something the UN warns could be a war crime (Knell et al. 2022).

We write this in late 2023 during Israel's genocidal campaign of violence on the Gaza Strip, and attacks by Israeli settlers have increased significantly in the West Bank. OCHA has reported that settler violence against Palestinians have resulted in trespassing, harassment, property damage, and personal injury, blocking the movement of Palestinians and damaging water resources that herding communities rely on—all increasing pressure on Palestinians to leave their land. The Israeli military still does not take steps to stop these attacks. On the contrary, the UN reports that in half of the cases, the Israeli military has "accompanied or actively supported" settler violence (OCHA 2023).

This exploration of settler colonialism and Indigenous resistance has made the case for investing agency in both the Palestinian communities and their relation with the land of historic Palestine as an inseparable part of those communities—defining enduring indigeneity in political and economic terms that defy the logics of settler colonialism and capital. In occupied Palestine, in particular, this resistance and refusal takes the form of *sumud*, or steadfastness, as an expression of enduring indigeneity in a struggle about the land where Palestinian communities refuse to leave. As one community organizer of the area described it:

> We are a living people. We move everywhere despite closures and checkpoints, the arrests, the demolitions. We are still on our own land, and we will never leave. This

is a kind of determination for everyone in this area, steadfastness, *sumud*. This is *sumud*. (At-Tuwani community organizer)

This resistance does not only take the form of being rooted in the land through "active not-leaving," but it is also expressed in the maintenance of an Indigenous, place-based lifestyle, which at the same time rejects capitalist logics of production and consumption. On the other hand, this type of resistance is constantly tested by the innovation of the techniques of domination and erasure that the settler state employs.

Notes

1. https://actionnetwork.org/letters/save-masafer-yatta/.
2. Israeli Ministry of Defense established the Civil Administration in 1981. This organ currently oversees all civilian matters for Israeli Jewish settlers and Palestinian residents in Area C of the West Bank as well as some administrative matters for Palestinians who live in other areas of the West Bank and Gaza Strip. Prior to the Oslo Accords, the Civil Administration was the governing body in all of the occupied Palestinian territories; since 1994, most of its functions have been transferred to the Palestinian Authority for civil matters in Areas A and B. Today, the Civil Administration is mainly responsible for issuing travel permits from the West Bank and Gaza to Israel and all inside the West Bank, work permits for Palestinians entering Israel to work, plus any type of construction or demolition permit in Israeli settlements and on Palestinian land in Area C (Human Rights Watch 2012, 21).
3. Coloniality is the logic animating "racialized and gendered socio-economic and political hierarchies according to an invented Eurocentric standard." The concept of decoloniality, then, "refers to analytic approaches and socioeconomic and political practices opposed to pillars of Western civilization: coloniality and modernity. This makes decoloniality both a political and epistemic project" (Mignolo 2011, xxiv).
4. The Oslo Accords II went into effect in 1995, officially dividing the West Bank into Areas A, B, and C. Area A is made up of the West Bank's major Palestinian population centers and falls under Palestinian Authority's civil and security control. In Area B, Palestinians have control over civil affairs, while Israel maintains security control. Area C falls under full Israeli control. Making up roughly 62 percent of the occupied West Bank, Area C is the only contiguous territory in the West Bank, containing the majority of Palestinian agricultural and grazing land as well as land reserves for future economic development. However, Palestinians are forbidden from creating permanent structures in Area C without a permit from the Israeli Civil Administration leaving around 150,000 Palestinians forced to reside in informal and nonpermanent encampments (MA'AN 2012; OCHA 2021).
5. https://rhr.org.il/eng/save-susya/.
6. Samaria is the central region of ancient Palestine. Samaria extends for about 40 miles (65 km) from north to south and 35 miles (56 km) from east to west. It is bounded by Galilee on the north and by Judaea on the south; on the west was the Mediterranean Sea and on the east the Jordan River. The mountain ranges of southern Samaria continue into Judaea with no clearly marked division. Interestingly, the Zionist

movement has historically called these regions by their original biblical names to erase the ancestral ties Palestinians have to the land.
7 https://blessedbuyisrael.com/.
8 http://weisshalivniwine.com/.
9 https://www.cityofdavid.org.il/.
10 http://atarsusya.co.il/.
11 See https://www.facebook.com/SumudCamp/ as well as +972 Magazine (2017).
12 The Oceti Sakowin Camp was one of several camps constructed at Standing Rock Sioux Reservation as a place of community, protest, and struggle against the Dakota Access Pipeline in 2016.

References

Abu El-Haj, Nadia (2001), *Facts on the Ground: Archaeological Practice and Territorial Self-Fashioning in Israeli Society*. Chicago: University of Chicago Press.
Al Tahhan, Zena (2022), "Israeli Forces Demolish Palestinian School in Masafer Yatta." *Al Jazeera*, November 23. https://www.aljazeera.com/news/2022/11/23/israeli-forces-demolish-palestinian-school-in-masafer-yatta.
Al Tahhan, Zena (2023), "Palestinian Villagers in Masafer Yatta Face Immediate Expulsion." *Al Jazeera*, January 4. https://www.aljazeera.com/news/2023/1/4/palestinian-villagers-masafer-yatta-face-immediate-expulsion-explainer.
Amnesty International (2022), "Israel's Apartheid against Palestinians." https://www.amnesty.org/en/latest/campaigns/2022/02/israels-system-of-apartheid/.
Amoruso, Francesco, Ilan Pappé, and Sophie Richter-Devroe (2019), "Knowledge, Power, and the "Settler Colonial Turn" in Palestine Studies." *Interventions: International Journal of Postcolonial Studies*, 21 (4): 452–63.
Barakat, Rana (2017), "Writing/Righting Palestine Studies: Settler Colonialism, Indigenous Sovereignty and Resisting the Ghost(s) of History." *Settler Colonial Studies*, 8 (3): 349–63.
Beaumont, Peter (2015), "Israeli Rights Groups Join Battle to Save Symbol of Arab Resistance to Evictions." *The Guardian*, June 6. https://www.theguardian.com/world/2015/jun/06/palestinians-israel-court-evictions-khirbet-susiya-resistance.
Benvenisti, Meron (2000), *Sacred Landscape: Buried History of the Holy Land Since 1948*. Berkeley: University of California.
B'Tselem (2013), "The South Hebron Hills." January 1. https://www.btselem.org/south_hebron_hills.
B'Tselem (2018), "Khirbet Susiya – A Village under Threat of Demolition." July 4. https://www.btselem.org/south_hebron_hills/susiya.
Corntassel, Jeff (2012), "Re-envisioning Resurgence: Indigenous Pathways to Decolonization and Sustainable Self-Determination." *Decolonization: Indigeneity, Education & Society*, 1 (1): 86–101.
Coulthard, Glen Sean (2014), *Red Skin, White Masks: Rejecting the Colonial Politics of Recognition*. Minneapolis: University of Minnesota Press.
Estes, Nick (2019), *Our History is the Future: Standing Rock versus the Dakota Access Pipeline, and the Long Tradition of Indigenous Resistance*. London: Verso.
Hawari, Yara, Sharri Plonski, and Elian Weizman (2019), "Settlers and Citizens: A Critical View of Israeli Society." *Settler Colonial Studies*, 9 (1): 1–5.

Human Rights Watch (2012), "'Forget About Him, He's Not Here': Israel's Control of Palestinian Residency in the West Bank and Gaza." February. https://www.hrw.org/sites/default/files/reports/iopt0212webwcover.pdf.

Johansson, Anna and Stellan Vinthagen (2014), "Dimensions of Everyday Resistance: An Analytical Framework." *Critical Sociology*, 42(3): 417–35.

Kauanui, J. Kēhaulani (2016), "'A Structure, Not an Event': Settler Colonialism and Enduring Indigeneity." *Lateral*, 5 (1). http://csalateral.org/wp/issue/5-1/forum-alt-humanities-settler-colonialism-enduring-indigeneity-kauanui.

Kedar, Alexandre (2003), "On the Legal Geography of Ethnocratic Settler States: Notes towards a Research Agenda." *Current Legal Issues*, 5: 401–41.

Khalidi, Rashid (2020), *The Hundred Years' War on Palestine: A History of Settler Colonialism and Resistance, 1917–2017*. New York: Metropolitan Books.

Knell, Yolande, Melanie Marshall, Rajai Khateeb, and Jimmy Michael (2022), "The Palestinians Facing Mass Eviction in the West Bank" (video). *BBC World Service*, August 28. https://www.bbc.com/news/av/world-middle-east-62635675.

MA'AN Development Center (2012), "Towards a Just Model of Palestinian Development: Reassessing International Aid Conditions." *MA'AN Development Center Position Paper*, January. http://www.maan-ctr.org/old/pdfs/FSReport/PP/PP-towards.pdf.

Mignolo, Walter (2011), *The Darker Side of Western Modernity: Global Futures, Decolonial Options*. Durham: Duke University Press.

OCHA (2020), "West Bank Demolitions and Displacement | December 2020." https://www.ochaopt.org/content/west-bank-demolitions-and-displacement-december-2020.

OCHA (2021), "Most Palestinian Plans to Build in Area C Not Approved." *OCHA: The Humanitarian Bulletin*, January–May. https://www.ochaopt.org/content/most-palestinian-plans-build-area-c-not-approved.

OCHA (2022), "Fact Sheet: Masafer Yatta Communities at Risk of Forcible Transfer | June 2022." https://www.ochaopt.org/content/masafer-yatta-communities-risk-forcible-transfer-june-2022.

OCHA (2023), "The Other Mass Displacement: Settlers Advance on West Bank Herders." OCHA Report, November 1. https://www.ochaopt.org/content/other-mass-displacement-while-eyes-are-gaza-settlers-advance-west-bank-herders.

Pappé, Ilan (2017), *Ten Myths about Israel*. London: Verso Books.

Patel, Yumna (2018), "Decades-long Battle Continues, as Susiya Braces for More Israeli Demolitions." *Middle East Eye*, February 17. https://www.middleeasteye.net/news/decades-long-battle-continues-susiya-braces-more-israeli-demolitions.

Qumsiyeh, Mazin B. (2011), *Popular Resistance in Palestine: A History of Hope and Empowerment*. London: Pluto.

Salaita, Steven (2016), *Inter/Nationalism: Decolonizing Native America and Palestine*. Minneapolis: University of Minnesota Press.

Salamanca, Omar Jabary, Mezna Qato, Kareem Rabie, and Sobhi Samour (2012), "Past is Present: Settler Colonialism in Palestine." *Settler Colonial Studies*, 2 (1): 1–8.

Sayegh, Fayez (1965), *Zionist Colonialism in Palestine*. Beirut: Research Center of the Palestine Liberation Organization.

Scott, James C. (1985), *Weapons of the Weak: Everyday Forms of Peasant Resistance*. New Haven: Yale University Press.

Seidel, Timothy (2017), "'We Refuse to Be Enemies': Political Geographies of Violence and Resistance in Palestine." *Journal of Peacebuilding and Development*, 12 (3): 25–38.

Seidel, Timothy (2019), "Sovereign Bodies, Sovereign States: Settler Colonial Violence and the Visibility of Resistance in Palestine." In *Palestine and Rule of Power: Local Dissent vs. International Governance*, edited by A. Tartir and T. Seidel, 47–70. New York: Palgrave Macmillan.

Seidel, Timothy (2021), "Settler Colonialism and Land-Based Struggle in Palestine: Towards a Decolonial Political Economy." In *Political Economy of Palestine: Critical, Interdisciplinary, and Decolonial Perspectives*, edited by A. Tartir, T. Dana, and T. Seidel, 81–107. New York: Palgrave Macmillan.

Seidel, Timothy (2023), "'Emigrantes, Palestinos, Estamos Unidos': Anticolonial Connectivity and Resistance along the 'Palestine-Mexico' Border." *Postcolonial Studies*, 26 (1): 94–111.

Simpson, Leanne Betasamosake (ed.) (2008), *Lighting the Eighth Fire: The Liberation, Resurgence, and Protection of Indigenous Nations*. Winnipeg: Arbeiter Ring Pub.

Tartir, Alaa, Tariq Dana, and Timothy Seidel (eds.) (2021), *Political Economy of Palestine: Critical, Interdisciplinary, and Decolonial Perspectives*. New York: Palgrave Macmillan.

Tartir, Alaa and Jeremy Wildeman (2020), "Peace in Palestine Cannot Be Achieved Amid Unlawful Demolitions." *Al Jazeera*, November 20. https://www.aljazeera.com/opinions/2020/11/20/israeli-crimes.

Wolfe, Patrick (2006), "Settler Colonialism and the Elimination of the Native." *Journal of Genocide Research*, 8 (4): 387–409.

Zaru, Jean (2008), *Occupied with Nonviolence: A Palestinian Woman Speaks*. Minneapolis: Fortress.

+972 Magazine (2017), "Palestinians, Israelis and Diaspora Jews Build West Bank Protest Camp." *+972 Magazine*, May 19. https://www.972mag.com/palestinians-israelis-and-diaspora-jews-build-west-bank-protest-camp/.

Part IV

Epistemic

Local Knowledge and Global Norms

In the final part of our volume, we explore *epistemic* sites of domination and resistance, highlighting the ways norms, narratives, and knowledge production itself can demonstrate a commitment to liberation and freedom or perpetuate control and domination. Chapters in this part examine the definitions, methods, and frameworks used to study and teach as well as analyze policies and norms about Palestine that challenge the liberal peace.

In "International Holocaust Remembrance Alliance, Academic Censorship, and the Politics of Settler Colonial Erasure," Somdeep Sen looks at the adoption of the IHRA definition of anti-Semitism at institutions of higher education, analyzing IHRA and academic censorship in view of the wider ideology and politics of settler colonialism. Sen notes that the IHRA definition seeks to circumscribe scholarship and pedagogical approaches that recognize the legitimacy, existence, and persistence of the Palestinian national cause as doing so undermines the myth of *terra nullis*—namely that Israel was built on a "land without a people for a people without a land." Sen concludes that IHRA is an extension of the settler colonial urge to erase the evidence of Indigenous existence. And its adoption across universities in the Global North is only evidence of the globalization of the politics of settler colonialism.

Next, Jeremy Wildeman traces how the intervention of Western liberal democracies has benefited Israeli settler colonial state-building, at the expense of Palestinian statehood and peace. His chapter "Liberal Packaging and Colonial Approaches: Problematizing Western Intervention in Palestine" explores how this process has unfolded, focusing on examples from three periods: the UN partition of Palestine (1940s), the Oslo peace process (1990s), and Western-led Palestine state-building after the Second Intifada (mid-2000s/2010s). This Western intervention has happened in an age of global decolonization and Western-driven global liberalism, where racist colonial ways of thinking remained inherent with how Western powers approached Palestine-Israel, demonstrably favoring the more "Europeanized" Israelis at the expense of the "Orientalized" Palestinians. The consistency with which Western states have prioritized Israeli perspectives and reinforced its illiberal settler colonial regime raises questions if Palestinians can trust Western intervention in the region.

In the book's final chapter "Palestinian Popular Education Post-Oslo," Melanie Meinzer takes a close look at the ways Palestinian NGOs' dependence on foreign aid during Oslo redirected civil society's energies toward donor priorities and weakened Palestinian resistance movements. Meinzer then argues that despite these obstacles, the spirit and pedagogies of the Intifada-era popular education movement are alive today and serve as a bulwark against cultural erasure under donor-enabled Israeli settler colonialism. Drawing on interviews and surveys, she shows how NGOs, community-based organizations, and educators have reconstituted the popular education movement by using political theater, visual arts, debate, and storytelling to conscientize and mobilize young people. She concludes that while aid dependence restricts Palestinian self-determination, popular education continues to be a vehicle for personal and collective liberation.

11

International Holocaust Remembrance Alliance, Academic Censorship, and the Politics of Settler Colonial Erasure

Somdeep Sen

Introduction

In fall 2021, I received an email from a high-ranking administrator of a European university where I was told that I was allowed to deliver a planned book talk, as long as I did not say anything that would breach the country's anti-terrorism legislation. The administrator noted that, in an earlier communication to the university, I had agreed that my presentation "would keep to the argument presented in the book." I was also reminded that the "university has adopted the IHRA [International Holocaust Remembrance Alliance] working definition of antisemitism." This email came after a complaint from the university's student-led Jewish Society regarding the title and content of my lecture. The Jewish Society had expressed its concerns to the hosting department and claimed that my lecture would lead to negative repercussions for Jewish students. Following this complaint, I was asked to provide additional information about the content of my talk, such as the main points of my presentation and/or presentation slides. I was told that this information would be used to reassure the students and resolve the matter.

The insinuation that a public presentation on a scholarly, peer-reviewed book could be deemed anti-Semitic or sympathetic to a terrorist organization may seem extraordinary. However, this use of the terrorism discourse (Collins and Glover 2002; Collins and Sen 2021) as well as the charge of anti-Semitism have become commonplace tools for censoring criticism of Israel. More recently though, institutions of higher education have become the battleground where the institutional adoption of the International Holocaust Remembrance Alliance (IHRA) working definition has led to severe curbs on critical scholarship and scholarly discourse on Palestine/Israel. Seeing as the IHRA working definition conflates criticism of Zionism and Israel with anti-Semitism, many have long insisted that its use would threaten "the pursuit of knowledge and academic freedom" (Gordon and LeVine 2021. See also: Ayyash 2020; Cook 2021; Gould 2020). In 2019, one of the original drafters of the working definition

Kenneth Stern also acknowledged that it is being used to attack free speech (Stern 2019). In this sense, the IHRA's working definition[1] could be considered an extension of long-standing Zionist efforts to censor all forms of Palestine solidarity activism.

However, in this chapter I argue that what we are witnessing is not just censorship. The adoption of the IHRA working definition at institutions of higher education and the subsequent attacks on critical scholars and scholarship are also animated by the wider ideology and politics of settler colonialism that is premised on the myth of Indigenous nonexistence (Wolf 2006, 387–409). The foundational impetus of Israel's project of settler colonialism is to then eliminate (evidence of) the existence of Palestine and Palestinian-ness. In the same vein, the IHRA definition also seeks to circumscribe any attempt to recognize the legitimacy, existence, and persistence of the Palestinian national cause—not least since any recognition of the existence of Palestine and Palestinian-ness would undermine the core founding myth of the State of Israel that proclaims that it was built on *terra nullius* (Masalha 2012; Shalhoub-Kevorkian 2015).

The chapter begins with a brief discussion of Israel's settler colonial urge to erase Palestine as a cause and Palestinians as a people. Subsequently, I deliberate the way the IHRA definition works to perpetuate and materialize the settler colonial myth of Indigenous nonexistence.

On Settler Colonial Erasure

The politics of erasure was very much written into the foundation of the State of Israel. In general, the establishment of a settler society is premised on the myth of the settled land being *terra nullius* and devoid of any significant Indigenous presence. As a means of then materializing this myth, the erasure of the native becomes necessary for building the settler society (Veracini 2016, 174–9; Veracini 2013, 313–3; Gordon and Ram 2016, 20–9; Calderon 2014, 313–38). Though, discursively, erasure is rationalized through a racialized conception of Indigenous presence being antithetical to and incompatible with the nature and purpose of the settler society (Wolfe 2006, 387). Also, in the settler narrative, the demise of Indigenous communities is deemed inevitable as the natives seemingly lack the ability or resources to arrest "the advancing tide" of the settler's "superior technology, military prowess, and centralized state" (Jacobs 2009, 6–7). This discourse (and myth) of the inevitable native demise is followed by efforts to dismantle all that evidences the existence of the Indigenous as a people with a distinct and recognizable peoplehood (Sen 2020, 137). Here, it is not to say that the structures and practices of domination one expects to see in a colonial condition are entirely missing in a settler colonial context. However, the expectation of settler colonizers is distinctive in that they do not just say to the native "you, work for me." They also demand that the native "go away" (Veracini 2011, 1)—thus, making any evidence of Indigenous existence particularly unsettling to the very basis of the settler society, as by simply "staying at home," the native can get "in the way" of the settler colonial endeavor (Rose 1991, 42).

Returning to Palestine/Israel, this settler colonial politics of erasure was very much the impetus of Theodor Herzl's utopian vision for a modern Jewish state in *Altneuland*, where he declared, "If I wish to substitute a new building for an old one, I must demolish before I construct" (Herzl 1902, 3). For European Jewish settlers this vision corroborated their right to "exclusive control, ownership and domination of the land" (Masalha and Isherwood 2014; 2014; see also Benvenisti 2002, 2). Also, it served to "reinforce the claim that Palestinians were/are not a people" (Shalhoub-Kevorkian 2015, 5)—at least, not a people with a distinct (or singular) enough peoplehood (Sen 2020, 7) to warrant recognition of their (national) claim to the land. The process of systematically destroying the native society (Wolfe 2006, 388) began with the *Nakba* of 1948 when Palestine and Palestinians were erased from the landscape (Masalha 2012, 2). Zionist military forces employed methods such as "large-scale intimidation; laying siege to and bombarding villages and population centers; setting fire to homes, properties and goods; expulsion; demolition; and, finally, planting mines among the rubble to prevent any of the expelled inhabitants from returning." These measures confirmed that, for the settler, Palestinians simply "had to go" to make way for the new settler society (Pappe 2006, xi), and the demise of Palestinian society was also seen as all but inevitable. This perception was evident in the matter-of-fact tone that Israeli military leader Moshe Dayan once declared, "Jewish villages were built in the place of Arab villages. You do not even know the names of these Arab villages, and I do not blame you because geography books no longer exist—not only do the books not exist, the Arab villages are not there either" (Khalidi 1992, xxxi).

To be sure, the violence that underpinned the establishment of the State of Israel and led to the forced expulsion of 750,000 Palestinians (Masalha 2012, 2)—representing 80 percent of the Palestinian population living on the now, occupied land (Abu-Lughod and Sa'di 2007, 3)—personified the settler colonial urge to replace the Indigenous community (Seidel and Tartir 2019, 4). But the politics of erasure is not just a matter of the past. It is also a matter of the present, seeing as Palestinians (and Palestinian-ness) have persisted by "staying home" and "getting in the way" of Israeli efforts to make the myth *terra nullius* a reality. For instance, the urge "to displace and replace the Indigenous" (Sen 2020, 27) is what animates the spatial politics of the Israeli settler colonial regime. Whether it is Palestinian home demolitions that introduce a sense of precarity to the Palestinian presence in the landscape (Joronen and Griffiths 2019, 561–76), the concerted effort to de-Palestinize/Judaize Jerusalem, or the Israeli settlement movement that fractures and ghettoizes Palestinian communities across the "Holy Land" (Zink 2009, 122–33; Quraishy 2009; Hodgkins 1996)—these initiatives strive to trigger the demise of the native society. As Sari Hanafi argues, this manner of erasure is not unlike the ethnic cleansing of Palestinians that happened during the *Nakba*, in that these measures also "target [the] land" and "Palestinian living spaces" in a way that makes the "transfer of the Palestinian population" all but inevitable (Hanafi 2009, 107; see also Hanafai 2012, 190–205).

The settler colonial urge to erase the signature of Palestine existence also drives Israeli efforts to destroy or appropriate Palestinian national-cultural symbols, folklore, and artifacts. Uprooting the cactus tree—a symbol of Palestinian resilience and patience—is meant to unsettle the Palestinian claim to the landscape. Prior to the *Nakba*, the Jaffa orange was a "source of [national] pride" as a "Product of Palestine" recognized across the world. But, after 1948, this evidence of Palestinian existence was appropriated as an emblem of the "new Israel" and, for Palestinians, "became the symbol of loss, a robbed nationhood" (Abufarha 2008, 349). There is also the appropriation of the symbolism of the olive tree or the claiming of Palestinian dishes like hummus, falafel, and shakshuka *as* Israeli. It is not without reason then that this manner of cultural appropriation has "long angered Palestinians" (Abunimah 2012)—especially since these artifacts serve as the basis for validating and sustaining Palestinian national consciousness among an occupied, colonized, and exiled national people (Bascuñan-Wiley 2019, 100–29; Said 1986, 63–80; Alsaafin 2018).

Finally, we can also look to the biological elimination of Palestinians (and their Palestinian-ness) wherein physical violence serves as a mode of suppressing any rebellious expression of Indigenous existence and persistence (Sen 2020, 33–4). The insistent manner in which Palestinians participants, who carried out stabbing attacks during the so-called "Knife Intifada" in 2015–16, were killed—often *after* being disarmed—was an example of this manner of elimination (Amnesty International 2016). By simply engaging in stabbing attacks, these young, rebellious Palestinians displayed an indomitable commitment to the Palestinian national struggle and an insistence that the land was not terra nullius (Sen 2020, 20–1). So, their extrajudicial killing—sometimes by armed Israeli civilians—was meant to underline that Palestinians simply "had to go." The unrelenting siege of the Gaza Strip also reflects this effort at the biological elimination of Palestinians. Gaza was transformed by the establishment of the State of Israel into a place where the majority of the population were refugees, carrying the memory and trauma of the *Nakba* (Roy 1995, 13; Gunning 2007, 27; Efrat 2006, 167). As a result, it has historically been the "training ground" for Palestinian revolutionaries and revolutionary activism and has a penchant for giving rise to popular uprisings (Roy 2011, 21; Gunning 2007, 27). Edward Said thus deemed Gaza to be at the "core" of the Palestinian struggle, "always a center of resistance" (Said 1995, 47). Unsurprisingly then, Israeli politicians and military leaders have had nothing but disdain for the coastal enclave. Yitzhak Rabin once said that he hoped Gaza would "sink into the sea," while Naftali Bennett once described the enclave as a "fortress of terror" (Sen 2021). Though, it is even more unsurprising that Gaza has been under siege since 2007 and the target of ritual Israeli military campaigns. All these efforts are meant to suppress and erase all expressions of Palestinian persistence and a revolutionary national spirit (Sen 2020, 32–4).

Censorship as Settler Colonial Erasure

Those that are antagonistic to the Palestinian liberation struggle frequently use censorship as a way of punishing critics of Israel and suppressing any expressions of Palestine solidarity. But such efforts are not just meant to restrict or control the circulation of particular ideas (Lebow 2016, 356; Jones 2015, xii) and standpoints on the politics of Palestine/Israel. This manner of censorship can also be viewed as animated by the politics of erasure I have described earlier. Herein, expressions of

Palestine solidarity face the ire of the settler colonial regime because any recognition of the Palestinian right to liberation is also tantamount to recognizing the existence of Palestinians as a distinct national community, which, in effect, undermines the settler colonial myth of Indigenous nonexistence.

This was the case, for instance, in 2014 when Palestinian-American professor Steven Salaita's job offer from the University of Illinois at Urbana-Champaign (UIUC) was rescinded after the university's Board of Trustees voted to block his appointment. The decision followed a campaign by pro-Israel students, faculty members, and donors who deemed Professor Salaita's tweets criticizing Israel's military onslaught on Gaza to be anti-Semitic (Mackey 2014). Some donors also threatened to "stop giving" to the university (Des Garennes 2014). The university president Robert Easter agreed with the decision of the Board of Trustees and said, "Professor Salaita's approach indicates he would be incapable of fostering a classroom environment where conflicting opinions would be given equal consideration" (Mackey 2014). The university was, however, censured by the American Association of University Professors (AAUP). And the chair of AAUP's Committee on Academic Freedom and Tenure Henry Reichmann noted, "The dismissal of Professor Salaita has roiled the UIUC community and much of academia; it is one of the more significant violations of academic freedom this decade" (AAUP 2015).

Undoubtedly, this violation of Professor Salaita's academic freedom was meant to restrict the circulation of his political standpoint on Palestine/Israel. Activists campaigning for the dismissal of Professor Salaita found it problematic that he deemed a pro-Israel stance to be indefensible,[2] and that anyone supporting Israel was "hopelessly brainwashed."[3] One student activist noted, "It's about feeling safe on campus ... This is a professor who tweeted that if you support Israel, you're an awful person." Another student claimed that the *lack* of civility in Professor Salaita's tweets "is a mechanism for silencing alternative views" (Mackey 2014). However, what was most egregious (for pro-Israel activists) was that—in both his 2014 tweets during the Israeli military campaign in Gaza[4] and his scholarship (Salaita 2011; Salaita 2016)—Professor Salaita's critique of Israel was foundationally framed by his view of the conflict as one between a colonizer (i.e., Israel) and an Indigenous people (i.e., Palestinians). Then, in this sense, UIUC's rescinding of the job offer was not just meant to suppress Professor Salaita's expression of solidarity with the Palestinian struggle. It was meant to censure his expression of Palestinian indigeneity and, with it, his insistence on the existence of Palestine and Palestinian-ness that stands as contrary to the settler colonial narrative.

A similar incident took place at the University of Toronto after a selection committee decided to appoint Dr. Valentina Azarova as director of the International Human Rights Program at the university's Faculty of Law. Eventually, the dean of the faculty blocked the appointment, citing immigration issues (Page 2021). However, a review of the decision, commissioned by the university (Anielska 2021), found that the dean blocked the appointment after receiving a phone call from David Spiro—a major donor to the faculty and a former board member of the pro-Israel lobby group Centre for Israel and Jewish Affairs—where he expressed his reservations regarding Dr. Azarova's appointment (Azizi 2022). Citing her academic works critical of the State of Israel, Spiro warned that hiring Dr. Azarova would lead to "a public protest campaign

[that] will do major damage to the university, including in fundraising" (McQuaig 2021). The Canadian Association of University Teachers (CAUT) voted to censure the University of Toronto noting that "the decision to cancel Dr. Valentina Azarova's hiring was politically motivated, and as such constitutes a serious breach of widely recognized principles of academic freedom" (CAUT 2021). CAUT suspended its censure when the university reoffered the position to Dr. Azarova, who subsequently "declined the offer" (Nasser 2021).

The children's book *P Is for Palestine* and its author Golbarg Bashi faced a similar manner on censure as pro-Israel activists and organizers seemed to view the ABC book's celebration of Palestinian history, culture, and the liberation struggle—that is, *its* inherent recognition of Palestine and Palestinian-ness—to be synonymous with "anti-Semitic propaganda" (Dorn and Pagones 2017). Bashi's book provides an "illustrated 'alphabetic adventure to Palestine'" (Palestine Legal 2018) and includes phrases such as "B is for Bethlehem," "C is for Christmas," "D is for Dabkeh," "F is for Falafel," and "K is for Kuffiya" (Elia 2017). However, those calling for the banning of *P Is for Palestine* took offense to "Palestine" appearing in the title of the book as well as the phrase "I is for Intifada" (Palestine Legal 2018). In late 2017 when a branch of the bookseller Book Culture announced that it would host a book reading by Bashi, it faced "threats of mayhem, violence, obstruction, boycotting . . . from emails, in person and phone calls" (Abunimah 2018). Eventually, copies of the book had to be hidden behind the cash register. Later Book Culture was pressured into making a statement where they apologized for supporting the book and condemned the Boycott, Divestment and Sanctions (BDS) movement. In December 2017, the Jewish Defense League (JDL) also disrupted a "P Is for Palestine" Hannukah party as uniformed members of the organization started harassing and filming the children when they sat down for a reading of the book (Gelman 2017). In 2019 reading of the book was also canceled (Insider NJ 2019; Middle East Monitor 2019) by the Highland Park Public Library in New Jersey after facing attacks from members of the local Jewish community. Rabbi Bernhard Rosenberg criticized the decision of the library to host the reading and said, "It's a symbol, it says that it's OK to have books that teach little children to hate." He added that the book was "anti-Semitic" and that "it's being used to teach little children about how great the Palestinians are, and we should murder the Jews" (ABC 7, 2019).

Of course, this way of weaponizing the charge of anti-Semitism to suppress any evocation of Palestinian (right to) existence is at the core of the modus operandi of the IHRA working definition of anti-Semitism. The nonlegally basic definition reads as follows:

> Antisemitism is a certain perception of Jews, which may be expressed as hatred toward Jews. Rhetorical and physical manifestations of antisemitism are directed toward Jewish or non-Jewish individuals and/or their property, toward Jewish community institutions and religious facilities. (IHRA 2016)

This definition was originally formulated in 2005 by the Vienna-based, European Monitoring Center on Racism and Xenophobia (EUMC) that was established by the Council of the European Union. The definition was removed from the website of the EUMC in 2013 (Gould 2020, 825), only to be adopted by the IHRA Plenary in Bucharest in 2016 (IHRA 2016). According to the lead drafter of the definition Kenneth Stern it was primarily meant to be used for "data classification"—specifically as a guideline and tool for the police to be able to "classify antisemitic crimes as hate crimes" (Gould 2020, 826). The IHRA definition is also complemented with a set of eleven contemporary examples "of antisemitism in public life, the media, schools, the workplace, and in the religious sphere" (IHRA 2016). As such, critics have pointed out, the working definition is "deeply flawed, and definition, not a definition" (Lerman 2018). The scholar of anti-Semitism Antony Lerman deemed it to be "a linguistic mess" that is not "not fit for purpose." "If antisemitism is a 'certain perception [of Jews],'" he asks, "what is that perception? If it's a 'certain' one, why not spell it out?" (Lerman 2018). Equally, the IHRA working definition states that anti-Semitism "*may* be expressed as hatred towards Jews [emphasis added]." However, Lerman argues that the use of the term "may" means that anti-Semitism could also *not* be expressed in this manner. He therefore asks, "So if it may not be expressed as hatred, how else might it be expressed? Shouldn't we be told?" (Lerman 2018). In a similar vein, British barrister Hugh Tomlinson notes that there is an "obvious problem with the wording." He adds that phrases like "a certain perception" or terms like "may" are too vague and confusing for the IHRA working definition to have any significant value in identifying and combatting anti-Semitism (Tomlinson 2017, 3).

The most problematic, and therefore divisive, aspect of the working definition is the way this vague conception of anti-Semitism operates in conjunction with the eleven contemporary examples of anti-Semitism. Notably, seven out of the eleven examples refer to the State of Israel (Sedley, Janner-Klausner, Bindman, Rose, and Kahn-Harris 2018). This makes the IHRA definition "a tool of choice" for pro-Israel activists and organizations as it represents a marked shift in the "meaning of anti-Semitism"—one that extends beyond the "traditional focus on hatred of Jews" to being tied to "how critical one is towards" the State of Israel and its (settler) colonialism (Gordon and LeVine 2021). In general, this conflation of criticism of Israel with anti-Semitism (Sedley 2017) reduces the highly complex politics of Palestine/Israel to the "single dimension [of]…antisemitism" (Ulrich 2019, 15), which in turn—when weaponized—can limit "freedom of speech with respect to disfavored positions on Israel" (Ulrich 2019, 3). Still, the IHRA working definition can be considered to be doing more than just censoring Israel critics. By drawing a synonymy between criticism of Israel and anti-Semitism, it works to limit the scope, vocabulary, and possibilities for expressing the Palestinian (right to) existence—not least since any such expression would need to be articulated as a critique of the Israeli state's settler colonial attempts to erase the signature of Palestine and Palestinian-ness from the landscape.

This politics of erasure was very much at play when my talk was charged as being anti-Semitic and potentially in violation of anti-terror law. Notably, while the title of my talk—that is, "Decolonizing Palestine"—was visible online, the content of my talk was not yet publicly available at the time of the complaint; this, despite the Jewish Society's claim that the content of my presentation would put the Jewish students on campus at risk. However, the title alone represents a commitment to Indigenous existence and persistence in the face of settler colonial rule, contra to the myth of *terra nullius*. And, consequently, the charge of anti-Semitism framed by the university's adoption of the IHRA working definition as well as the university administrator's insistence that I must keep to argument around the book were meant to limit the vocabulary and possibilities of stating the existence and persistence of Palestine and Palestinian-ness during my presentation.

In 2020, the IHRA's settler colonial politics was equally on display when an article published in the University of Glasgow's online postgraduate journal *eSharp* was deemed anti-Semitic by pro-Israel activists. The essay titled "Advocating Occupation: Outsourcing Zionist Propaganda in the UK" was published in 2017 and studies grassroots Zionist advocacy activities in the UK. Specifically, it argues that the State of Israel has "outsourced" its propaganda activities to pro-Israel grassroots advocacy organizations in the UK that help perpetuate pro-Israel discourses and undermine Palestine solidarity activism (Jackman 2017, 48). In doing so, the essay concluded, these grassroots organizations "reinforce from below the British government's long-standing support for Israel" (Jackman 2017, 55). While the article was peer-reviewed, pro-Israel activist David Collier deemed it to be "laden with conspiracy, antisemitism and errors." As such, he posited, the "entire [peer-review] process is rife with heavy antisemitism" and that the paper "should be hung on the walls at Glasgow university as a reminder of the shame that they ever allowed this to be published" (Collier 2020). Faced with this criticism, the University of Glasgow released a statement noting its adoption of the IHRA working definition and that it "takes a zero-tolerance approach to antisemitism and hate speech of any kind" (JC Reporter 2020). The university inserted a preface at the beginning of the article that apologizes for the "considerable offense" that it had caused. It added that the essay showed a "biased selection of sources," a "misrepresentation of data," and "promote[d] an unfounded anti-Semitic theory regarding the state of Israel and its activity in the United Kingdom" (Winstanley 2021). Subsequently, the university faced widespread criticism from prominent scholars for undermining academic freedom and eventually retracted the "anti-Semitic" label. A new preface now says that the article "promote[s] what some would regard as an unfounded theory regarding the State of Israel and its activity in the United Kingdom" (Gayle 2021).

In a way, the *eSharp* affair is prototypical of the political effect of the working definition's widening of the traditional definition of anti-Semitism to also include criticism of the State of Israel. Herein the concern of the essay was not Jewish people or Jewish life. Rather, its critique squarely focuses on the Israeli state's grassroots advocacy in the UK. However, framed by the IHRA definition, the University of Glasgow as well as pro-Israel activists considered this criticism to be synonymous with "hatred of Jews," thus once again limiting the possibility of expressing Palestinian right to existence seeing as such an expression necessarily requires a critique of the State of Israel and its colonial policies.

"Chilling Effect" and Its Limits

In this chapter I have sought to tie efforts to censor Palestine solidarity activism to the wider settler colonial effort at erasure of Palestine and Palestinians. Israeli authorities are of course aware of the detrimental impact of censorship on Palestinian advocacy efforts. It is not without reason then that the Israeli cabinet recently allocated $30 million for covert advocacy efforts in the United States and other Western countries (Benzaquen and The Seventh Eye 2022). A key target of these efforts has been the BDS movement and its supporters. The Palestinian-led movement calls for "freedom, justice and equality" and is driven by the "simple principle that Palestinians are entitled to the same rights as the rest of humanity" (bdsmovement.net). However, in response to this simple call for equality in accordance with international law Israeli authorities have engaged in a concerted effort to undermine (and erase) the BDS movement's forefronting of the Palestinian narrative—often through the charge of "terrorism" or "anti-Semitism." This was the case, for instance, in 2019 when the Israeli Ministry of Strategic and Public Diplomacy[5] published a report titled "Terrorists in Suits" that claimed ties between BDS-supporting NGOs and terrorist organizations (Ministry of Strategic Affairs and Public Diplomacy (State of Israel) 2019). Later that year, it published another report titled "Behind the Mask" that argued that the BDS campaign was anti-Semitic (Ministry of Strategic Affairs and Public Diplomacy (State of Israel) 2019). This report was officially revealed at the European Parliament (Ministry of Foreign Affairs (State of Israel) 2019).

But while it would seem that the space for advocating for Palestinian rights is shrinking, we may also be witnessing the limits of this manner of censorship and settler colonial erasure. In January 2022, Palestinian academic and activist Shahd Abusalama was suspended from her teaching position at Sheffield Hallam University, following a pro-Israel smear campaign that claimed that her social media posts critical of Israel were anti-Semitic. Silencing a prominent advocate of Palestinian liberation in and of itself contributes to the settler colonial politics of erasure, though, such acts of censorship also work to erase an evocation of Palestine and Palestinian-ness by having a "chilling effect" that makes any advocate for Palestinian rights *persona non grata* and the Palestinian cause itself *too* polemic to support. Reacting to the suspension Abusalama noted, "The Zionist defamation campaign by Jewish News, Campaign Against Antisemitism and Jewish Chronicle joins a historical pattern where the Zionist colonial narrative is consistently privileged over the narratives of the oppressed" (Middle East Monitor 2022). Citing its adoption of the IHRA working definition (Sheffield Hallam University 2021), the university initially defended its decision. However, Abusalama received widespread support and the university was forced to reinstate her employment a week after her suspension (Charrett 2022).

In November 2021, the Canadian Association of University Teachers (CAUT) passed a motion rejecting the IHRA definition, adding that the association "supports the academic freedom of its members and recognizes the need to safeguard the rights of scholars to develop critical perspectives on all states, including the state of Israel, without fear of outside political influence, cuts to funding, censorship, harassment, threats, and intimidation" (CAUT 2021). Driven by similar concerns regarding censorship, the IHRA definition was also rejected by, among others, the University of Toronto (The Palestine Chronicle 2021), the Jewish Faculty Network in Canada (Appel 2021), the Massachusetts House of Representatives (Harrison and Auerbach 2021), and the University College of London's (UCL) Academic Board that made an advisory recommendation to the UCL's governing body that it find an alternative to the IHRA definition that was adopted by the university in 2019 (UCL 2021). While it may be early days, these developments reveal a growing mainstream awareness of the existence of a concerted effort to censor critical discourse on Israel and advocacy for Palestinian rights. And, for many, the weaponization of the charge of anti-Semitism may have revealed the uncompromising nature of the settler narrative and its inability to grant any semblance of recognition to Palestine as a cause and Palestinians as a people.

Notes

1. As a response to the IHRA working definition being used to stifle criticism of Zionism and the State of Israel, a group of scholars formulated the Jerusalem Declaration on Antisemitism (JDA) that explicitly states that support of Palestinian rights, criticism or opposition to Zionism, criticism of the State of Israel, and support for Boycott, Divestment and Sanctions movement are not, in and of themselves, anti-Semitic (see guidelines 6–15 of JDA: https://jerusalemdeclaration.org).
2. See tweet here: https://twitter.com/stevesalaita/status/486718092933099520?ref_src =twsrc%5Etfw%7Ctwcamp%5Etweetembed%7Ctwterm%5E486718092933099520 %7Ctwgr%5E%7Ctwcon%5Es1_&ref_url=https%3A%2F%2Fwww.nytimes.com %2F2014%2F09%2F13%2Fworld%2Fmiddleeast%2Fprofessors-angry-tweets-on-gaza -cost-him-a-job.html.
3. See tweet here: https://twitter.com/stevesalaita/status/490673766373265408?ref_src =twsrc%5Etfw%7Ctwcamp%5Etweetembed%7Ctwterm%5E490673766373265408 %7Ctwgr%5E%7Ctwcon%5Es1_&ref_url=https%3A%2F%2Fwww.nytimes.com %2F2014%2F09%2F13%2Fworld%2Fmiddleeast%2Fprofessors-angry-tweets-on-gaza -cost-him-a-job.html.
4. See tweet here: https://twitter.com/stevesalaita/status/489835145185476608?ref_src =twsrc%5Etfw%7Ctwcamp%5Etweetembed%7Ctwterm%5E489835145185476608 %7Ctwgr%5E%7Ctwcon%5Es1_&ref_url=https%3A%2F%2Fwww.nytimes.com %2F2014%2F09%2F13%2Fworld%2Fmiddleeast%2Fprofessors-angry-tweets-on-gaza -cost-him-a-job.html.
5. The Israeli Ministry of Strategic and Public Diplomacy merged with the Ministry of Foreign Affairs in 2021.

References

AAUP (2015), "Summary Rejection of Professor's Appointment Violated Principles of Academic Freedom and Tenure." April 28. https://www.aaup.org/media-release/ summary-rejection-professor's-appointment-violated-principles-academic-freedo m-and#.YtyDky8RpQI.

ABC7 (2019), "Children's Book 'P is for Palestine' Stirs Controversy in New Jersey Town." *ABC 7*, May 18. https://abc7ny.com/p-is-for-palestine-abcs-alphabet-book-controversy /5305695/.

Abufarha, Nasser (2008), "Land of Symbols: Cactus, Poppies, Orange and Olive Trees in Palestine." *Identities: Global Studies in Culture and Power*, 15: 343–68.

Abu-Lughod, Lila and Ahmad H. Sa'di (2007), "Introduction: The Claims of Memory." In Ahmad H. Sa'di and Lila Abu-Lughod (eds.), *Nakba: Palestine, 1948, and the Claims of Memory*, 1–24. New York: Columbia University Press.

Abunimah, Ali (2012), "Hummus and Falafel Are Already 'Israeli'. Now They're Coming for Palestine's Olive Oil Too." *Electronic Intifada*, January 16. https://electronicintifada.net/blogs/ali-abunimah/hummus-and-falafel-are-already-israeli-nowtheyre-coming-palestines-olive-oil-too.

Abunimah, Ali (2018), "New York Bookseller Bowed to Israel Supporters after Threats." *The Electronic Intifada*, February 13. https://electronicintifada.net/content/new-york-bookseller-bowed-israel-supporters-after-violent-threats/23301.

Alsaafin, Linah (2018), "I Eat, Therefore I am: Palestinian Cuisine as Cultural Idenity." *TLS. Times Literary Supplement*, 6006. https://go.gale.com/ps/i.do?id=GALE%7CA634285434&sid=googleScholar&v=2.1&it=r&linkaccess=abs&issn=0307661X&p=AONE&sw=w&userGroupName=anon%7Ed2dc1a1c.

Amnesty International (2016), "Israel/OPT: Pattern of Unlawful Killings Reveals Shocking Disregard for Human Life." September 28. https://www.amnesty.org/en/latest/news/2016/09/israel-opt-pattern-of-unlawful-killings-reveals-shocking-disregard-for-human-life/.

Anielska, Marta (2021), "IHRP Controversy Report Concludes External Pressure Did Not Influence Hiring Decision." *The Varsity*, April 4. https://thevarsity.ca/2021/04/04/ihrp-controversy-report-concludes-external-pressure-did-not-influence-hiring-decision/.

Appel, Jeremy (2021), "A New Canadian Jewish Faculty Group Opposes the IHRA Definition of Antisemitism." *The Canadian Jewish News*, December 12. https://thecjn.ca/news/a-new-canadian-jewish-faculty-group-opposes-the-ihra-definition-of-antisemitism/.

Ayyash, Mark Muhannad (2020), "The IHRA Definition Will Not Help Fight Anti-Semitism." *Al Jazeera English*, November 23. https://www.aljazeera.com/opinions/2020/11/23/the-ihra-and-the-palestinian-struggle-for.

Azizi, Ghazal (2022), "Rolling the Dice on Academic Freedom." *McGill Tribune*. https://www.mcgilltribune.com/rolling-the-dice-on-academic-freedom/.

Bascuñan-Wiley, Nicholas (2019), "*Sumud* and Food: Remembering Palestine Through Cuisine in Chile." *Mashriq & Mahjar: Journal of Middle East and North African Migration Studies*, 6 (2): 100–29.

Benvenisti, Meron (2002), *Sacred Landscape. The Buried History of the Holy Land since 1948*. Berkeley: University of California Press.

Benzaquen, Itamar and The Seventh Eye (2022), "The New Hasbara Campaign Israel Doesn't Want You to Know About." *+972 Magazine*, January 25. https://www.972mag.com/hasbara-funding-foreign-agents/.

Calderon, Dolores (2014), "Uncovering Settler Grammars in Curriculum." *Educational Studies*, 50 (4): 313–38.

CAUT (2021), "CAUT Council Imposes Rare Censure Against University of Toronto Over Azarova Hiring Controversy." April 22. https://www.caut.ca/latest/2021/04/caut-council-imposes-rare-censure-against-university-toronto-over-azarova-hiring.

Charrett, Catherine Chiniara (2022), "How a Palestinian Academic Defeated a Campaign to Silence Her." *Al Jazeera English*, February 10. https://www.aljazeera.com/opinions/2022/2/10/how-a-palestinian-academic-defeated-a-campaign-to-silence-her.

Collier, David (2020), "Glasgow University Publishes Antisemitic Conspiracy Theory." December 11. https://david-collier.com/glasgow-university/.

Collins, John and Ross Glover (eds.) (2002), *Collateral Language: A User's Guide to America's New War*. New York: New York University Press.

Collins, John and Somdeep Sen (eds.) (2021), *Globalizing Collateral Language: From 9/11 to Endless War*. Athens: University of Georgia Press.

Cook, Jonathan (2021), "How the IHRA Definition Became a Pro-Israel Cudgel." *Mondoweiss*, April 27. https://mondoweiss.net/2021/04/how-the-ihra-antisemitism-definition-became-a-pro-israel-cudgel/.

Des Garennes, Christine (2014), "Salaita Prompted Donors' Fury." *News Gazette*, September 2. https://www.news-gazette.com/news/salaita-prompted-donors-fury/article_7c90ef7b-f622-5492-9bab-ab7efeac1ce8.html.

Dorn, Sara and Stephanie Pagones (2017), "Kid's Book Called 'P Is for Palestine' is Stirring Up Outrage Among Mom." *New York Post*, November 17. https://nypost.com/2017/11/19/kids-book-called-p-is-for-palestine-enrages-jewish-moms/.

Efrat, Elisha (2006), *The West Bank and Gaza Strip: A Geography of Occupation and Disengagement*. New York: Routledge.

Elia, Nada (2017), "P is for Palestine: The Children's ABC Book Pro-Israel Bullies Tried to Ban." *Middle East Eye*, December 15. https://www.middleeasteye.net/fr/node/68005.

Gayle, Damien (2021), "Glasgow University Retreats Over 'Antisemitic' Label for Journal Article." *The Guardian*, November 10. https://www.theguardian.com/education/2021/nov/10/glasgow-university-retreats-over-antisemitic-label-for-journal-article.

Gelman, Emmaia (2017), "We had a 'P Is for Palestine' Party for Kids, and the JDL Showed Up." *Forward*, December 27. https://forward.com/opinion/390530/we-had-a-p-is-for-palestine-party-for-kids-and-the-jdl-showed-up/.

Gordon, Neve and Mark LeVine (2021), "Was Einstein an Anti-Semite?." *Inside Higher Ed*, March 26. https://www.insidehighered.com/views/2021/03/26/problems-increasingly-dominant-definition-anti-semitism-opinion.

Gordon, Neve and Moriel Ram (2016), "Ethnic Cleansing and the Formation of Settler Colonial Geographies." *Political Geography*, 53: 20–9.

Gould, Rebecca Ruth (2020), "The IHRA Definition of Antisemitism: Defining Antisemitism by Erasing Palestinians." *The Political Quarterly*, 91 (4): 825–31.

Gunning, Jeroen (2007), *Hamas in Politics: Democracy, Religion, Violence*. London: Hurst & Company.

Hanafi, Sari (2009), "Spacio-cide: Colonial Politics, Invisibility, and Rezoning in Palestinian Territory." *Contemporary Arab Affairs*, 2 (1): 106–21.

Hanafi, Sari (2012), "Explaining Spacio-Cide in the Palestinian Territory: Colonization, Separation, and State of Exception." *Current Sociology*, 61 (2): 190–205.

Harrison, Cole and Elsa Auerbach (2021), "Massachusetts House Rejects Distorted Definition of Antisemitism." *Massachusetts Peace Action*, April 30. https://masspeaceaction.org/massachusetts-house-rejects-distorted-definition-of-antisemitism/.

Herzl, Theodor (1902), *Old – New Land*, trans. Lotta Levensohn. New York: M. Wiener.

Hodgkins, Allison (1996), *The Judaization of Jerusalem—Israeli Policies since 1967*. Jerusalem: Palestinian Academic Society for the Study of International Affairs.

International Holocaust Remembrance Alliance (IHRA) (2016), "What is Antisemitism? Non-Legally Binding Working Definition of Antisemitism." https://www.holocaustremembrance.com/resources/working-definitions-charters/working-definition-antisemitism.

Jackman, Jane (2017), "Advocating Occupation: Outsourcing Zionist Propaganda in the UK." *eSharp*, 25 (1): 45–58.

Jacobs, Margaret D. (2009), *White Mother to a Dark Race. Settler Colonialism, Maternalism, and the Removal of Indigenous Children in the American West and Australia, 1880–1940*. Lincoln: University of Nebraska Press.

JC Reporter (2020), "Glasgow University Criticised Over 2017 'Zionist Lobbyists' Paper." *The Jewish Chronicle*, December 11. https://www.thejc.com/news/uk/glasgow-university-criticised-over-2017-zionist-lobbyists-paper-1.509617.

Jewish Voice for Palestine (2019), "JVP Chapter Condemns NJ Library Censorship of Children's Book 'P is for Palestine.'" *Insider NJ*, May 30. https://www.insidernj.com/press-release/jvp-chapter-condemns-nj-library-censorship-childrens-book-p-palestine/.

Jones, Derek (2015), *Censorship: A World Encyclopedia*. London: Routledge.

Joronen, Mikko and Mark Griffiths (2019), "The Affective Politics of Precarity: Home Demolitions in Occupied Palestine." *Environment and Planning D: Society and Space*, 37 (3): 561–76.

Khalidi, Walid (1992), *All That Remains: The Palestinian Village Occupied and Depopulated by Israel in 1948*. Washington, DC: Institute for Palestine Studies.

Lebow, Richard Ned (2016), "Self-Censorship in International Relations and Security Studies." *Journal of Global Security Studies*, 1 (4): 356–60.

Lerman, Antony (2018), "Labour Should Ditch the IHRA Working Definition of Antisemitism Altogether." *Open Democracy*, September 4. https://www.opendemocracy.net/en/opendemocracyuk/labour-should-ditch-ihra-working-definition-of-antisemitism-altogether/.

Mackey, Robert (2014), "Professor's Angry Tweets on Gaza Cost Him a Job." *The New York Times*, September 12. https://www.nytimes.com/2014/09/13/world/middleeast/professors-angry-tweets-on-gaza-cost-him-a-job.html.

Masalha, Nur (2012), *The Palestine Nakba: Decolonising History, Narrating the Subaltern, Reclaiming Memory*. London: Zed Books.

Masalha, Nur and Lisa Isherwood (2014), "Introduction." In Nur Masalha and Lisa Isherwood (eds.), *Theologies of Liberation in Palestine-Israel: Indigenous, Contextual and Postcolonial Perspectives*, xi–xviii. Eugene: Pickwick Publications.

McQuaig, Linda (2021), "University of Toronto Hiring Fiasco Shows Reliance on Donors Limits University's Role in Challenging 'Cherished Beliefs.'" *Toronto Star*, July 1. https://www.thestar.com/opinion/contributors/2021/07/01/university-of-toronto-hiring-fiasco-shows-reliance-on-donors-limits-universitys-role-in-challenging-cherished-beliefs.html.

Middle East Monitor (2019), "Protests in US Against Children's Book 'P is for Palestine.'" October 25. https://www.middleeastmonitor.com/20191025-protests-in-us-against-childrens-book-p-is-for-palestine/.

Middle East Monitor (2022), "Palestinian Academic Suspended by UK University Using Controversial Definition of Anti-Semitism." January 27. https://www.middleeastmonitor.com/20220127-palestinian-academic-suspended-by-uk-university-using-controversial-definition-of-anti-semitism/.

Ministry of Foreign Affairs (State of Israel) (2019), "Ministry of Strategic Affairs Report Exposes the Antisemitic Nature of BDS at the European Parliament in Brussels." September 25. https://www.gov.il/en/Departments/General/ministry-of-strategic-affairs-report-exposes-the-antisemitic-nature-of-bds-at-the-european-parliament-in-brussels-25-septem.

Ministry of Strategic Affairs and Public Diplomacy (State of Israel) (2019a), *Terrorists in Suits: The Ties Between NGOs Promoting BDS and Terrorist Organizations*. https://www

.gov.il/BlobFolder/generalpage/terrorists_in_suits/en/De-Legitimization%20Brochure.pdf.

Ministry of Strategic Affairs and Public Diplomacy (State of Israel) (2019b), *Behind the Mask the Antisemitic Nature of BDS Exposed*. https://www.gov.il/BlobFolder/generalpage/behind_the_mask/en/strategic_affairs_Behind%20The%20MAsk_en.pdf.

"Motions from the 91st CAUT Council Meeting." https://council.caut.ca/sites/default/files/motions_resolutions_for_caut_council_website-en.pdf.

Nasser, Shanifa (2021), "Censure Against U of T Temporarily Suspended After School Reverses Course in Hiring Controversy." *CBC News*, September 17. https://www.cbc.ca/news/canada/toronto/u-of-t-censure-university-of-toronto-azarova-1.6179705.

Page, Michael (2021), "University of Toronto's Leadership Draws Fire Over Academic Freedom." *Human Rights Watch*, April 28. https://www.hrw.org/news/2021/04/28/university-torontos-leadership-draws-fire-over-academic-freedom.

Palestine Legal (2018), "Palestine Children's Book: Threats & Censorship." February 20. https://palestinelegal.org/case-studies/2018/2/20/palestine-childrens-book-threats-censorship.

Pappe, Ilan (2006), *The Ethnic Cleansing of Palestine*. Oxford: One World.

Quraishy, Samira (2009), *The Judaization of Jerusalem: A Review of Israel's Escalating Campaign of Land Seizures, House Demolitions, and Eviction of Palestinians*. London: Middle East Monitor.

Rose, Deborah Bird (1991), *Hidden Histories: Black Stories from Victoria River Downs, Humbert River and Wave Hills Stations*. Canberra: Aboriginal Studies Press.

Roy, Sara (1995), *The Gaza Strip. The Political Economy of De-development*. Washington, DC: Institute of Palestine Studies.

Roy, Sara (2011), *Hamas and Civil Society in Gaza: Engaging the Islamist Social Sector*. Princeton: Princeton University Press.

Said, Edward (1986), "On Palestinian Identity: A Conversation with Salman Rushdie." *New Left Review*, 160: 63–80.

Said, Edward (1995), *Peace and Its Discontents: Essays on Palestine in the Middle East Peace Process*. New York: Vintage Books.

Salaita, Steven (2011), *Israel's Dead Soul*. Philadelphia: Temple University Press.

Salaita, Steven (2016), *Inter/Nationalism: Decolonizing Native America and Palestine*. Minneapolis: University of Minnesota Press.

Sedley, Stephen (2017), "Defining Anti-Semitism." *London Review of Books*, 39 (9). https://www.lrb.co.uk/the-paper/v39/n09/stephen-sedley/defining-anti-semitism.

Sedley, Stephen, Laura Janner-Klausner, Geoffrey Bindman, Jacqueline Rose, and Keith Kahn-Harris (2018), "How Should Antisemitism be Defined?" *The Guardian*, July 27. https://www.theguardian.com/commentisfree/2018/jul/27/antisemitism-ihra-definition-jewish-writers.

Seidel, Timothy and Alaa Tartir (2019), "The Rule of Power in Palestine: Settler Colonialism, Neoliberal Governance, and Resistance." In Alaa Tartir and Timothy Seidel (eds.), *Palestine and the Rule of Power: Local Dissent vs. International Governance*, 1–19. New York: Palgrave Macmillan.

Sen, Somdeep (2020), *Decolonizing Palestine: Hamas Between the Anticolonial and the Postcolonial*. Ithaca: Cornell University Press.

Sen, Somdeep (2021), "Why Israel Hates Gaza." *Foreign Policy*, December 26. https://foreignpolicy.com/2021/12/26/why-israel-hates-gaza/.

Shalhoub-Kevorkian, Nadera (2015), *Security Theology, Surveillance, and the Politics of Fear*. Cambridge: Cambridge University Press.

Sheffield Hallam University (2021), "Sheffield Hallam Adopts the IHRA Definition of Antisemitism." February 3. https://www.shu.ac.uk/news/all-articles/latest-news/university-statement-ihra-definition-of-anti-semitism.

Stern, Kenneth (2019), "I Drafted the Definition of Antisemitism. Rightwing Jews are Weaponizing it." *The Guardian*, December 13. https://www.theguardian.com/commentisfree/2019/dec/13/antisemitism-executive-order-trump-chilling-effect.

The Palestine Chronicle (2021), "Toronto University Rejects IHRA Definition of Antisemitism." December 15. https://www.palestinechronicle.com/toronto-university-rejects-ihra-definition-of-antisemitism/.

Tomlinson, Hugh (2017), "Opinion: In the Matter of the Adoption and Potential Application of the International Holocaust Remembrance Alliance Working Definition of Antisemitism." March 8. https://freespeechonisrael.org.uk/wp-content/uploads/2017/03/TomlinsonGuidanceIHRA.pdf.

UCL (2021), "UCL Statement on IHRA." *UCL*, February 12. https://www.ucl.ac.uk/news/2021/feb/ucl-statement-ihra.

Ullrich, Peter (2019), *Expert Opinion on the 'Working Definition of Antisemitism' of The International Holocaust Remembrance Alliance*. Berlin: Rosa Luxemburg Stiftung.

Veracini, Lorenzo (2011), "Introducing Settler Colonial Studies." *Settler Colonial Studies*, 1 (1): 1–12.

Veracini, Lorenzo (2013), "'Settler Colonialism': Career of a Concept." *The Journal of Imperial and Commonwealth History*, 41 (2): 313–33.

Veracini, Lorenzo (2016), "Afterword: A History of the Settler Colonial Present." *Settler Colonial Studies*, 6 (2): 174–9.

Winstanley, Asa (2021), "Scottish College Censors Israel's Critics." *The Electronic Intifada*, November 4. https://electronicintifada.net/blogs/asa-winstanley/scottish-college-censors-israels-critics.

Wolfe, Patrick (2006), "Settler Colonialism and the Elimination of the Native." *Journal of Genocide Research*, 8 (4): 387–409.

Zink, Valerie (2009), "A Quiet Transfer: The Judaization of Jerusalem." *Contemporary Arab Affairs*, 2 (1): 122–33.

12

Liberal Packaging and Colonial Approaches

Problematizing Western Intervention in Palestine

Jeremy Wildeman

Introduction

This chapter assesses the approach and impact of Western liberal democracies on Palestinian development, sovereignty, and Palestinian-Israeli peacebuilding. It specifically considers why their engagement has not improved Palestinian well-being or Palestine-Israel peace. It does this cognizant of the fact the Middle East Peace Process (MEPP), which got underway between Israelis and Palestinians at Madrid in 1991, and specifically the Oslo Peace Process that began within the MEPP in 1993 have been the most important peace efforts for Palestine and Israel since the end of British colonial rule in 1948. Those efforts have failed to establish peace despite significant financial and political resources invested by Western governments. Instead, once the MEPP began Israeli settlement building accelerated in the occupied Palestinian territory (oPt). Palestinian lands in the West Bank (including East Jerusalem) were carved into a discontiguous smattering of semiautonomous cantons that are surrounded and cut off from each other, and from the outside world, by Jewish-Israeli settlement communities, military installations, transportation infrastructure, industrial infrastructure, and separation barriers (Haddad 2020). Meanwhile, Palestinian society has been scarred by deep-set structural violence, precipitous declines in public well-being (Bhaiwala 2015; Giacaman et al. 2009), and an ongoing forced demographic transformation caused by forced population transfers that are illegal under international law (Lynk 2018). From 2007, Gaza was strictly blockaded behind a suffocating Israeli and Egyptian siege, while being exposed to frequent military assaults, rendering it next to uninhabitable (UNCTAD 2015, 3). Gross insecurity and humiliation at the hands of Israeli security personnel are part of everyday Palestinian life in the oPt (OCHRC 2022), and the basic movement of people and goods is strictly controlled and largely limited to meeting Israel's needs. Palestinian industry long ago de-developed to a point where foreign assistance has been "a" and all too often "the" primary driver of Palestinian economic and institutional life. Yet, that "assistance" has simultaneously contributed to the securitization of Palestinians and further colonization of their lands (Tartir 2018).

Israeli politics has been dominated since the mid-1990s by a Likud political party that is hostile to key aspects of the MEPP, notably the establishment of an autonomous Palestinian state in the oPt. Though all Israeli governments have contributed to the development of settlement infrastructure within the oPt, including the Yitzhak Rabin Labor-led government (1992–5), Likud governments have been prominent champions of the settlement movement. In 2018, a Benjamin Netanyahu Likud-led government passed a quasi-constitutional Basic Law declaring Israel an exclusive homeland for the Jewish people where "The state views the development of Jewish settlement as a national value and will act to encourage and promote its establishment and consolidation" (Wootliff 2018). In January 2020, encouraged by the announcement of a Trump Peace Plan, the Netanyahu government proposed a formal annexation of approximately 30 percent of the oPt. It only backed down from formal annexation with the advent of the Abraham Accords, which offered Israel a normalization of diplomatic relations with the UAE and Bahrain (Badarin 2020, 6; Lazaroff 2020). By 2022, Netanyahu was able to form a government again after a brief period out of power, when the settlement movement became prominent in a Likud-led coalition forming the most right-wing government in the history of Israel (Al Jazeera and News Agencies 2022). The de facto annexation of oPt lands remained ongoing throughout, while Western donors regularly laud Israel's desire for peace (Berman 2014; EEAS Press Team 2022).

While Israelis and Palestinians live de facto in a single state under Israeli government rule, the government of Israel refuses to grant Palestinians equal political rights or cease the process of ongoing displacement of Palestinians from their land. Many leading analysts now characterize this system of rule as apartheid (Carter 2007; Dugard 2018; Falk 2014, 67; Falk and Tilley 2017; Tilley 2018; Tutu 2002) and/or an ongoing process of ethnic cleansing (Avnery 2010; Falk 2014, 67; Masalha 2012b; Santos 2016; Zureik 2003). In that system, the development of normal Palestinian economic and political institutions is impossible. Not only do Palestinians face a complex matrix of debilitating socioeconomic obstacles under Israeli rule but, as this chapter explains, their right to self-determination is undermined by the occupier and Western peacemaker alike. Even the Palestinian right to build their own institutions as they see fit is frequently denied.

To explore the role Western (liberal) states have played in Palestine, this chapter begins by looking at the original peace model they developed for Israelis and Palestinians, based on partition in a nascent United Nations (UN) in the late 1940s. There Western actors largely ignored the Indigenous Palestinian voice, and partition immediately contributed to decades of violence while undermining Palestinian self-determination. The second section explores the liberal ideological framework by which Western democracies have most often approached Palestinian-Israeli peacebuilding. It looks at how the approach favors the concerns of the colonizer, Israel, and how that may be consistent with Western liberalism's historical cohabitation with colonialism. The section also looks more specifically at liberalism's historical cohabitation with settler colonialism, how this contributes to the elimination of the Palestinian narrative, and how it reinforces analytical ignorance among Western policymakers. The third section describes how liberal models can only be sustained through decontextualized analysis and the use of false narratives. These permeate Western development programming that is run, in theory, to support development and peace in the Middle East. The section also provides examples of how the decontextualization of aid causes harm and reinforces a violent, deleterious status quo. The chapter concludes by noting that Western peacemakers would need to radically redefine their approach if they are interested in fostering Middle East peace and truly addressing the Palestinian humanitarian crisis. However, it questions if, based in their track record, this will happen and suggests Palestinians should be wary of Western intervention into their lands.

Colonial Partition

Imperial Europe and the United Nations Partition of Palestine

When Israel and the PLO signed the Oslo I Accord in 1993, there was global optimism this would lead to a lasting peace based on a two-state solution with an exchanging of land for peace. The accord hearkened back to the plan prescribed by United Nations General Assembly (UNGA) Resolution 181 (II) in 1947 (United Nations General Assembly 1947). Responding to "strife" in what was British colonial ("Mandatory") Palestine, the UNGA's solution had been to partition the land and peoples into separate states: one for Jews (including Jewish Palestinians) and one for non-Jewish Palestinians (heretofore referred to as Palestinians). Under that plan, those two states would be bound together in a sort of economic federation and Jerusalem granted special status as a UN-administered international regime. A largely urban Jewish community that constituted less than a third of the population, occupied less than 7 percent of the land and were comprised of mostly recently arrived settlers would be allocated 55.5 percent of the land and prime agricultural areas (Khalidi 1997, 11). The Indigenous Palestinians, who made up the majority of the population and owned most land, were allocated only 45.5 percent of Palestine (Khalidi 1997, 11).

Informed observers were aware that Palestinians and Arabs bitterly opposed a partition they considered unjust and against the interest of Palestinians (Husseini 2008, 46; Newport 2014, 134). They understood implementing UNGA 181 (II) would almost certainly require the use of force against the Indigenous Palestinians (Khalidi 1997, 15). Western diplomats and analysts, like Canada's Elizabeth MacCallum, warned such a deal would inevitably lead to a long-term protracted conflict (Newport 2014, 147–50). The US State Department and Sovietologists within the department feared that partition would work against US regional interests and provide the Soviet Union an entry point into the Middle East (Brecher 2012, 227). Yet, in the wake of the horrors of the Holocaust, Western political leaders were swayed by humanitarian concerns to establish a homeland for the Jewish people (Husseini 2008, 49; Tauber 1998, 93–4, 1999, 230–1). This included powerful actors like US president Harry Truman (Brecher 2012, 229), his ruling Democratic Party (Democratic Party, 1948), and Canada's Under-Secretary of State for External Affairs Lester B. Pearson (Labelle 2018, 171), all key architects of a new liberal international order that was being embodied within the nascent United Nations.

This was the tail end of an age of imperialism where Europeans had long ignored and deliberately trampled upon the aspirations of colonized peoples. Decolonization was on the horizon, but the UN was itself still very European in nature, while Zionism would emerge from the twilight of Imperial Europe shaped, as Dana and Jarbawi write, by three fundamental traits: nationalism, colonialism, and anti-Semitism (2017, 198). The Zionist movement deliberately disregarded the presence of the Indigenous people of the land, just like how Palestinian aspirations were largely ignored by Western leaders who did not concern themselves if the UN was being asked to violate Palestinian rights (Pappé 2006, 32) or why Palestinians were being asked to pay for Europe's genocidal crimes against European Jewry. Even the creation of any Palestinian state seemed to be of secondary importance to Western powers (Husseini 2008, 47). Despite the anti-colonial idealism imbued within Communism, the Soviet approach to Israel and Palestine was pure Realpolitik, supporting the foundation of Israel out of competition with the capitalist West, with an eye on establishing a presence in the Middle East (Krammer 1973, 103; Newport 2014, 363).

From an Indigenous Palestinian perspective, European powers were siding with a minority community that only recently came to settle in Palestine (Yusuf 2002, 43). With the rapid evacuation of British forces in 1948, regional Arab forces clashed with the paramilitary forces striving to establish an Israeli state, which were backed by the resources, advanced technology, and military techniques of both the capitalist and communist European camps. The result was an even more unfair outcome than envisaged in UNGA 181 (II) with an Israeli state established on 78 percent of historic Palestine (Pappé 2016, 404), 750,000 Palestinians forcibly expelled from it (United Nations 2008, 10), and Jordanian-Egyptian rule extended over the remaining 22 percent of Palestine.¹

Despite this outcome, UNGA 181 (II) remained intact as a conceptual framework for future peacebuilding, which was based on the principle of establishing separate national homes for Israelis and for Palestinians in historic Palestine. This model was reinforced after Israel occupied the remaining 22 percent of Palestine in the 1967 Arab-Israeli War and through two more decades of significant regional conflagrations like the Jordanian Civil War (1970/1), the 1973 Arab-Israeli War, and the Lebanese Civil War (1975–90). Unlike in the 1940s, when Israel's military gains and very creation were mostly legitimized at the UN, in subsequent conquests Israel faced opposition from that same body and an international community that, at least rhetorically, opposed any further extension of Israeli sovereignty into Arab lands. This included pressure for Israel to leave Gaza after first conquering it in 1956, and after the 1967 war, as iterated in UN Security Council (UNSC) Resolution 242 (United Nations Security Council 1967) and UNSC Resolution 338 (United Nations Security Council 1973). Those UNSC resolutions called for a ceasefire, Israel's right to exist in security in the region, for Israel to withdraw from territories it seized in 1967, and for negotiations to get underway in search of a lasting peace.

By 1981, the UN Secretary-General observed that the "Palestinian problem" and Israel-Arab conflict had probably claimed more of the UN's time than any other international problem over thirty-five years (*Part I of Three YB 1982 Excerpts* 1982, 3). It was a much different world in 1981 than in 1947. Already by the time of the 1967

UNSC votes, the violent and hard-fought struggles of innumerable colonized peoples had resulted in a global process of decolonization that saw international bodies, such as the UN, come to better represent the characteristics of the broader international community (Prashad 2008, xvi)—rather than just the European imperial powers that once dominated it. The West was changing, too, and support for overt colonialism ebbed among electorates that were becoming more and more liberal, and diverse through immigration from the Global South. When the Palestinian people began to rise up against Israeli rule in the First Intifada (1987–93), in a mostly unarmed movement which Israel met with extreme force, the Palestinians garnered global sympathy that extended through a Western Europe that had in the 1970s become increasingly sympathetic to the Palestinian lot. As the Soviet Union, by that point a key supporter of the Palestinian cause, began to unravel in the 1980s under the weight of the Cold War, in 1988 the Palestinian leadership in exile, the PLO, gave up on its foundational aim to liberate and unite all historic Palestine into one multireligious state (Palestine Liberation Organization, 1968). Instead, they acceded to negotiations for a Palestinian state on just the lands Israel occupied militarily in 1967. This approach was based on the logic of the UN formulas in UNGA 181 (II), UNSC Resolution 242, UNSC Resolution 338, and by incorporating UNGA 194 (Article 11) into final status talks, which in 1948 had guaranteed the right of Palestinian refugees to return to their homes as soon as possible (United Nations General Assembly 1948). This decision was made as Western liberal democracies emerged out of the Cold War hegemonic in global affairs and the stage was set for direct talks between Palestinians and Israelis at Madrid in 1991, Moscow in 1992, and Oslo in 1993, setting the peace process into motion.

Liberalism and Colonialism in Palestine

Western Liberalism and the Deconstruction of Modern Palestine

Though not the only normative framework under which Western powers organize themselves, since the end of the Second World War liberalism and its variation neoliberalism have been mostly dominant. The UN, which helped partition Palestine, and its predecessor League of Nations, which "awarded" Palestine to Britain as a mandate to "govern in the interests of the colonized," are ontological constructs of Western liberalism. They are, in theory, international bodies dedicated to cooperation between states (at least Western ones), the peaceful resolution of disputes among states, and the prevention of conflict. Today, many of the world's leading liberal bodies are engaged actors in the context of Israel's colonization of Palestine. They and Western liberalism have in the process cohabitated with, obscured, and even contributed to the military occupation of and settler colonization of Palestine.

Liberalism holds an inherent faith in the innate goodness of the individual, the capacity for political institutions (governments) to promote social progress, and the idea that states are capable of meaningful cooperation (Keohane and Nye 1998, 10–11). Depending on their interpretation, liberals may espouse a number of different values (Bell 2014), which may include: free markets, individual liberties and human rights, racial and gender equality, limitations on the power of government, freedom of speech and the press, freedom of religion, and a separation of religion from state. Liberals often espouse the right of a people to self-determination (Hobhouse 1964, 25), and to democratic self-governance, the latter of which is considered the superior form of civilized governance. In Anglo-American politics and in their political theory, Bell argues that liberalism has become so hegemonic that "most who identify themselves as socialists, conservatives, social democrats, republicans, greens, feminists, and anarchists have been ideologically incorporated, whether they like it or not" (Bell 2014). Both the West and ideological liberalism became particularly dominant in global affairs after the fall of the Soviet Union took place in the early 1990s (Keohane 2012).

Mostly internationalist by nature, liberals support global institutions and accords to promote cooperation and facilitate trade, which is meant to leave everyone better off while rendering the costs of war prohibitive (Keohane and Nye 1998). Liberals also believe a predilection for peace exists among democracies, because such states are responsible to their citizens, and their citizens will consider the costs of war to be irrational. Liberals believe that this responsiveness by democratic states to their citizens imbue those states with an inherent peaceful rationalism (Doyle 1983, 225), whereby these states come to realize they have more to gain by working together than struggling on their own in competition with each other. Within the logic of this framework, if both Israelis and Palestinians were to have a liberal democracy, they would realize they have more to gain working together peacefully than in conflict. Since Western policymakers already considered Israel to be a fellow liberal democracy, imbued with the accoutrements of modernity, the search for peace would naturally come through reforming and changing the nature of the Palestinians so that they could become liberal and democratic, too.

Yet, ambiguities have characterized the way liberal thought has dealt with illiberal acts. Political theorists like Bell, McNally, and Pitts have argued that liberalism is itself a handmaiden to destructive, autocratic Western imperialism (Bell 2016; McNally 2014; Pitts 2000). Bell and Pitts point out that great liberal thinkers, such as Tocqueville and Mill, were advocates of the virtues of imperialism (Bell 2016; Pitts 2000). Williams (2020) notes that liberal thinkers in the eighteenth and nineteenth centuries were well aware of the human cruelties involved in European colonialism, in a foundational period for the birth of liberalism. John Locke, often referred to as the father of liberalism, worked on behalf of slavery and colonialism, too. Some contemporary scholars emphasize that Locke was concerned about private property above all else, including slaves (Brewer 2018). Others have suggested that "Western" ideas about democracy and rights simply serve as cover for imperialism and the oppression of Indigenous peoples (Brewer 2018).

Israel is the product of state-building in a European settler colony whose sole aim was to found a national home for the Jewish people (Herzl 2008). It was nurtured primarily by a British metropole and then by the United States with other Western states. The process of settler colonialization is closely connected with landownership, dispossession, and the replacement of existing populations. It is only made possible through first taking land away from Indigenous peoples (Rodriguez Martin 2019, 489), and this leads to a zero-sum struggle for land and life, for colonizer and colonized alike (Wolfe 2006, 387). Thus, Israel's creation was done at great cost to the Indigenous Palestinians, and these actions put Israel in a family of like-minded settler colonial states, including the United States, Canada, Australia, and New Zealand. Meanwhile, like those states, Israel is regularly described as liberal and democratic but rarely as a settler-colonial (Hilal 2015, 353). This is the case even as Israel obviously imposes on Palestinians a colonial system of control that combines features of apartheid with features of the "reserve" system used to colonize and control Native Americans and Australian Aboriginals.

Despite very clear evidence of ongoing dispossession, Western policymakers assume Israel is naturally predisposed toward peace, because it is a liberal state, like themselves. Lloyd argues that when Westerner's look at Israel they see a fellow liberal democracy seeded by a European metropole, which is inherently superior to other societies in an otherwise "backward region" (Lloyd 2012, 65). While identifying with Israel as a fellow liberal democracy, Western policymakers have assumed that the broader problems of conflict and violence lay with the "less developed" and "illiberal" Arabs and Muslims. Within that logical framework, Israel's security emerged as a central discursive element in all peace negotiations (Pappé 2016, 409), notably when peace talks broke down into violence during the Second Intifada in the early 2000s. Meanwhile, the same concern for the security of Palestinians does not exist among Western governments, and the onus on building peace through an abstention from violence is placed almost solely on the Palestinians. Take for example how US Secretary of State Anthony Blicken iterated in May 2021, the US position is that they "believe strongly that Israel has a right to defend itself," and that it is a false equivalence to compare a "terrorist group—Hamas—that is indiscriminately launching rockets at civilians and Israel, which is responding to those attacks" (Magid 2021).

Israel is always assumed to have a right to defend itself and the Palestinians largely to be the aggressor and Israeli violence invariably tolerated, if not justified, while violent acts by Palestinians are only categorized as a threat to peace (Ignatieff 2002, 1146). Israeli colonization through settlement building accelerated in the oPt in the 1990s, a period that should have been dedicated to building goodwill for peace negotiations and where a foundational precept for peacebuilding was premised on Palestinians establishing an autonomous state in the oPt (Shlaim 2013). Michael Lynk, former UN Special Rapporteur on the situation of human rights in the Palestinian territories, points out, "no country creates civilian settlements in occupied territory unless it has annexationist designs in mind," and this is why the international community has designated the practice of "settler-implantation as a war crime, as per Rome Statute of 1998, Article 8(1)(b)(viii)" (Lynk 2018, 14).

Even with 1949 armistice lines that set Israel up on 78 percent of Palestine, and despite various UN interventions, there was always a strong impulse by Israel to colonize all historical Palestine (Masalha 2012a; Pappé 2006). Though Israeli settler colonization has been strategically consistent over time, with its characteristic tendencies to expel and replace Palestinians, and to "de-Arabize" conquered lands (Pappé 2006, 49), the way this has been done has been adapted to different contexts in different eras. Thus, while the mass expulsion of Palestinians at gunpoint in 1948/9 is no longer considered acceptable in the contemporary era, expulsion remains a formative part of Israeli settler colonialism, even when being carried out at a reduced speed and with more indirect methods (Wolfe 2006, 401). Those methods include a combination of measures, such as the creation of internal borders in the oPt and forcing Palestinians off the majority of their land (in Areas B and C) into small, overcrowded, and economically nonviable "Bantustans" (in Area A). Now most of Area C has been allocated to Israeli settlements or the Israeli military, at the expense of Palestinian communities (*OCHA* n.d.). By 2019, Area C was home to a population of 325,500 Israeli settlers living in 125 settlements and approximately 100 outposts, compared to an estimated 180,000 to 300,000 Palestinians (*B'Tselem* n.d.). Such settlement building is illegal under international law and the UN has called on Israel to "cease all settlement activities in the Occupied Palestinian Territory, including East Jerusalem" (United Nations Security Council, 2016). This has happened under the watchful gaze of most Western liberal democracies, whose greatest resistance to such an illiberal act as settler colonialism is to bleat about their concern with Israel's actions or unilateral measures by "both sides." Some, like former Canadian prime minister Stephen Harper, have, when questioned on Israeli settlement building, said they think it is inappropriate to single out and criticize Israel, a fellow liberal democracy, for how it chooses to govern itself (Payton 2014).

Liberalism and Settler Colonialism

For Palestinians, their daily life is defined by an ongoing life-or-death process of settler colonialism (Badarin 2015; Weizman 2007). From a normative liberal perspective, settler colonialism should appear to be among the greatest crimes against humanity and one of the most easily recognized forms of oppression in the world (Waziyatawin 2012). It was an integral part of the colonial European expansion that shaped the contemporary world, leaving the Global South de-developed and poor and the North (the West) rich. Recovery from the ravages of colonialism defines the modern identity of some of today's greatest emerging powers, India and China, that prior to European subjugation were powerhouses in manufacturing that met their own needs (McQuade 2017). They were impoverished when their economies were plundered and production redirected to benefit Europe. The North-South dynamic was also shaped by the violent elimination of colonized societies. Entire regions were "rebirthed" as lands of the European West. The United States, today's global superpower and mediator of the MEPP, came into existence out of the brutal settler colonization of North America's Indigenous societies (Brown 2012). Canada and Australia emerged from similar processes, as well.

Europeans were once convinced about the greater good of imperial expansion, as an enlightened act of progress (Bell 2010; Kipling 1998; Speetjens 2016). Perhaps an echo of their past convictions, or possibly guilt, Western scholars and analysts tend today to gloss over and ignore the legacies of colonial atrocities. Some engage in revisionism like the pernicious argument that colonialism helped to develop colonized societies (Dahlgreen 2014; Gilley 2017; Kipling 1998). What can be said with certainty is that the early liberal societies with empires, like the French, Dutch, and British, forcibly pacified native peoples who resisted colonization, leaving colonized peoples with duties but few rights (Conklin 1998, 419).

Liberalism has a history of cohabitation with settler colonialism. It is well-known in the field of settler colonial studies that a settler colony can be simultaneously predisposed toward conflict and eliminatory violence against Indigenous peoples, yet apply liberal organizing principles to the settlers it considers citizens (Veracini 2010, 3). Thus, the government of a settler state routinely denies public goods and markets to Indigenous inhabitants ("noncitizens") as part of the process of their dispossession, while providing goods and markets to people it considers citizens.

Meanwhile, the framework of colonialism that undergirds Israel and defines its relationship with the Palestinians is almost purposefully forgotten (Gordon 2009, 59). Badarin writes that denying responsibility toward the victims of settler colonial displacement is deeply rooted in Israeli society and something peacemakers work around (Badarin 2016, 129–30). Thus, Palestinian memory and experiences are recast by Western peacemakers as obstacles, treated like irrelevant features (Pappé 2016, 402), rather than integral realities. In this way, liberal institutions like the World Bank will describe how they avoid descriptive terminology about the occupation in order to focus on positive dialogue and avoid "deconstructive recriminations" about past actions (The World Bank 2012). Hawari notes that the demand to leave the past behind "as bygones" is a "tactic often invoked by those in positions of power in peace process discourses around the world, particularly in contexts of colonialism and settler colonialism" (Hawari 2018, 172).

Alternate Facts to Maintain the Status Quo

Technocratic Development Aid

Combined with liberalism's inherent faith in the ability to "develop" societies through good policy, liberalism has long occupied a functional capacity to engage in endless state-building processes, while obscuring underlying imperial or colonial processes that are underway. This is why development aid became intrinsic to the two-state model of peacebuilding in the MEPP. There development aid has been rhetorically used as a means to "equip" Palestinians with liberal, democratic, and capitalist institutions (Amundsen, Giacaman and Khan 2004), thereby creating a modern Palestinian state that Israel can securely cohabitate with, establishing peace. This operated on racist, Orientalist logic that puts the onus on Palestinians to prove they are capable of managing a state (Hilal 2015, 353), without any pressure on Israel to fundamentally change its ways. Meanwhile, this approach assumes that Western "experts" can provide necessary oversight to redevelop Palestinian state and society, as though the Palestinians are uniquely less capable than other peoples in countries like Kuwait, the United States, or Romania. Conveniently, this approach leaves it up to Israel and its Western allies to determine when and if the Palestinians have that capacity for independence.

Relying on the World Bank as their guide, Western donors driving the MEPP decided that development aid should be separated from politics to build confidence among Palestinians in the peace process through economic growth (Tartir and

Wildeman 2013; Wildeman and Tartir 2021). Development aid could thus act as a "peace dividend" to encourage Palestinian participation in peacebuilding with Israel (Le More 2008, 89). The approach was built on the false perception that Palestinians are the primary drivers of violence, and it required stripping away the contextual analysis that explains why Palestinians might engage in violence. Bereft of the context of Israel's violent settler-colonial project, Western donors could then develop policy based on an idea that Palestinians just need to be convinced that violence is not an appropriate way to interact with liberal democratic states like Israel, while the radical modernization of Palestinian society under Western oversight takes hold. Pappé refers to this "business-like approach" by Western peacemakers (Pappé 2016, 402) as one where they operate on the belief that policy can be designed in a technocratic and neutral manner, independent of politics, which is thus able to foster an environment conducive to peace. Yet, those technocrats and that power are never truly impersonal or free from subjectivity, while the approach conveniently allows Israel and its Western allies to determine when and if the Palestinians have been "well-enough developed" for peace.

The World Bank is one of the leading liberal bodies that Western donors tasked with creating the conditions for peace through Palestinian reform and development. The Bank advised from the onset of the Oslo process that Palestinian economic turmoil, when juxtaposed against Israeli success, would be a clear impediment to peace (The World Bank 1993, 1). In other contexts, Easterly describes such an approach as "an illusion that poverty is purely a technical problem, distracting attention away from the real cause: the unchecked power of the state against poor people without rights" (Easterly 2014). Thus, donors came first to look at Palestinian poverty as the primary issue that needed to be resolved in order to foster peace, rather than the political reasons for Palestinian poverty existing in the first place. Meanwhile, the racist Western myth that the "less developed" Palestinians were the drivers of violence reinforced a sense that Palestinians could not be trusted with self-rule until the process of development had been seen through. Until that happened, a prevailing viewpoint was that Palestinians would need to remain under Israeli rule, for the alternative could be much worse (Turner 2012, 494).

Thus, the onus was left solely on Palestinians to become better, finally ready for peaceful cohabitation with Israel. This one-sided Western fixation on providing security for Israel, a state they are effectively allied with and most identify with in the Middle East, exists in the face of Western peacemakers arguing that they are able to deliver impersonal and technocratic solutions (Monaghan 2016). Yet, analysis this author conducted on five US Government Accountability Office (GAO) reports concerning American aid programming in the oPt, produced between 2010 and 2015, reveals a fixation on violence committed by Palestinians but not against Palestinians, the clearly weaker and militarily occupied party (Wildeman 2018, 143).

After the Second Intifada (2000–6) took place, security supplanted poverty reduction as the priority in Western institution building in the oPt. As with poverty reduction, however, security was problematized as issues of capacity and institution building, stripped away from the political context that explains why violence is taking place to start with (Bahdi and Kassis 2016, 2015). Thus in new ways and in new contexts,

Western liberal democracies and their foreign "aid" further entrench Israel's rule over the oPt (Bahdi and Kassis 2016) through the development of new security structures maintaining control over the Palestinian population while settler colonialism takes place largely unabated. To make matters worse, the large inflow of foreign aid into the captive oPt economy allows Israel to benefit economically from its settler colonization (Hever 2010, 2015; Hilal 2015, 354). This leaves Israel with little pressure to change its colonial ways but many financial incentives to maintain the status quo.

Ignoring Empirical Reality

A never-ending occupation and deleterious settler colonization of the oPt is far from the outcome most hoped for with the MEPP, if they took its liberal rhetoric at face value. For Western advocates of that MEPP to maintain their policy course without any fundamental change, in the face of evidence that it is both failing and causing harm, requires a great deal of structural ambiguity and cognitive dissonance. This can only be maintained by an ongoing process of misreading, poor analysis, and decontextualization to alter perceptions of empirical realities. This actually began near the onset of the MEPP. When Western policymakers in 1993 created a development model meant to prepare Palestinians for autonomy, they did so in a way that was specifically ignorant of the context of settler colonialism (Bahdi and Kassis 2016, 2015). Their decontextualization was in fact so extreme that they did not even properly account for the continuing Israeli military occupation and absence of Palestinian sovereignty in their models (Le More 2005, 996). This misreading and poor analysis extended to economics.

Prior to the MEPP, ample indicators suggested the oPt economy was suffering from its connection to Israel. Sara Roy (1987) found, for instance, that Gaza's economy was becoming poorer because Israeli rule had been structurally designed for the sole developmental benefit of Israel. Palestinians were used as cheap labor for Israeli economic growth and their earnings then used to buy Israeli goods while allowing Israel to free up Jewish labor from menial jobs to develop advanced industry (Tamari 1988; Wolfe 2006, 390). Palestinians meanwhile could not develop their own economic sectors for their sole benefit, and Israeli policy was designed to undermine Palestinian sectors that might compete with Israeli equivalents (Roy 1995, 6, 146). Simultaneously, the oPt became Israel's most important export market: tariff-free and noncompetitive, with Palestinian goods regularly prevented from entering Israel. Roy (1995, 4) called this the "deliberate, systematic deconstruction of an Indigenous economy by a dominant power." Rather than challenge and restructure this colonial economic arrangement, to see more equitable economic outcomes that could better sustain peace and improve Palestinian standards of living, donors then decided they needed to reinforce Israeli-Palestinian economic interlinkages. This was in theory meant to build and strengthen peace but would in reality reinforce an ongoing process of economic dispossession.

An unwillingness to deal with reality and challenge, or even acknowledge Israel's colonialism, is reflected in donors' language. During the 1990s, the term "occupation" vanished almost entirely from the international discourse, despite it being a universally accepted description of Israeli rule over the oPt, as per UN Security Council Resolutions 298 (1971), 446 (1979), and United Nations General Assembly resolution 32/5 (October 28, 1977). Quite a number of international organizations collectively came to substitute the term "occupied Palestinian territory" with appellations like "West Bank and Gaza Strip," "Palestinian territories," or even "Palestinian Authority" (Le More 2008, 29). Even the World Bank has been reluctant to refer to the oPt as occupied. For instance, in eighteen World Bank reports from 2009 to 2017 to the Ad Hoc Liaison Committee (AHLC), a grouping where major donors meet on a biannual basis to determine Palestinian funding, the word "occupation" is only mentioned nineteen times and "occupied" thirty-five times throughout 500 pages of analysis (Wildeman 2018, 112). References to the occupation disappeared altogether from 2012 to 2017, even though the occupation/colonization intensified and continued to define Palestinian life (Wildeman 2018, 112). Astonishingly, in a 239-page evaluation of its work in the oPt 2001–9 (Garcia-Garcia et al. 2009), the World Bank only uses the word "occupation" twice, both in references to a Palestinian Authority plan called "Palestine: Ending the Occupation, Establishing the State." In that report, the word "occupied" is mentioned sixteen times, but only three are clear references to an act carried out by Israel, while the other thirteen are secondary citations of "occupied," often in a report title (Wildeman 2018, 113).

An example of how this process of decontextualization leads to bad policy support appeared on the World Bank's "West Bank and Gaza" website in 2017 (October 27). There the Bank offered water policy guidance for Palestinians using the example of Israeli water management. The blog entitled "Israel: How meeting water challenges spurred a dynamic export industry" described how water has become a US$2-billion rapid growth industry for Israel, with an increase in exports of almost 200 percent in just three years (Moore 2017). In the blog, the author extols the virtues of Israeli government policy and its "progressive" approach to water pricing and conservation (Moore 2017). Lest the benefits of this "success story" be lost on an oPt audience he observes,

> The Israeli example shows that it's possible to turn severe water scarcity into an economic opportunity with the right investments in technology, financing, policy, and institutions. For World Bank client countries that are severely affected by water scarcity, the case of Israel suggests that investing in a combination of sound policy incentives and technology can create substantial rewards, not only in the water sector, but more broadly for innovation-led economic growth as well. (Moore 2017)

It should be alarming to see the World Bank offer this guidance. Palestinian-Israeli water sharing of resources from the oPt is highly iniquitous (Zeitoun 2013, 145), and this has long been understood to be the case. Israel's colonial appropriation of Palestinian water resources has been catastrophic for Palestinians (Dana and Jabawi 2017, 209; Selby 2003), and the World Bank has decades of experience on the ground to have seen this in action. As the Israeli NGO B'Tselem stated,

> In 1967, Israel seized control of all water resources in the newly occupied territories. Israel retains exclusive control over all the water resources between the

Jordan River and the Mediterranean Sea, except for a small section of the coastal aquifer in the Gaza Strip. Israel uses the water as it sees fit, ignoring the needs of Palestinians in the West Bank and in the Gaza Strip, subjecting them to a mostly man-made water shortage. Neither area is supplied enough water. In Gaza, even the water that is supplied is substandard and not potable. (B'Tselem 2017)

Selby uses water as an example of how sanitizing facts leads to oppressive practices that are "discursively repackaged and represented as instances of Israeli-Palestinian 'cooperation'" (Selby 2003, 123). Thus, after the Oslo Accords were signed, iniquitous Israeli control over Palestinian water resources was relabeled "cooperation," even though nothing in the power dynamics changed. The Israeli Mekorot water company retained ownership over the West Bank's water infrastructure, as it had since 1982, supplying rapidly growing Israeli settlements while relying on the newly "liberated" Palestinians to act as middlemen enforcing Israel's discriminatory water distribution and collecting bills among Palestinian communities (Selby 2003, 128). In this way, Israeli water companies can turn an export profit using Palestinian resources, including by reselling oPt water to Palestinians at unfair rates. It is therefore bizarre to see a blog implying that the Palestinians might learn from the Israeli water management policy. It is an example of how the ambiguities and language of liberalism, like cooperation, have been used to obscure illiberal colonial practices beneath the liberal rhetorical framing.

Conclusion

If Western actors are to contribute to peacebuilding and genuine Palestinian development, such as the European Union and member states in their state-building efforts, the starting point is to acknowledge, account for, and oppose an Israeli colonialism that is inimical to a just and lasting peace in the Middle East, a Palestinian state, and Palestinian life. As this chapter describes, that requires Western scholars, analysts, and policymakers to challenge their inherent, colonial biases that favor Israel. Meanwhile, Palestinians have become dependent on foreign aid that contributes to their de-development and further entrenched Israel's colonial infrastructure. Suddenly withdrawing that aid without alternatives could have catastrophic short-term consequences for Palestinians.

Mandy Turner (2020) asks if in the absence of Palestinian sovereignty, international donors can play a progressive role in what is clearly "a situation of settler colonialism and accelerating apartheid." Her conclusion is that it may be possible if donors are "forced to be progressive by a clear and consistent plan and strategy from the Palestinian leadership and Palestinian civil society groups" that create a framework of preconditions under which they are willing to accept donor money (Turner 2020). Bahdi and Kassis further offer a warning that engaging at development and peace on donors' existing terms amounts to "neo-colonial co-optation" (2016, 2011). Yet, a question remains to what extent Palestinians can develop a coherent national strategy while under foreign rule, given the great extent to which Israel and the West interfere in Palestinian institutions and society. Regardless, one point remains clear: without a radical change in their approach, Western states will continue to underwrite and provide security for Israeli settler colonialism, within a rhetorical liberal framework. Meanwhile, the historical consistency with which Western liberals have prioritized Israel's political interests and underwritten its settler colonial cause raises questions to what extent Palestinians can rely on Western actors as sponsors of peace and to what extent Palestinians should disaggregate Western state actors from Israel.

Note

1 The Palestinian Central Bureau of Statistics places the number of Palestinians expelled at 800,000 of a population of 1.4 million Palestinians, with 531 villages destroyed and 15,000 people killed (*PCBS* 2019).

References

Al Jazeera and News Agencies (2022), "Israel's Netanyahu Reaches Coalition Deal with Pro-settler Party." *Al Jazeeera*, December 1. https://www.aljazeera.com/news/2022/12/1/israels-netanyahu-reaches-coalition-deal-with-far-right-party

Amundsen, Inge, George Giacaman, and Mushtaq Husain Khan (2004), *State Formation in Palestine: Viability and Governance During a Social Transformation*. London and New York: Routledge.

Area, C. (n.d.), *[United Nations]*. UN-OCHA. Retrieved September 10, 2019, from https://www.ochaopt.org/location/area-c.

Area, C. (n.d.), *B'Tselem*. Retrieved September 10, 2019, from https://www.btselem.org/topic/area_c.

Avnery, Uri (2010), "Slow-Motion Ethnic Cleansing." In William A. Cook (ed.), *The Plight of the Palestinians: A Long History of Destruction*, 255–7. New York: Palgrave Macmillan US. https://doi.org/10.1057/9780230107922_32.

Badarin, Emile (2015), "Settler-Colonialist Management of Entrances to the Native Urban Space in Palestine." *Settler Colonial Studies*, 5(3): 226–35. https://doi.org/10.1080/2201473X.2014.955946.

Badarin, Emile (2016), *Palestinian Political Discourse: Between Exile and Occupation*. New York: Routledge.

Badarin, Emile (2020), "Israel Annexation Plan: Jordan's Existential Threat." *Middle East Eye*. http://www.middleeasteye.net/opinion/israel-annexation-why-jordan-problem-too.

Bahdi, Reem and Mudar Kassis (2016), "Decolonisation, Dignity and Development Aid: A Judicial Education Experience in Palestine." *Third World Quarterly*, 37 (11): 2010–2027. https://doi.org/10.1080/01436597.2016.1181521.

Bell, Duncan (2010), "John Stuart Mill on Colonies." *Political Theory*, 38(1): 34–64. https://doi.org/10.1177/0090591709348186.

Bell, Duncan (2014), "What Is Liberalism?" *Political Theory*, 42(6): 682–715. http://www.jstor.org/stable/24571524.

Bell, Duncan (2016), "The Dream Machine: On Liberalism and Empire." In Duncan Bell (ed.), *Reordering the World: Essays on Liberalism and Empire*. Princeton: Princeton University Press.

Berman, Lazar (2014), "Harper: Support for Israel is Morally and Strategically Right." *Times of Israel*, January 20. http://www.timesofisrael.com/harper-canada-stands-for-israel-because-it-is-right-to-do-so/

Bhaiwala, Zahra (2015), "Health Under Occupation: Constraints on Access to healthcare in the Palestinian Territories." *Mondoweiss*, August 14. https://mondoweiss.net/2015/08/constraints-palestinian-territories/.

Brecher, Frank W. (2012), "US Secretary of State George C. Marshall's Losing Battles Against President Harry S. Truman's Palestine Policy, January–June 1948." *Middle Eastern Studies*, 48 (2): 227–47.

Brewer, Holly (2018), "Does Locke's Entanglement with Slavery Undermine His Philosophy?" *Aeon*, September 12. https://aeon.co/essays/does-lockes-entanglement-with-slavery-undermine-his-philosophy.

Brown, Dee (2012), *Bury My Heart at Wounded Knee: An Indian History of the American West*, 1st ed. New York: Open Road Media.

B'Tselem (2017), "Water Crisis." *B'Tselem*, November 11. http://www.btselem.org/water.

Carter, Jimmy (2007), *Palestine: Peace Not Apartheid*. New York: Simon and Schuster.

Conklin, Alice L. (1998), "Colonialism and Human Rights, A Contradiction in Terms? The Case of France and West Africa, 1895–1914." *The American Historical Review*, 103 (2): 419–42. https://doi.org/10.2307/2649774.

Dahlgreen, Will (2014), "The British Empire is 'Something to be Proud of.'" *YouGov, Lifestyle Politics and Current Affairs*. https://yougov.co.uk/topics/politics/articles-reports/2014/07/26/britain-proud-its-empire.

Dana, Tariq and Ali Jarbawi (2017), "A Century of Settler Colonialism in Palestine: Zionism's Entangled Project." *The Brown Journal of World Affairs*, 24(1): 197–220. https://www.jstor.org/stable/27119089

Democratic Party (1948), *1948 Democratic Party Platform*. The American Presidency Project. https://www.presidency.ucsb.edu/documents/1948-democratic-party-platform.

Doyle, Michael W. (1983), "Kant, Liberal Legacies, and Foreign Affairs." *Philosophy & Public Affairs*, 12 (3): 205–35. doi:10.2307/1960861

Dugard, John (2018), *Confronting Apartheid: A Personal History of South Africa, Namibia and Palestine*. Auckland Park: Jacana Media.

Easterly, William (2014), "The New Tyranny." *Foreign Policy*, March 10. http://www.foreignpolicy.com/articles/2014/03/10/the_new_tyranny.

EEAS Press Team (2022), *Israel: Statement by the High Representative Josep Borrell on Prime Minister's Support for a Peace Agreement with Palestinians*. European External Action Service. https://www.eeas.europa.eu/eeas/israel-statement-high-representative-josep-borrell-prime-minister%E2%80%99s-support-peace-agreement_en.

Falk, Richard (2014), *A/HRC/25/67 Report of the Special Rapporteur on the Situation of Human Rights in the Palestinian Territories Occupied Since 1967, Richard Falk* (Twenty-Fifth Session A/HRC/25/67; Agenda Item 7). UN General Assembly Human Rights Council.

Falk, Richard and Virginia Tilley (2017), *Israeli Practices Towards the Palestinian People and the Question of Apartheid (E/ESCWA/ECRI/2017/1)*. UN-ESCWA. https://electronicintifada.net/sites/default/files/2017-03/un_apartheid_report_15_march_english_final_.pdf.

Garcia-Garcia, Jorge, Konstantin Atanesyan, Jumana Farah, George Polenakis, Tarek Kotb, Gita Gopal, Miguel Angel Rebolledo Dellepiane, Svetlana Markova, Nawaf Ibrahim Abu Sitta, and Christopher Willoughby (2009), *The World Bank Group in* the West Bank and Gaza, 2001–2009: Evaluation of the World Bank Group Program (No. 100011), 1–239. The World Bank. http://documents.worldbank.org/curated/en/144151467998201026/The-World-Bank-Group-in-the-West-Bank-and-Gaza-2001-2009-evaluation-of-the-World-Bank-Group-program.

Giacaman, Rita, Rana Khatib, Luay Shabaneh, Assad Ramlawi, Belgacem Sabri, Guido Sabatinelli, Marwan Khawaja, and Tony Laurance (2009), "Health in the Occupied Palestinian Territory 1: Health Status and Health Services in the Occupied Palestinian Territory." *The Lancet*, 373: 837–49.

Gilley, Bruce (2017), "The Case for Colonialism. Retraction by Publisher." *Third World Quarterly*, 1–17. https://doi.org/10.1080/01436597.2017.1369037.

Gordon, Todd (2009), "Canada, Empire and Indigenous People in the Americas." *Socialist Studies/Études Socialistes*, 2 (1). http://socialiststudies.com/article/view/23795.

Haddad, Mohammed (2020), "Palestine and Israel: Mapping an Annexation." *Al Jazeera*, June 26. https://www.aljazeera.com/news/2020/6/26/palestine-and-israel-mapping-an-annexation.

Hawari, Yara (2018), "Palestine Sine Tempore?" *Rethinking History*, 22 (2): 165–83. https://doi.org/10.1080/13642529.2018.1451075.

Herzl, Theodor (2008), *The Jewish State*. Wildside Press LLC.

Hever, Shir (2010), *The Political Economy of Israel's Occupation: Repression Beyond Exploitation*, 1st ed. Pluto Press: London.

Hever, Shir (2015), *How Much International Aid to the Palestinians Ends up in the Israeli Economy?* Aid Watch. http://www.aidwatch.ps/sites/default/files/resource-field_media/InternationalAidToPalestiniansFeedsTheIsraeliEconomy.pdf.

Hilal, Jamil (2015), "Rethinking Palestine: Settler-colonialism, Neo-liberalism and Individualism in the West Bank and Gaza Strip." *Contemporary Arab Affairs*, 8 (3): 351–62. https://doi.org/10.1080/17550912.2015.1052226.

Hobhouse, Leonard Trelawny (1964), *Liberalism*. Oxford: Oxford University Press.

Husseini, Hassan (2008), "A 'Middle Power' in Action: Canada and the Partition of Palestine." *Arab Studies Quarterly*, 30 (3): 41–55. http://www.jstor.org/stable/41858551

Ignatieff, Michael (2002), "Human Rights, the Laws of War, and Terrorism." *Social Research*, 69 (4): 1137–58. http://www.jstor.org/stable/40971599

Keohane, Robert O. (2012), "Twenty Years of Institutional Liberalism." *International Relations*, 26(2): 125–38. https://doi.org/10.1177/0047117812438451.

Keohane, Robert O. and Joseph S. Nye (1998), "Power and Interdependence in the Information Age." *Foreign Affairs*, September/October. http://www.foreignaffairs.com/articles/54395/robert-o-keohane-and-joseph-s-nye-jr/power-and-interdependence-in-the-information-age.

Khalidi, Walid (1997), "Revisiting the UNGA Partition Resolution." *Journal of Palestine Studies*, 27 (1): 5–21. https://doi.org/10.2307/2537806.

Kipling, Rudyard (1998), "The White Man's Burden." *Peace Review*, 10 (3): 311–12. https://doi.org/10.1080/10402659808426162.

Krammer, Arnold (1973), "Soviet Motives in the Partition of Palestine, 1947–48." *Journal of Palestine Studies*, 2 (2): 102–19. JSTOR. https://doi.org/10.2307/2535483.

Labelle, Maurice J. (2018), "Not So Nobel: Arab Perceptions of Lester B. Pearson and Canada." In Asa McKercher and Galen Roger Perras (eds.), *Mike's World: Lester B. Pearson and Canadian External Relations, 1963-68*, 169–88. UBC Press: Vancouver.

Lazaroff, Tovah (2020), "Netanyahu Pledges Annexation, Plans to Open School Year in a Settlement." *The Jerusalem Post*, August 31. https://www.jpost.com/israel-news/netanyahu-pledges-annexation-plans-to-open-school-year-in-a-settlement-640647.

Le More, Anne (2005), "Killing With Kindness: Funding the Demise of a Palestinian State." *International Affairs (Royal Institute of International Affairs 1944–)*, 81 (5): 981–99. https://doi.org/10.2307/3569071.

Le More, Anne (2008), *International Assistance to the Palestinians After Oslo*. Routledge: London; New York.

Lloyd, David (2012), "Settler Colonialism and the State of Exception: The Example of Palestine/Israel." *Settler Colonial Studies*, 2 (1): 59–80. https://doi.org/10.1080/2201473X.2012.10648826.

Lynk, Michael (2018), *A/73/45717 Situation of Human Rights in the Palestinian Territories Occupied Since 1967—Advance Unedited Version* (Seventy-Third Session, Item 74 (b) of the Provisional Agenda A/73/45717; Item 74 (b)). UN General Assembly Human Rights Council.

Magid, Jacob (2021), "Reiterating Israel's Right to Defend Itself, Blinken Criticizes 'False Equivalence' Being Made Between Israel, Hamas." *Times of Israel*, May 17. https://www.timesofisrael.com/liveblog_entry/blinken-reiterates-israels-right-to-defend-itself-theres-false-equivalence-being-made-between-israel-hamas/.

Masalha, Nur (2012a), *Expulsion of the Palestinians: The Concept of "Transfer" in Zionist Political Thought, 1882–1948*. Institute for Palestine Studies.

Masalha, Nur (2012b), *The Palestine Nakba: Decolonising History, Narrating the Subaltern, Reclaiming Memory*. Zed Books Ltd: London.

McNally, David (2014), "The Blood of the Commonwealth." *Historical Materialism*, 22 (2): 3–32. https://doi.org/10.1163/1569206x-12341359.

McQuade, Joseph (2017), "Colonialism was a Disaster and the Facts Prove it." *The Conversation*, September 26. http://theconversation.com/colonialism-was-a-disaster-and-the-facts-prove-it-84496.

Monaghan, Jeff (2016), "Security Development and the Palestinian Authority: An Examination of the 'Canadian Factor'." *Conflict, Security & Development*, 16 (2): 125–43. https://doi.org/10.1080/14678802.2016.1153310.

Moore, Scott Michael (2017), "Israel: How Meeting Water Challenges Spurred a Dynamic Export Industry." *The Water Blog*, October 27. http://blogs.worldbank.org/water/israel-how-meeting-water-challenges-spurred-dynamic-export-industry.

Newport, Richard (2014), *The Outsider: Elizabeth P. MacCallum, the Canadian Department of External Affairs, and the Palestine Mandate to 1947*. Thesis, Carleton University, Ottawa. https://curve.carleton.ca/785df807-2bff-442e-a284-011959d005fe.

OCHRC (2022), *Israel: UN Experts Condemn Record Year of Israeli Violence in the Occupied West Bank*. Office of the United Nations High Commissioner for Human Rights. https://www.ohchr.org/en/press-releases/2022/12/israel-un-experts-condemn-record-year-israeli-violence-occupied-west-bank

Palestine Liberation Organisation (1968), *1968—Palestinian National Charter*. Bureau of Public Affairs Department of State. The Office of Electronic Information. https://2001-2009.state.gov/p/nea/rls/22573.htm.

Pappé, Ilan (2006), *Ethnic Cleansing of Palestine*. Oneworld Publications: Oxford.

Pappé, Ilan (2016), "Historiophobia or the Enslavement of History: The Role of the 1948 Ethnic Cleansing in the Contemporary Peace Process." *Arab Studies Quarterly*, 38 (1): 402–17. https://doi.org/10.13169/arabstudquar.38.1.0402.

Payton, Laura (2014), "Stephen Harper Vows Loyalty to Israel in Speech to Knesset." *CBC*, January 20. http://www.cbc.ca/news/politics/stephen-harper-vows-loyalty-to-israel-in-speech-to-knesset-1.2503393.

PCBS (2019), *On the 70th Annual Commemoration of the Palestinian Nakba*. Palestinian Central Bureau of Statistics. http://www.pcbs.gov.ps/post.aspx?lang=en&ItemID=3137.

Pitts, Jennifer (2000), "Empire and Democracy: Tocqueville and the Algeria Question." *Journal of Political Philosophy*, 8 (3): 295–318. https://doi.org/10.1111/1467-9760.00104.

Prashad, Vijay (2008), *The Darker Nations: A People's History of the Third World*. Reprint edition. New York: The New Press.

Rodriguez Martin, Endika (2019), "Settler Colonial Demographics: Zionist Land Purchases and Immigration During the British Mandate in Palestine." *Interventions*, 21 (4): 486–509. https://doi.org/10.1080/1369801X.2018.1547214.

Roy, Sara (1987), "The Gaza Strip: A Case of Economic De-Development." *Journal of Palestine Studies*, 17 (1): 56–88. https://doi.org/10.2307/2536651.

Roy, Sara (1995), *The Gaza Strip: The Political Economy of De-Development*. Institute for Palestine Studies: Washington, DC.

Santos, Madalena (2016), "Palestinian Narratives of Resistance: The Freedom Theatre's Challenge to Israeli Settler Colonization." *Settler Colonial Studies*, 8 (1): 96–113. https://doi.org/10.1080/2201473X.2016.1206698.

Selby, Jan (2003), "Dressing up Domination as 'Cooperation': The Case of Israeli-Palestinian Water Relations." *Review of International Studies*, 29 (1): 121–38. https://doi.org/10.1017/S026021050300007X.

Shlaim, Avi (2013), "It's Now Clear: The Oslo Peace Accords Were Wrecked by Netanyahu's Bad Faith." *The Guardian*, September 12. https://www.theguardian.com/commentisfree/2013/sep/12/oslo-israel-reneged-colonial-palestine.

Speetjens, Peter (2016), "Alexis de Tocqueville: The Father of Western Liberalism was also an Advocate for Colonising Algeria." *Middle East Eye*, May 29. http://www.middleeasteye.net/opinion/alexis-de-tocqueville-father-western-liberalism-was-also-advocate-colonising-algeria.

Tamari, Salim (1988), "What the Uprising Means." *Middle East Report*, 152: 24–30. https://doi.org/10.2307/3012098.

Tartir, Alaa (2018), "The Limits of Securitized Peace: The EU's Sponsorship of Palestinian Authoritarianism." *Middle East Critique*, 27(4): 365–81. https://doi.org/10.1080/19436149.2018.1516337

Tartir, Alaa and Jeremy Wildeman (2013), "Can Oslo's Failed Aid Model Be Laid to Rest?" *Al-Shabaka*. http://al-shabaka.org/node/672.

Tauber, Eliezer (1998), "Elizabeth P. MacCallum and the Arab-Israeli Conflict." *Journal of Israeli History*, 19 (2): 93–107. https://doi.org/10.1080/13531049808576130.

Tauber, Eliezer (1999), "The Jewish and Arab Lobbies in Canada and the UN Partition of Palestine." *Israel Affairs*, 5 (4): 229–44. https://doi.org/10.1080/13537129908719539.

The World Bank (1993), *Developing the Occupied Territories: An Investment in Peace*. World Bank.

The World Bank (2012), *Towards Economic Sustainability of a Future Palestinian State: Promoting Private Sector—Led Growth* (Report No. 68037-GZ). World Bank. http://siteresources.worldbank.org/INTWESTBANKGAZA/Resources/GrowthStudyEngcorrected.pdf.

Tilley, Virginia (2018), "Prof Virginia Tilley at 'Oslo at 25: A Legacy of Broken Promises' Conference." *Middle East Monitor*, October 5. https://www.middleeastmonitor.com/20181005-prof-virginia-tilley-at-oslo-at-25-a-legacy-of-broken-promises-conference/.

Turner, Mandy (2012), "Completing the Circle: Peacebuilding as Colonial Practice in the Occupied Palestinian Territory." *International Peacekeeping*, 19(4): 492–507. https://doi.org/10.1080/13533312.2012.709774.

Turner, Mandy (2020), "International Aid in the Absence of Palestinian Sovereignty: Notes towards a Strategy in the Aftermath of the Trump 'Peace Plan.'" *Jadaliyya*, February 19. https://www.jadaliyya.com/Details/40706.

Tutu, Desmond (2002), "Apartheid in the Holy Land." *The Guardian*, April 29. http://www.theguardian.com/world/2002/apr/29/comment.

UNCTAD (2015), *TD/B/62/3 Report on UNCTAD Assistance to the Palestinian People: Developments in the Economy of the Occupied Palestinian Territory* (Report on UNCTAD Assistance to the Palestinian People TD/B/62/3; Trade and Development Board, Sixty-Second Session, Geneva, 14–25 September 2015, Item 10 (b) of the Provisional Agenda). United Nations Conference on Trade and Development. http://unctad.org/meetings/en/SessionalDocuments/tdb62d3_en.pdf.

United Nations (2008), *The Question of Palestine and the United Nations*. United Nations Department of Public Information. https://unispal.un.org/pdfs/DPI2499.pdf.

United Nations General Assembly (1947), *A/RES/181(II) of 29 November 1947* [UN General Assembly Resolution]. Retrieved August 17, 2014, from http://unispal.un.org/unispal.nsf/0/7F0AF2BD897689B785256C330061D253.

United Nations General Assembly (1948), *A/RES/194*. https://www.securitycouncilreport.org/un-documents/document/ip-ares-194.php.

United Nations Security Council (1967), *S/RES/242 (1967) of 22 November 1967* [Security Council Resolution]. https://unispal.un.org/DPA/DPR/unispal.nsf/0/7D35E1F729DF491C85256EE700686136.

United Nations Security Council (1973), *S/RES/338 (1973) of 22 October 1973* [Security Council Resolution]. https://unispal.un.org/DPA/DPR/unispal.nsf/0/7FB7C26FCBE80A31852560C50065F878.

United Nations Security Council (2016), *S/RES/2334 (2016) of 23 December 2016* [Security Council Resolution]. https://www.un.org/webcast/pdfs/SRES2334-2016.pdf.

Veracini, Lorenzo (2010), *Settler Colonialism: A Theoretical Overview*. Palgrave Macmillan: Houndmills, Basingstoke, New York.

Waziyatawin (2012), "Malice Enough in Their Hearts and Courage Enough in Ours: Reflections on US Indigenous and Palestinian Experiences Under Occupation." *Settler Colonial Studies*, 2 (1): 172–89. https://doi.org/10.1080/2201473X.2012.10648831.

Weizman, Eyal (2007), *Hollow Land: Israel's Architecture of Occupation*. Verso: London.

Wildeman, Jeremy (2018), *Donor Aid Effectiveness and Do No Harm in the Occupied Palestinian Territory*. Aid Watch Palestine. http://www.aidwatch.ps/sites/default/files/resource-field_media/Aid%20Effectiveness%20%26%20Do%20No%20Harm%20in%20OPT-%20Final-compressed_1.pdf.

Wildeman, Jeremy and Alaa Tartir (2021), "Political Economy of Foreign Aid in the Occupied Palestinian Territories: A Conceptual Framing." In Alaa Tartir, Tariq Dana, and Timothy Seidel (eds.), *Political Economy of Palestine: Critical, Interdisciplinary, and Decolonial Perspectives*, 223–47. Cham: Springer International Publishing. https://doi.org/10.1007/978-3-030-68643-7_10.

Williams, David (2020), *Progress, Pluralism, and Politics*. McGill-Queen's University Press: Montréal, Québec.

Wolfe, Patrick (2006), "Settler Colonialism and the Elimination of the Native." *Journal of Genocide Research*, 8 (4): 387–409. https://doi.org/10.1080/14623520601056240.

Wootliff, Raoul (2018), "Final Text of Jewish Nation-state Law, Approved by the Knesset Early on July 19." *The Times of Israel*, July 19. https://www.timesofisrael.com/final-text-of-jewish-nation-state-bill-set-to-become-law/.

Yearbook of the United Nations 1982 (excerpts I) (1982), United Nations. https://www.un.org/unispal/document/auto-insert-205341/.

Yusuf, Muhsin (2002), "The Partition of Palestine (1947)—An Arab Perspective." *Palestine - Israel Journal of Politics, Economics, and Culture*, 9 (4). https://search.proquest.com/openview/71017ec62a49d42c7784418efed515ed/1?pq-origsite=gscholar&cbl=26627.

Zeitoun, Mark (2013), "Global Environmental Justice and International Transboundary Waters: An Initial Exploration." *The Geographical Journal*, 179 (2): 141–9. https://www.jstor.org/stable/43868544

Zureik, Elia (2003), "Demography and Transfer: Israel's Road to Nowhere." *Third World Quarterly*, 24 (4): 619–30. https://doi.org/10.1080/0143659032000105786.

13

Palestinian Popular Education Post-Oslo

Melanie Meinzer

Introduction

As my shared taxi lurched around the hairpin turns of the dizzyingly steep Wadi al-Nar highway between the Palestinian city of Ramallah and the southern West Bank, I glimpsed one of the ubiquitous US Agency for International Development (USAID) signs announcing that this road was "a gift from the American people." The Palestinians are the recipients of this gift, whose dubious nature becomes apparent as the highway winds alongside the barbed wire-topped Israeli separation wall and Ma'ale Adumim, the largest Israeli settlement in the occupied West Bank.

During the Second Intifada (2000–5), Israel built checkpoints along the Wadi Al-Nar road, further restricting Palestinians' freedom of movement.[1] Like the Wadi Al-Nar highway, the many donor-funded infrastructural, cultural, and educational interventions in the occupied West Bank made in the name of democracy, development, and peacebuilding are fraught with these kinds of ambivalences. In the fall of 2015, a Palestinian youth theater director explained to me that her organization refused to apply for USAID funding because the United States hypocritically enabled the expansion of Israeli settlements on Palestinian land. "They give money for roads," she said, "but these roads separate us even more than before."[2]

Since the 1993 Oslo Accords, the Palestinians have been among the world's highest per capita recipients of foreign nonmilitary aid (Wildeman and Tartir 2021). This aid was meant to further the peace process with Israel through humanitarian relief, economic development, Palestinian state-building, and by cultivating a democratic civil society. Rather than advancing peace, the past thirty years of donor aid has amounted to what Turner (2015) calls "peacebuilding as counterinsurgency" by facilitating Israeli settler colonialism through subduing and securing the Palestinians.

Education is a cornerstone of the donor-funded Palestinian Authority's (PA) state-building efforts and a nexus of conflict with donors and Israel, each having their own vision of what Palestinian education should achieve. For donors, funding education after the Oslo Accords was a means of reasserting the status quo after the Intifada (Al-Rozzi 2022). The first Palestinian Ministry of Education was founded in 1994, ostensibly bringing the school curriculum under Palestinian control for the first time. Supported by foreign aid, the ministry published its first curriculum in 2000. Shortly thereafter, a watchdog NGO[3] claimed that the textbooks were anti-Semitic and incited violence against Israel. This portrayal of Israel as the victim of Palestinian aggression is part of a larger narrative that frames Israel and the Palestinians as locked in binary conflict, rather than as resisting settler colonialism amidst enormous asymmetries in the power to inflict harm (Jong 2018; Matar 2017). Italy canceled its support for the curriculum, and the World Bank demanded that the PA divert its textbook funding to other projects (Moughrabi 2001). Several joint Israeli-Palestinian and US studies later discredited these allegations, but the textbook controversy showed how donors and other actors could intervene in the Palestinian curriculum.

Donor and Israeli interference has largely sanitized the PA textbooks of any controversial political content. Revolutionary Palestinian historical figures were removed from the Palestinian textbooks, along with maps showing Jerusalem as the future capital of Palestine (Moughrabi 2001). The word Nakba, referring to Israel's expulsion of Palestinians in 1948, is not mentioned in the PA textbooks until the fifth grade (Ali 2013). Attempting to mediate between the Palestinians and the Israeli occupiers, donors championed coexistence through what they called "peace education." However, education that relies on cultural and historical erasure is directly opposed to education for liberation, which would equip Palestinian students with the awareness and skills they need to resist Israeli settler colonialism (Al-Rozzi 2022). Decoupling education from liberation and resistance has been a divide-and-conquer strategy used by colonial and occupying forces in Palestine and continues today under the guise of development.

Under the British Mandate (1920–48) and Jordanian (1948–67) and Israeli military rule (1967–present), common tactics for repressing Palestinian nationalism included limiting Palestinian leadership in the formal education system, restricting the textbooks teachers could use or publish, requiring teachers to sign nonpolitical statements, and punishing teacher and student activists. Even under the PA, the education system perpetuated much of the earlier imperial and colonial suppression of Palestinian identity by failing to integrate the people's history with the PA's narrative of history and national identity. This incomplete and self-censored curriculum does not reflect the realities of life under the Israeli occupation and fails to connect with the historical knowledge and sense of identity that Palestinian students acquire from hearing stories from their friends, families, and communities. Caught between overlapping regimes of aid dependence and settler colonialism, the PA curriculum is simultaneously "too political" for donors, yet not political enough for the society for which it is intended.

Adwan rejected donors' expectations that Palestinian textbooks reflect a "culture of peace" in the absence of a functioning peace process, observing that "children cannot be duped into believing or learning the opposite of what they see and experience" (2001, 68). Besides, no amount of historical omissions in the textbooks could negate the importance of everyday experiences of oppression in shaping Palestinians' political consciousness. As Moughrabi noted, "the Israeli occupation, with its daily cruelty and humiliation, is a far more powerful text than any schoolbook could ever be" (2001, 18). As long as formal schooling fails to connect with what Palestinians experience, there will be the need for popular education to preserve historical memory as a basis for collective struggle.

During the First Intifada (1987–93), the Israeli military closed Palestinian schools and universities for months to years at a time, fearing that they would become spaces for political organizing. This forced education underground, as popular committees created informal neighborhood schools, which reunited education with resistance (Fasheh 1990). After the Oslo Accords, activists from the popular education movement who were among the leftist groups excluded from the PA went on to form nongovernmental organizations (NGOs).

This chapter tells the story of several Palestinian educational NGOs and community-based organizations that use arts-based, participatory pedagogies to raise critical consciousness and carry on the work of the popular education movement in the post-Oslo period. These NGOs receive a small amount of educational aid relative to the PA but play a significant role in sustaining, advancing, and institutionalizing the Intifada-era critical pedagogies and historical knowledge missing from the official Palestinian curriculum. Together with Palestinian students, teachers, and families, these NGOs cocreate what one educational activist called the "hidden curriculum."[4] As he described it,

> The hidden curricula are much more important than the official curricula. If the curriculum didn't give me a space to explain my history, I will bring my history. The people didn't give up. Before the [Oslo] peace agreement, we—as Palestinians—protected our history through popular education.

This hidden curriculum is a body of critical historical knowledge and contemporary political and social identities whose diverse political imaginaries converge around the collective struggle for cultural sovereignty and survival. It centers the tradition of oral history and storytelling to preserve collective memory and cultural identity under Israeli settler colonialism (Hastings 2016). Popular education in occupied Palestine is part of a global struggle against state and settler colonial projects that attempt to culturally erase Indigenous people and minorities. The Black Panthers, Zapatistas, Irish hedge schools, and ethnic studies programs in the United States all used critical pedagogy and popular education to build collective political consciousness and connect awareness of injustice to activism.[5]

This chapter draws on thirteen interviews and 240 surveys conducted with Palestinian educators, activists, and students in the West Bank in 2014 and a ten-month period in 2015–16 to better understand how foreign aid influences the political consciousness of Palestinian students through Palestinian educational NGOs. The data show that Palestinian students and activists see education as a site of donor and Israeli intervention, and turn to their families and friends as trustworthy sources of knowledge about Palestinian history and current events. Throughout this chapter several students will reflect on what it means to build and maintain a critical awareness of oppression while living under Israeli settler colonialism in a donor-funded education system that normalizes the occupation.

The Palestinian educational NGOs in this study demonstrate their understanding of the importance of informal sources of knowledge by organizing communities through popular education. These NGOs carve out spaces in a heavily censored and policed education system to carry on the work of the popular education movement. They also cocreate, publish, and spread the hidden curriculum among students and communities by equipping them with the reflective and artistic skills they need to tell their stories through political theater, graphic novels, and personal testimonies written as short stories. These educational NGOs are part of a larger ecosystem of activists, educators, students, and "solidarity donors" (see Meinzer 2019) who are committed to decolonizing the mind by cultivating critical awareness as a foundation for resistance.

Education as a Site of Intervention

Nearly all of the NGOs in this chapter operated in Area A, an administrative division that refers to the 18 percent of the West Bank that is under PA control. Area C, which makes up 60 percent of the West Bank, is under full Israeli civil and military control. The few Palestinian groups organizing cultural resistance in Area C spoke of the primary need for the most basic educational spaces—schools, which Israel often demolished and then denied the permits needed to rebuild. When asked about the depoliticization of the PA textbooks, an NGO representative working in Area C said, "We start from zero. Give us the school, and give us the teachers, allow us to have classes, and *then* we can quarrel about the curriculum."[6]

Palestinian students saw schools and the PA curriculum as sites of Israeli and foreign intervention, which rendered knowledge in the formal education system suspect. Raghda,[7] a university student, described education in the West Bank as "awful, misleading, and controlled by Israelis." She said that Israel interfered in the Palestinian textbooks by presenting partial truths, or "fake facts."[8] Miriam, another university student, said that the occupation targets Palestinian education by reformulating school subjects to fit Israel's narrative. Palestinian students become "spaces for reformation" through revisionist history. As she explained,

> It used to be a crime to put Israel in the history books for kids. Nowadays, you see Israel, Tel Aviv . . . but Tel Aviv used to be "Tele Rabia" for us . . . if kids are getting the Israeli narrative, how is that not being controlled somehow? Foucault says knowledge is very important. The more you know, the more power you have. We're an occupied people. You read in history papers that we're living with Israel in peace and all of this normalization. How does the Palestinian Authority allow this? If people are taught things that are not correct, then how do you expect them to grow? Instead of fighting the power structures oppressing them, they start accepting it, normalizing it.[9]

Referencing Foucault, Miriam linked knowledge, power, and resistance and saw the PA as complicit in Israel's efforts to shape Palestinian consciousness. Another university student, Nadia, whose father was living in Lebanon shortly before the 1982 Sabra and Shatila massacre, criticized the PA's history curriculum for minimizing violence against the Palestinians. She said that the curriculum mentions the Sabra and Shatila massacre but does not include pictures or convey the magnitude of Israel's violence.

She maintained that the textbooks should reflect that reality, and that these omissions were partly why her classmates were unaware of the scale of the ongoing violence in the West Bank and Gaza.[10] These students' suspicion of official sources of information underscored the need for a point of comparison between what was presented in school and what they know and experience in daily life.

The Importance of Firsthand Experience

A survey[11] of 240 Palestinians (largely university students) was conducted for this study to uncover how they learned about Palestinian history and identity and the relative importance of each source of knowledge. The survey findings reinforced that direct experience was the most reliable way of knowing about Palestinian history and identity. Seventy percent of respondents considered personal experiences of life under the Israeli occupation to be the most important factor influencing their sense of identity as Palestinians, while only 33 percent saw school and textbooks as playing a role. Other important factors influencing identity were family (65 percent) and friends (45 percent). In terms of learning about Palestinian history, interpersonal sources such as family (53 percent) and teachers (53 percent) mattered about as much as school and textbooks (50 percent) (see Table 13.1).

The student interviews supported the survey finding that firsthand experience mattered more than school when it came to learning about Palestinian history and the occupation. When asked if she learned about politics in school, a university student replied: "no, not from school, from personal experience—*tajarib shakhsia* . . . School . . . it's *ishii thanawia*—secondary."[12] Another student sided with her grandparents' stories over what she learned in class. She said, "We hear from our grandfather or grandmother [who] lived these things, as we live these events right now, so they knew what happened. You hear it from them, and find that not everything is real. Education is not honest, not really."[13]

Table 13.1 Sources of Knowledge About Palestinian History and Identity

Source	Percent Who Said This Influenced Their Palestinian Identity	Percent Who said This Influenced Their Knowledge About Palestinian History
Personal experiences under the occupation	70	—*
Family's experiences	65	53
Friends' experiences	45	24
Teachers	—	53
Books (non-textbooks)	33	52
School and textbooks	33	50
Internet/media	39	37
Political parties	10	15
Educational NGOs and civic groups	11	12

* The answer "personal experiences under the occupation" was not included as a response option for the question about the factors influencing one's knowledge of Palestinian history.

The centrality of direct experience supports Moughrabi's (2001) observation that the Israeli occupation is a more powerful tool for raising political consciousness than any textbook could be. The importance of direct experience—whether one's own or in one's inner circle—reflects students' low degree of trust in official sources of information like the curriculum. While a relatively low number of students (11 percent) saw NGOs and civic groups as a significant influence on their knowledge of history and sense of identity, these NGOs play an important role in channeling resources toward creating and distributing the "hidden curriculum" and, by doing so, help sustain the critical knowledge and participatory pedagogies that the popular education movement used to raise critical consciousness and mobilize resistance.

A flyer titled "My Right to Choose My Curriculum," created by an educational NGO working in occupied East Jerusalem, supported the survey finding that students learn most from people they trust. The flyer was part of a campaign against Israel's efforts to impose its curriculum in Palestinian schools in East Jerusalem, which have been under the Israeli Municipality's jurisdiction since Israel annexed the city during the 1967 war. In 2013, the Israeli Municipality began pressuring Palestinian schools to adopt the Israeli curriculum and matriculation exam. Palestinian schools were offered monetary incentives to adopt the Israeli curriculum (Haaretz 2016). Israel's education minister said this would "aid the process of Israelization," presumably to extend Israel's annexation of Palestine into the realm of cultural consciousness.

The flyer, written in colloquial Arabic, begins with the boy asking his mother (a trusted source) about children's rights. She tells her son that he has the right to play, the right to housing, and the right to education. They then talk about how the Israeli curriculum portrays the Palestinians as new arrivals and divides them up into minority groups—Muslims, Christians, and Bedouins—rather than as Indigenous Palestinians with collective rights. She points out that his textbooks teach him about Israeli heroes like Herzl (founder of the World Zionist Organization) and Ben-Gurion (Israel's first prime minister) but not Palestinian leaders like Abd Al Qader Al Huseini (the Palestinian Arab nationalist who fought in the 1936-9 Arab revolt and 1948 war) and Mahmoud Darwish (the renowned poet). The mother tells her son, "You [Palestinian students] read that [the Israeli curriculum] in school and start thinking that this is true, stop saying Palestine is our country, and become Israeli citizens." Her son replies, "I am Palestinian and I will remain Palestinian . . . [they should] just change their books." In the rest of the flyer, the boy realizes more about how the Israeli curriculum tries to influence his identity and resolves to read about Palestinian historical figures and tell his friends.

This NGO published another flyer titled "The Israeli Curriculum Distorts Palestinian National Identity," which depicts a Star of David made out of barbed wire imprisoning the Palestinian flag, symbolizing Israeli repression of Palestinian identity. Below the flag, a snapshot from an Israeli textbook written in Arabic shows three students—Dina, Ahmad, and Khaled—celebrating Israeli Independence Day by singing the Israeli national anthem. Text on the blackboard below reiterates that the Israeli curriculum elevates Jewish figures and Western art at the expense of Islam and Palestinian culture. The last paragraph warns "the [Israeli] curriculum works to erase Palestinian resistance, and to fully divide Arab culture. This is what happened to the Palestinians inside [Israel] between 1948-1967."

Another part of the flyer seems to echo Miriam's observation about knowledge and power by saying that the Israeli curriculum "distorts the civilizational identity and culture of Palestinian students . . . isolating them from their reality, history, culture and identity." At the end of the passage, it raises the rhetorical question: "Which curriculum do we want? My curriculum is my identity. My curriculum is Palestinian." Despite its limitations, the PA textbooks, unlike the Israeli curriculum, portray the Palestinians as one people with collective rights and claims to the land. NGOs like this one do the foundational work in East Jerusalem of organizing communities and raising critical consciousness in order to sustain a sense of common purpose needed for cultural survival.

Cocreating Knowledge: The Hidden Curriculum

Palestinian educational NGOs carve out spaces for the "hidden curriculum," an alternative body of knowledge about Palestinian history and identity missing from the donor-funded PA textbooks. According to a Palestinian NGO representative, Palestinians "need to learn about heritage, culture, history and about our own geography so we can defend our rights and demand them."[14] Palestinian educational NGOs push back against the depoliticization of education by reinserting historical knowledge and by cultivating collective Palestinian identity, continuing the work of the neighborhood schools from the popular education movement.

The hidden curriculum draws on Palestinians' everyday experiences under the occupation and what young people learn about Palestinian history and identity from their families. Palestinian NGOs perform "memory work" (Schlund-Vials 2012) by compiling these stories into a larger narrative. For example, an NGO developed a program for students in Ramallah who were unable to visit Jerusalem due to the many legal and physical barriers erected by Israel to keep Palestinians in the West Bank from visiting. Instead of making the physical journey to the city, the children completed a reading passport to learn about prominent Palestinians and collected oral histories from relatives who had lived there.[15] This imaginary field trip used participatory learning (in this case storytelling) to build students' attachment to the land and connections between family members and communities. The children submitted their completed reading passports to their librarians and were awarded a "visa" for having completed this assignment from the hidden curriculum. This NGO also published books and stories written by children, which they then distributed to Palestinian schools and libraries free of charge.[16] Gathering and sharing this cultural knowledge helps restitch the social fabric of Palestinian communities fragmented by Israeli settler colonialism.

Mujawarah: Deconstructing Hierarchies and Producing Collective Knowledge

A core value underlying many popular education projects in the post-Oslo era is that knowledge is produced collaboratively and in community with others. This is in contrast to the top-down model where the teacher "deposits" information from state-sanctioned textbooks into students' minds, what Freire called the "banker's approach" to education, where students become passive learners, rather than critical thinkers with the agency to imagine and explore alternative perspectives and futures.

One NGO representative called this deconstruction process "unlearning." Unlearning means critically reflecting on your own education and experiences to reconsider what you know and believe. He recalled a discussion in which his group deconstructed the "key of return," a popular symbol of Palestinian refugees' demand to return to the villages and homes from which they were expelled in 1948. Through reflecting on the symbol of the key, he realized that it was connected to imperialist discourses on private property, which implied that the goal of return was to live a prosperous life in capitalist terms—by living in fancy houses. Through reflecting on the key, he arrived at an alternative, which was that the Palestinians should "return to the common." Critical reflection led him to imagine alternative ways of realizing Palestinian liberation.

This NGO's group-based process of unlearning was based on their practice of community deliberation, called *mujawarah*, which means "neighboring" in Arabic. According to the NGO representative, *mujawarah* is a way of teaching and studying with one another where

> A group of people meet in a situation in which there is no hierarchy. Everyone is a source of knowledge, everyone has something to pass to the other. When we invite a professor to come speak, we have a circle. "Ah, what's your name?" And usually it's "I am doctor Rachel," and then it's "Oh, hi Rachel!" Seriously, first hear us, then we will hear you. We have so much to give you, and it's way more than what you will give us. It has to be based on that.

Mujawarah flattens social hierarchies and insists that every person in the community is a source of knowledge, which turns the top-down banker's model of education on its head and undermines the authority of Israel and the PA to narrate the conflict and determine what Palestinian resistance and liberation could or should look like.

Critical Reflection: Oral Histories, Books, and Graphic Novels

Project Hope is an NGO that was founded in 2003 in Nablus during the Second Intifada to provide educational and community activities for Palestinian children unable to go to school due to curfews and Israel's siege of the city. From 2010 to 2014, Project Hope trained Palestinian university students in graphic storytelling, expecting that these students would go on to teach young people in their communities how to create graphic novels. Project Hope's graphic novel project illustrates the hands-on, collaborative approach that Palestinian educational NGOs take cocreating and curating the hidden curriculum with the community. The graphic novels, published in three digest-sized volumes, provide an outlet for self-expression, and because they are written in English,

Figure 13.1 Excerpt from Ahmed Masri's "On This Earth We Deserve Life."

they give outsiders a glimpse into how young Palestinians experience life under the occupation. The graphic novels also lend insight into how NGOs encourage students to critically reflect on their everyday experiences.

For example, Figure 13.1 from "On This Earth We Deserve Life" shows Ahmed Masri's circuitous route from his home in Ramallah to An Najah University in Nablus. This 37-mile (60-kilometer) journey can take up to two and a half hours, because, as his drawing shows, the direct route between the two cities is blocked by Israeli checkpoints and settlements. The solid and dashed lines show the winding roads that drivers must take around these obstacles. This drawing reflects Ahmed's understanding of the necessary and unjust obstacles he faces in accessing education.

In "Curfew Challenge," Sherien Habibah shows how education continued in Nablus when schools were closed during the Second Intifada. Figure 13.2 shows a student passing along the good news that her neighbor is opening a school in his house. The story ends with the girls entering their makeshift school. The final caption reads "education continues . . .". Project Hope's graphic novels show how Palestinian educational NGOs can engage students in participatory learning and produce the cultural artifacts that make up the hidden curriculum.

These graphic novels also preserve and circulate personal narratives of the sort that are shared between friends, family, and trusted teachers. The hidden curriculum draws heavily on personal experience and the stories of friends and family as a more reliable way of knowing about Palestinian history. The hidden curriculum spreads Palestinian culture in an environment where Palestinian political consciousness is repressed by donors' and Israeli interventions. As discussed in Meinzer (2019), when Palestinian educational NGOs retain creative control over the content of their materials, aid can support rather than obstruct Palestinians' agency, because it allows NGOs to produce and distribute books and other components of the hidden curriculum on a larger scale.

Figure 13.2 Excerpt from Sherien Habibah's "Curfew Challenge."

In Their Words: "Not a Liberal, But a Radical"

Palestinian educational NGOs use participatory learning to help students integrate their life experiences under the Israeli occupation into a cohesive and critical awareness of oppression. This chapter concludes with Palestinian students' reflections on activism and decolonizing the mind. A common theme across the student interviews was that an internal transformation within each person was necessary for collective liberation. For Hasan, a theater student, freedom started inside each individual. He observed that

> everybody knows there is occupation in Palestine, but there is a lot of occupation inside each person, inside me, inside my mind, in everything I do ... make yourself free. Bring freedom for yourself, and then you can bring freedom for your land.[17]

Decolonizing the mind means being able to recognize contradictions and imagine different futures—the ability to compare what is with what could be. Students' framing and reframing of the conflict are evidence of critical reflection. For example, Nadia referred to the British Mandate period as the "British occupation," noting that while others did not call it that, Palestine was nevertheless occupied by a foreign government.[18]

Miriam pointed to the depth of the Israeli occupation's sometimes invisible reach into Palestinian society:

> It's psychological warfare. We are treated like we are in prison: "we give you malls and other things," but you're still controlled. Even in these prisons, you have mini-

prisons, then mini-mini-prisons, and then you have actual prisons. Then they tell you: "we want peace with you."

Miriam recognized the contradiction between the "peace process" and the daily violence of the occupation. She concluded: "They are smart, the people who colonize. But they're stupid at the same time, to think that we're not as smart as they are, to understand what they are doing."[19] Miriam had been involved in NGO programs since she was a teenager, which she used as a platform to educate foreigners (including me) about the conflict.

Palestinian educational NGOs and students shared this discourse of decolonizing the mind through popular education, indicating that despite their dependence on foreign aid, NGOs have not lost touch with grassroots priorities. According to one NGO representative, the Palestinians were "not only subjected to physical colonization and occupation, but also mental colonization and the occupation of the mind . . . that is much more toxic."[20] NGOs provide the context to make sense of lived experience and equip students with the tools to take action against oppression. They engage students in cultural production to recreate and reclaim lost or obscured knowledge. The alternative narratives that emerge from the hidden curriculum help students to see the contradictions between what they know from informal sources and what they are told to believe by the media and formal education system.

While Palestinian educational NGOs are not the only factor influencing student activism, they provide spaces and networks to learn new ways to engage. For Asma, volunteering at an educational NGO at her university was pivotal in her joining the Boycott, Divestment, Sanctions (BDS) movement. She heard of the NGO through a friend who said it would be a good place to fulfill the required volunteer hours at her university.

Asma traced her political thinking back to her cultural studies classes and time volunteering at the NGO. After starting these courses, she began talking about politics with her father, who taught her more about Palestinian history. Prior to this, she said that "politics was a zero subject at our house." After two years of volunteering at the NGO, Asma began boycotting Israeli products. While volunteering, she began reading more about the BDS movement's impact and was amazed at the difference it made. She then persuaded her family to join the boycott. "I'll never buy Israeli products," she said. "I don't eat them, I don't use them. I know they hate us. How are you going to buy something from them?"[21] This NGO provided the collective action frame of boycott as a way to resist the occupation, and Asma's experience shows that NGOs can change the way students perceive and take political action.

Other students I interviewed sought out NGOs after already gaining a degree of political awareness. Two students joined a theater NGO because they were dissatisfied with their high school and university educations. Hasan left his public school for the theater NGO's program at age fifteen against his family's wishes because he wanted to better understand Palestinian society and culture, and Amjad joined the theater because he wanted to learn more about Palestinian history and identity.[22] Both students saw the theater NGO as providing a cultural education that the mainstream education system could not.

I met Miriam through an educational NGO. She had been volunteering with NGOs since she was a teenager. These NGO programs gathered Palestinians and foreigners to discuss the Palestinian struggle. Miriam found that the foreigners she met had a limited understanding of the situation in Palestine, and she felt obligated to help them understand the conflict as a way of helping her country. Through these conversations, she challenged their beliefs and her own. She concluded that one could only ever have partial knowledge of an issue, so the process of questioning and deconstructing knowledge was what mattered most.[23]

Finally, it is important to note that the work of Palestinian educational NGOs extends beyond the individual organizations, as the students, teachers, and communities who participate in their programs become multipliers who spread critical consciousness beyond the initial group. Several student interviewees recounted times when they challenged their teachers or raised their classmates' political awareness around the Israeli-Palestinian conflict. This reflected their desire to spread their critical consciousness to others, a key way that popular education can mobilize people.

In eleventh grade, Nadia argued with her teacher over whether the 1993 Oslo Accords were positive for the Palestinians, because it was under the Accords that Palestinian president Mahmoud Abbas conceded the Palestinian refugees' right of return. When Nadia asked why the Palestinian Authority did not issue passports for Palestinians living abroad, her teacher replied that those who went abroad would not want to live in the West Bank. Nadia challenged her teacher because she grew up hearing her father's stories about living abroad in Beirut near the Sabra and Shatila refugee camps in the 1980s. She knew from her parents' experiences that Palestinians living in exile wanted to return, as did the refugees, so for the teacher

> to tell me that what we are doing now is best for us [the Palestinians] was unacceptable after hearing my father's experience. My father has been there in Beirut; he has seen the Palestinian camps. He has seen how the refugees were living, so for her to tell me that Oslo is in our favor—Oslo is not in our favor.

Nadia also tried to educate her classmates. She wrote a political play for a theater competition at her high school, about a man whose land was confiscated by Israel. She also memorized the names of those killed in Gaza in 2014, and in the ongoing wave of violence in 2015–16, so that the dead would be remembered as people, not as numbers. She also gave a presentation at her university warning other students that if they did not learn about the violence in Gaza, they would be next.[24] Although Nadia did not participate in NGO programs, her independent learning and efforts to educate her classmates through presentations and theater parallel the activities that educational NGOs use to raise political consciousness.

Miriam also became an expert critical educator during her year as an exchange student at an American high school, through confronting American stereotypes of Muslims and Palestinians. After deciding to give a class presentation on Palestine, she was called to the principal's office where she had to reassure him that her presentation would not promote terrorism or be "anti-Israel." She confronted a classmate's prejudice about Muslims in a measured way, asking her to "assess" her belief that Muslims deserved to be collectively blamed for the September 11, 2001, attacks.[25] Like Nadia, Miriam's activism was to use critical thinking to help others deconstruct what they thought they knew. When I asked Miriam what she wanted for the future, having just completed her university degree in international law with a focus on human rights, she concluded:

> No, not a liberal, I don't want to become that. Maybe something new. Not a liberal, not a conservative. Maybe a radical.

Notes

1. "A Trip Through the Palestinian Road Network" in *This Week in Palestine*, August 9, 2014. http://archive.thisweekinpalestine.com/details.php?id=3673&ed=205&edid=205.
2. NGO Interview, December 2, 2015.
3. The Center for Monitoring the Impact of Peace (CMIP) is a US-based NGO founded in 1998 by Itamar Marcus (a resident of the West Bank settlement of Efrat). In 2000, the NGO was renamed the Institute for Monitoring Peace and Cultural Tolerance in School Education (IMPACT). The NGO has examined textbooks from Iran, Egypt, Israel, the Palestinian Territories, Saudi Arabia, Syria, and Tunisia.
4. The use of hidden curriculum here differs from its original usage in the critical education literature as a set of implicit norms, values, and beliefs that students absorb through the routines and social structures of the classroom (Giroux 1983). The hidden curriculum also reproduces class relations and the authority of the teacher over the student (Willis 1981, Martin 1976). Vallance (1973) called this "latent curriculum" "simply what schooling does to people" (Kentli 2009). I interpret the interviewee's use of the term as referring to knowledge and practices that sustain resistance and subvert Israeli or Palestinian efforts to control what students learn about their culture, history, and identity. His use of the term "hidden curriculum" applies here.
5. For more on the Irish hedge schools in Tudor England see Lyons (2016) as well as Peck (2001) on the Black Panther Liberation Schools in the United States in the late 1960s. See also Paulo Freire's work on education and critical consciousness (1973, 1993), the landless workers' movement in Brazil (Carter 2003), and the Zapatistas' autonomous education in Chiapas (Baronnet 2008).
6. NGO Interview, November 5, 2015.
7. Participants' names have been changed to protect their privacy.
8. Student Interview, February 29, 2016.
9. Student Interview, December 23, 2015.
10. Student Interview, February 28, 2016.
11. Surveys were collected using snowball sampling.
12. Student Interview, February 28, 2016.
13. Student Focus Group Interview, February 29, 2016.
14. NGO Interview, December 10, 2015.
15. NGO Interview, January 8, 2014.
16. NGO Interview, January 8, 2014.

17 Student Interview, May 11, 2016.
18 Student Interview, February 28, 2016.
19 Student Interview, December 23, 2015.
20 NGO Interview, October 20, 2015.
21 Student Interview, March 7, 2016.
22 Student Interviews, May 11, 2016.
23 Student Interview, December 23, 2015.
24 Student Interview, February 28, 2016.
25 Student Interview, December 23, 2015.

References

Adwan, Sami (2001), "Schoolbooks in the Making: From Conflict to Peace; A Critical Analysis of the New Palestinian Textbooks for Grades One and Six." *Palestine-Israel Journal of Politics, Economics, and Culture*, 8 (2): 57.

Ali, Zarefa (2013), "The Missing Narratives in Palestinian Schoolbooks." *Al Shabaka: The Palestinian Policy Network*. https://al-shabaka.org/commentaries/the-missing-narratives-in-palestinian-schoolbooks/.

Al-Rozzi, Mohammed. (2022), "A New Intifada: Education." *Al Shabaka: The Palestinian Policy Network*. https://al-shabaka.org/scenario-analyses/education-scenario-4/.

Baronnet, Bruno (2008), "Rebel Youth and Zapatista Autonomous Education." *Latin American Perspectives*, 35 (4): 112–124.

Carter, Miguel (2003), *The Origins of Brazil's Landless Rural Workers' Movement (MST): The Natalino Episode in Rio Grande Do Sul (1981–84). A Case of Ideal Interest Mobilization*. Oxford: University of Oxford Centre for Brazilian Studies.

Fasheh, Munir (1990), "Community Education: To Reclaim and Transform What Has Been Made Invisible." *Harvard Educational Review*, 60 (1): 19–36.

Freire, Paulo (1973), *Education for Critical Consciousness*, trans. M. Bergman Ramos. New York: Continuum.

Freire, Paulo (1993), *Pedagogy of the Oppressed*. New York: Continuum.

Giroux, Hemry A. (1983), *Theory and Resistance in Education: A Pedagogy for the Opposition*. Amherst: Bergin and Garvey.

Habibah, Sherien (2010), "Curfew Challenge." In R. Cox (ed.), *The West Bank: A Collection of Graphic Novels*, 46–52. Project Hope. https://projecthope.ps/projecthope/images/sampledata/graphicnovel/2009/Graphic%20Novel%202010.pdf.

Hastings, Thayer (2016), "Palestinian Oral History as a Tool to Defend Against Displacement." *Al Shabaka: The Palestinian Policy Network*. https://al-shabaka.org/commentaries/palestinian-oral-history-tool-defend-displacement/.

Jong, Anne de. (2018), "Zionist Hegemony, the Settler Colonial Conquest of Palestine and the Problem with Conflict: A Critical Genealogy of the Notion of Binary Conflict." *Settler Colonial Studies*, 8 (3): 364–383.

Kashti, Or and Nir Hasson (2016), [Newspaper Article] "Israel's Education Ministry to Pay East Jerusalem Schools to 'Israelize' Curriculum." *Haaretz*, 29 January. https://www.haaretz.com/israel-news/.premium-israel-to-pay-e-jlem-schools-to-israelize-curriculum-1.5397288.

Kentli, Fulya Damla (2009), "Comparison of Hidden Curriculum Theories." *European Journal of Educational Studies*, 1 (2): 83–88.

Lyons, Tony (2016), "'Inciting the Lawless and Profligate Adventure'—THE HEDGE SCHOOLS OF IRELAND." *History Ireland*, 24 (6): 28–31.

Martin, Jane R. (1976), "What Should We Do with a Hidden Curriculum When We Find One?" *Curriculum Inquiry*, 6 (2): 135–151.

Masri, Ahmed (2010), "On This Earth We Deserve Life." In R. Cox (ed.), *The West Bank: A Collection of Graphic Novels*, 62–67. Project Hope. https://projecthope.ps/projecthope/images/sampledata/graphicnovel/2009/Graphic%20Novel%202010.pdf.

Matar, Dina (2017), "Whose 'Ethnic Cleansing?': Israel's Appropriation of the Palestinian Narrative." *Al Shabaka: The Palestinian Policy Network*. https://al-shabaka.org/commentaries/whose-ethnic-cleansing-israels-appropriation-palestinian-narrative/.

Meinzer, Melanie (2019), "Solidarity Donors and Popular Education in the West Bank." In A. Tartir and T. Seidel (eds.), *Palestine and Rule of Power: Local Dissent vs. International Governance*, 175–202. London: Springer International Publishing.

Moughrabi, Fouad (2001), "The Politics of Palestinian Textbooks." *Journal of Palestine Studies*, 31 (1): 5–19.

Peck, Craig (2001), "'Educate to Liberate': The Black Panther Party and Political Education." Unpublished Doctoral Dissertation, Stanford University, Stanford. http://elibrary.ru/item.asp?id=5255695.

Schlund-Vials, Cathy J. (2012), *War, Genocide, and Justice: Cambodian American Memory Work*. Minneapolis and London: University of Minnesota Press.

Turner, Mandy (2015), "Peacebuilding as Counterinsurgency in the Occupied Palestinian Territory." *Review of International Studies*, 41 (1): 73–98.

Vallance, Elizabeth (1973), "Hiding the Hidden Curriculum: An Interpretation of the Language of Justification in Nineteenth-Century Educational Reform." *Curriculum Theory Network*, 1: 5–21.

Wildeman, Jeremy and Alaa Tartir (2021), "Political Economy of Foreign Aid in the Occupied Palestinian Territories: A Conceptual Framing." In *Political Economy of Palestine: Critical, Interdisciplinary, and Decolonial Perspectives*, 223–47. Cham: Springer International Publishing.

Willis, Paul E. (1981), *Learning to Labor: How Working Class Kids Get Working Class Jobs*. New York: Columbia University Press.

Contributors

Nijmeh Ali is a fellow at the National Centre for Peace and Conflict Studies, at the University of Otago. Her research focuses on resistance and activism within oppressed groups, particularly among Palestinian activists in Israel. In a comprehensive view, her research provides a critical perspective on studying resistance and revolution in non-Western societies. It also deals with exposing strategies used by oppressed and marginalized groups in resisting their subjugation; therefore, it applies to women, minorities, refugees, and migrants.

Yara M. Asi, PhD, is an assistant professor at the School of Global Health Management and Informatics at the University of Central Florida in the United States. She is a visiting scholar at the FXB Center for Health and Human Rights at Harvard University in her capacity as codirector of the Palestine Program for Health and Human Rights. She also serves as a nonresident fellow at the Arab Center Washington, DC; a 2023–4 nonresident fellow at the Foundation for Middle East Peace; and a 2020––1 US Fulbright Scholar to the West Bank. Her research agenda focuses on health, human rights, and development in conflict-affected and fragile settings. Her first book, *How War Kills: The Overlooked Threats to Our Health*, will be published in January 2024.

Tariq Dana is Associate Professor of Conflict and Humanitarian Studies at the Doha Institute for Graduate Studies. He serves as associate editor of *Middle East Critique*. He is a policy advisor for Al-Shabaka: The Palestinian Policy Network. He is coeditor of *Political Economy of Palestine: Critical, Interdisciplinary, and Decolonial Perspectives* (2021).

We'am Hamdan is currently a PhD candidate in education at the University of Cambridge. Her research concerns the navigational journeys of Palestinian ICT graduates from higher education and EdTech Hubs into the labor market under colonial domination. She completed her MSc in comparative and international education at the University of Oxford with distinction. We'am is interested in how education can be used to reconstruct systems, countries, and persons impacted by conflict and the effectiveness of the incipient ICT industry in supporting economic growth and positive life experiences for Palestinian citizens and young people in particular.

Anas Iqtait specializes in the political economy dynamics shaping governance and fiscal policy of the Palestinian Authority and the political economy and geoeconomics of the wider region. He serves as an assistant professor of economics and political economy of the Middle East at the Australian National University (ANU), Australia. Previously, Anas worked in Palestine with the United Nations Office for the Coordination of

Humanitarian Affairs (OCHA), Oxfam, and the Korean International Cooperation Agency and served as a research fellow at Birzeit University in 2017. He is a cofounder and chief editor of the ANU-based Near East Policy Forum and serves as a nonresident scholar with the Middle East Institute (United States) and a research associate with the Economic Research Forum. His academic publications include *Funding and the Quest for Sovereignty in Palestine* (2022).

Gabi Kirk is a PhD candidate in geography with a designated emphasis in feminist theory and research at the University of California, Davis. Working between political ecology, feminist geography, and geographies of colonialism, her dissertation project examines how Palestinian farmers and sustainable development organizations in the northern West Bank use agroecology in projects of identity formation and struggles for sovereignty. She also studies the settler-colonial history of agricultural science, examining the transnational circuits of agricultural and infrastructural expertise between California and Palestine from the nineteenth century onward. She has a personal and intellectual interest in interrogating Zionist claims to "Jewish indigeneity" through environmentalism. She has published, solo and collaboratively, both academic and popular pieces, including in *Jewish Currents*, *Historical Geography*, *Journal of Political Ecology*, *Society and Space*, and *PROTOCOLS*.

Paul Kohlbry is a postdoctoral associate in the Department of Anthropology at Cornell University. His research brings together critical agrarian studies, political ecology, and legal anthropology. Since 2013, he has carried out archival and ethnographic research on issues around peasant agriculture, property law, land privatization, anti-colonialism, and agrarian transformation in the Middle East, primarily in Palestine and Israel.

Melanie Meinzer is an independent scholar and the learning and impact strategist at the Center for Cultural Power. Her research examines the political economy of foreign aid, education, and social movements in the Israeli-occupied West Bank. Her writing has appeared in academic journals and edited volumes and in *Jadaliyya*, *Alliance Magazine*, and *Inside Higher Ed*. She holds a PhD in political science from the University of Connecticut.

Colin Powers (PhD Johns Hopkins School of Advanced International Studies) is a senior researcher and MENA Program chief editor for Noria Research in Paris. He is a two-time recipient of the Fulbright Grant. His research centers on political economy with a regional focus on the Middle East and North Africa.

Timothy Seidel is an associate professor of peacebuilding, development, and global studies and the director of the Center for Interfaith Engagement at Eastern Mennonite University in Harrisonburg, Virginia. He is the coeditor of *Political Economy of Palestine: Critical, Interdisciplinary, and Decolonial Perspectives* (2021) and *Palestine and Rule of Power: Local Dissent vs. International Governance* (2019).

Somdeep Sen is an associate professor in international development studies at Roskilde University, Denmark. His research focuses on race and racism in international relations, liberation movements, spatial politics, settler colonialism, and postcolonial studies. He is the author of *Decolonizing Palestine: Hamas between the Anticolonial and the Postcolonial* (2020) and coeditor of *Globalizing Collateral Language: From 9/11 to Endless War* (2021). His work has also appeared in *The Washington Post*, *Al Jazeera English*, *Foreign Policy*, *The Huffington Post*, *Open Democracy*, *Jacobin*, *The London Review of Books*, *The Palestine Chronicle*, and *The Disorder of Things*.

Federica Stagni is a PhD candidate at the Faculty of Political Sciences and Sociology at Scuola Normale Superiore, Italy, under the supervision of Donatella della Porta and Lorenzo Bosi. Her research focuses on social movements in Israel and Palestine. Federica holds a degree in International and Diplomatic Sciences from the University of Bologna and a master's degree in European and International Studies from the School of International Studies of Trento. She worked as a research assistant for ACLED. Her PhD focuses on anti-demolition and anti-eviction movements in Israel and Palestine. Previous publications of hers include the original article "When Feminism Redefines National Liberation: How Tal'at Movement Brought Feminism to the Core of the Palestinian National Liberation Struggle," which appeared this year in *Critical Sociology*.

Hebatalla Taha is an associate senior lecturer at the Department of Political Science and the Center for Advanced Middle Eastern Studies at Lund University in Sweden. Heba's work lies at the intersection of political economy and security in the modern Middle East. Her doctoral research dealt with contemporary Israeli economic development policies toward Palestinians of 1948, analyzing at the mutual production of Palestinians as subjects of Israeli capitalism and colonialism. More recently, Heba is researching nuclear histories and technologies in the Middle East. Heba is also an affiliate at the Nuclear Knowledges research collective in the Center for International Studies at Sciences Po Paris. Heba previously taught at SUNY Binghamton, the American University in Cairo, and Leiden University.

Alaa Tartir is a senior researcher and the director of the Middle East and North Africa Programme at Stockholm International Peace Research Institute (SIPRI). Tartir is also a research associate and academic coordinator at the Geneva Graduate Institute, a global fellow at the Peace Research Institute Oslo (PRIO), a program and policy advisor to Al-Shabaka: The Palestinian Policy Network, and a governing board member of the Arab Reform Initiative (ARI). Among other positions, Tartir was a visiting professor at Sciences Po, a fellow at the Geneva Centre for Security Policy, and a researcher in international development studies at the London School of Economics and Political Science (LSE), where he earned his PhD. He is the coeditor of *Political Economy of Palestine: Critical, Interdisciplinary, and Decolonial Perspectives* (2021) and *Palestine and Rule of Power: Local Dissent vs. International Governance* (2019). Tartir can be followed on Twitter (@alaatartir), and his publications can be accessed at www.alaatartir.com.

Jeremy Wildeman, PhD (Exeter), is a fellow at the Human Rights Research and Education Centre at the University of Ottawa and an adjunct professor at Carleton

University. His teaching responsibilities have included Middle East politics, development, and international relations. His research includes comparative analysis of Western donor development programming toward the Palestinians and the Middle East in a multipolar world. He wrote his doctoral thesis on Canada's foreign aid in the Occupied Palestinian Territory, after a decade providing humanitarian support in the region. He is the author of numerous peer-reviewed papers on Middle East politics, has co-guest edited a special issue *Canadian Foreign Policy Journal*, "What Lies Ahead: Canada's Engagement with the Middle East Peace Process and the Palestinians" (2021), and has coedited the books *Advocating for Palestine in Canada* (2022) and *Canada as a Settler Colony on the Question of Palestine* (2023).

Index

accountability 58, 61–2, 132
agriculture 97–8, 121, 143–7, 152–5, 166
aid (development, donor, foreign, international) 21, 31, 69, 93, 99–102, 117, 120, 126–9, 132–6, 146, 202–6, 214–16, 222, 224
annex/annexed 17–18, 23–4, 121 n.1
annexation 17–18, 195, 219
antisemitism 179, 184–8
apartheid 55, 61, 165, 170, 195, 200, 207
authoritarian/authoritarianism 31–2, 52, 128, 131
autonomy 7, 9, 17–32, 52, 73, 76, 84, 144, 161, 204

banks/banking 82, 98, 108–23
blockade 10, 37–99, 56, 77, 108, 194
border/borders 23–6, 29, 39, 41–3, 46, 60, 69–70, 82, 84, 96, 100, 102, 110, 116, 121 n.1, 135, 145, 150, 152, 201
boycott, divestment, sanctions (BDS) 184, 187, 188 n.1, 224

capital/capitalist 4, 8, 70, 74, 77, 79, 81, 111–12, 115–22, 143–7, 153–6, 162, 167, 169–71, 197, 202, 221
capitalism 8–9, 52, 69–71, 83, 85, 92–3, 98, 101–2, 148, 155, 163–4
censor/censorship 179–80, 182, 185–8, 216
civil society 8, 60–1, 132, 206, 214
class 2, 9, 25, 71, 99, 108, 120, 144–5, 153, 156 n.1, 226 n.4
climate 9, 46, 143, 150, 152–5
colonialism 2, 56, 62, 92–3, 99, 103 n.2, 152, 195, 197–9, 201–2, *see also* coloniality; colonization; settler colonialism
coloniality 3, 5–6, 94, 172 n.3
colonization 3, 17–18, 20, 28–31, 51–3, 56–7, 63, 89, 94, 110, 145, 147, 164, 168, 194, 198, 200–1, 204–5, 224, *see also* colonialism; coloniality; settler colonialism
corruption 60, 75, 78

debt 8, 89, 108–9, 114–23, 147
decolonial 2–5
decolonization 10, 18, 20–1, 91–4, 100–1, 163, 177, 197–8, 217, 223–4
de-development 5, 8, 56, 75, 81, 206, *see also* development
democracy 10, 194–5, 198–201, 204, 214
dependency 24–5, 31, 73, 83–4, 110, 144–5
depoliticizing 102, 217, 220
development 6–7, 22, 31, 51–2, 55–6, 62–3, 68–71, 74, 78, 80, 83–4, 91–103, 127–33, 135, 144–7, 150, 155–6, 165, 172 n.4, 194–6, 202–4, 206, 214–15, *see also* de-development

economy 22–5, 28, 31, 68–70, 75, 79, 81, 83–4, 95–9, 108–13, 116–20, 122 nn.3, 8, 11, 126–7, 133–4, 144, 146–8, 162, 165–6, 204, *see also* political economy
education 7, 19, 32, 55, 68, 70–1, 75, 78–9, 83–5, 112, 120, 130, 169, 179–80, 214–26
electricity 75, 77–8, 82–4, 123 n.12, 130, 165
environment, environmental 5, 9, 59, 71, 75–83, 153–6
European Union (EU) 82, 184, 206

finance 8, 108–9, 112, 117, 120–1, 128
fragmented/fragmentation 8, 22, 29, 31, 38, 55, 72, 75, 80–1, 84–5, 165, 220

Gaza Strip   10, 18, 22, 25–7, 36, 38–46, 54–6, 58, 68–72, 74, 76–7, 81–2, 84–5, 103, 109–10, 113, 116–17, 119, 121–2, 126, 131–2, 134–5, 150, 152, 165, 172 n.2, 182–3, 194, 197, 205–6, 218, 225
gender   9, 41, 69, 71, 75, 146, 172 n.3, 199
globalization   10, 28, 58, 60, 146
governance   20–1, 24–6, 37, 45, 56, 93, 99, 109–10, 127–32, 135–6, 152, 199

Hamas   37, 40–5, 109, 114, 131, 200
health   4, 7, 36–47, 59, 115, 126, 130, 149, 165
human rights   8, 10, 36–41, 45–7, 56–63, 69, 84, 165, 169, 198, 200, 226, *see also* rights

immigration   22, 70, 183, 198
imperial/imperialism   2, 8, 145, 164, 196–202, 215, 221
indigeneity   4, 141, 161–4, 167, 171, 183
Indigenous   4, 20, 37, 52–3, 84, 92, 95, 99, 108, 143, 148, 161, 163–71, 180–3, 185, 195–7, 199–202, 204, 212, 219
inequality   8, 52, 89, 109, 113, 121
informal/informality   112, 121, 162, 172 n.4, 216
Information and Communication Technology (ICT)   8, 56, 68–86
integration (economic)   28, 70, 84, 94–5, 97, 99, 126–7, 144, 147
International Holocaust Remembrance Alliance (IHRA)   9, 179–80, 184–8
Intifada
   first *Intifada*   27–8, 39, 144–5, 198
   second *Intifada*   10, 29, 39–40, 42, 144, 149, 200, 203, 214, 216, 221–2

Jerusalem   1, 18, 22, 24, 29–31, 38, 41, 44, 56–7, 59, 70, 73, 75–6, 79–82, 110, 121 n.1, 151, 165, 167, 181, 188 n.1, 194, 196, 201, 215, 219

law
   humanitarian law   10, 46–7, 165

international law   18, 75, 165, 187, 194, 201, 226
Israeli law   41, 54, 57, 63 n.4, 73, 91, 152, 195
legitimacy   9, 28, 29, 46, 57, 130, 131, 135, 166, 177, 180
liberalism   10, 177, 195, 198–202, 206

Masafer Yatta   4, 162, 164–71
migration   37, 146

Nakba   54, 91, 94–5, 145, 148, 154, 181–2, 215
neoliberalism   5, 75, 131, 145, 198
nongovernmental organizations (NGOs)   10, 46, 75, 78, 83, 85, 129, 131–2, 150, 187, 216–25

oil   128–9
olives   144–5, 147–50, 155, 166
   olive oil   143, 147–50, 155
   olive trees   147–51, 156 n.2, 166, 169–71, 182
Oslo Accords   5, 7, 17–18, 23, 26, 28–32, 56, 69, 72–5, 79, 82, 109, 113, 121, 126, 131–4, 145–6, 153, 165, 172 nn.2, 4, 177–8, 194, 196, 198, 203, 206, 214–16, 225

pacification   20, 24, 25, 31
Palestine Liberation Organization (PLO)   7, 25–30, 109, 196, 198
Palestinian Authority (PA)   7–8, 21, 26, 28–32, 37, 56, 69–75, 77–8, 82, 89–90, 118, 123 n.12, 126–7, 130–6, 146, 153, 165, 172 nn.2, 4, 205, 214–17, 221, 225
Palestinians in Israel or '48 Palestinians   54–5, 91, 96, 101
Paris Protocol   8, 109, 113, 115–16, 126, 135
peacebuilding   21, 31, 194–5, 197, 200, 202–3, 206, 214
permit(s)   7, 54, 82, 171, 172 n.2
   medical   11, 36–47
political economy   4–5, 16, 68, 71, 75, 83, 93, 144–6, 148, 152, 155, *see also* economy
poverty   94, 120, 168, 203

proletarianization 92, 94, 102, 145
protest 10–11, 32, 64 n.5, 169, 171, 173 n.12, 183
Protocol on Economic Relations, *see* Paris Protocol

race 100, 163
racial 23, 30–1, 52, 59, 81, 100, 146, 148, 199
racist 145, 170, 177, 202–3
refugees 9, 23, 29, 54–5, 70, 96, 111, 154, 182, 198, 221, 225
rents 73, 129
repression 19, 56, 128, 219
resistance 1–7, 10–11, 20, 27, 51, 53, 63, 68, 70–1, 75, 85, 92–4, 103, 144, 148–50, 152, 154, 161–2, 164, 169–71, 182, 201, 215–19, 221, *see also* struggle
revenues (clearance and public) 9, 31–2, 69, 74, 81–2, 90, 114–15, 117–18, 123 n.12, 126–36
rights 11, 19, 21–2, 26, 30, 32, 59, 73, 95, 148, 171, 187–8, 195, 197, 199, 203, 219–20, *see also* human rights

securitization 37, 59, 102, 131, 135, 194
security 7, 20, 23–4, 26, 28, 30, 32, 36–47, 52–3, 55–7, 59–60, 62–3, 78, 82, 92, 102, 131–4, 149, 171, 172 n.4, 194, 197, 200–7
self-determination 9, 18–19, 21, 161, 163, 195, 199
settlements 4, 18, 23–6, 28–30, 39, 53, 55, 73, 94–7, 99, 112, 115, 120, 126, 134, 149, 151–3, 161–2, 165–6, 168–9, 171, 172 n.2, 181, 194–5, 200–1, 206, 214, 222, 226 n.3
settler colonialism 2–6, 21, 36–8, 46, 51–2, 55, 57, 61–2, 69, 94–5, 99–101, 108, 121, 127, 148, 161–4, 167, 169, 171, 180, 185, 195, 201–2, 204, 206–7, 214–16, 220, *see also* colonialism; coloniality; colonization

solidarity 4, 6, 92, 97, 102, 143, 148–9, 153, 155, 164, 180, 182–3, 186, 217
sovereignty 9, 17–20, 24–5, 29–30, 45, 85, 141, 152, 161, 164, 194, 197, 204, 206, 216
state-building 10, 127, 130–1, 135, 146, 153, 177, 199, 202, 206, 214
status quo 21, 22, 29, 31, 32, 37, 78, 81, 196, 202, 204
steadfastness 7, 9, 148, 161–2, 164, 171–2, *see also sumud*
struggle 4–6, 21, 101, 144–6, 148, 152, 155, 161–5, 168–9, 171, 182–4, 198, 200, 215–16, 225
sumud 9, 148, 161–2, 164, 168–71, *see also* steadfastness
surveillance 6, 51–63

tax, taxes 9, 27, 31–2, 74, 80, 90, 110, 115, 122 n.7, 123 n.12, 126–30, 134–6
taxation 32, 126–31, 134–6
trade 27, 74, 85, 111–12, 119, 126, 134–6, 143–4, 149, 155, 199
transnational 9, 92–4, 143–4, 147–50, 153, 155–6, 164
two-state solution 28, 116, 196, 202

violence 4, 10, 32, 38, 40, 55, 98, 131, 145–6, 148, 181–2, 184, 195, 200, 202–3, 215, 217–18, 224–5
    settler violence 4, 9, 161–5, 169, 171
    structural violence 36–8, 46, 69, 194

wall (separation/apartheid) 31, 38–41, 214
water 29, 53, 120, 123 n.12, 130, 151–4, 161, 165, 171, 205–6
women 40, 42, 55, 101, 119, 154, 162, 168, 170
World Bank 69–70, 73–4, 80–2, 85, 112, 120, 130–3, 202–5, 215
Zionism/Zionist 17–18, 23, 52–5, 57, 59, 93–100, 102, 147, 150, 154, 164, 166–7, 179–81, 186–8, 197, 219

www.ingramcontent.com/pod-product-compliance
Lightning Source LLC
Chambersburg PA
CBHW071827300426
44116CB00009B/1467